Albert J. Beveridge

ALBERT J. BEVERIDGE

American Nationalist

John Braeman

THE UNIVERSITY OF CHICAGO PRESS • CHICAGO AND LONDON

International Standard Book Number: 0–226–07060–3
Library of Congress Catalog Card Number: 75–142041

The University of Chicago Press, Chicago 60637
The University of Chicago Press, Ltd., London

To My Mother and the Memory of My Father

Contents

false CONTENTS

Preface

I was drawn to write this biography of Albert J. Beveridge through an interest in the progressive movement of which he was a part. I began with the supposition that he was a typical progressive. But research and reflection have convinced me that there is no such thing as "a typical progressive"—no such thing, in fact, as a "progressive movement" with a coherent program and ideology.

Why, then, a biography of Beveridge? He was not one of Sidney Hook's heroes in history who decisively altered the course of human affairs. But he was a significant figure of his day who did make important contributions both in politics and the writing of history. And though he was not simply his times writ large, his life story does illuminate the complexity of those years.

I started work on this project more years ago than I care to remember as a Ph.D. dissertation at Johns Hopkins University. I am indebted to my advisers at Hopkins, Professor Charles A. Barker and Professor Wilson Smith, the latter now at the University of California–Davis, for their many kindnesses then and since.

I would like to thank the following for generous financial assistance that made possible the completion of this work: the Midwest Research Grants Program of the Lilly Endowment, Inc., the American Philosophical Society, the American Council of Learned Societies, and the Research Council of the University of Nebraska. I wish to acknowledge particularly my gratitude to Dr. James C. Olson, then dean of the Graduate College of the University of Nebraska and now chancellor of the University of Missouri–Kansas City, who was instrumental in arranging a semester off with pay for me in the spring of 1968.

Let me also express my appreciation to those librarians—too many to name individually—whose assistance was indispensable in my research.

I am grateful to the following for permission to reprint in revised form materials first published as articles: Professor Donald F. Carmony, for "The Rise of Albert J. Beveridge to the United States Senate," *Indiana Magazine of History* 53 (December 1957): 355–82, and "Albert J. Beveridge and the First National Child Labor Bill," ibid. 60 (March 1964): 1–36; Harwood P. Hinton, for "Albert J. Beveridge and Statehood for the Southwest, 1902–1912," *Arizona and the West* 10 (Winter 1968): 313–42; and Weldon E. Kefauver, for "The Square Deal in Action: A Case Study in the Growth of the 'National Police Power,'" in *Change and Continuity in Twentieth-Century America,* edited by John Braeman, Robert H. Bremner, and Everett Walters (Columbus, Ohio, 1964; © 1964 by the Ohio State University Press).

And, above all, I wish to take this opportunity to express publicly my debt to my parents—to whom this volume is dedicated—and my wife Kathy and daughter Beth. Their love sustained me throughout my labors on this book.

ABBREVIATIONS USED IN NOTES

BP   Beveridge Papers (Library of Congress)
IHS   Indiana Historical Society
ISL   Indiana State Library
LC   Library of Congress
LL   Lilly Library, Indiana University
AHR   *American Historical Review*
CR   U.S., Congress, *Congressional Record.* All references unless otherwise noted are to the Senate proceedings.
IMH   *Indiana Magazine of History*
MVHR   *Mississippi Valley Historical Review*
SEP   *Saturday Evening Post*

References to Beveridge's magazine articles are cited simply by the magazine name, volume and/or date, and pages, while his published speeches are cited only by their short title. Full details are in the Bibliographical Notes.

Typographical errors in newspapers or typed letters have been silently corrected. Spelling and punctuation in handwritten letters have been followed exactly.

Introduction

The growing body of research into the years 1900 to 1917 has undermined the handy generalizations that historians were prone to make about the progressive movement. Today we have to discard the very notion of a movement in the sense of a unified entity. Rather, we are faced with what Otis Graham, Jr., has aptly termed "the vexatious variety of progressivism." And we find diverse and even contradictory personalities, movements, and ideas bearing, in their own appraisal no less than in that of historians, the label "progressive."

Given this diversity within progressivism—and among progressives—biography provides a good medium for illuminating the complexity of that epoch in American history. For the biographer has a twofold task: to show how the environment shapes the individual and how the individual influences his environment. There is no one man who can be singled out as the archetypical progressive. But Albert J. Beveridge (1862–1927) was part of many of the streams that flowed together to constitute the larger progressive movement. By examining what he did and what he did not do, what moved him and what did not, what he believed in and what he rejected, we can gain fuller insight into the forces at work during the first three decades of the twentieth century.

Beveridge's achievements while in the Senate were sufficient to place him among the front rank of progressives. He was the author of the meat inspection law passed by Congress in the wake of the uproar created by Upton Sinclair's *The Jungle*—a measure that represented a precedent-shattering expansion of federal authority over business. He introduced the first national child labor bill, and his agitation of the question prepared the ground for the later adoption of the Keating-Owen Act under the Wilson administration. He was the leading congressional champion of the establishment of a tariff commission to put tariff making upon a "scientific" basis. He was one of the leading Republican "insurgents" in the fight over the Payne-Aldrich tariff bill which did so much to split the G.O.P. He led the fight to unseat Senator William Lorimer of Illinois—a landmark in the battle to safeguard the electoral process from corruption.

Perhaps even more important, Beveridge epitomized many of the paradoxes with which progressivism abounded. He was an ardent imperialist who called upon the United States to play a major role in world affairs; yet he was an "irreconcilable" on the League of Nations. He was an advocate of military preparedness; yet he balked at Wilson's defense of American neutral rights. He was an Anglo-Saxon supremacist vis-à-vis lesser breeds across the seas; yet he shied away from the nativism of the Ku Klux Klan. He was elected to the Senate a staunch defender of the status quo; yet he moved to reform in his anxiety over popular discontent and the danger of social upheaval. He was an admirer of big business and big businessmen; yet he came to demand the strengthening of the federal government to prevent corporate wrongdoing. In the heyday of his progressivism he defended unions as the workers' first line of self-defense; yet after the Adamson Act he turned violently against organized labor as a new and more dangerous brand of special privilege. He was a loyal protectionist; yet he broke with his party's leadership over the Payne-Aldrich tariff bill. He was an ambitious politician consumed by dreams of the presidency; yet twice when his political future lay at stake—in 1910 and in 1922—he placed principle above expediency. He was an arch-Republican partisan; yet he followed Theodore Roosevelt into the Progressive Party. He was a leading opponent of amalgamation between the Progressives and the G.O.P.; yet he tried for a political comeback in 1922 as the foe of much of what the Progressive Party had espoused.

Turning to the study of history after his defeat for reelection to the Senate, Beveridge made his mark in the world of scholarship. Despite—or perhaps because of—his lack of professional training, he swore allegiance to the gospel of nineteenth-century "scientific history." But few historians have shown more strikingly in their work the influence of their own values, predispositions, and attitudes. Yet notwithstanding its pro-Federalist bias, his monumental, four-volume

Life of John Marshall remains to this day the standard biography of the great chief justice. And though death cut short his biography of Abraham Lincoln, his posthumously published first two volumes were a landmark in Lincoln scholarship—a starting point for all later students of the man and his times.

1

Youth

The men who assumed political leadership at the beginning of the twentieth century had been reared upon, and inculcated with, the values of individualism, self-reliance, and American manifest destiny held dear by their fathers. But they had grown to maturity in a rapidly urbanizing and industrializing America, an America with a widening gulf between the new masters of capital and the poor in the slums of the burgeoning metropolises, an America wrecked by violent strikes and bitter farm discontent. Their problem was to reshape the traditional values drawn from a simpler and bygone age to fit this new America. Among the leaders in this reshaping was Senator Albert J. Beveridge of Indiana.

The Beveridge name was an ancient and widely known surname in Scotland. And the senator would throughout his life boast of his Scottish ancestry. His grandfather, Thomas Beveridge, was born in Loudoun County, Virginia, on 16 February 1771, the son of John Beveridge and the former Susannah Noble. Thomas Beveridge married Tacy Roberts, and a son named Thomas Henry was born on 10 February 1818. After Thomas's death in 1827, his widow moved to Ohio with most of her children. But Thomas

Henry was left in Virginia under the guardianship of an uncle, Noble Beveridge. Chafing under his uncle's harsh ways, the youngster ran off to join his mother in Ohio.

Biographical data about Thomas Henry Beveridge is scanty. He married Elizabeth Lamb, the daughter of a farmer near Zanesville. The 1840 census listed him as living in Adams County, in southwestern Ohio. In 1847, he purchased a 107½-acre farm along the west fork of Brush Creek, about three miles south of the village of Sugartree Ridge in neighboring Highland County. Over the next fifteen years, he succeeded in more than doubling the size of his holdings. For the 1860 census, he estimated his worth at $4,000 in real estate and $1,100 in personal property. His house—a rambling, solidly built structure with a white-columned, Virginia-style portico— bespoke a man of substance in the community.

Of his nine children, four boys and three girls survived infancy. After his wife died, leaving without a mother four youngsters under eighteen, he wed a thirty-seven-year-old widow, Frances Eleanor Parkinson Doyle, on 2 January 1862.

Frances was born on 25 September 1824, the daughter of George Washington Parkinson and his wife Rebecca. Frances's maternal grandfather, "Squire" Oliver Ross, had migrated from northern Ireland after the American Revolution and was a pioneer settler and leading citizen of Highland County. Her father was a hatmaker. In 1841 she married Philip Doyle, the local carpenter and builder. The couple had three surviving children—two daughters and a son. When her mother was widowed in 1849 and left nearly penniless, Frances took her, as well as a younger sister, into her home. Five years later, her own husband died, leaving her with the burden of supporting the family. For the next eight years, until her marriage to Thomas Henry Beveridge in January 1862, she did so with a firmness of spirit worthy of her Scotch-Irish forebears.

Albert Jeremiah Beveridge was born to Thomas and Frances on 6 October 1862 at the Ohio farmhouse. The child inherited the dominant Beveridge features—steel-blue eyes, a very clear complexion, a large nose, a strong chin, very straight hair, and—he would boast—a spirit of daring and adventure. In later years, he was fond of telling how he had found carved into the wall of the Tower of London the name of a sixteenth-century Beveridge imprisoned for "obstinacy in Religious opinions"—another family trait.

When the boy was born, his father was away serving in the Union army. Although forty-four years of age, Thomas Beveridge had enlisted as a first lieutenant in the Eighty-Ninth Regiment, Ohio Volunteer Infantry, in August 1862, when the Confederate army invading Kentucky had advanced within striking distance of the Ohio River. After the Confederate drive was turned back, he resigned from the army because of his age and troubles at home. He had borrowed heavily to expand his farm, and his army service plunged him deeper into debt. Selling off a large chunk of his property, he moved to the town of Level in nearby Warren County and opened a general store. But the venture was a disaster. In February 1866 he went into bankruptcy, and his remaining Highland County land and even his personal belongings were sold to pay his debts.

Joining the westward trek, Thomas leased a farm near the village of Chipps Station, Moultrie County, in east central Illinois. His 1867 tax return showed no real estate and personal property valued at only sixty-five dollars. Hit by the postwar agricultural depression, he gave up farming and moved into Sullivan—the county seat—where he worked as a butcher. Although he managed to buy a home, he continued to struggle in the morass of debt. In 1874 he went into business in partnership with his new son-in-law, Aaron Miley, the local postmaster and Republican leader. But the business failed to prosper, back taxes mounted, and the partners had to sell out for a fraction of their investment. Thereafter Thomas eked out a living by farming and doing odd jobs around town. After his death in October 1895, his home had to be sold at auction to pay his debts and back taxes.

The family's poverty cast its pall upon the spirited and restless son. Albert was his mother's favorite, and she encouraged him in his dreams and aspirations. Throughout her life, until her death in 1918, mother and son remained in close touch. But Thomas Beveridge was a stern and forbidding man, soured by his tribulations. Between father and son there was scant warmth of feeling, while his half-brothers resented him as their stepmother's pet. This alienation from his father and half-brothers—with its resulting identity problems for the growing boy—were contributory factors in his lifelong need for public recognition and approval.[1]

---

1. For his mother's always encouraging him, see Beveridge to George H.

In the family's straits, the youngster had to shoulder his share of the burden. He would boast in later years that he had plowed and harvested every field around Sullivan but one. He worked as a section hand on a railroad being constructed through the country. Then he worked as a logger and teamster in a lumber camp and so impressed his boss that he was placed in charge of a team of men older and more experienced than himself. While in the lumber camp, he picked up the "art of profanity"—a habit that stuck with him throughout his life. Every cent earned went into the family coffers for food and clothing.

The unhappy days of his boyhood instilled in him a fierce determination to make his mark in the world. And as far back as he could remember, he dreamed of becoming a lawyer. Tocqueville's observation that the closest thing to an American aristocracy was to be found in the bar was borne out by the standing of lawyers in rural Illinois of the 1870s. Albert spent hours at the county court house watching the great men in action and would then go into the woods to copy their gestures and repeat the half-understood words. Fired by his dreams of glory, physically toughened by labor, he acquired the discipline and resourcefulness needed to fulfill his ambitions.

Albert's formal education began at the Two-Mile School not far from his father's farm. It was a one-room wooden schoolhouse that had only one teacher for all the classes. After the family moved into Sullivan, Albert attended the graded Sullivan Free School and then its two-year high school. In these schools, he mastered McGuffey's *Readers,* Goodrich's *Histories,* and Raye's *Arithmetic.* Although the high school taught no Greek and scant Latin, Albert completed the rest of the standard pre-college program: English grammar and composition, algebra and plane geometry, American history, English literature, and a smattering of the natural sciences.

Most important, he came under the influence of a remarkable teacher, Mrs. Lotta Webster, who encouraged him in his dreams and protected him from the jibes of his schoolmates, who resented what they regarded as his insufferable egotism. He participated en-

---

Lorimer, 16 December 1915, Lorimer Papers (Historical Society of Pennsylvania). On his hostility toward his Beveridge half-brothers, see: T. L. Beveridge to Benjamin Harrison, 22 June 1900, Harrison Papers (LC); Beveridge to T. L. Beveridge, 25 June 1900, Beveridge Papers (LC); *Indianapolis News,* 31 March 1900. On his feelings toward his father, see: MS Autobiography, BP.

thusiastically in the weekly debates and declamations in school. He had his first taste of glory when the Francis Murphy Temperance Movement swept over Moultrie County, and he became a popular speaker at its meetings. The applause of his audiences proved a heady wine.

Frances and Thomas Beveridge gloried in Methodism's promise of man's redemption from sin through divine grace, and young Albert was reared in the belief in God's providential design for the world and himself. The Methodist circuit riders of the middle border preached a gospel of hard work, thrift, and prudence. His school texts were filled with stories of the rewards that come to those who pursued such virtues and the ills that befell those guilty of idleness, vice, and gambling.

Love of country was instilled with love of God. Thomas Beveridge had named one daughter America, another Columbia. Romanticizing his wartime service, he recalled for Albert the glorious days of the struggle to save the Union. Memorial Day celebrations awakened each year anew the memories of that conflict. Stories glorifying liberty, independence, resistance to tyranny, and the heroes of the American past abounded in his school books. Ministers rejoiced in their sermons that God had picked this land for his chosen people. Fourth of July speakers proclaimed this nation's destiny to spread its blessings around the globe to less fortunate peoples.

And the youngster identified love of country with loyalty to the Grand Old Party. His brother-in-law was the local postmaster and the leading Republican in the county, and his father as a Union veteran was a devoted party man. Bands, drum corps, uniformed marching companies, torchlight parades, "bloody shirt" speeches, and victory barbecues kept partisan feelings at a fever pitch in the years after the Civil War. At the Republican meetings to which his father took the boy, party spellbinders lashed the Democracy for its disloyalty to the flag and hailed the Republican party as the savior of the Union and friend of the loyal soldier. Abraham Lincoln was Albert's boyhood hero, and the youth grew up in the belief that the G.O.P. was God's helper in building a happier, nobler land.

Beveridge graduated from Sullivan high school in the spring of 1881. Having read glowing accounts of the benefits of a college education, he dreamed of going on to college. His situation, however, appeared hopeless. In his last year of high school, his brother-in-law had obtained for him a clerkship at the post office. Although he had saved nearly every penny of the $40.50 paid him, that amount was not sufficient for college. A possible alternative was West Point. A military career appealed strongly to a youth reared upon tales of military glory, and he took the competitive examination given by the local congressman to determine the appointment to the military academy. But a penalty for his laughter at a whispered joke cost him the prize.

Seeing his despair, a friendly lumberman for whom he had worked, Edward Anderson, offered to lend him fifty dollars. With this sum added to the forty dollars he had saved, he set out in September 1881 for Indiana Asbury University (renamed DePauw University in 1884 in honor of its wealthy benefactor Washington C. DePauw) in Greencastle, Indiana. "Old Asbury," as the school was called, had been founded in the 1830s under the auspices of the Methodist Episcopal Church. At the time of Beveridge's arrival, it was the largest and most influential institution of higher learning in Indiana.

Albert had picked Indiana Asbury because its kindly president, Alexander Martin, had replied personally to his postcard of inquiry and encouraged him to come. He arrived at the campus, a fellow student recalled, "a strong, straight figure, short rather than tall, dressed in a baggy old suit that yet somehow deceived you into thinking it was all right; a pallid, keen, alert face with a powerful jaw and gray-blue eyes that suggested a runner in sight of the goal; long-ish, fair hair, a perfect mop of it." He was afire with ambition. "I would be willing," he exclaimed to a schoolmate, "to go to hell if I could make a reputation as great as that of Napoleon."[2]

Money remained a continuing worry throughout his four years at Asbury. He was so poor when he arrived at Greencastle that he borrowed a wheelbarrow and carted his trunk the two miles to the campus. Since the school lacked dormitories and a commons, the undergraduates roomed in town. Beveridge arranged to share a room with a fellow student named George Nolin, and to save money, the two did their own cooking. In the spring, he joined the Delta Kappa Epsilon fraternity—the "Dekes" as they were called—and to reduce his expenses organized a fraternity boarding-house and became its steward.

---

2. David Graham Phillips, "Albert J. Beveridge," *Success Magazine* 8 (August 1905): 526. Clarence W. Hall, *Samuel Logan Brengle, Portrait of a Prophet* (New York, 1933), p. 43.

To earn pocket money, he did odd jobs around Greencastle. But his financial salvation was the cash prizes awarded the winners of the school's oratorical contests. Every day he would stand before a full-length mirror, repeating the speeches of past masters, practicing sound and cadence, and rehearsing gestures. His greatest triumph was winning the Interstate Oratorical Contest in the spring of his senior year. At his return from the finals in Columbus, Ohio, he was the local hero. Classes were dismissed, the Cadet Battery fired a five-gun salute as his train pulled into the station, and the DePauw Band and Cadet Drum Corps led his triumphant march to the campus.

On his first summer vacation he returned to Sullivan and worked on the surrounding farms. The next summer he took a job selling door to door a volume on exotic religions entitled *Error's Chains*. He was so successful that the publishing firm made him sales manager for Iowa for the following summer, and he recruited about thirty of his fellow students to canvass the Hawkeye state. Not all were successful. A story in the *DePauw Monthly* reported that many went "busted" and roundly swore at "Boss B-V-rge." Beveridge himself, however, saved $250 to pay his way through his senior year. He was even able that spring to establish his own oratorical contest with a twenty-five dollar prize.

At the same time, he was compiling a highly successful academic record. He entered with a deficiency in Latin, but he managed to make up the deficiency while simultaneously taking and passing the regular freshman Latin course. Lacking any training in Greek, he took German as his second language. The rest of his studies followed the time-hallowed pattern: heavy doses of Latin, rhetoric, logic, and moral philosophy, with smaller doses of history, literature, mathematics, and the natural sciences. Beveridge received grades of 90 or more in almost all his courses. In the examination for honors in belles lettres and history he was awarded second class honors at the end of his sophomore year and first class honors at the end of his junior year.

He found most of his classes dull, mere recitation from memory. Far more stimulating than his formal studies were the activities of the college literary societies—the Platonian and its rival, the Philological. Within a few months of his arrival, he became a leader in "Old Plato." Each spring the two societies vied against each other in formal debates. A fellow student recalled how Beveridge, "manifesting power before he said a word," won his audience by his unshakable air of self-confidence. Throughout the year, the members of the societies would meet each week for informal debates that ranged through literature, science, religion, philosophy, and politics.

Beveridge was a wide reader. A classmate remembered that "you could always find 'Bev' in the library." Shakespeare was his favorite, followed by Burns, Dickens, and Thackeray. His college addresses showed a familiarity with the writings of John Stuart Mill, Rousseau, Herbert Spencer, Henry George, and even Karl Marx, but his knowledge of these thinkers remained largely superficial. The dominant atmosphere at Indiana Asbury served to reinforce the moral, religious, and political teachings of his boyhood.

That atmosphere was of a strongly denominational college with compulsory daily chapel and compulsory church attendance in "Sabbath forenoon." Early in his junior year, "evangelistic meetings" were held at the Locust Street Methodist Church across from the campus. One by one the campus leaders were caught up in the revivalist fervor. But Beveridge stood aloof. Then one day his friend Sam Brengle—who would become a top officer in the Salvation Army— sat down to "argue it out with him" and won him over. The next day he attended the church services and was "led" to the altar.

The chief text in his senior year course in belles lettres and history was Francis Wayland's *Elements of Political Economy*. From Wayland, Beveridge imbibed the tenets of nineteenth-century "clerical laissez-faire." Taking "Capital and Labor" as his topic for the Interstate Oratorical competition, he lamented the growing unrest simmering beneath the surface, "bursting into riots and strikes, like the complaining murmurs of a coming storm," warned that extremists were on the march who "demand the overthrow of our social system," and even prayed: "God grant that ere socialism visit us with torch and sword some Caesar, some Cromwell, some Napoleon shall rise and save us from ourselves!" In the United States, industry, thrift, and godliness reaped their just reward. "Vice, sloth and attendant wretchedness prevail, not because of poverty; poverty prevails because of them. It is the old, old problem of human nature and its frailty."[3]

At DePauw, devotion to the Union, love of country, and loyalty to

3. Herold T. Ross, "Albert Jeremiah Beveridge at DePauw" (unpublished ms., 1935; microfilm copy in the DePauw University Archives), pp. 117–34.

the Republican party were articles of faith shared by faculty and students. So Dr. Martin gave Beveridge permission to take a month off from classes in the fall of 1884 to campaign for the G.O.P. A local party leader in Greencastle arranged with the Republican State Committee to schedule him to some lesser places. Although his youthfulness often took his audiences aback when he first appeared, he was a tremendous success. A report to the state's leading Republican newspaper, the *Indianapolis Journal*, hailed him as the G.O.P.'s "young man eloquent."[4] When the special campaign train carrying presidential nominee James G. Blaine came to Indiana, Beveridge was included in the delegation of prominent Republicans that joined the train and accompanied the "Plumed Knight" across the state.

His multifarious activities were made possible by an hour-by-hour budgeting of his time. In his room he hung the slogan "NO TIME TO WASTE."[5] He walked across campus with a rapid stride that left his companions breathless. Although enjoying a lark with his friends, he had no time to waste in idle talk. Many students resented his drive and ambition as reflecting a swaggering vainglory. The *DePauw Monthly* spoke of Beveridge's giving "the plan upon which the universe was created his unqualified personal indorsement."[6] But the sheer force of his personality won a host of admirers. "There always was a fascination for me in strength," fellow student and future novelist David Graham Phillips recalled of his first meeting with Beveridge, "and this new acquaintance of mine, with his unkempt hair and his burning eyes and his voice like a trumpet, was obviously strong mentally and physically."[7]

The years at DePauw were happy ones. There he met his future wife; there he found friendships that would last his lifetime; and there he gained new confidence in his own powers and abilities. In June 1885, he graduated with the degree of Bachelor of Philosophy. The university would look upon him as one of its most successful sons and bestow upon him all the honors at its disposal. For his part, he would give unstintingly of his time and money to advance its welfare.

---

4. *Indianapolis Journal*, 6 October 1884.
5. Handwritten sign, Box 326, BP.
6. Ross, "Beveridge at DePauw," p. 51.
7. Phillips, "Beveridge," p. 526.

2

Indianapolis Lawyer

After graduation, Beveridge's first task was to restore his health, which had been impaired by too much work and too little sleep. With the idea of recovering his strength by life in the outdoors, he went to the town of Dighton in western Kansas. A spiraling land boom was underway at the time of his arrival, and he formed a partnership with an ex-cowboy named Dave McClelland to locate new settlers upon their tracts. Caught up in the land fever, he began to speculate in buying and selling abandoned homesteads. Although his prospects for financial success appeared bright, he returned to Indiana in the fall of 1886 to follow through with his dream of studying for the bar.

He arrived in the middle of the 1886 congressional campaign and promptly took to the stump to denounce the Cleveland administration as a government by Wall Street, Britain, and a reawakened Confederacy.[1] While campaigning two years before, he had met Benjamin Harrison, the state's leading Republican and top-ranking lawyer. Counting upon his acquaintanceship, the youth asked Harrison for a job as a clerk with his firm. The reserved and austere Harrison

---

1. *Indianapolis Journal*, 5, 7, 11 October 1886.

brushed aside his request with a coldness and curtness that Beveridge never forgot. He turned in desperation to Indianapolis's next ranking law firm, McDonald, Butler, & Mason. The firm's senior partner, ex-Democratic Senator Joseph E. McDonald, listened sympathetically. He welcomed the youth to stay and read law, but said he could pay no salary and give no promises. Although his savings from Kansas were nearly exhausted, Albert stayed.

The first few weeks were hard, but he had gained the friendship of many of the Republican legislators while campaigning, and they obtained for him a job as reading clerk for the Republican-controlled Indiana House of Representatives. The salary from this job allowed him to continue his studying for admission to the bar. After six months, he was put on a salary of twenty dollars a month. When the firm's junior partner retired with a nervous breakdown, McDonald offered Beveridge the position of managing clerk with the job of handling the ailing man's duties.[2] The salary raise accompanying this promotion allowed him to marry his college sweetheart, Kate Maude Langsdale, the daughter of the publisher of the *Greencastle Banner*, on Thanksgiving Day, 24 November 1887. The following month, on 21 December 1887, he was formally admitted to the bar.

He left McDonald and Butler in 1899 to start practice on his own. His first office was a tiny backroom that he shared with another young lawyer, and he had money enough to last only two months. As with many beginning lawyers, the backbone of his practice was the collection of minor debts. But the times—and the place—were ripe for his advancement. The 1890s were "the golden age" of Indianapolis. The discovery in the late 1880s of extensive gas fields to the northeast of the city sparked a boom that even the depression of 1893–96 failed to halt. Although the gap between rich and poor widened, society remained fluid.

Beveridge's first important break came when his father-in-law took advantage of political and family connections to have Beveridge engaged to assist the state attorney general, Louis T. Michener, in pleading before the Indiana Supreme Court the governor's side in the dispute over appointments between Republican chief executive Alvin P. Hovey and the Democratic-controlled legislature. The deci-

---

2. On his affection for McDonald and Butler, see *Indianapolis News*, 24 June 1891, 18 September 1895.

sion of the court upholding the governor gave Beveridge's career a
boost. Even more important was his resulting friendship with the
influential Michener, a key figure in winning the presidency for
Benjamin Harrison. Taking a fatherly interest in the younger man,
Michener gave him political advice, helped arrange out-of-state
speaking engagements for him, and gave him entry into top political
circles.

In 1892, he was engaged to represent the state in a suit brought by
the Indiana railroads challenging the increased assessments made by
the newly established State Board of Tax Commissioners. When the
Indiana Supreme Court upheld the State Board, the railroads appealed to the United States Supreme Court, and thus Beveridge had
his first experience pleading before the high tribunal.[3] The case was
highly publicized. According to newspaper stories, more money was
involved than in any tax case ever tried in the United States. Beveridge's role in the case earned him a handsome fee—a reported five
thousand dollars—and the decision of the Supreme Court upholding
the State Board marked another step up for Beveridge. To prospective
clients he would send copies of his brief in the case to demonstrate his
legal talents.

The work of the young lawyer caught the attention of one of the
city's foremost business leaders, Theodore P. Haughey, founder and
president of the Indianapolis National Bank, and Haughey befriended
Beveridge.[4] Haughey's financial empire, however, rested upon shaky
foundations. The first sign of trouble came in 1892 when his National
Accident Association went into liquidation, and Beveridge as the
association's counsel had the unpleasant task of settling the outstand-
ing claims. Then, in July 1893, came the shocking news of the crash of
the Indianapolis National Bank. Investigation by the bank examiners
uncovered grave irregularities. Indictments charging misappropria-
tion of funds were handed down in December against Haughey, his
son Schuyler C. Haughey, and two business associates. With Bev-

---

3. *Pittsburgh, Cincinnati, Chicago and St. Louis Railway Company* v. *Backus,
Treasurer, et al.,* 133 Ind. 625; *Cleveland, Cincinnati, Chicago and St. Louis
Railway Company* v. *Backus, Treasurer,* 133 Ind. 513. *Pittsburgh, Cincinnati,
Chicago and St. Louis Railway Company* v. *Backus,* 154 U.S. 421; *Cleveland,
Cincinnati, Chicago and St. Louis Railway Company* v. *Backus,* 154 U.S. 439.
   4. See, for example, Theodore P. Haughey to Beveridge, 15 August 1892, BP.

eridge by his side as his personal lawyer, Haughey pleaded guilty in April 1894 and was sentenced to six years in prison.[5]

Beveridge succeeded, however, in saving the son. Arguing that the younger Haughey had not acted with criminal intent but had simply followed the instructions of his trusted and respected father, he concluded with an eloquent appeal for mercy. At stake, he pleaded, was the happiness of Schuyler Haughey's young wife. Shall she walk "the future's unknown paths" hand-in-hand with her husband or must she tread "that dark highway alone—no, not alone, but with the ghosts of grief and memory for her companions"? At stake was the future of his little son—"God bless him! God help him!" Shall he have the opportunity of working out his career "without the penitentiary's shadow ever on him" or must he face "a destiny blacker than midnight without moon or star"? At stake was the heart of a mother "whose soul is nightly whipped by the fiends of humiliation and suspense." And at stake was the last hope of his father—a man broken in health and spirit whose only wish was to see his son exonerated for a crime he did not commit. "Will you shut out this little ray of sunshine and leave him forever in the night?" When the jury brought in a verdict of "not guilty," the disgusted prosecutor blasted the jury for allowing their emotions to becloud their judgment.[6]

But Beveridge's success at the bar had more solid foundations than simply the tricks that blinded juries. He brought to each case thorough preparation, a remarkable grasp for details, an almost photographic memory, and a mastery of the law; and these qualities attracted a growing and profitable clientele. He hired a full-time secretary and even took on a law clerk, a young Jewish boy from Connersville, Indiana, Leopold G. Rothschild, who would play an important role in his future political career. In 1893, he moved to a larger office—the same rooms formerly occupied by McDonald and Butler. At that time, he estimated that his was "the second best single practice in town." The following year, the *Indianapolis News* in its special twenty-fifth anniversary issue featured him in its list of "leaders in Indianapolis business and professional life."[7]

---

5. *Indianapolis News,* 9–10 April 1894.
6. Ibid., 19, 21 October 1895.
7. Beveridge to John C. Shaffer, 22 November 1893, Shaffer Papers (ISL). *Indianapolis News,* 6 December 1894. For a complimentary appraisal of Bev-

Beveridge played an increasingly prominent role in the life of his adopted city. He was active in the Commercial Club, the major force for civic progress in the growing city; in the Young Men's Christian Association; in the Meridian Street Methodist Episcopal Church; in the May Music Festival Association; and in the Indianapolis Art Association. He served as attorney for the city's Board of School Commissioners. He could be counted upon to assist in local charity drives. He was elected a member of the prestigeful Indianapolis Literary Club, whose membership of one hundred was composed of the leading business and professional men of the city.

He was a devoted theatergoer and sometimes acted as secret critic for the *Indianapolis Journal*. He even wrote a paper for delivery to the Indianapolis Literary Club seeking to prove that Sir Walter Raleigh had written Shakespeare's plays.[8] In another paper, he lambasted French fiction from Balzac on for its "materialism," "decadence," and lack of "purifying ideals."[9] In the fall of 1894, he made his first trip to Europe and wrote up his impressions for a local newspaper under the title "Notes of a Hasty Journey."[10] He was a popular and sought-after speaker at commencement exercises, Memorial Day celebrations, and patriotic functions. His growing reputation as a speaker led to invitations from the nation's centers of wealth and power—Chicago's Union League, Hamilton, and Marquette Clubs, the Pittsburgh Bar Association, the New York City Republican Club, the Alger Republican Club of Detroit, Philadelphia's Clover Club, the New England Society of Saint Louis, and Boston's Middlesex Club.

During these years, Beveridge formed many of the friendships that would play an important part in his future career. He first met John C. Shaffer when Shaffer was president of the local street railway and he was still an unknown young lawyer. Representing a boy whose leg had been cut off by one of the traction company's horse cars,

---

eridge's abilities as a lawyer by Federal District Judge John H. Baker, see *Dinner and Toasts in Honor of Senator Albert J. Beveridge . . . January 13, 1899* (Indianapolis, 1899), pp. 17–19.

8. Claude G. Bowers, *Beveridge and the Progressive Era* (Boston, 1932), pp. 52–54. Beveridge submitted a copy of the paper to the *Century Magazine*, but the editor was not convinced. C. C. Buell to Beveridge, 21 January 1896, BP.

9. "The Decay in French Fiction" [5 January 1891], BP.

10. "Notes of a Hasty Journey," *Indianapolis News*, September–December 1894, Scrapbook, BP.

Beveridge pleaded personally with Shaffer for a prompt settlement to save the family the expenses of a court fight. Shaffer was so impressed that he engaged Beveridge as attorney for his far-flung traction and utility interests.[11]

In the late 1880's, he was introduced to George W. Perkins, then Inspector of Agencies for the New York Life Insurance Company with headquarters in Chicago. The two men struck up an immediate friendship. Sending Perkins his photograph, Beveridge hailed the insurance company executive as "a flowing bowl of human champagne, sparkling with an effervescing joy which infects, intoxicates and permeates one's entire being with mighty cheer." Reciprocating with a photograph of himself, Perkins predicted that Beveridge— "the handsomest man in the world"—was destined for the presidency of the United States and he would become his secretary of state.[12]

His friendship with Perkins was responsible for Beveridge's engagement in the last major case of his legal career. In 1897, the State Board of Tax Commissioners ruled that life insurance polices were subject to the state's personal property tax. Perkins, at that time third vice-president of New York Life, was so impressed with the lengthy brief Beveridge prepared and sent him challenging the legality of the State Board's action that he sent a copy over to the company's lawyers, and New York Life engaged him to file a test case. He received a five thousand dollar fee for his services, and the decision of the Indiana Supreme Court in favor of the insurance companies attracted nationwide attention.[13] A leading New York law firm even offered Beveridge a partnership. "I don't want to be rich," he replied. "I have other ambitions!"[14]

These ambitions were political. Beveridge had picked the law as his profession largely because the law was the seedbed of the nation's

---

11. See the remarks by John C. Shaffer in *Dinner and Toasts in Honor of Senator Albert J. Beveridge*, p. 45, and *Addresses at the Dinner in honor of Albert J. Beveridge February fifth Nineteen seventeen* (Indianapolis, 1917), p. 23. On his handling of Shaffer's legal business, see Box 278, BP, and the Shaffer Papers.

12. Beveridge to George W. Perkins, 24, 28 October 1897, Perkins Papers (Columbia University Library). Perkins to Beveridge, 25, 30 October 1897, BP.

13. *State Board of Tax Commissioners et al.* v. *Holliday et al.*, 150 Ind. 216. The Armstrong investigation of insurance company practices revealed that New York Life had paid Beveridge $5,204.75 for "law expenses" in 1898. *Chicago Record-Herald*, 17 June 1906.

14. Robert Shackleton, "The New Senator from Indiana," *SEP*, 8 September 1900, p. 10.

political leaders. In every campaign, he left his legal practice and took the stump for the Republican party. He won an enthusiastic following and became one of the state's most popular and sought-after campaigners. "My first desire," he assured a G.O.P. leader, "is to do whatever may be the best for the party so far as I can do, and I shall, at all times and ever, be more than happy to subordinate my own personal desires to what may seem to be the best interests of that great party, upon whose success hangs the welfare of the country and therefore the future of civilization itself."[15]

Like so many Republican stump orators of the days, Beveridge waved the "bloody shirt" with gusto.[16] But more than memories of the struggle to save the Union shaped his political loyalties. As a rising young lawyer, he supported the Grand Old Party as the defender of property and its rights and the bulwark of free enterprise. The swiftness of his own rise had confirmed for Beveridge that any man with the proper qualities could win fortune and that poverty reflected personal faults—idleness, drunkenness, and vice—rather than social ills. "Down with the demagogic cry against wealth," he told a political rally. "I am in favor of everybody being rich. . . . And if we cannot all be rich I am in favor of as many being rich as possible."[17]

He stood firmly for sound money. And he extolled the protective tariff as the foundation stone of national prosperity and well-being. Behind protection's ramparts, the wheels of industry sped forward, agriculture prospered, the American standard of living was safeguarded from foreign pauper labor, and the native genius had full sway to carry the nation to grander vistas of wealth and power. All this would be destroyed by Democratic free trade. "Every time we have had a high tariff," he reminded his audiences, "the country has dined at the Delmonicos of prosperity. Every time we have had a low tariff the land has had commercial delirium tremens."[18]

His popularity on the campaign trail won him increasing political importance. The *Indianapolis News* picked him out as one of the most

---

15. Beveridge to Louis T. Michener, 17 September 1892, Michener Papers (LC).

16. See, for example, *Indianapolis Journal,* 5 November 1892.

17. Campaign Speech 1894, BP.

18. *Indianapolis News,* 5 November 1892.

prominent—and promising—younger Republicans in the state.[19] Aspirants for office sought his endorsement.[20] In 1893, the state's top political leaders approached him to run for state attorney general at the upcoming election. The prize was tempting—the office paid between thirty and thirty-five thousand dollars a year in fees. But after much soul-searching, he turned down the offer. "It is firing my gun off too soon," he confided to John C. Shaffer. "I think that there may be something higher ahead for me—but I shall not care even for that unless I can [do] . . . my country good in the better & nobler sense."[21]

Beveridge's prospects were good in the 1890's. But millions of his fellow Americans had scant grounds for cheer. Never before, not even in the violence-ridden depression of the 1870s, had the outlook appeared so bleak. The drought that had struck the western plains in 1887 returned summer after summer for five years. As wheat fell below fifty cents a bushel and corn to twenty-eight cents, thousands of farms went beneath the auctioneer's hammer. In the South, cotton fell to five cents a pound. In the cities, the panic of 1893 left thousands jobless. A series of spectacular strikes—the Homestead strike of 1892, the Pullman strike of 1894, the warfare along Colorado's Cripple Creek—alarmed middle-class America.

The unrest spilled over into Indiana. In 1894, the coal miners went out in a strike marked by violence and property damage. When Democratic governor Claude Matthews sent in the state militia to restore order in the strike region, Beveridge hailed the governor for his courage "in these days of demagogy." The Populist revolt, the popularity of the free-silver heresy, the march of Coxey's army appeared to Beveridge the portents of social upheaval. "This is the hour," he lamented to Chicago's Union League Club on Washington's birthday, 1895, "of partisanship degenerated into faction, of opinions unsettled, of vagaries abounding, of lawlessness infecting the very air we breathe."[22]

The year 1896 was for Beveridge and like-minded Americans the

---

19. Ibid., 13 November 1894.
20. See, for example, Jno. H. Gillett to Beveridge, 19 April 1892, BP.
21. Beveridge to Shaffer, 20, 22 November 1893, Shaffer Papers.
22. Beveridge to William Scott [June 1894?], BP. *Indianapolis News,* 23 February 1895.

year of crisis. And the Hoosier took to the stump to repel the forces of anarchy. The high point of his campaigning was his address at the Chicago Auditorium under the auspices of the Marquette Club—a speech that won him praise from so influential a national G.O.P. leader as Senator Matthew Quay of Pennsylvania. At stake in the election, he warned, were "all our standards of morals, all our notions of right and wrong, all our ideas of mine and thine, all our belief in the powers and purposes of our government." The nation's future lay in the balance. "Elect Bryan," he exclaimed, "and reap the harvest of destruction, drink the wine of dissolution, and tell history that we are another one of liberty's failures, another Greece, another Rome, another beautiful dream dissolved, another fond experiment of freedom failed."[23]

The Republican landslide in 1896 relieved Beveridge's alarm for the nation's immediate safety. Yet his former bouyancy never returned. The six million votes cast for the Democracy were a warning of the dangers ahead. "The Huns and vandals" of society "are on the march," he told the New York Republican Club on Lincoln's birthday, 1898. Preachments of "piracy" were heard on every side. Demagogues "awaken expectations which nothing but the abolition of property and the reversal of civilization can fulfill." He railed against those who would set labor against capital, the farmer against the banker, the South against the North, the West against the East. Let there be, he appealed, no classes, no sections dividing the American people. All beneath the stars and stripes were brothers, whose destiny and well-being were inextricably joined.[24]

Beveridge romanticized war, rebelled at mere money-making, and lamented the materialism of the age. Even before the depression of 1893, he was a high-flying expansionist and called for extending United States dominion northward over Canada and southward over Mexico, for a powerful navy, for strengthening the merchant marine, for an American-controlled Nicaraguan canal, for acquisition of Cuba and Santo Domingo—"keys to the Gulf, to the Mississippi, to the future Isthmus canal"—for annexation of Hawaii, and for a string of coaling stations "in the Pacific Ocean and in the Australian seas."[25]

---

23. *Chicago Inter Ocean*, 30 October 1896.
24. *Indianapolis Journal*, 13 February 1898.
25. "Our Diplomatic Relations" [13 January 1890], BP.

The European powers, he warned a businessmen's group in June, 1893, "seize island and archipelago and new territory everywhere to make monopolies for their markets and fortresses for their flags," while the United States remained "without a single naval rendezvous in any sea."[26]

The crisis of the 1890s spurred his imperialism. The conquest of new markets abroad for the surplus of farm and factory would restore prosperity. National self-assertion in the world theater would show that the United States had not lost its capacity for growth. Shouldering the white man's burden would give the nation's young manhood a nobler and more uplifting vision than the mere pursuit of gain. As the Cuban crisis came to a head, he had only scorn for those businessmen who demanded "peace at any cost," and he lamented how "the commercial spirit" had "gangrened the heart of patriotism." When the popular clamor forced President William McKinley to send Congress his war message on 11 April, Beveridge was exultant. "At last," he rejoiced to the Republican county convention, "God's hour has struck. The American people go forth in a warfare holier than liberty —holy as humanity."[27]

Amid the shouts of martial fervor, political unrest vanished. Amid the drums of marching soldiery, prosperity returned. William Jennings Bryan interrupted his preachment of free silver to lead the Nebraska volunteers against the Spaniards. At the same time, the conflict marked the final stage in the reconciliation of North and South after the Civil War as Confederate veterans led by "Fighting Joe" Wheeler rallied to the flag. "The present war," Beveridge told a southern newspaper editor, "has been one of the three great national blessings that God's watchful providence has given to his chosen people. . . . No sections any more but a Nation. At last, my friend, a Nation. No, not *a Nation* but THE *Nation. The Nation,* God's chosen people."[28]

The American people had gone to war to free Cuba. The president in his war message had disclaimed any ambition for territorial gains, and Congress in the Teller Resolution had foresworn annexation of

---

26. Speech at the Opening of the Republican Commercial Travellers' Association, 3 June 1893, BP.

27. Beveridge to Perkins, 17 March 1898, BP. *Indianapolis Journal,* 17 April 1898.

28. Beveridge to John Temple Graves, 13 July 1898, BP.

Cuba. But Beveridge had grander dreams. On 27 April—two days after the formal declaration of war by Congress—he startled Boston's Middlesex Club with the blunt declaration that "the first gun of our war for civilization is also the morning gun of a new day in the republic's imperial career." And he painted a glowing word-picture of "the stars and stripes" over an isthmian canal, over Hawaii, "over Cuba and the southern seas."[29]

The newspaper reports of this speech—based upon the advance copies Beveridge had supplied—made no reference to the Philippines. But seeing newspaper reports about Admiral George Dewey's fleet steaming across the Pacific, he included at the last minute a ringing declaration that "the Philippines are logically our first target."[30] After the smashing American victory at Manila Bay, he added the island to his list of impending acquisitions. Although weak-kneed and short-sighted politicians might hesitate, Beveridge had no doubts about God's providential design for his chosen people. "It may be," he exulted to his friend George W. Perkins, "that *we* will not annex the Philippines, Hawaii and Cuba: but *events* will annex them."[31]

Different motives for overseas expansion reinforced one another in Beveridge's mind. There was his own pride of race: the American people were descended from the Teutons of old—a conquering race—and the spirit of their fathers, men who had tamed the wilderness and conquered the continent, lived on. There was America's Christian duty to bring the blessings of its advanced civilization to backward peoples. There was the Darwinian struggle for survival underway "in the world of human society and affairs" as "in the vegetable and animal world,"[32] and this country dared not lag behind in the worldwide race for colonies. There was the need to find markets abroad for the nation's surplus to prevent future depressions with their danger of revolutionary upheaval.

By mid-July, Congress had approved the annexation of Hawaii; Theodore Roosevelt and his Rough Riders had won the battle of San

---

29. *Boston Globe*, 28 April 1898. *Boston Herald*, 28 April 1898. *Boston Post*, 28 April 1898. *Indianapolis News*, 28 April 1898.

30. Beveridge, *"Grant, The Republican." Address . . . At the Banquet of the Middlesex Club of Massachusetts, Boston, Mass., . . . April 27, 1898* [Boston, 1898].

31. Beveridge to Perkins, 7 May 1898, BP.

32. Beveridge to Graves, 13 July 1898, BP.

Juan Hill; the battle of Santiago had broken the back of the Spanish naval power in the Caribbean; Dewey's spectacular victory had focused public attention on the Philippines; and American troops were on their way across the Pacific. Alarmed by the threatened partition of China, business leaders saw in the Philippines the gateway to the Far East. Religious spokesmen and periodicals saw in the islands new fields for missionary endeavor. The imperialist tide was running strongly. To resist, Beveridge warned a Democratic newspaper editor, "is as hopeless as it would be for me to throw myself in the Atlantic and attempt with outstretched arms to turn the course or stay the progress of the Gulf Stream."[33]

---

33. Ibid.

3

Election to the Senate

When hostilities broke out in 1898, Beveridge's first impulse was to volunteer for the army.[1] But he soon abandoned his military ambitions for a bolder undertaking. For years he had looked forward to the time when the United States would embark upon a program of overseas expansion. But he had not expected such a program for at least another ten years. Now with the war that day was at hand, and the prospect that he must "idly sit and witness the procession of events" gave him "a spell of political blues." "I would rather," he exclaimed, "take part in organizing our colonial system than to do anything else on this earth. I would rather map out and advocate the imperial policy of the Republic than to have been the leading statesman of the late war. It means more for humanity, more for our country and a larger place in history."[2]

Not the man to give up his dreams without a fight, he broached to a group of personal friends the possibility of his running for the United States Senate if the Republicans carried the legislature. The meeting was held in mid-May at the law office of James W. Noel.

---

1. Beveridge to Charles G. Dawes, 25 April 1898, BP.
2. Beveridge to Dawes, 10 May 1898, BP.

Present besides Noel were fellow lawyers Frank L. Littleton and Larz A. Whitcomb, and an up-and-coming young businessman, A. M. Glossbrenner. His friends were stunned for a moment by the daring of the scheme. He was not yet thirty-six years of age; he had never held any elective office; he was not backed by any of the state's leading politicians. Despite these handicaps, Beveridge had an abiding faith in his own destiny and succeeded in transmitting that confidence to his friends.

Littleton had served in the last session of the legislature, and had previously filed for renomination. Following this discussion, Noel, Glossbrenner, and Whitcomb agreed to run for the Indiana house of representatives to support Beveridge in his bid for the Senate. A few days later, they induced another friend, Frederick A. Joss, to run for the state senate. Beveridge had made no mistake in his choice of supporters. Though all were still in their late twenties or early thirties, they had made their mark as leaders of the younger Republicans centered in the Marion Club, which had become a major force in the Marion County G.O.P. In June, a county legislative convention nominated Noel, Whitcomb, Glossbrenner, and Littleton for the state house of representatives. Two months later Joss won his senatorial nomination.

Looking to capitalize upon his popularity as a speaker, Beveridge angled for an invitation to deliver the keynote address at the Republican state convention in August. The theme of his speech would be expansion, and he hoped to win personal acclaim that would boost his senatorial ambitions. But the state's top Republican office holder, Senator Charles W. Fairbanks, insisted upon that honor for himself. Beveridge was bitterly disappointed. "Had I conducted the convention today," he fumed, "I would have, in this single day, done seventy-five percent of the work which will be on our shoulders this Fall and Winter."[3]

He strove to recover the lost ground while campaigning that fall. By the time, a spirited debate was underway over the disposal of the fruits of American victory. When he opened the state campaign at a rally at Indianapolis's Tomlinson Hall on 16 September, he added his voice to the growing clamor for acquisition of the Philippines. An onlooker was struck with how "pale and very intense" his face

---

3. Beveridge to John C. Wingate, 4 August 1898, BP.

appeared when he rose to speak, how "every nerve seemed at its highest tension," and how he spoke with such "intense vehemence" that he "fairly hissed out some words with set jaws."[4]

Shall the United States, he asked the crowd, abandon its future greatness across the seas? Shall "the march of the flag"—a march that had taken the American people across a great continent—stop at the water's edge? He reminded his listeners of America's God-given duty to uplift their fellow men. He pictured the Filipinos as children incapable of self-government. He appealed to national pride. "We cannot fly from our world duties," he cried; "it is ours to execute the the purpose of a fate that has driven us to be greater than our small intentions. We cannot retreat from any soil where Providence has unfurled our banner; it is ours to save that soil for liberty and civilization."[5]

An unimpressed young Democrat in the audience thought the speeech "a great string of sophistries and inconsistencies covered by Rhetoric."[6] But the crowd applauded wildly. Thousands more thrilled to his words in the newspapers the next day, and the Republican state committee broadcast three hundred thousand reprints throughout the Middle West. The favorable reaction encouraged him to devote all his campaign speeches to the advocacy of American expansion. His speechmaking helped to prepare the ground for the popular response President McKinley found when he toured the Middle West that fall testing public sentiment on retaining the Philippines.

While stumping, he approached local politicians about his possible senatorial candidacy. The response was heartening, and as rumors began to spread about his plans, promises of support began flowing in from politicians anxious to climb on the bandwagon. After the Republican sweep in the election, he made formal announcement of his candidacy and opened campaign headquarters in the Hotel Denison to greet the politicians flocking into Indianapolis from throughout the state. John C. Wingate of Montgomery County, a skillful and popular political veteran, was placed in charge. He was assisted by two other professionals—Sid Conger of Shelby County and John R.

---

4. Holman Hamilton and Gayle Thornbrough, eds., *Indianapolis in the "Gay Nineties": High School Diaries of Claude G. Bowers* (Indianapolis, 1964), pp. 201–2.

5. *Indianapolis Journal,* 17 September 1898.

6. Hamilton and Thornbrough, *Indianapolis in the "Gay Nineties,"* p. 202.

Bonnell of Montgomery County. "I do not propose to make any blustering fight," Beveridge reported, "but am going to put up the strongest, most vigorous and most unceasing contest you ever heard of. It shall, however, be dignified throughout. It was decided today that my *personal* work was done and that, from now on, my friends must do the rest of the work for me."[7]

One of the first tasks was to overcome the prejudice against a young man barely thirty-six years of age who had previously held no elective office. When he heard that South Bend wagon manufacturer Clem Studebaker had expressed doubts about his age, Beveridge urged a mutual friend to remind Studebaker "that Thomas Jefferson was only 33 years of age when he wrote the Declaration of Independence; that Hamilton was only 32 when he was Secretary of the Treasury; that Andrew Jackson was in the Senate at 30; Henry Clay . . . at 30; Albert Gallatin . . . at 32." His friend District Judge John H. Baker in letters and personal talks testified to his qualifications for the Senate.[8]

A graver handicap was his place of residence. With United States Senator Fairbanks also from Indianapolis, many Hoosier politicians grumbled about the "hoggish propensities of the Indianapolis Republicans."[9] Beveridge's friend Frank Littleton was a candidate for speaker of the Indiana house of representatives, and in mid-December a rumor circulated that his rivals for the senatorship planned to throw their support to Littleton. Supporters worried about antagonism toward Indianapolis pleaded with Beveridge to ask Littleton to withdraw. "Gentlemen," he replied, springing to his feet, "not another word; not one other word. Frank Littleton is one of the best friends I have in the world. . . . I would rather go down to defeat than to imperil by any selfish action of mine the chance of my friend for the office which he seeks."[10]

Although Littleton was elected speaker by acclamation when the legislature met, his election failed to deflate the Beveridge boom. Perhaps Beveridge's rivals had even given him a boost. The speaker-

---

7. Beveridge to Dawes, 10 November 1898, BP.
8. Beveridge to John C. Shaffer, 17 December 1898, BP. On Baker's efforts: Bowers, *Beveridge and the Progressive Era*, pp. 86–87; George W. Steele to Charles W. Fairbanks, 12 November 1898, Fairbanks Papers (LL).
9. *Indianapolis Journal,* 17 November 1898.
10 *Indianapolis News,* 12 January 1899.

ship, with its influence upon committee assignments and legislation, in the hands of a supporter gave Beveridge an advantage in appealing to uncommitted legislators. But rumors persisted that Senator Fairbanks thought the election of another Indianapolis man would not be in his interest. And Beveridge saw the senator's hand behind the announcement on 10 January—the day of the Republican legislative caucus—of the appointment of Addison C. Harris *of Indianapolis* as minister to Austria-Hungary.[11]

Although few Hoosier politicians had taken his candidacy seriously at the start, Beveridge surprised experienced observers by showing unexpected strength. A group of Indianapolis businessmen, led by millionaire carriage manufacturer David M. Parry and banker Charles E. Coffin, organized a "Business Men's Association" for Beveridge, with a membership of over a hundred men from all over the state. Working behind the scenes, Beveridge's managers traded promises of future patronage for votes in the legislature. Most importantly, he alone of all the candidates remained unscarred by the bitter factional rivalry dividing Indiana Republicans.

This factional rivalry dated from 1888. Most of Indiana's top Republicans, headed by John C. New, the publisher of the *Indianapolis Journal,* supported Benjamin Harrison for the Republican presidential nomination. A thirty-six-year-old millionaire railroad lawyer and speculator named Charles Warren Fairbanks, however, led a group of younger Republicans in a fight to pledge the state's delegation to the national convention to Judge Walter Q. Gresham. This round went to the Harrison men. But Fairbanks, spending freely from his personal fortune, continued active in local politics, built up his personal following, and took advantage of the Republican defeat in 1892 to take over the party leadership in the Hoosier state.

With his eye on a senatorial seat, Fairbanks joined the McKinley-for-president movement in 1886. This moved the factional in-fighting to a fever pitch. The Harrison men accused McKinley of having plotted in 1892 to block Harrison's renomination. But the Ohio man's supporters carried the day. In reward for his services to the winning

---

11. Although Fairbanks denied that the announcement of Harris's appointment had been arranged to injure Beveridge's chances, Beveridge remained unconvinced: Fairbanks to Harry S. New, 14 January 1899, New Papers (LC). Beveridge to Dawes, 2 March 1899, BP.

side, Fairbanks was McKinley's personal choice for temporary chairman of the G.O.P. national convention. In January 1897, when the Republican controlled legislature met to choose a successor to replace Democrat Daniel Vorhees, the president-elect threw his support behind Fairbanks. As the only Republican senator from Indiana, all the top federal officeholders in the state were his appointees and looked to him for leadership.[12]

After his election, Fairbanks moved to smooth over party factionalism. Indiana was so closely divided politically that G.O.P. divisions could throw the state to the Democrats, and Fairbanks required the solid backing of his home state to realize his presidential ambitions. But the long-standing antagonisms within the party would not down. A bitter struggle took place over the state chairmanship at the beginning of 1898. And this same factional rivalry flared anew in the contest over the senatorial seat to which Beveridge was aspiring. Had Fairbanks taken an active hand, he probably could have had his way. Unwilling, however, to antagonize any of the senatorial candidates and their backers, he personally followed a strictly hands-off policy.

The front runner in the 1899 senatorial contest was J. Frank Hanly of Lafayette. Though not yet thirty-five, he had served in the Indiana senate from 1890 to 1894, followed by a term in Congress. Supporting him were most of the politicians belonging in the past to the Fairbanks wing of the party. His leading supporters—Marion County political manipulator Joseph B. Kealing, Kealing's law partner, state senator Martin Hugg, and former State G.O.P. chairman George F. McCulloch—were now reported hostile to the senator because of patronage squabbles; but many of his top federal appointees—led by Robert J. Tracewell, Controller of the Treasury, and David W. Henry, the Collector of Internal Revenue at Terre Haute—joined Congressman James A. Hemenway of the First District, James E. Watson of the Sixth District, and Charles L. Henry of the Eighth District in backing the Lafayette man.

While no longer politically active, Harrison personally favored Judge Robert S. Taylor of Fort Wayne for the Senate. A leading

---

12. See, for examples, Fairbanks to David W. Henry, 13 November 1897; to A. E. Nowlin, 23 June 1898; Albert W. Wishard to Fairbanks, 5 March 1898, Fairbanks Papers (LL). S. E. Kercheval to Fairbanks, 14 June 1897, Fairbanks Papers (IHS).

patent attorney and former judge, Taylor had served as a member of the Mississippi River Commission since 1881 and was Harrison's closest friend. He had run—with Harrison's blessing—for the Senate against Fairbanks in 1897. Although highly respected for his ability, Taylor's chilly personality, lack of an adequate organization, and aloofness from the vulgar pushing of the politicians were fatal handicaps.

Seven-term Congressman George W. Steele of Marion was backed by Harry S. New, the son of John C. New and his successor as publisher of the *Indianapolis Journal*. A Civil War veteran, Steele was the favorite of the "old soldier" element. Although he had supported Fairbanks in the 1897 senate contest, he was a former Harrison man. His running cut into Taylor's support; but the two would join in a showdown to block Hanly. And New, in sharp rivalry with Joseph B. Kealing for mastery of the Marion County G.O.P. organization, was determined to beat the Lafayette man at any price.

A fourth candidate was ex-Congressman Francis B. Posey of Evansville, from "the pocket" in southwestern Indiana. Posey had long belonged to the anti-Fairbanks wing of the party. He had scant hopes of winning. Southern Indiana was largely Democratic territory, with few Republicans in the legislature. He was in the race for one purpose —to have revenge on his rival for leadership in the first congressional district, Representative James A. Hemenway. With Hemenway in the Hanly camp, Posey was drawn into the anti-Hanly bloc.[13]

This situation was tailor-made for Beveridge. In 1888, he had supported Gresham, even going to Chicago in hopes of stampeding the G.O.P. national convention from the galleries.[14] But he was too young to have played a major role in the fight. Nor was he personally or politically close to Fairbanks.[15] His friendship with Harrison campaign manager Louis T. Michener had transformed him into an enthusiastic supporter of Harrison's renomination in 1892. And at Michener's behest, he stayed out of the hassle over the 1896 presi-

---

13. My conclusions about the line-up in the 1899 senatorial contest are based upon examination of the *Indianapolis News, Indianapolis Journal*, Fairbanks Papers (LL and IHS), David W. Henry Papers (ISL), Robert S. Taylor Papers (ISL), and Harry S. New Papers (ISL).

14. Beveridge to Walter Q. Gresham, 26 June 1888, Gresham Papers (LC).

15. For Beveridge's anxiety about Fairbanks's possible hostility, see Beveridge to Dawes, 10 November 1898, BP.

dential nomination, thus avoiding the bitterness that followed.[16] Taking as his motto "Keep sweet," he strove to line up second choice pledges from all camps.[17]

As the showdown approached, the Hanly forces continued to exude confidence. Hanly's managers claimed thirty-five members of the legislature—only ten short of a majority—pledged to their man before even the legislature met. But Harry S. New took the lead in arranging for a meeting of representatives of Beveridge, Taylor, Steele, and Posey. An agreement was reached that all would stay in the race until the caucus to keep their pledged votes from shifting to Hanly, and that in the balloting they would throw their support to the strongest candidate to block Hanly.

In the days that remained before the caucus, Beveridge swung his campaign into high gear. A flood of Beveridge-for-senator telegrams signed by the state's top businessmen poured in upon wavering legislators. To give the impression that he was the workingmen's favorite, Beveridge's backers arranged for straw votes at railroad shops and manufacturing plants, and all showed Beveridge the favorite. To stimulate a bandwagon psychology, his managers arranged for one legislator after another to announce publicly his support. On the night before the caucus, fifteen legislators met and pledged to vote for him as long as the contest lasted.

On Tuesday night, 10 January 1899, the eighty-nine Republican members of the General Assembly gathered at the State House to select a United States senator. Beveridge sat in his law office with a few friends, while a lieutenant telephoned the results of each ballot from the caucus. The report of the first ballot shocked him. He had polled only thirteen votes—a disloyal pair had deserted his standard. Shaken by their desertion, Beveridge temporarily despaired of his chances. Thirteen was his unlucky number. But picking up second-choice votes on succeeding ballots, he climbed into second place behind Hanly. As the deadlock continued on ballot after ballot, his confidence returned. "That amounts to nothing," he insisted when his vote dropped two on the eighth ballot. "I'll be nominated."

---

16. Beveridge to Louis T. Michener, 10 June 1892, Michener Papers. Michener to Beveridge, 17, 23 March 1896, BP.

17. Bowers, *Beveridge and the Progressive Era,* p. 89.

The deadlock continued until the ninth ballot. Then suddenly gaining three votes, Hanly polled thirty-seven votes—only eight short of a majority. This was the moment of crisis. No rival except Beveridge remained within striking distance of his lead. Amid heightening tension, the tenth ballot was thrown out because of an error. On the next ballot, the supporters of Judge Robert S. Taylor threw their votes to Beveridge. The backers of Major George W. Steele followed on the twelfth, and final, ballot. Putting down the telephone, Beveridge turned to his friends and calmly announced "Gentlemen, I am nominated." Then he called his wife to tell her the news. "Kitty," he said, "I am nominated, thank God."[18]

His formal election came a week later, on Tuesday, 17 January. The following day, in his speech of acceptance, he set forth the credo that would guide him in Washington:

> I shall fearlessly stand in the Senate of the United States for the business interests of this country, when that means the welfare of all the people; I shall fearlessly stand by the labor interests of the land, when that means the prosperity of all the people; and I shall just as fearlessly stand against the demands of any class, when those demands do not involve the interests of the entire American people and the ongoing of the imperial American republic.[19]

There was a pride about the new senator. Of medium height, he was muscularly built, with broad shoulders; his bearing was easy and confident, his stride rapid—"the step of an alert mind," wrote a friendly reporter; his face thin with a set jaw and flashing blue eyes— "the face of a man who has aimed high and fought hard." Self-conscious about his youthful appearance, he took pains with his dress to impress the world with his importance and dignity. Even before his election to the Senate, an Indianapolis high school student recorded in his diary how Beveridge "seems to have just steped [sic] out of a band box when he rises to deliver an address." Most of his fellow lawmakers had adopted informal attire—Mark Hanna's baggy suits set the new style. But Beveridge retained the formal Prince Albert coat,

18. Charles F. Remy, "The Election of Beveridge to the Senate," *IMH* 36 (June 1940): 131–33.

19. *Journal of the House of Representatives of the State of Indiana . . . 1899* (Indianapolis, 1899), pp. 253–58.

gray-striped trousers, high, stiff collar, and black tie, thus winning the sobriquet of "the fashion plate" of the Senate.[20]

He had planned while running for the Senate to arrange a law partnership whereby his partner would do most of the work while his name attracted the clients. When the preliminary negotiations broke down, however, he reconsidered, turned over his pending business to a friend, and retired from further practice. The abandonment of his law practice was a financial sacrifice. Fortunately, he found that he had a flair for magazine writing, and he turned out on the average ten articles a year at five hundred to a thousand dollars per article.

He would tolerate no commitments that might compromise his political independence or interfere with his duty as a public servant. Although most of his fellow lawmakers accepted railroad passes without a second thought, he would not. While campaigning, he paid all his own expenses and refused reimbursement from the party organization. When one of his closest personal friends, financier George W. Perkins, sent him a personal contribution of $30,000 to assist his reelection in 1904, he returned the money. "The more I see how money is spent by men in politics," he explained to Perkins, ". . . the more firmly determined am I to either win or lose on my merits."[21]

At the same time, he was a political realist. Patronage was the lubricant that kept a political organization going, and Beveridge scrambled to gain his share. For a man without a private fortune, patronage was the only possible way by which he could reward political supporters or even meet personal obligations. Thus, after the death of his first wife, he arranged for a position in the Indianapolis post-office for his father-in-law. And after his second marriage, he badgered the president to find a suitable ministerial post for his new brother-in-law, who was first secretary of the American Embassy in Berlin.

He had a facile mind schooled in the court room. He could absorb and commit to memory with amazing speed materials that came before him. One of his secretaries recalled how he would memorize a major speech at a single reading.[22] Despite a sharp, metallic-sounding

---

20. Shackleton, "The New Senator from Indiana," p. 8. Hamilton and Thornbrough, *Indianapolis in the "Gay Nineties,"* p. 198. Ross, "The Oratorical Career of Albert Jeremiah Beveridge," pp. 91–93.

21. Beveridge to George W. Perkins, 3 October 1904, BP.

22. Bowers, *Beveridge and the Progressive Era,* pp. 159–60.

voice, he was one of the nation's most popular speakers at a time when political spellbinding was highly admired and rewarded. And he worked hard at his speech making, polishing and repolishing what he had to say, rehearsing every detail of his presentation and voicing, and exhibiting a "uniform seriousness" on the platform. His speeches, wrote a veteran Indiana newspaperman, "are linguistic masterpieces, carefully weighed and finished in advance."[23]

He kept up an extensive personal correspondence with personal friends and political lieutenants. He had to attend to the thousand and one errands and favors that his constituents demanded of him. Every campaign he took the stump for the Grand Old Party. He was often up until the early hours of the morning going over official reports, studying proposed new legislation, or preparing an article or speech. He spent his summers away in the country "to get strength from Mother Earth";[24] but even while on vacation he would put in hours each day with a stenographer, writing letters, dictating speeches and articles, and correcting proofs.

His struggle upward had left its mark. The swiftness of his rise left him with a continuing dread of being thrown from his high place. No man was more anxious about his public reputation. He was aggressive in trying to place favorable stories in the newspapers. Thus, he instructed a friendly writer to stress in the biographical sketch he was preparing "my success as a lawyer," "the devotion which my friends have always manifested toward me," "my hard working industry," and the "absolute correctness of my dress."[25] He was even touchy about the photographs that appeared. Time and again he would complain how this newspaper had maligned him, how that newspaper had failed to recognize his achievements. He would boast of his speaking triumphs and claimed an instinctive understanding of, and sympathy with, the man in the street.[26]

Not everyone could warm to Beveridge. He was a highly self-centered person, and, like most self-centered people, he could be

23. Louis Ludlow, *From Cornfield to Press Gallery: Adventures and Reminiscences of a Veteran Washington Correspondent* (Washington, 1924), pp. 285–86.

24. Beveridge to Albert Shaw, 9 July 1902, BP.

25. Beveridge to David Graham Phillips, 2 February 1899, BP.

26. See, for examples, Beveridge to Perkins, 20 October 1900; to Hilton U. Brown, 9 January 1903; to John R. McLean, 5 October 1905, BP.

insensitive to others' feelings. His insistence upon unstinting loyalty and devotion made him difficult to work for. Even his most loyal aides at times rebelled at his unreasonable demands, and there were those who after working for him complained bitterly that no man could serve Beveridge and retain his self-respect. "You are a scholar and a great statesman," one of his closest friends admonished, "but as I have studied your characteristics and achievements it has seemed to me that the alloy in your mental make-up is shown in your lack of receptivity to suggestions or criticisms offered by others to your plans and purposes."[27]

Although he could unbend with a few personal friends and even laugh at himself, the impression he gave outsiders, even before his election to the Senate, was of an "overpowering self esteem." Elbert Hubbard's biting *The Philistine* quoted "a jaundiced gentleman from Terre Haute" on how "Beveridge has the Big-Head, and puts in his spare time comparing himself with Lincoln." Jealous Senate colleagues resented his success "in advertising himself." His posturing, his zeal for the limelight, and his theatrical manner inspired jibes about "the Grand Young Man of Indiana." Washington newspapermen at their annual Gridiron Dinner satirized his never missing an opportunity to make a speech; indeed, he "had made a great many when there were no opportunities."[28]

Even many who sympathized politically with the Hoosier were put off by his vanities. Though convinced that "inside" Beveridge was "a noble soul," Kansas editor William Allen White found his "grand manner"—his "stroking himself on the back with a pride in his oracular wisdom"—"sometimes a bit ridiculous." Secretary of commerce James R. Garfield admitted that Beveridge was right "at heart," but thought him "shallow" and "to[o] full of his own importance." Long before their break, President William Howard Taft complained to his military aide that he could not understand how so "honest and able" a man could be "such a selfish pig. He never talks. He only preaches." *Saturday Evening Post* roving correspondent Samuel G. Blythe, while

---

27. Shaffer to Beveridge, 3 January 1912, BP.
28. Hamilton and Thornbrough, *Indianapolis in the "Gay Nineties,"* p. 198. *The Philistine* 15 (August 1902): 72. Henry Cabot Lodge to Theodore Roosevelt, 14 June 1906, Roosevelt Papers (LC). Louis Brownlow, *A Passion for Politics: The Autobiography of Louis Brownlow, First Half* (Chicago, 1955), p. 398. *Indianapolis Star,* 19 February 1911.

extolling his "courage," "integrity," "splendid mind," and "large grasp of public questions," conceded that he was "something of an egoist, given to vainglorious conversation and declamation," with "an extreme faculty for irritating many with whom he comes in contact."[29]

At the same time, however, he had that mysterious something that inspired and maintained abiding loyalties. His oldest and "most intimate" friend was the novelist David Graham Phillips.[30] Phillips had been one year behind Beveridge at Indiana Asbury. Although Phillips went off to Princeton after his sophomore year, they kept in touch. In his standpat days, Beveridge took Phillips to task for exaggerating the darker aspects of American life at the expense of "the nobler and sweeter and more constructive side and achievements." Phillips dissented from Beveridge's high-flying imperialism and chided him for defending the indefensible in Beveridge's article on the Senate for the *Saturday Evening Post*.[31] But these differences did not affect their feelings toward one another. Beveridge rejoiced in Phillips's growing reputation. And when he could, he ran up to New York to visit with the novelist "to talk and talk . . . and live again a few hours out of the golden past."[32]

Phillips modeled the hero of his political novels, Hampden Scarborough, upon Beveridge. Scarborough works his way through college, has the magical power to sway multitudes with his voice, becomes the leader of the "forces of honesty in his party" against the "forces of the machine," triumphs over the conspiracy of privilege, wins the presidency, and leads the country "back toward what the republic used to be before differences of wealth divided its people . . . [and] made equality before the law a mockery."[33] When Beveridge

---

29. William Allen White, *The Autobiography of William Allen White* (New York, 1946), p. 389. James R. Garfield to Lucretia R. Garfield, 7 October 1906, James R. Garfield Papers (LC). [Archibald W. Butt], *Taft and Roosevelt: The Intimate Letters of Archie Butt, Military Aide* (2 vols., Garden City, N.Y., 1930), 1: 58. Samuel G. Blythe, "Insurgent Indiana," *SEP*, 2 April 1910, p. 4. I am grateful for the Garfield reference to Professor Jack Thompson of the University of Massachusetts.

30. Beveridge to Jesse F. Salyers, 22 June 1922, BP.

31. Beveridge to Phillips, 27 November 1903; Phillips to Beveridge, 31 July 1906, BP. Beveridge's article is "The Senate: A Mirror of Our National Ideals," *SEP*, 14 July 1906, pp. 3–4, 24.

32. Beveridge to Phillips, 13 November 1906, BP.

33. Kenneth S. Lynn, *The Dream of Success: A Study of the American Imagination* (Boston and Toronto, 1955), pp. 140–44.

moved toward progressivism, Phillips was delighted that his friend had become the Hampden Scarborough of his fiction. Phillips's death in January 1911 came as a devastating shock. "The loss grows heavier with the days," he wrote to the novelist's sister. Time did not soften the loss. "How I loved him!" he exclaimed; "it can't be spoken of."[34]

Next to Phillips his dearest friend was John C. Shaffer. Even after Shaffer moved to Chicago, they communicated almost daily. Entering the newspaper field, Shaffer built up a far-flung empire, comprising at its height the *Chicago Evening Post;* the *Indianapolis, Muncie,* and *Terre Haute Stars;* the *Denver Rocky Mountain News* and *Times;* and the *Louisville Herald.* Shaffer's lifelong ambition was to see Beveridge in the White House, and he devoted his time and newspapers to advancing his friend's political career. "There isn't anything," Shaffer assured him, ". . . that can ever affect my *esteem, regard* and *affection* for you." Beveridge returned that affection. "It is impossible for one human being to know another better than I know him," he confided, "and the more I know him, the greater is my love and admiration for him."[35]

The third member of his inner circle was George W. Perkins. Beveridge admired Perkins's "mighty ability," "splendid initiative," "dash & elan," and "resistless enthusiasm," and took pride in his meteoric rise in the business world to become a partner in J. P. Morgan & Company. "I rejoice in your triumphs," he congratulated the financier, "as in my own." He praised Perkins as the exemplar of the new breed of businessmen-statesmen for instituting an employee profit-sharing and stock-ownership plan to reduce labor turnover at the United States Steel Corporation. When Perkins came under fire during the Armstrong Committee's investigation of insurance company practices, Beveridge never wavered in his support. "In all this trial," he assured Perkins, "my heart is always with you as it always has been with you."[36]

After his nomination by the G.O.P. legislative caucus, Beveridge wanted Perkins to come to Indianapolis for his formal election. When his first wife died, he turned to Perkins for solace. After his second

---

34. Beveridge to Mrs. Carolyn Frevert, 27 April[?] 1913, 18 June 1915, BP.

35. Shaffer to Beveridge, 13 March 1914; Beveridge to B. F. Lawrence, 19 September 1923, BP.

36. Beveridge to Perkins, 26 March 1901, 30 September 1905 [— April 1907], Perkins Papers.

marriage, he asked Perkins's advice about investing the new Mrs. Beveridge's money. When his son was born, Perkins was the godfather. And when Beveridge was in financial straits after his defeat for reelection, Perkins hastened to offer his assistance. Worried that Perkins was overworking himself, Beveridge repeatedly warned him to watch his health and take vacations. With Perkins, Beveridge could even joke at himself. He talked freely of his presidential ambitions and promised to make Perkins his secretary of state. "There is only one thing that is exacted in advance," he reminded Perkins goodnaturedly, "and that is that you will recognize who is really boss."[37]

After becoming senator, Beveridge sought out Albert Shaw, editor of the *American Monthly Review of Reviews*. Attracted by Shaw's fervent defense of American expansion, Beveridge wrote Shaw how his articles had "been a great help—even an inspiration" and introduced himself. There followed a long and intimate relationship in which they exchanged personal confidences and views on the political affairs of the day. "There are," Beveridge found, "few as fine & true & loyal & able men as Albert Shaw." "It does me," Beveridge assured Shaw, "a whole lot of good to get a letter from you every week or two; no matter if you have nothing to write about it is a tonic to see your signature."[38]

There was a remarkable intellectual rapport between the lawmaker and editor. On question after question, Beveridge would find Shaw's views identical with his own. Shaw relied on Beveridge for inside information about Washington developments for his "Progress of the World" section. In turn, he boosted the Hoosier in the pages of his magazine. When Shaw ran a piece applauding Beveridge for his "industry, courage, and sheer ability," the lawmaker hailed Shaw as "Dear Old 'Loyalty'" and promised that "when my ship comes to port, dear old man, you'll be with me."[39] So highly did Beveridge regard Shaw's political wisdom that he even sent him advance copies of his speeches for Shaw's approval. When he turned to his historical

---

37. Beveridge to Perkins, 14 May 1903, ibid.
38. Beveridge to Albert Shaw, 27 January 1899, BP. Beveridge to Perkins, 12 July 1905, Perkins Papers. Beveridge to Shaw, 4 December 1911, Shaw Papers (New York Public Library).
39. *American Monthly Review of Reviews* 26 (August 1902): 147. Beveridge to Shaw, 4 August [1902], Shaw Papers.

work, he continued to rely upon Shaw for Shaw's critical judgment and contacts with many of the country's leading historians.

After Beveridge's return from the Philippines in 1899, David Graham Phillips introduced him to George H. Lorimer, the editor-in-chief of the *Saturday Evening Post*. On the lookout for new contributors, Lorimer asked Beveridge to write for the *Post* on his experiences in the Philippines. The articles were so well received that Lorimer welcomed Beveridge as a regular contributor. Beveridge became a frequent visitor to Lorimer's home outside Philadelphia. As with Perkins, he could with Lorimer unbend, joke at himself, and reveal a playful side outsiders never saw.[40]

Beveridge's other, less intimate, companions were largely drawn from the newspaper and magazine world. Sensitive to newspaper criticism, and aware of the powerful influence of the fourth estate in politics, Beveridge deliberately cultivated contacts among the press. Perhaps the most important of these was publisher Frank A. Munsey. Munsey had been favorably attracted by Beveridge's ardent imperialism, and the two men became lifelong friends.[41] But most of his journalist friends were working newspapermen. Beveridge enjoyed their rough-and-tumble company and their hard-drinking, fast-paced life.

His friends saw beneath the surface vanities that repelled so many. They found a man of tremendous driving force, power, and magnetism—a man even of brilliance. And he came to the Senate filled with promise of future greatness. Beveridge, Controller of the Currency Charles G. Dawes recorded in his private journal, "is Presidential timber if he can restrain his immense energies and commanding talents and have the patience to exercise tact and discretion."[42]

---

40. John Tebbel, *George Horace Lorimer and the Saturday Evening Post* (Garden City, N.Y., 1948), pp. 167–69.

41. *Munsey's Magazine* 24 (December 1900): 461.

42. Charles G. Dawes, *A Journal of the McKinley Years*, ed. Bascom Timmons (Chicago, 1950), p. 185.

4

The High Tide of Empire

Beveridge came to the Senate with an all-consuming ambition for the presidency; he even dreamed of the 1904 nomination as within his grasp. With a mixture of arrogance and naïveté, he strove for the limelight. He asked for assignment to the most prized committees of the upper chamber: Foreign Relations, Finance, Judiciary, and the chairmanship of the new Committee on the Philippines. His heart's desire was a seat on the Foreign Relations Committee so that he could shape American policy in the years ahead. To strengthen his hand, he decided to visit the Philippines before Congress met in December 1899. He shared the popular excitement over America's sudden emergence as an imperial power and wished to see at first hand the archipelago. And with his flair for the dramatic, he foresaw the publicity value of the trip.

Beveridge arrived in the Philippines accompanied by his wife, the beginning of May 1899. First he talked with American and foreign businessmen and wealthy Filipinos in Manila; then he made a tour of the front lines to visit with the troops. Everywhere he went he jotted down in his little red notebook details about the resources of the islands, the healthfulness of the climate, the political incapacity of the natives, and the importance of strong measures to suppress the insurgents without delay. Leaving the Philippines, he stopped at Hong Kong to speak with officials and businessmen familiar with the Far Eastern situation, and then went to Japan where he had a lengthy interview with Japanese elder statesman Marquis Ito.

Returning in August, Beveridge declined to grant any interview but went immediately to the Rocky Mountain resort of Banff, for his wife, who had become ill on the trip, needed rest. He arrived in Indianapolis at the beginning of September. Though besieged by newspaper reporters, he continued his refusal to make any public statement. The president, anxious for firsthand news from the islands, invited him to Washington. Beveridge boasted of the "extraordinary" impression he had made upon the chief executive in their talks. Even more gratifying were the newspaper headlines he had won. "You cannot imagine how I have 'caught on' to the country," he reported to George W. Perkins. The press "now calls me the Sphinx."[1]

At the same time, he was pulling strings to obtain his hoped-for committee assignments. He had local businessmen write to Senate leader Nelson W. Aldrich extolling Beveridge's political soundness. George W. Perkins set the Washington lobbyist of the New York Life Insurance Company at work in his behalf. Charles G. Dawes joined in promoting the Hoosier. He so impressed Theodore Roosevelt that the New York governor wrote to his friend, Senator Henry Cabot Lodge of Massachusetts, recommending the newcomer for the Foreign Relations Committee. He haunted the White House to solicit McKinley's backing.

Although not given the vacant place on the Foreign Relations Committee, he was assigned to the new Committee on the Philippines as a reward for his trip. But many senators resented his pushiness. Stories about his vanity and overbearing manner circulated around the capital. The kindly, but well-informed, McKinley regretted that the Hoosier "was hurting his standing here by his unwise methods of securing recognition," and even he found Beveridge "sometimes tiresome."[2]

---

1. Beveridge to George W. Perkins, 16, 30 September 1899, BP.
2. George B. Cortelyou Diary, 23 December 1899, 4 January 1900, Cortelyou Papers (LC).

Statesmen of the past, so Beveridge had been taught, had shaped the nation's destiny by flights of eloquence on the floor of the Senate. And so he hoped to fulfill his dream of guiding America's colonial policy by exploiting his trip in a major speech on the Philippines. To set the stage, he drew up a resolution "declaring our purpose to retain the Islands permanently and administer the government as the situation demands."[3] But after consultation with party leaders, he reluctantly deleted the word "permanently." With the text thus watered down, he succeeded after last-minute scurrying around in winning the lukewarm approval of top G.O.P. lawmakers, and introduced the resolution on 4 January.[4]

When presenting the resolution, he announced that he would deliver a full-dress speech in its support on 9 January. An hour and a half before the Senate met that day, the galleries were already filled, and at noon, when the session began, people were still lining up to get in. A hush settled over the crowd when Beveridge made his appearance. Nervous and pale, he appeared younger than his thirty-seven years. But his listeners sat in rapt silence for two hours as he called upon the nation to fulfill its destiny across the seas.

He appealed to the American people to continue the onward march of the flag; he extolled the nation's historic duty of selfless aid to struggling mankind; he proclaimed the superiority of the Anglo-Saxon race, divinely called to spread its civilization over benighted lands. God, he exclaimed, "has marked the American people as His chosen Nation" to lead "in the regeneration of the world." To uplift "savage and senile peoples" was "the divine mission of America." He told of the archipelago's wealth, its nearness to the vast markets of China, and reminded his listeners of the dangers ahead unless the United States found new outlets for its surplus of farm and factory. Duty and destiny, profit and power, he cried, required that this nation retain the Philippines—"hold it fast and hold it forever."

He ridiculed the arguments of the anti-imperialists. The Declaration of Independence applied to civilized men who were qualified for self-rule. But the Filipinos were "a barbarous race"—"Orientals, Malays, instructed by Spaniards in the latter's worst estate." Nor did

---

3. Beveridge to Perkins, 29 December 1899, BP.
4. Cortelyou Diary, 4 January 1900, Cortelyou Papers. *CR*, 56th Cong., 1st sess., 1899–1900, 33, pt. 1: 644.

the Constitution impose any bar. The Constitution expressly gave Congress the authority to "make all needful rules and regulations respecting territory belonging to the United States." No more sweeping language could be imagined. Even in the absence of this provision, Congress would have the authority to administer the new possessions "in any manner the situation demands." Such power was implicit in the Constitution, "not merely because it is a power inherent in and an attribute of nationality," but "because it is the power most necessary for the ruling tendency of our race—the tendency to explore, expand, and grow."

He accused the anti-imperialists of encouraging the insurgents in their resistance. There must be no halt in military operations, no sign of hesitation or weakness. This country could not withdraw from the islands without loss of its honor and betrayal of its sacred duties. "What shall history say of us?" the Indiana lawmaker asked.

> Shall it say that we renounced that holy trust, left the savage to his base condition, the wilderness to the reign of waste, deserted duty, abandoned glory, forgot our sordid profit even, because we feared our strength and read the charter of our powers with the doubter's eye and the quibbler's mind? Shall it say that, called by events to captain and command the proudest, ablest, purest race of history in history's noblest work, we declined that great commission?[5]

As he resumed his seat amid thunderous applause from the galleries, the drama was heightened when the aged senator George F. Hoar rose to answer. The Massachusetts senator regarded the administration's Philippine policy as a betrayal of the historic principles upon which the republic had been founded. He had not intended to speak, he told the Senate, but he could not sit and allow Beveridge's words to pass without a reply. "As I heard his eloquent description of wealth and glory and commerce and trade," he lamented, "I listened in vain for those words which American people have been wont to take upon their lips in every solemn crisis of their history. I heard much calculated to excite the imagination of the youth seeking wealth or the youth charmed by the dream of empire. But the words Right, Justice, Duty, Freedom were absent."[6]

Correspondents dashed from the press galleries to write up the

---

5. *CR*, 56th Cong., 1st sess., 1899–1900, 33, pt. 1: 704–12.
6. Ibid., p. 712.

clash for the front pages of their newspapers. The anti-imperialist
Springfield Republican charged that Beveridge "talks like a young
Attila come out of the West" and warned that "if his Americanism is
now the true brand, then indeed is the republic no more." Democratic
newspapers jeered that his plea for retention of the islands "forever"
contradicted the president's promises about preparing the natives for
self-government. But a people still intoxicated with dreams of imperial glory thrilled to his words. " 'Twas a speech ye cud waltz to,"
conceded the hostile Mr. Dooley. Congratulatory letters poured in
by the thousands. "After Hoar's reply," Theodore Roosevelt wrote,
"I felt like sending him Whittier's Ichabod." The Republican National
Committee reprinted a million copies of the speech for distribution
throughout the country. The newcomer, wrote the correspondent of
the *Chicago Times-Herald,* has seized "the psychological moment in
the tide of our national affairs, and makes himself famous at a leap."[7]

But the rumblings grew louder. The public acclaim given the new
senator inflamed the jealousy of his colleagues. And even many supporters of the administration's policy were disturbed by the speech,
with its talk of racial superiority, its demand that the United States
retain the islands "forever," and its emphasis upon trade and wealth.
Stung by Democratic jibes that Beveridge had spoken for the administration, McKinley took pains to reassure the public that American
rule over the Philippines would bring not exploitation but "liberty
and justice and good government."[8] When anti-imperialists in Congress seized upon Beveridge's resolution in order to embarrass the
G.O.P., administration spokesmen refused to take the bait.

Too excited by the newspaper headlines he was making to pay
these rumblings any attention, Beveridge plunged headlong into the
debate over American policy toward another of its new acquisitions,
Puerto Rico. The island was in desperate plight. Puerto Rican tobacco,
sugar, and coffee had lost their former Spanish market, while the
prohibitive rates of the Dingley tariff closed the United States to
island products. Complicating the situation was the larger question of

---

7. *Springfield Republican,* 10 January 1900. *Indianapolis Sentinel,* 10 January
1900. Finley Peter Dunne, *Mr. Dooley's Philosophy* (New York, 1900), 129–33.
Theodore Roosevelt to Beveridge, 13 January 1900, BP. *Chicago Times-Herald,*
10 January 1900.
8. Margaret Leech, *In the Days of McKinley* (New York, 1959), p. 486.

the constitutional status of the new possessions. Although denying that the Constitution automatically followed the flag, McKinley, in his annual message of December 1899, did urge free entry of Puerto Rican products to save the island from starvation.

But the House Ways and Means Committee disregarded the president's appeal and reported a bill imposing duties of 25 percent of the Dingley rates on trade between Puerto Rico and the mainland. Under pressure from diehard protectionists led by the tobacco and sugar-beet growers, and worried about setting a precedent for the Philippines, McKinley reversed his stand and gave the Ways and Means Committee bill his support. To soften the blow, the tariff was reduced to 15 percent of the Dingley rates and limited to two years' duration.

When the measure came before the upper chamber, Beveridge promised the chief executive his support. He even defended the Indiana congressmen under attack for voting for the measure in the House. Congress, he replied to protesting constituents, had "a free hand to legislate as the wisdom of circumstances demand for our new possessions." If not—if, as the Democrats held, "the Constitution extends itself, without action of Congress, over Porto Rico, Hawaii and the Philippines, and they become parts of the United States, with ultimate statehood at the end of the syllogism"—then "we had better abandon them at once. Porto Rican, Filipino and Hawaiian Senators and Congressmen are not a refreshing prospect."[9]

Nor did he look upon the measure as a betrayal of the welfare of our wards. All the money to be raised would be spent for the benefit of the island. Since Puerto Rico had no internal revenue system, Congress had no alternative but the tariff to raise the funds for support of the island's government. It must be understood, he wrote to another constituent, "that every dollar of this tariff comes out of the pockets of the sugar and tobacco barons of Porto Rico; that hardly any of it comes off of the people; and that every dollar of it goes to the island, the people, and the improvement of both."[10]

The popular uproar, however, would not down. Newspapers throughout Indiana, Republican and Democratic, joined in attacking

---

9. Beveridge to Harry ——, 7 March [1900]; to Larz A. Whitcomb, 7 March [1900], BP.
10. Beveridge to Frank Littleton, 1 March [1900], BP.

the bill as a betrayal of the administration's promises of benevolent treatment of the new dependencies. Public meetings resounded with protests. A flood of letters poured into the offices of Indiana lawmakers warning of G.O.P. defeat in the upcoming elections if the Puerto Rican tariff were adopted. Local politicians reported that in the eyes of the man in the street the island was as much a part of the United States as Arizona or New Mexico and deserved the same treatment. In a flash, the issue illuminated the simmering discontent at the increasing rate of trustification. The president's sudden reversal was denounced as a surrender to the ultraprotectionists, and suspicions were rife that "improper trust influence" was behind the measure.[11]

Beveridge wavered before this storm. What should he do: defy public opinion or antagonize party leaders? Finally, his anxiety to ride the popular tide prevailed. On Monday, 19 March, he presented an amendment to the bill for removal of all duties between the island and the mainland. The Senate, he explained, had approved—and the House was expected to concur—an emergency grant of over two million dollars for the relief of the island. That sum would suffice until a system of local taxation could be set up. So the plea that adoption of the tariff was required as an emergency revenue measure no longer applied. The constitutional question, he declared, could be safeguarded by passing a declaratory provision reaffirming "that the Constitution of the United States is not extended over Puerto Rico."[12] He promised to deliver a full-dress speech on 22 March in support of his amendment. With this step, the Hoosier had joined a bloc of roughly ten Republican senators in revolt against the party leadership.

Indiana newspapers were loud in their praise. But his action sparked a backlash at home and in Washington. The state's Republican congressmen, all but one of whom had voted for the bill, were infuriated at his retreat when the storm came his way. His colleague in the Senate, Charles W. Fairbanks, stood by the administration. Local politicians complained bitterly about his muddying the political waters. In Washington, the resentment against his pushiness was

---

11. Frederick A. Joss to Beveridge, 13 March 1900, BP.
12. *CR*, 56th Cong., 1st sess., 1900, 33, pt. 4: 3024.

deeper than ever. Even McKinley complained about his "egotism."[13] His fellow senators chuckled at a rhyme going around the capital that pictured Beveridge none too flatteringly:

> There was once a pretty goslin,
> But his friends were very few,
> For he thought that there was nothing
> In the world but what he knew.
> So he always in the barnyard
> Had a very forward way,
> Telling all the hens and turkeys
> What they ought to do or say.[14]

Tremendous pressures were brought to bear upon him. The administration could not afford to retreat: defeat on the Puerto Rican tariff could jeopardize its entire legislative program. The president himself appealed to Beveridge to postpone his speech in the hope that a satisfactory compromise might be worked out. A rumor circulated that Senate leaders would read him out of the party if he gave his speech. Party leaders in Indiana urged him to cease stirring up popular feeling. Giving way, he agreed to postpone his speech until 30 March. Days of indecision followed. He angrily denied that he had surrendered. But in the same breath he expressed his hopes for a compromise which all Republicans could support. The praises of the newspapers turned to jeers. Seeing how the wind was blowing, the bill's floor manager assured the White House that Beveridge "will be all right in the end."[15]

He was scheduled to speak on 30 March, but moved the date up a day so he could leave for the bedside of his wife, who was desperately ill with the dysentery contracted during their Philippine trip. She had been too sick to accompany him to Washington in December but had stayed on in Indianapolis and then went to Asheville, North Carolina, for treatment. When she failed to respond, she was transferred to a Dansville, New York, sanitarium. Distraught over her worsening illness, Beveridge was tempted to go without speaking.

---

13. Cortelyou Diary, 18 March 1900, Cortelyou Papers.
14. *Indianapolis Press*, 23 March 1900.
15. Ibid.

But his friends warned that this would leave him open to accusations of cowardice.[16]

The pressures upon him continued to mount. Senator Joseph B. Foraker of Ohio, the chairman of the committee for the Pacific Islands and Puerto Rico, had tacked on to the tariff measure his bill providing a civil government for the island. And to smooth the return of the bolters, the Senate leaders amended the bill to remove all duties as soon as the new insular government set up a system of local taxation. A political lieutenant reported from Indiana the "unanimous" feeling among the members of the Republican State Committee that Beveridge's refusal to vote for the measure would be "unwise."[17]

On the evening of 28 March, Beveridge's friends Charles G. Dawes and George W. Perkins came over and urged him to fall into line. At their behest, he prepared an addition to his speech backing the measure. But he continued to waver—unwilling, perhaps unable, to decide between a temporary loss of popularity and standing by his party. After a sleepless night, he made his choice. Although the bulk of his speech was a strong, even impassioned, defense of free trade between Puerto Rico and the United States, he concluded by announcing his support of the legislation. The bill, he rationalized, "does establish a working civil government which must not be delayed another moment, and does insure early reciprocity, and so is a step in the right direction in our progress as an administering Nation."[18]

But the speech boomeranged. As he spoke, one after another of the members of the Senate rose and marched noisily from the chamber. Only a half-dozen remained to hear his speech through. At the end, the Hoosier fled in tears from the hall. Supporters of the bill complained that his attacks on the tariff would further inflame popular feeling. Opponents were bitter that he had yielded to party leadership. Indiana political observers found him "very materially depreciated in public estimation." Indiana mugwump and civil-service reformer Lucius B. Swift complained to his wife that Bever-

---

16. Leopold G. Rothschild to Beveridge, 26 March 1900 (telegram) BP.
17. Henry W. Bennett to Beveridge, 28 March 1900, BP.
18. *CR*, 56th Cong., 1st sess., 1900, 33, Appendix: 279–86.

idge was "after all as we always thought nothing but sounding brass."[19]

His departure on the evening of the twenty-ninth for Dansville saved him from worse humiliation. For, on the following day, seventy-nine-year-old Senator Edmund C. Pettus of Alabama rose and delivered a parody of what he called "our great orator" and his "wonderful declamation." Mimicking Beveridge's way of buttoning the top of his coat, his gestures and mannerisms, the aged senator conveyed a picture of ridiculous pomposity. "When you get a genuine orator," Pettus drawled, "he is absolutely absolved from all rules of logic or common sense."[20]

Few senators had ever suffered so rude a handling. None of the eight Republicans who held out and voted against the bill were treated so insultingly. The retaliation was personal, not political. Beveridge thought his political career ruined. But the uproar over the Puerto Rican tariff passed swiftly. Anxious to mend the party's wounds, the administration took no retaliatory action against the bolters. And the Hoosier had learned his lesson. In the future, he would save his speech-making for the stump. Time would heal his wounds. The moment, however, was a bitter one—and was made the more bitter by personal tragedy.

When he arrived at Dansville, he found his wife rapidly sinking. Her death, in mid-June, brought Beveridge close to a breakdown. "I cannot think of anything," he exclaimed in anguish to their former minister, "but that her words come before me, always noble, helpful, for the best. I cannot go any place that I do not see her. . . . It is coming to the point where when I awaken in the morning, it is very close up to the border of insanity for a little while. She is not there, you know, and never will be." Gradually, he found comfort. "I have abandoned thought, analysis and philosophy," he wrote Charles G. Dawes, "—they are good for nothing. I have just come back to that old formula of our mothers which we thought so very shallow in our 'smart' days but which has the very profundity of profoundness in it,

---

19. Albert W. Wishard to Charles W. Fairbanks, 2 April 1900, Fairbanks Papers (LL). Lucius B. Swift to Mrs. Ella B. Swift, 1 April 1900, Swift Papers (ISL).

20. *CR*, 56th Cong., 1st sess., 1900, 33, pt. 4: 3509–10.

namely, 'I believe, help thou mine unbelief.'" He would not lose his grip, he promised his worried friends. He would continue with his career. "There is nothing in this life worth while but love and duty. Duty alone remains to me. . . . I *am* going to try to do what she would have me do."[21]

In the fall of 1900, partially recovered from his grief, he took off upon the campaign trail. When Democratic presidential nominee William Jennings Bryan made imperialism the leading issue in his campaign, Beveridge hastened to take up the challenge. In speech after speech, he sounded the same appeal: that Anglo-Saxons had a God-given duty to uplift benighted peoples across the seas; the country's mounting surplus demanded new markets abroad; the national honor forbade the lowering of the flag. And he was exultant at the G.O.P.'s triumph. "When you run up against the instinct of the American people for national power, expansion and wealth," he gloated to a Democratic leader, "you are running up against a great natural human ocean current, resistance to which is perfect folly. Please remember that we are at bottom English, or to go still deeper, Teutonic."[22]

The McKinley-Roosevelt victory hastened the fullfillment of the nation's long-standing ambition of building a transisthmian waterway joining the Atlantic with the Pacific. No one had been more enthusiastic about the project than Beveridge.[23] But the more he studied the draft convention agreed to in February 1900, whereby Britain was to remove the limitations upon the United States imposed by the Clayton-Bulwer treaty of 1850 and permit an American-built and American-controlled canal, the more upset he became. He started out with an emotional anti-British animus—a legacy perhaps of the Fourth of July orations of his youth, which he would retain throughout his life. And he saw in the Hay-Pauncefote treaty another example of how wily British diplomats had outfoxed their inexperienced and unsuspecting American cousins.

The United States, he protested, would spend millions of dollars to build the canal but would be prohibited under the treaty from reaping any benefit. Under the nonfortification provision of article 2,

---

21. Beveridge to Horace A. Cleveland, 25 June 1900; to Charles G. Dawes, 29 June [1900], BP. Beveridge to Perkins, 26 June 1900, Perkins Papers.

22. Beveridge to John Temple Graves, 26 November 1900, BP.

23. See, for example, *Indianapolis Journal,* 7 February 1900.

the United States could not even stop an enemy fleet during wartime from sailing through the canal to attack San Francisco or New Orleans. The invitation in article 3 to the other powers to adhere to the pact violated the Monroe Doctrine by involving European nations in the affairs of the Western Hemisphere. Most disturbing to Beveridge was that the new pact simply amended, rather than abrogated, the Clayton-Bulwer treaty, thus leaving in force the provision in the 1850 treaty barring both Britain and the United States from colonizing any part of Central America and dooming his dreams of American expansion southward.

Beveridge longed to awaken his fellow lawmakers to these dangers he saw in the treaty. But remembering his humiliation in the Puerto Rican tariff battle, he dared not make a full-dress speech. In this quandary, he decided to make his appeal indirectly. Did the new pact, he asked the floor managers for the treaty, abrogate the Clayton-Bulwer treaty with its bar against United States expansion in Central America? If foreign powers adhered to the treaty, would not their approval be required for its future amendment? The leaders of the fight against the treaty praised him for his "admirable tact and discretion" in raising questions that "alone ought to be enough to kill the whole scheme."[24]

In face of the commotion in and out of the Senate, the upper chamber adopted three amendents: the first stipulated that article 2 should not apply "to measures which the United States may find it necessary to take for securing by its own forces the defense of the United States and the maintenance of public order"; the second formally abrogated the Clayton-Bulwer treaty; and the last struck out article 3. Beveridge wished to go further. Thus he voted for an amendment giving this country a free hand to acquire any territory "as the United States may deem best in its own interests." And he supported another amendment to permit discriminatory charges in favor of American ships engaged in the coastwise trade. But even though these amendments were defeated, he had learned his lesson and voted yea on final ratification.[25]

24. Frederick W. Holls to Stephen B. Elkins, 12 December 1900, Holls Papers (Columbia University Library). Albert Shaw to Beveridge, 15 December 1900, BP.

25. U.S., Congress, Senate, *Journal of the Executive Proceedings*, 56th Cong., 20 December 1900, pp. 619–25.

The British government's refusal to accept the amendments threatened to destroy the budding friendship between the two countries.
But the two powers signed, in November 1901, a second Hay-Pauncefote treaty meeting the American demands. Thereafter the pace of
activity on the canal increased. Beveridge hailed the adoption of the
Isthmian Canal Act in the spring of 1902 as bringing "the dream of
the American people for decades" nearer fulfillment. And he applauded Theodore Roosevelt's intervention in support of the Panama
revolutionists after the Colombian Senate rejected the Hay-Herran
treaty. "After decades of delay," he told the 1904 G.O.P. national
convention, "when the people want a thing done, they want it done."[26]

While the Senate was debating the first Hay-Pauncefote treaty,
the administration and Congress had to deal with another legacy of
the Spanish-American War, Cuba. The Teller amendment to the
declaration of war had promised the Cubans their independence.
But would this promise be kept? Beveridge was a leading champion
of retaining the island. He dismissed the Teller amendment as a
sentimental mistake approved by Congress in a moment of excitement. Cuba lay too near this country's southern coastline and the
soon-to-be-built isthmian canal for the United States to give her up.
And the Cubans were Latins lacking the Anglo-Saxon genius for self-
government. If the United States withdraws, he warned a G.O.P.
rally in the fall of 1900, "revolution will succeed revolution" until the
island falls into anarchy.[27]

McKinley reaffirmed that the promise of Cuban independence was
a sacred pledge. But the administration insisted that the island's
constitution include a provision giving the United States the right to
intervene for the preservation of Cuban liberty and independence
and the protection of life and property. When the Cubans balked, the
chief executive resolved to ask Congress to take action.

Many congressional leaders were doubtful whether action could
be taken, since the Supreme Court had recently decided that Cuba
was a foreign country. Not Beveridge, however. He rushed about
buttonholing senators and pleading that the troops not be withdrawn
until the Cubans gave in. "I hope you'll come out hard on Cuba," he

---

26. *Indianapolis Journal*, 4 July 1902. *Indianapolis News*, 23 June 1904.
27. *Indianapolis Journal*, 26 September 1900.

told Albert Shaw of the *Review of Reviews,* "—Am CONTROL of foreign relations, fortifications, finance [,] sanitation, nothing short of this & the right to intervene in domestic administration at our option. Also hit hard the idea that Congress has no power to act."[28]

The president was consulting with congressional leaders along similar lines. On 25 February, Senator Orville H. Platt of Connecticut tacked an amendment on to the army appropriation bill continuing military occupation of the island until the Cuban constitutional convention yielded to the administration's demands. Both houses gave their swift approval. Beveridge was overjoyed. The Platt Amendment, he boasted, gave the United States over Cuba "the most perfect suzerainty now existing in the world"—stronger than Britain's over Malaya or even that of the Dutch over the East Indies. "For weeks & months even," he wrote Shaw, "I have been quietly laboring for just this. I have never dared to hope that it could be secured now. But it has been & it is great."[29]

When the Democrats attacked the administration for betraying American pledges to Cuba, Beveridge rushed to the defense. The United States, he contended in an article in the *North American Review* that brought him praise from Senate Republican leaders, had a duty to protect the Cubans from foreign interference and from the even graver danger of anarchy. The Platt Amendment was required to uphold the law and order indispensable for the preservation of Cuban liberty.[30] Privately, however, he saw the Platt Amendment as a giant stride toward his goal of annexing the island. Independence would result in anarchy within a few years, and this country would have to intervene. When that happened, the United States would remain permanently. "The Platt Amendment," he prophesied, "never will be abrogated except by a still stronger relation."[31]

---

28. Beveridge to Shaw, 16 February [1901], Shaw Papers.
29. Beveridge to Shaw [— February 1901], ibid. Beveridge to Harry S. New, 10 March 1902, BP.
30. *North American Review* 172 (April 1901): 535–50.
31. Beveridge to New, 10 March 1902, BP.

5

The Ebbing of Imperialism

Until the time came for annexation of Cuba, Beveridge turned his attention to the future of the Philippines. In January 1900, President McKinley had appointed William Howard Taft, a former federal judge from Ohio, to head a commission to take over the administration of the islands from the military. Following the crushing of insurgent resistance, Taft was formally inaugurated civil governor on 4 July 1901. The commission, in its report that fall, recommended establishment of a bicameral legislature composed of an appointive upper house and an elected assembly. His aim, Taft explained to the Senate Committee on the Philippines in February 1902, was to train the Filipinos to "a condition where they will be able to maintain a stable government to protect life, liberty, and property, and if they desire ultimately—it is in the distant future—to maintain a national government of their own."[1]

Beveridge could never accept this possibility. In his eyes, more than lack of training and education disqualified the Filipinos for self-government. Their disqualification was

_____

1. U.S., Congress, Senate, Committee on the Philippines, *Affairs in the Philippine Islands. Hearings*, 57th Cong., 1st sess., 17 February 1902, S. Doc. 331, pt. 1: 331–49.

racial; it was fixed in their blood now and forever. "We cannot change racial characteristics by a season of education," he bluntly told Lyman Abbott of *The Outlook*. His own pride of race would not permit any different answer; his sense of national honor would not tolerate the dishonor of lowering the flag. Beyond any arguments, he exclaimed, "it is our racial instinct to acquire and to *hold*. This may be said to be the inherited wisdom of hundreds of generations. It never can and never will be overcome." When *Review of Reviews* editor Albert Shaw admonished that "never" was a long time, Beveridge stood his ground. "I believe it to be true that 'a people of our blood never leave a land they have once occupied.' According to my present belief, I think we will never quit the Philippines."[2]

When Taft appeared before the Committee on the Philippines, Beveridge cross-examined him about the dangers of a popular assembly for the islands. Would not native demagogues exploit the assembly to fan anew the flames of revolt? Would not obstructionism by the assembly paralyze the administration and bring a host of ills in its wake? Were the Filipinos prepared for the responsibility of so much self-government? His warnings had their impact. There was, committee chairman Henry Cabot Lodge reported to Taft, "a great deal of objection" within the committee to a popular assembly. Taft was disturbed at the news, and he blamed Beveridge, "who," he complained, "thinks he knows more about the Philippines than anyone else."[3]

While discussing the Philippines government bill, the committee had to face a more explosive issue. Stories had filtered back to the United States about army brutality toward the natives in suppressing the rebellion, and the Democrats and anti-imperialists, sensing a campaign issue, filled the halls of Congress and the newspapers with accounts of military atrocities. Beveridge had no patience with these attacks upon the American forces. After his return from the Philippines, he had extolled the bravery and gallantry of the American fighting men in his *Saturday Evening Post* articles. And he had kept in touch with many of the officers and men he had met while there.

When the committee was forced to undertake a full investigation,

2. Beveridge to Lyman Abbott, 7 February, 10, 17 March 1902; to Albert Shaw, 12 February 1902, BP.

3. Henry Cabot Lodge to William H. Taft, 22 March 1902; Taft to Luke Wright, 11 April 1902, Taft Papers (LC).

Beveridge rushed to the army's defense. Given a free hand by committee chairman Henry Cabot Lodge, he prompted friendly witnesses to testify how kindly the army had behaved toward the natives, and brow-beat, ridiculed, and cut short hostile witnesses. He denounced the Democrats and the anti-imperialists for encouraging the insurgents and prolonging the fighting by their attacks upon the administration's policy. Although even he had to admit that acts of brutality had taken place, he replied that such excesses could not be avoided in a guerilla war with a savage foe and insisted that the guilty individuals had been punished. The army as an army fought no war of terror, and Democratic charges of widespread atrocities were an insult to the American fighting men.

Beveridge's counterattack succeeded in blunting the atrocity issue. But the overheated tempers in the Senate chamber exploded over a side issue. Assailing the failure of the State Department to protect the interests of one of his constituents in Mexico, Senator Joseph W. Bailey of Texas denounced the department's solicitor, William L. Penfield of Indiana, as "grossly incompetent" or "shamefully indifferent to the rights of an American citizen in a foreign land." Rising to defend his fellow Hoosier, Beveridge called Bailey's remarks an "unjust and ill-considered attack" upon "a most honorable and able gentleman." The hot-tempered Bailey demanded that Beveridge withdraw his "insinuation." When Beveridge refused, Bailey cried that he had been insulted. There followed a bitter exchange of words. The climax came when Bailey snapped that he could "fathom the intelligence of every other man in the Senate Chamber except that of the Senator from Indiana." "I am very glad to find the Senator beyond his depth," Beveridge retorted amid laughter from the gallery.[4]

The Senate adjourned a few minutes later. Beveridge remained in his seat smoking a cigar and chatting with friends when Bailey came over and demanded that he retract his statement that Bailey was guilty of making an unwarranted attack. When Beveridge refused, Bailey exclaimed, "Then, damn you, I'll make you!" and lunged at the Hoosier.[5] One account had Bailey grabbing Beveridge by the throat with both hands, ripping his collar, and tearing his necktie before Senators John C. Spooner of Wisconsin and Louis E. McComas

---

4. *CR*, 57th Cong., 1st sess., 1902, 35, pt. 8: 7657–67.
5. *New York Times*, 1 July 1902.

of Maryland and the assistant sergeant-at-arms pulled him away. Beveridge reported that Bailey had been caught before reaching him. Paying scant attention to the incident, the Hoosier went that evening to the theater with Senator Orville H. Platt of Connecticut. But the newspapers played up the story, and congratulations flowed in praising him for his coolness and self-restraint.

As the debate over the Philippine atrocities raged, another debate over the Philippine civil government bill went on within the Committee on the Philippines. Making a last-ditch appeal to the committee, Taft dismissed as "altogether unfounded" the idea that a Philippine assembly would fan a new insurrection. The suffrage requirements would limit the franchise to the pro-American propertied classes, while the appointed council would have the authority to vote appropriations if the assembly balked. With the assembly thus deprived of that power over the purse used so effectively in this country's own past to bend royal governors to the colonial assemblies' wills, the advantages outweighed the possible dangers. Nothing, said the governor, would do more to reassure not only the Filipinos but many Americans about this country's benevolent intentions toward the islands.[6]

But his pleas failed to move Beveridge. And, with Lodge's behind-the-scenes support, he prevailed in the committee. The bill that was reported on 31 March simply provided for a census when peace was restored "to enable Congress to establish intelligently a permanent popular representative government for all the islands." No date was given when this step would be taken.[7] Democratic sniping delayed final action until 3 June when the Senate gave its approval.[8] To avoid any backlash, Beveridge kept in the background during the debate on the Senate floor—but the triumph was his.

From the Senate the bill went to the House Committee on Insular Affairs where its fate remained in question. The stand taken by the administration would be decisive. Theodore Roosevelt had succeeded to the presidency in 1901, and that ardent imperialist personally shared the Indiana lawmaker's doubts about a popular assembly for

6. Taft to Lodge, 26 March 1902, Taft Papers.
7. U.S., Congress, Senate, Committee on the Philippines, *Administration of Civil Government in the Philippines, Etc.: Report . . . to Accompany S. 2295,* 57th Cong., 1st sess., 1902, S.Rept. 915, p. 1.
8. *CR,* 57th Cong., 1st sess., 1902, 35, pt. 6: 6227–31.

the Philippines. But Taft, "very much disappointed," was threatening to resign unless the assembly were approved,[9] and secretary of war Elihu Root backed the governor and brought the chief executive around. In line with the administration's wishes, the House committee rejected the Senate measure and reported a substitute providing that "whenever the existing insurrection in the Philippine Islands shall have ceased," the Philippine Commission should hold "a general election for the choice of delegates to a popular assembly."[10]

Beveridge was enraged. Even the "very best" of the Filipinos, he asserted, "are like children."[11] But as a junior member of the Senate committee he was not among the conferees appointed to reconcile the differences between the Senate and House bills. The House conferees stood fast, and, with the session rapidly drawing to a close, the Senate conferees had to yield or have Congress adjourn without any legislation. When the president intervened in behalf of the House substitute, Lodge reluctantly backed down and accepted the House bill amended to require a two-year waiting period of "general and complete peace" before election of the assembly.[12] Beveridge lamented to newspaper publisher Whitelaw Reid that to give the Filipinos a popularly elected assembly was "a frightful mistake." As soon as "it gets into operation it will be fruitful of all sorts of trouble for us."[13]

With the passage of the Philippine Organic Act of 1902 bill, the archipelago faded from public attention. Symptomatic was the repeated defeat of bills to relieve Philippine tobacco and sugar from the high duties of the Dingley tariff. In accordance with his paternalistic attitude toward the republic's wards, Beveridge supported Philppine reciprocity. But the protests of domestic sugar and tobacco producers resounded more loudly in the halls of Congress. Not merely was the public apathetic, but the worsening relations with Japan disillusioned many formerly ardent imperialists about the wisdom of having acquired the islands. Beveridge never shared these doubts.

9. Taft to Henry A. Cooper, 2 April 1902, Taft Papers.
10. U.S., Congress, House, Committee on Insular Affairs, *Civil Government in the Philippine Islands: Report to Accompany S. 2295*, 57th Cong., 1st sess., 1902, H. Rept. 2496, pp. 1–4, 16–17. For House approval, see *CR* (House), 57th Cong., 1st sess., 1902, pt. 8: 7486–87.
11. Beveridge to Harry S. New, 23 June 1902, BP.
12. *CR*, 57th Cong., 1st sess., 1902, pt. 8, 7668–73, 7735–39.
13. Beveridge to Whitelaw Reid, 21 April 1903, BP.

He continued to hail American acquisition as "the most fortunate event that has ever happened or could possibly happen to the inhabitants of these Islands," to rail against the folly of "going too fast in crowding New England's self-government down the throats of Malays who are not prepared to digest it," and to preach that "'What we have we hold' is the motto of our blood."[14]

Beveridge valued the Philippines for their own wealth; but their greatest attraction lay in their strategic location as the gateway to China. Since the 1890s he had been haunted by the dangers of an ever-growing surplus glutting the American market and he looked to China's teeming millions for the solution. By the spring of 1901, however, China appeared on the brink of partition among the powers. The Boxer Rebellion had given the Russians the pretext for moving troops into Manchuria to protect their Chinese Eastern Railway, and an international expeditionary force had captured Peking. Delaying withdrawal of their troops after the suppression of the Boxers, the Russians tightened their grip upon Manchuria. With world attention focused upon the Far East, Beveridge resolved to visit that troubled area. "The Oriental question," he confided to Albert Shaw, "is the world question from now on for the next quarter of a century. . . . This trip will make me easily the authority on the Orient in American public life."[15]

He left New York in May 1901, made stopovers in London, Paris, and Berlin, where he spoke with top government officials, and arrived in Saint Petersburg at the beginning of June. He remained there about a week, then traveled southward to Moscow. He was amazed—even awed—at the vastness of the land, the richness of its soil, and its rapid industrial growth. Taking the recently built Trans-Siberian railroad to Vladivostock, he proceeded southward along the Russian-controlled railroads in Manchuria. The Russian government had promised him a free hand in pursuing his investigations, and he spent a month looking over the situation there. From Manchuria, he went on to Peking; then to Shanghai, to talk with business leaders in the China trade; to Tokyo, to interview Japanese political leaders; and to

---

14. Beveridge to Taft, 15 March 1905, BP. *The Reader* 10 (July 1907): 149, 152.

15. Beveridge to Albert Shaw, 2 May 1901, BP.

the Philippines, to check the changes since his previous visit. How
to keep the Chinese market open for this country's surplus of farm
and factory, he told reporters upon his return to the United States in
October, "is the largest question of our immediate future."[16]

Awaiting his return was a note from the new president, Theodore
Roosevelt, inviting him to the White House to report on his findings.
He took the first train east to impress upon the chief executive the
significance of the Far Eastern situation for the United States. He
bombarded the Senate leaders with pleas for assignment to the
Foreign Relations Committee. The party chieftains were sympathetic.
To his disappointment, however, his factional rival within the Indiana
Republican organization, Charles W. Fairbanks, took advantage of his
seniority to demand the vacant place.

But he could still influence, through his pen, the shaping of American policy. To finance the trip, he had contracted with the *Saturday
Evening Post* to write a series of articles about the Far East. The
articles ran from November 1901 to April 1903, and drew so favorable
a response that he expanded them into a full-length book, which
Harper & Brothers published in December 1903 under the title *The
Russian Advance*. The threat of war across the Pacific made the book
into a best seller, with twenty thousand copies sold within six weeks
of publication.

The message contained in his articles, books, and private talks
and correspondence was simple. The partition of China could not be
long delayed. Not the Open Door notes, but the jealousies of the
powers had saved the Celestial Empire so far. The stalemate could not
last forever. But if the United States backed the winning side, American traders and manufacturers could, in return, gain privileges not
granted to their foreign rivals. And Beveridge had no doubts which
was the winning side. Even before making his trip he had called for
a deal between the United States and Russia. He returned from the
Far East more convinced than ever that Russia was "the great power
of the future"—"the coming autocrat of all the Asias."[17]

An apostle of the "white man's burden," Beveridge came back from
the Far East convinced that Russia was performing in Manchuria the
same civilizing mission that the United States was performing in the
Philippines. Glorifying force, discipline, and authority, he had re-

16. *Indianapolis Journal,* 8 October 1901.
17. *SEP,* 7 December 1901, p. 3.

mained blind during his whirlwind tour to the deep-seated weaknesses in the empire of the czar. The people he had met during his trip were mostly supporters of the regime—government ministers, army officers, nobles, landowners, bankers, merchants, and manufacturers—and their views colored his judgment.

The shortcomings of his outlook were revealed in his contrasting portraits of Witte, Pobedonostsev, and Tolstoy. He hailed Witte as the examplar of an American-style success story—a man of the people who had risen by the sheer force of his abilities to sit at the right hand of czar, an administrative genius who, single-handed, was transforming Russia into a modern industrial power. He was almost as impressed with the reactionary Pobedonostsev. "The whole man is assertion!" Beveridge recorded admiringly. The nationalism of the procurator of the Holy Synod was after his own heart. His distate for Tolstoy, on the other hand, was evident in everything he wrote about him. Tolstoy's surroundings and the man struck Beveridge as neglected, even dirty; "Poverty, want of care, rebellion at system are visible on every side."[18]

Misjudging csarist Russia's stability, Beveridge misjudged the staying power of the csarist drive in the Far East. He saw that war between Russia and Japan was inevitable. Japan could not permit Russia to absorb Manchuria, Korea, and northern China without a fight. But who would win? In his articles and books, Beveridge hedged, but his pro-Russian bias could be read between the lines.[19] Privately, he was more blunt. He dismissed the Anglo-Japanese alliance of 1902 as a weak reed. Britain, he told Senator Orville H. Platt of Connecticut, would not fight when the showdown came. The Japanese had waited too long to act, and the Russians had grown too strong for Japan to defeat unaided. "The first thing for us to do is to have a special understanding with Russia that whatever she does as to other nations, Manchurian ports and Siberian ports shall be open to American goods. I think she would be only too happy to make such an arrangement. And since she is going to hold the province anyhow, why had we not better make the best of the situation."[20]

But his pro-Russian sympathies made scant impression in top ad-

---

18. Beveridge, *The Russian Advance* (New York and London, 1903), pp. 428, 455.

19. See, for example, *SEP*, 8 February 1902, pp. 1–3.

20. Beveridge to Orville H. Platt, 2 May 1903, Platt Papers (Connecticut State Library).

ministration circles. Washington welcomed the signing of the Anglo-Japanese alliance in January 1902 as a counterweight to the Russians, and suspicions were rife, in this country and abroad, that there was a secret agreement between the United States, Britain, and Japan. These rumors disturbed Beveridge. He had long distrusted the secretary of state John Hay and Roosevelt's friend Henry Cabot Lodge as Anglophiles. Now the president, despite their talk after his return from the Far East, was falling into the same trap. To back the Anglo-Japanese alliance would be to support the losing side. "I am awfully afraid," he wrote to Albert Shaw, "that our people will make some commitment in this matter that will rise up to plague us a little later on."[21]

The crisis came in the spring of 1903, when the Russians failed to carry out the second phase of their promised withdrawal of troops from Manchuria and instead made new and sweeping demands upon China. Beveridge hastened to Oyster Bay to make a personal appeal to the president not to join with Britain and Japan in protesting the Russian action. "I never presented a proposition or series of propositions to any one in my life any better than I did this whole business to our Chief," he reported to Shaw. Yet he could make no headway with Roosevelt. "There will be no receding from his Russian determinations. It is an exceedingly critical and far-reaching hour in American diplomacy."[22]

This country's anti-Russian, pro-Japanese policy helped to steel the Japanese to begin war with Russia in February 1904. At the outbreak of the war, public feeling in the United States was strongly in sympathy with Japan. Beveridge was disturbed. Propaganda, he complained, had misled the American people.

> The whole case can be put in three sentences:
> First. A christian nation against a pagan nation.
> Second. A white nation against a yellow nation; and in its larger consequences, the white race against the yellow race.
> Third and most immediately important. A nation which cannot supply its own markets in European Russia itself with manufactured goods and will not be able to do so for the next seventy-five years . . . against a nation, which has manufacturing establishments from one

---

21. Beveridge to Shaw, 12 February 1902, BP.
22. Beveridge to Shaw, 6, 16 July 1903, BP.

end of the Empire to the other, within half a day's sail of China, whose markets we want. In short, a nation which is not our competitor in the sale of manufactured goods, but is a purchaser, and could be made at least twenty times as great a purchaser as it is now, against a nation which is not only a competitor but the only great competitor with us for Oriental trade.

With its growing population and high degree of industrialization, Japan had to monopolize the Chinese market to maintain its own prosperity. Since the United States could not prosper without foreign markets for its surplus, another irrepressible conflict lay ahead. "Should Japan win in this war," he warned, "our next great row will be with her, and no statesmanship can prevent it any more than it has been able to prevent the war between Japan and Russia."[23]

As Japan won victory after victory, growing doubts were expressed in the United States whether the Empire of the Rising Sun would act so differently from Russia in the Far East. Anxious to preserve the Far Eastern balance of power, Roosevelt stepped in to bring peace. Beveridge was heartened by this belated realization of the Japanese threat. And in December 1905 he attained his long-cherished ambition of membership on the Senate Foreign Relations Committee. But his hopes of making the committee a springboard from which to influence American foreign policy proved illusory. By 1906, there was little interest in foreign problems. The enthusiasm of the days of the Spanish-American war had faded. Developments in the Caribbean would show how far the public mood had changed.

Beveridge had long preached that national security required American hegemony in the Caribbean. Thus he applauded Roosevelt's forcefulness in upholding the Monroe Doctrine when, in the winter of 1902–3, the German navy blockaded Venezuela to force the payment of debts to its nationals. His praise was even louder for the so-called Roosevelt corollary. But his long-range aim differed from the administration's. Roosevelt's purpose was to prevent European intervention in the Western Hemisphere; he disclaimed any wish to acquire new territory. Beveridge looked forward to extending American "suzerainty" over the entire Caribbean. "These islands," he told a G.O.P. rally, "are geographically the territory of the United States."[24]

23. Beveridge to John H. Baker, 17 March 1904, BP.
24. *Indianapolis Star*, 23 September 1906.

The key was Cuba—and over Cuba the differences between Beveridge and the White House came to the front. Beveridge had never lost faith that Cuba would relapse into anarchy and that American troops would be forced to return. In the meantime, he urged for adoption of reciprocity with Cuba to strengthen the economic and financial bonds tying the island to the United States. He applied for a place on the Committee on Relations with Cuba whenever a vacancy should occur, and in December 1905 he was given the place. The following summer a revolt broke out against the government of President Estrado Palma. Palma, helpless to suppress the revolt, requested in September 1906 that the United States intervene.

Beveridge rushed to Oyster Bay to urge Roosevelt to send in troops and take over the island. The president, sensing that the country's ardor for imperialist adventures had passed, listened with annoyance. Undaunted, Beveridge took to the stump during the election campaign to appeal directly to the people. The United States, he exhorted G.O.P. rallies, had fulfilled its pledge, foolishly given, to grant the island independence. Now that the Cubans had shown their inability to maintain that independence, let the United States return, and this time "to stay," to save the island from anarchy.[25] His calls for annexation of Cuba, he reported to the president, bring "a response very much like the wild enthusiasm that preceded the Spanish War."[26]

But Beveridge was carried away by his own enthusiasm. Newspaper after newspaper warned that any United States intervention under the Platt Amendment should be temporary. Although the breakdown of negotiations between the warring Cuban factions forced him to intervene, Roosevelt pledged withdrawal of American troops as soon as order was restored. When Beveridge protested that "it is nonsense to keep on setting up one Cuban government after another," the president described him as "perfectly rabid" on the question. "*One* Cuban government has been tumbled over," Roosevelt warned Beveridge. "It would come perilously near bad faith if we do what would amount to seizing this excuse immediately to conquer the island."[27]

---

25. Ibid.
26. Beveridge to Theodore Roosevelt, 1 October 1906, BP.
27. Roosevelt to Taft, 4 October 1906, Roosevelt Papers. Roosevelt to Beveridge, 5 October 1906, in Elting E. Morison, et al., eds., *The Letters of Theodore Roosevelt* (8 vols., Cambridge, Mass, 1951–54), 5: 444–45.

Beveridge was bitterly disappointed. The Cubans were incapable of self-government, he insisted, and the United States would again be forced to intervene. The president's stand had simply delayed annexation for a few more years. But the day of further expansion had passed. The excitement and enthusiasm following the Spanish-American war had given way to apathy toward—and disillusionment over—overseas responsibilities. Exaggerated hopes of new markets abroad had proved to be largely illusory. And the return of prosperity relieved the anxieties that had spurred imperialism in the 1890s. As revived confidence for the future replaced the grim despair of the years of farm revolt and labor strife, building an overseas empire appeared to most Americans a meaningless diversion, a waste of energies that could more profitably be devoted to securing more progress within the United States.

Beveridge retained the imperialist fever of the turn of the century. He continued to dream of "A Continental Republic" with the stars and stripes over Canada and Central America, continued to preach "American control of the Pacific," continued to proclaim the "duty" of the United States as an "administering" nation to bring civilization to backward people.[28] But his pleas for annexation of Cuba, his demand that the United States retain the Philippines forever, his calls for an active Far Eastern policy gradually ceased to be echoed or heeded. And he was too shrewd and ambitious a politician to hang onto a fading issue. Seeing that the public had lost interest in foreign affairs, he began to neglect his duties as a member of the formerly prized Foreign Relations Committee and spend his time on questions more in the limelight.

---

28. *SEP*, 5 September 1903, p. 4; 19 September 1903, p. 10. *The Reader* 7 (May 1906): 569.

6

Politics in State and Nation 1899–1904

Despite his nationwide fame as the champion of imperialism, Beveridge dared not rest upon his press clippings. To remain in the Senate, and even hope to attain his dream of the presidency, he had to build a solid power base in Indiana. The danger came not so much from the Democrats. Although the two parties had been closely balanced in the decades after the Civil War, 1896 inaugurated a long period of Republican ascendancy. Bryan's nomination led to the lasting defection of many sound-money Democrats, while long-term economic, social, and demographic developments—the return of prosperity, the heightened nationalism spurred by the Spanish-American war and its aftermath, growing industrialization and urbanization, rising farm prices and agricultural diversification, the lagging population growth of the traditionally Democratic southern part of the state, and the declining proportion of foreign-born in the state's population—solidified the Republicans' grip on Indiana. The all-important struggle took place within the Republican party between Beveridge and his fellow senator Charles W.

Fairbanks. That struggle would shape Indiana Republican politics for the next twenty years.

At the start, their rivalry involved no more than a struggle for power. Beveridge came to the Senate a loyal defender of the time-hallowed planks of the Grand Old Party. Haunted by the specter of social upheaval from the grim days of the 1890s, he denounced as "political catalines" those demagogues who "set brothers laboring in one calling against brothers laboring in another"; blasted class hatred as the arch-enemy of the republican government; pleaded for "American unity" against "the prophets of dissension." "The great truth of the hour," he told a bankers' meeting, "is this: the real interest of every American citizen is the true interest of every other American citizen; the ultimate good of any class is the final good of all. . . . The real prosperity of every industry and every calling rests on the prosperity of every other industry and calling in the Nation. When we injure one we injure all."

His overriding aim remained to restore that sense of national purpose, that spirit of national discipline he believed indispensable for the American people to attain their destined mastery in the world theater. He delivered strident appeals for discipline, solidarity, loyalty; he exalted the national purpose, the national will, and the national welfare. "As a nation of brothers, undivided by imaginary and needless differences," the United States could fulfill its imperial destiny. "But if we are divided among ourselves," he warned his audiences; "if we waste and scatter our forces which, united, are irresistible, we will, instead of achieving the mastery of the world, lose the mastery of ourselves."[1]

Thus he risked popular disapproval in Indiana to support Mark Hanna's ship subsidy bill. Few Hoosiers could see any profit in a subsidy for the merchant marine. That the major beneficiary would be the Morgan-dominated shipping trust reinforced middle western hostility. But the protests from Indiana did not move Beveridge. A strong merchant marine was required for national power and greatness. His complaint was that the measure approved by the Senate was too limited. He favored, he confided to his friend John C. Shaffer, a larger subsidy. "The reason why we do not adopt it," he

---

1. *Indianapolis Journal,* 7 February 1900.

exclaimed, "is because we fear the power of the demagogues among the people. I do not fear them and am prepared to vote for such a bill right now."[2]

The outcry first against the Puerto Rican tariff, then against the ship subsidy bill, were but symptoms of a growing uneasiness about the rapid pace of industrial consolidation and concentration. Another symptom was the increasing popularity of the "Iowa Idea" to remove tariff protection from trust-made goods. Beveridge was dismayed to find, while stumping the middle west in the fall of 1902, "many signs of a tide of semi-Populism rising within our party." There must be no faltering, he urged Senate leaders. "In thirty years we have not had more need for steady sanity in our party counsels than at this particular hour."[3] And he assured the editor of the arch-conservative *New York Sun* that he was "the most earnest of those who resist demagogical attacks upon property and property rights."[4]

Beveridge hailed the consolidation of business into larger and larger units as part of the onward march of progress. The trust had developed in response to the demands of modern life. He admired as modern heroes the J. P. Morgans, the Rockefellers, the Harrimans, who had transformed the United States from an agricultural nation to the world's foremost industrial power in the brief span of a generation. "The friendship and support of the great generals of affairs like yourself," he told the president of the mammoth New York Life Insurance Company, "—the men who by sheer force of imperial qualities, have compelled the recognition of the world—are to me very precious indeed."[5]

He had no patience with those doubters who saw in the rise of the giant corporation a threat to the historic American dream of opportunity. All that was required for success were the traditional virtues —industry, thrift, perseverance, and morality. This was the advice he gave to youthful inquirers, and this was the message he broadcast to the world, first in a widely read series in the *Saturday Evening Post* and then in a best-selling book *The Young Man and the World*. Do not be discouraged, he preached. "The great things have not all been

2. Beveridge to John C. Shaffer, 19 March 1902, BP.
3. Beveridge to Orville H. Platt, 27 August 1902; to John C. Spooner, 12 October 1902, BP.
4. Beveridge to Paul Dana, 14 September 1903, BP.
5. Beveridge to John A. McCall, 30 January 1899, BP.

done; scarcely have they been commenced." Even if you fail, regret not. "Be your deeds little or big, one thing you *can* do and be: *You can be a man.* . . . And to be a MAN, in our American meaning of that word, is glory enough for this earthly life."[6]

Beveridge admitted that evils, such as overcapitalization, unfair competition, and price manipulation, had accompanied the rise of the giant corporation. But he blamed a handful of wrongdoers. The public, he explained to a Nebraska audience, must distinguish between the "good" trust and the "bad" trust. "A trust is a good trust when it . . . produces better goods at cheaper prices and delivers them to the consumer more conveniently than a dozen different concerns could do." A "bad" trust "dishonestly" raised its prices "to satisfy the greed of its managers."[7] His model of a "good" trust was the United States Steel Corporation; his prototype of the new business-statesman was his friend George W. Perkins. And he waxed enthusiastic about the way more and more business leaders were looking upon their positions as public trusts.

Even Beveridge, however, had to grant that not all businessmen were "wise and honest." When there was business wrongdoing, the people's government had to step in to restrain "the foolish and criminal."[8] But in the same breath he warned against precipitate action that would upset the delicate mechanism of business. He had only scorn for "the wild and foolish proposition of the Democrats to destroy trusts."[9] Indiscriminate trust-busting was foolish and destructive. To break up the giant corporations would fatally handicap the United States in the worldwide struggle underway for overseas markets. "What we are all against," he proclaimed, "is the dishonest operation of these trusts, just as we are all against the dishonest conduct of any man. But the sensible thing is not to destroy them; the sensible thing is to remedy them."[10]

These views made Beveridge a much sought-after speaker before businessmen's gatherings. Speaker of the House of Representatives "Uncle Joe" Cannon thought his speech before the Indiana Bankers'

---

6. Beveridge, *The Young Man and the World* (New York, 1905), pp. 280, 309.
7. *Indianapolis Journal,* 29 September 1900.
8. *Denver Post,* 19 September 1902.
9. Beveridge to H. C. Pettit, 17 August 1902, BP.
10. *Indianapolis Journal,* 29 September 1900.

Association "hit the bull's eye." An executive of J. P. Morgan reported that he had heard praise on all sides for Beveridge's speeches on the trust question—even from the *Commercial and Financial Chronicle*, "one of our old, conservative and cranky papers." Railroad magnate James Hill applauded his 1902 Washington's Birthday speech for its "conservative forethought." A spokesman for the National Association of Manufacturers could find "no reason why this Association should not be one of the strongest endorsers of Senator Albert J. Beveridge."[11]

There was nothing in this political outlook that distinguished Beveridge from his colleague Charles W. Fairbanks. The only issue on which they differed was the Puerto Rican tariff, and that storm passed swiftly. Conflicting ambitions, not principles, lay behind their clash. After his election, Beveridge made no secret of his ambitions for the presidency. Fairbanks had his own presidential aspirations. Seeing Beveridge as a dangerous rival for the G.O.P. leadership in Indiana, he hastened to mend his political fences. "His friends," a lieutenant reported from Washington, "will have nothing to complain about respecting his readiness to get charge of the party organization in Indiana. In my judgment, he is at work right now, and will never let up until things are going right."[12]

In the upcoming struggle, the party structure favored the "ins." The key man in the political structure was the precinct committeeman. The precinct committeemen constituted the county committees and elected the county chairmen. At the beginning of even-numbered years, party members gathered in mass meetings to elect the precinct committeemen and delegates to the district conventions. The district conventions selected the district chairmen, one for each of Indiana's thirteen congressional districts. The district chairmen in turn made up the state committee, which named the state chairman. Before 1901, party organization was not regulated by law. In that year, the legislature required the election of precinct committeemen by ballot in the two counties—Marion (Indianapolis) and Vanderburgh (Evansville)—having a city with a population of fifty thousand or more. A 1905 law extended this requirement to Vigo County (Terre Haute).

---

11. Joseph G. Cannon to Beveridge, 15 September 1903; Charles Steele to Beveridge, 10 April 1902; George W. Perkins to Beveridge, 26 February 1902; John M. Maxwell to Beveridge, 16 January 1903, BP.

12. Robert J. Tracewell to David W. Henry, 23 January 1899, Henry Papers.

But even in these counties, the election machinery was left in the hands of existing party organizations.

The method of nominating local party candidates, by direct primary or by delegate convention, remained up to the county committees, even in the counties covered by the 1901 law. The single exception was Vigo County, where the 1905 law made the direct primary for such nominations mandatory. And nominations of congressmen and statewide officers were by delegate conventions. The delegates to these nominating conventions were selected by ballot or another round of mass meetings, at the call of the county committees, with the second the favored procedure outside of the larger cities. On paper, authority flowed upward from the rank-and-file party members. In practice, however, the permanent standing committees ran party affairs and dominated the nominating convention. The lubricant that kept this party machinery going was patronage to reward past services and guarantee future loyalty. But dissatisfaction over the distribution of the patronage was the leading source of hostility toward the "ins." With his election, Beveridge became the hope of the "outs" throughout the state. All those unhappy with the political status quo rallied to his banner.

But Beveridge faced an uphill fight. Fairbanks was a multimillionaire who spent freely to advance his political ambitions. Through his railroad connections, he arranged for free passes for his supporters. He had close personal and political ties with President William McKinley. He secretly owned a three-quarter interest in the *Indianapolis News*, the state's leading newspaper, and his cousin, Delavan Smith, was its publisher.[13] Aptly described as "a curious combination of mugwump-Fairbanks organ," the *News* was independent in national affairs but a Fairbanks booster when his ambitions were at stake,[14] and Beveridge repeatedly complained about its hostility. Nearly all the state's federal officeholders were Fairbanks appointees. Beveridge had to rely upon a handful of personal friends, who were businessmen and lawyers first and politicians second, to look after his interests in Indiana.

At the first test of strength—the party reorganization in January

13. *Indianapolis Star*, 6–8, 10 September, 3 October 1919.
14. William Dudley Foulke to Theodore Roosevelt, 7 March 1908, Roosevelt Papers.

1900—Fairbanks strengthened his grip upon the party machinery. In the spring of that year his long-time associate, Colonel Winfield T. Durbin, the Republican national committeeman from Indiana, easily captured the G.O.P. gubernatorial nomination. Reflecting the White House's wish to soft-pedal the Puerto Rican tariff issue, the platform adopted by the state convention simply endorsed the administration's colonial policies in broad terms without going into any details. But because of the resentment his stand had aroused among party regulars, Beveridge had to forego his ambition to serve as chairman and keynoter of the gathering.

The 1900 state convention marked the nadir of Beveridge's political fortunes. With the beginning of McKinley's second term came a reshuffling of the patronage. Forgiving Beveridge for his bolt on the Puerto Rican tariff, the chief executive assured him that he would divide the Indiana patronage "half and half."[15] Beveridge's share consisted of the postmastership in two of the four Democratic congressional districts plus the Collector of Internal Revenue for the Terre Haute District and United States Marshal. As collector, he named Crawfordsville postmaster John R. Bonnell. The marshalship went to Henry C. Pettit of Wabash, a former speaker of the Indiana House of Representatives.

With these appointments, Beveridge built the nucleus of a political machine manned by full-time professionals. Bonnell handled affairs in southern Indiana from his base in Terre Haute. A personal friend, Charles W. Miller of Goshen, who was elected state attorney general in 1902—"our strongest man," the senator called him—had charge of northern Indiana. Pettit, "the Moltke of our forces," had overall supervision of his affairs in the state.[16] Leopold G. Rothschild, nicknamed the "Baron," acted as liaison man between the senator and his Indiana lieutenants. Shortly after Beveridge had opened his law office, Rothschild had come seeking a job as a clerk, and taking an immediate liking to the younger man, Beveridge had taken him on. In return, Rothschild idolized Beveridge. His unquestioned loyalty and devotion made him Beveridge's most trusted confidant in his home state.

To gain the support of his constituents, Beveridge spent much of

---

15. Beveridge to Henry W. Bennett, 9 January 1901, BP.
16. Beveridge to Roosevelt, 16 June 1903, Roosevelt Papers. Beveridge to Gifford Pinchot [—— 1903], Pinchot Papers (LC).

his time and energy in performing the innumerable errands and favors Americans expect from their representatives. He worked to increase Indiana's share of the "pork-barrel" voted by Congress for federal buildings and river improvements. He introduced dozens of special pension bills on behalf of veterans who could not fulfill the general pension requirements. He pushed for the establishment of rural free delivery routes in Indiana. He sought to gain favor through distribution of the free seeds he received from the Department of Agriculture. He made repeated flying trips back to Indiana to meet with local politicians, attend Grand Army of the Republic meetings, speak to businessmen's clubs, local bar associations, and church groups.

But his colleague retained the advantage of his ties with the White House. When the Indianapolis postmastership became vacant while Beveridge was away at his wife's bedside, Fairbanks pushed through the appointment of his own man without his colleague being consulted. And he induced the president in the spring of 1901 while Beveridge was away on his Russian trip, to promote district attorney Albert W. Wishard to the post of solicitor of the Department of Interior to make a place for Joseph B. Kealing, the state's top political manipulator. The new district attorney wasted no time in forcing the resignation of state chairman Charles S. Hernly, who had become more and more suspect to the Fairbanks people, and replacing him by Kealing's hand-picked man, James P. Goodrich of Winchester.

The situation was abruptly transformed by the assassination of McKinley and the succession of Theodore Roosevelt. While vice-president, Roosevelt had regarded Fairbanks with suspicion as a rival for the 1904 presidential nomination. Now he was president and would brook no rival. Not that Fairbanks personally posed a serious danger. The threat came from Mark Hanna, the man who had made McKinley president and was now senator from Ohio and Republican national chairman. Whom would Fairbanks support in a showdown?

Beveridge was returning from his trip to the Far East when he learned of McKinley's death. He immediately saw its importance for his political fortunes, and with Albert Shaw, a long-time friend of Roosevelt's, acting as intermediary, he hastened to jump aboard Roosevelt's bandwagon. He hoped to join the inner circle around the new president and even purchased a horse in expectation of invitations to accompany Roosevelt on his famous jaunts through Rock

Creek Park. But Roosevelt could never warm personally to the Hoosier. Beveridge was too pushy, too puffed up with his own self-importance for his liking. "Thy servant is not a Beveridge," Roosevelt cracked to Henry Cabot Lodge, "and does not . . . expect you to keep in mind the different speeches that I make."[17]

Yet Indiana was a pivotal state, and as Roosevelt worked with Ohio's Joseph B. Foraker to undermine Hanna in his home state, so he played up to Beveridge to undermine another possible rival. Their alliance was sealed when the question arose of a successor to the late Judge William A. Woods of Indiana on the Federal Court of Appeals for the Seventh District. Beveridge recommended Judge Francis E. Baker of the Indiana Supreme Court. Baker was the son of Federal District Judge John H. Baker, and Beveridge never forgot the kindness the old judge had shown him in his early legal career. Taking up the challenge, Fairbanks refused to agree to Baker's appointment. All understood the stakes involved in this test of strength under the new administration. "This matter," Beveridge confided to John C. Shaffer, "is more important to me than anything that has arisen or will arise during my public life short of the one great event. My supremacy in Indiana would be fixed by this with more certainty and permanency than anything I can imagine."[18]

Beveridge's strategy was to identify his interests with Roosevelt's. Thus, he warned the latter of Fairbanks's continued presidential aspirations and told of his own efforts to keep Indiana in line for Roosevelt. But should his choice for the Federal Court of Appeals not be appointed, then his influence—and Roosevelt's position—in Indiana would be destroyed. The beneficiary would be Fairbanks, or worse, Hanna. These pleas struck a responsive chord with the president. The announcement on 10 December of Baker's appointment threw Indiana politics into a turmoil. The bandwagon politicians hastened to pledge their loyalty to the junior senator. Aspiring job seekers were advised to gain his backing since he was the man closer to the new president. Even the *Indianapolis News* conceded that the appointment was a blow to Fairbanks's prestige. Beveridge was exultant. "Everything in Indiana is fixed as well as it can be," he

17. Roosevelt to Henry Cabot Lodge, 16 October 1906, in Henry Cabot Lodge, ed., *Selections from the Correspondence of Theodore Roosevelt and Henry Cabot Lodge* (2 vols., New York, 1925), 2: 246–49.
18. Beveridge to Shaffer, 28 November 1901, BP.

wrote to Shaw. "It's not *just* as I would have it but nearly so as possible."[19]

This upset intensified the behind-the-scenes jockeying for position. Fairbanks was not willing to take second place to his younger rival. He was embarrassed and infuriated at stories in the newspapers relating how Beveridge had swung Indiana into line for Roosevelt, and he blamed Beveridge for inspiring the articles. For his part, Beveridge was disturbed by the continuing rumors of opposition to his reelection, with Governor Winfield T. Durbin most frequently mentioned as his would-be nemesis. "We cannot expect any fair, honorable or just treatment from the other side," he warned his supporters in Indiana. "All that can be done against us they will do."[20]

Adding to his anxieties was the Hoosier newspaper situation. His strongest newspaper champion, the *Indianapolis Press*, ceased publication in April 1901. He continued to receive sympathetic treatment in Harry New's *Indianapolis Journal*. But the *Journal*, with its partisan reputation, was in serious financial difficulties. Rumors in the summer of 1901 that the paper was for sale alarmed Beveridge. To prevent the *Journal* from falling into the hands of his colleague, he appealed to his friend John C. Shaffer, publisher of the *Chicago Evening Post*, to buy the paper. Unfortunately Shaffer could not raise the money. Although the publisher of record when the *Journal* was sold the following spring was former congressman and electric railway promoter Charles L. Henry, the understanding among Indiana politicians—and correctly so—was that Fairbanks himself had provided the bulk of the purchase money.[21]

More upsetting news came from Ohio. Just before the meeting of the Republican state convention in May 1903, Senator Joseph B. Foraker publicly demanded that the convention endorse Roosevelt for the presidential nomination. Hanna balked, protesting that such action was premature. The news alarmed Beveridge. The mainstay of his political strength in Indiana was his alliance with the White House. The possibility of a successful fight against Roosevelt's nomination heartened his factional rivals and threatened to undo his own

---

19. Beveridge to Albert Shaw [— January 1902], Shaw Papers.
20. Beveridge to Pettit, 15 May 1902, BP.
21. At the time of the sale of the *Journal* to George F. McCulloch in June 1904, Fairbanks owned over four-fifths of the capital stock: Charles L. Henry to Charles W. Fairbanks, 2 June 1904, Fairbanks Papers (LL).

efforts to win Indiana for the president and himself. "Hanna," he complained, "made a break and a bad one."[22]

The flurry passed swiftly. The president had previously undermined Hanna's strength in Ohio by his handling of the patronage. Now Roosevelt's insistence on publicly drawing the line between friend and foe forced Hanna to back down. Beveridge hastened to gain maximum political advantage from the collapse of the Hanna boom. "We are very busy now DOING necessary things," he reported to Roosevelt. "The organization *will be yours absolutely*." But, he warned, no risk must be taken. "DO NOTHING *affecting Indiana directly or indirectly or remotely or in any other way*," without consulting him. The moment was well chosen. "All right," the still nervous chief executive replied, "I shall do nothing about Indiana save after consultation with you."[23]

Encouraged by this promise, Beveridge pushed to take over the party leadership at the reorganization in January 1904 and to replace state chairman James P. Goodrich with his own man. But the political situation was too fluid for Beveridge or his rivals to risk a showdown. Durbin publicly disclaimed any ambition of running for the Senate. At the same time he warned that he would have to reconsider if Beveridge continued his fight against Goodrich. Taking the hint, Beveridge called off his supporters. At the Republican "love feast" at the end of December, Beveridge praised the state chairman as "trained, effective, unselfishly devoted to the party's interests." In return, the party's top leaders—"everybody," Beveridge reported, "from the State Chairman, senior Senator, Congressmen and all the speakers"—declared for Beveridge's reelection.[24]

Beveridge's retreat was a wise move. In three out of the four districts where the contests for the district chairmanship were not called off, the candidates he opposed were elected. Nor could he prevent the nomination of J. Frank Hanly for governor. But he had achieved his larger aim. The Republican state convention adopted a resolution endorsing his reelection and calling upon "the Republican delegation in the next General Assembly" to give him their "unanimous support."

---

22. Beveridge to Shaffer, 28 May 1903, BP.
23. Beveridge to Roosevelt, 16 June 1903, Roosevelt Papers. Roosevelt to Beveridge, 18 June 1903, BP.
24. *Indianapolis Journal*, 31 December 1903. Beveridge to Shaw, 31 January 1904, BP.

This resolution, he boasted to friends, marked "the first time in the history of the State of Indiana that any convention of any party ever took such action. Our State Convention two years ago did not do it for Fairbanks, and it was never done for Harrison, Morton, Hendricks or McDonald."[25]

Political expediency born of Indiana's political situation had inspired his adherence to Roosevelt. He was worried, however, about the new chief executive's reputation as an impulsive and not quite safe man. These doubts were heightened by rumors that Roosevelt would ask Congress in his first message to establish a Department of Commerce to supervise the activities of giant corporations. "Time is doing more to solve this question than anything else," he complained to George W. Perkins; "and if there be one defect in our system of legislation, it is the adoption of hasty and ill-advised laws. In such a co-operative industrialism as is now coming to exist in the United States most difficulties remedy themselves, if given sufficient time and sufficient freedom from ignorant experiments."[26]

But his anxieties swiftly passed. He seconded Roosevelt's affirmation that publicity was the first requisite for remedying trust "evils." And he extolled the administration's proposed Department of Commerce legislation as "an immense step toward a safe and sane control of organized industry by which the evils may be reduced without destroying the good." Most important, he found Roosevelt a man after his own heart, who wished to "check any improper or hurtful tendencies" without "disturbing and dislocating the business of the whole country," who shared his dream of a united America attaining mastery on the world stage, who was committed to his own vision of a powerful national government able to curb corporate wrongdoing, mediate between capital and labor, and remedy the worst abuses of modern industrial society, and who, devoted to the national welfare like himself, stood above the clash of selfish interests.[27]

Given his vanity, Beveridge was subject to fits of depression in which he complained about the president's lack of appreciation. But even he fell under the spell of Roosevelt's exuberant personality.

---

25. *Indianapolis News,* 27 April 1904. Beveridge to Perkins, 28 April 1904, BP.
26. Beveridge to Perkins, 31 October 1901, BP.
27. *Indianapolis Journal,* 12 September, 23 December 1902. *Indianapolis News,* 23 March 1903.

Theodore Roosevelt, he exclaimed to Chief Forester Gifford Pinchot, was a "peach."[28] Knowing his man, Roosevelt took pains to flatter Beveridge. He sent over advance copies of his speeches for him to read, asked his advice, and arranged for him to second his nomination at the G.O.P. national convention. In his speech, Beveridge pulled out all stops in his praise of the chief executive. "It was," he wrote Roosevelt, "from the very heart. And that was because you have earned it —deserved it."[29]

At the same time, his reputation as a Roosevelt man did not hurt his standing with the Senate's ruling quadrumvirate of Nelson W. Aldrich of Rhode Island, Orville H. Platt of Connecticut, William B. Allison of Iowa, and John C. Spooner of Wisconsin.[30] From his first days in the upper chamber, Beveridge had longed for their approval. He looked up to Allison as a guide. He thought Platt the foremost constructive statesman of his time. The Connecticut senator became as "dear and close" to him as if he were his own father, and years after his death Beveridge would continue to hang his picture in a place of honor in his study and write to his widow as his "Sweet New England Mother."[31] Watchful for promising younger men, the Senate leaders began grooming him for a more important role. His first step upward came in 1902 when he was picked to sit with Aldrich, Allison, Spooner, Mark Hanna, and Eugene Hale of Maine on the all-powerful Republican Steering Committee.

In June 1903, Aldrich casually invited Beveridge to join with the top Senate Republicans at his summer place that August to discuss the legislative program for the upcoming session. When no further word came from Aldrich, Beveridge was terribly upset. He even wrote to Aldrich, reminding him in none-too-subtle fashion of his invitation. Much to his relief Aldrich responded with a formal invitation. Beveridge was so pleased that he leaked the news to the newspapers. "The very fact of my meeting with the older, wiser and universally recognized conservative members of the Senate," he confided to Orville H. Platt, "will still further the correction now in such rapid progress

---

28. Beveridge to Pinchot, 23 June 1903, BP.
29. Beveridge to Roosevelt, 25 June [1904], Roosevelt Papers.
30. See, for example, the defense, even praise, of Roosevelt as a "conservative" by Senator Orville H. Platt: Platt to John H. Flagg, 30 December 1903, Platt Papers.
31. Beveridge to Shaw, 10 November 1904, BP. Beveridge to Mrs. Orville H. Platt, 29 July 1916, Platt Papers.

of the original impression given out when I entered the Senate that I was not a moderate and safe man."[32]

As his first term in the Senate neared its finish, Beveridge's political career looked promising. And all signs pointed to a Republican sweep. The Democrats were split, dispirited and saddled with the lackluster Judge Alton B. Parker as their candidate. Roosevelt's "square deal" had captured the public imagination. Chronically anxious over the future, Beveridge was more nervous about the results than most of his fellow Republicans. Rumors that the Democrats had given up on the presidential race and were concentrating upon the legislative contests alarmed him, and he was furious when the National Committee refused to send more money and speakers into Indiana. By mid-October, however, even his spirits revived amid the multiplying evidences of the Republican tide.

Stumping Indiana, Beveridge hailed the tariff as the bulwark of national prosperity and warned that a Democratic triumph would bring depression in its wake. He even played with the "bloody shirt," attacking the Democrats for opposing relief for the old soldiers. But he made his strongest appeals upon the Roosevelt record. The Northern Securities suit, the Department of Commerce bill, and the anthracite settlement marked the beginning of a new day of justice for all. Roosevelt's election, he told his audiences, "means that no power in this republic, however strong or rich, no organization, however numerous and determined, is too great for the sovereignty of the law; no citizen, however poor or humble, no interest, however small or weak, is too insignificant for the law's protection."[33]

The results surpassed the most optimistic forecasts. Roosevelt carried the state by over ninety thousand votes, J. Frank Hanly was elected governor by more than eighty thousand, and the G.O.P. captured the legislature by a five-to-one margin. So large was the Republican legislative majority that Beveridge claimed a personal victory. "I carried counties in this State for the Legislature that went for Parker and all the rest of the Democratic ticket except the legislative candidate," he boasted to Albert Shaw. "That is to say, our legislative victory is greater than the Presidential victory so far as the State is concerned."[34]

---

32. Beveridge to Platt, 13 July 1903, Platt Papers.
33. *Indianapolis Star,* 29 September 1904.
34. Beveridge to Shaw, 14 November 1904, BP.

7

Statehood for the Southwest

The accidents of Senate seniority—death,
retirement, defeat, and more attractive committee chairmanships—elevated Beveridge
to the chairmanship of the Senate Committee on Territories when Congress met in
December 1901. By that date, the entire
continental expanse of the United States
had attained statehood except for the territories of Oklahoma, New Mexico, Arizona,
and the still unorganized Indian Territory.
In the 1890s, aspirations for territorial statehood had foundered over the issue of free
silver. After the turn of the century, however, statehood activities took on renewed
life. And the Republican platform in 1900
declared in favor of "the early admission to
statehood of the Territories of New Mexico,
Arizona, and Oklahoma."[1]

Beveridge's background and sympathies
prejudiced him against southwestern aspirations. He remembered how in the 1890s the
senators from the sparsely settled Rocky
Mountain states had nearly forced the country into the dishonor of monetary repudiation and brought the republic to the verge of
anarchy. Suspicious of the Democratic lean-

---

1. Kirk H. Porter and Donald B. Johnson, eds.,
National Party Platforms (Urbana, Ill., 1961), p.
123.

ings of the territories, he feared lest their admission upset the balance of power in the Senate. With future relations of business and government, the protective tariff, and foreign policy at stake, no risk must be taken. "My present tendency," he confided to Albert Shaw upon becoming committee chairman, "is in favor of the admission of Oklahoma and the Indian Territory as a single State and the rejection of the applications of New Mexico and Arizona."[2]

The issue came up sooner than Beveridge had anticipated. In the House of Representatives, New Mexico's Republican delegate, Bernard S. Rodey, joined with Democrat Marcus A. Smith of Arizona to arrange bipartisan support for a so-called omnibus statehood bill for the admission of Oklahoma, New Mexico, and Arizona. The bill reserved to Congress the right to add the Indian Territory, wholly or in part, to Oklahoma, while an accompanying measure gave the Indian Territory territorial status for the present. The bill was reported from the House Committee on Territories and passed the lower chamber on 9 May 1902, after scant debate. And in the Senate, the powerful and ruthless Mathew S. Quay of Pennsylvania, whom Beveridge rated as "the greatest practical politician" of the time, was pushing for prompt approval by the upper chamber.[3]

Taken by surprise, Beveridge saw that his only hope of blocking passage of the bill lay in pigeonholing it in his committee. The committee members were split. Five Republicans led by Beveridge were against the bill; Quay and four Democrats were for it. The pivotal vote was that of Republican senator Thomas R. Bard of California. Bard was under heavy pressure from southern California business interests with ties in Arizona to support the admission of the territories, but his anti-Catholic bias made him adamant against the admission of New Mexico. At its meeting on 14 June, the committee voted to postpone action on the statehood bill until the next session. Although the bill's supporters moved to discharge the committee, Beveridge took advantage of senatorial tradition to block action until the next session. The Indiana senator thus won the first round—and breathing space in which to rally his forces.

Working in close touch with the Senate leaders, Beveridge gained

---

2. Beveridge to Albert Shaw, 10 January 1902, Shaw Papers.
3. For Beveridge's appraisal of Quay, see *Indianapolis Star*, 21 December 1921.

their support for his own statehood program: the admission of Oklahoma with the Indian Territory as one state while leaving New Mexico and Arizona as territories. He appealed to his friends in the magazine and newspaper field to hit the omnibus bill "right between the eyes," sought to round up witnesses who could testify in support of his stand, and arranged to lead a subcommittee in an on-the-spot investigation of the territories. "My thought is," he confided to Wisconsin's John C. Spooner, "that if we would look over the ground in person and with impartial and judicial severity, our report will carry great weight on the country at large and that will have some influence on certain Senators who want to kick over the traces."[4]

The four-man subcommittee—Beveridge, Republican senators Henry E. Burnham of New Hampshire and William P. Dillingham of Vermont, and Populist Henry Heitfield of Idaho—arrived in New Mexico on 12 November and finished twelve days later at Guthrie, Oklahoma Territory. As the subcommittee traveled from place to place holding its hearings, Beveridge gathered data on the population of the territories, the educational situation, and the agricultural industrial possibilities. Angry statehood boosters claimed that the Hoosier was more interested in defaming the people of the territories than in finding out the facts.[5]

Their anger was the more because Beveridge had found the ammunition he was looking for to resist the omnibus bill. His majority report from the Committee on Territories concluded that neither Arizona nor New Mexico was qualified for admission. Arizona had a population of only 123,000. Approximately one out of four of the territory's inhabitants did not speak English; 29 percent were illiterate in "any language whatever." Saloons and gambling houses were allowed to run day and night throughout the week, even on Sundays. Lack of water ruled out substantial agricultural development, and mining, its largest industry, could not provide a lasting base for future population growth. The issue, he told the Senate, was "the great fundamental principle of democratic government, to wit, that in

---

4. Beveridge to John C. Shaffer, 31 October 1902; to John C. Spooner, 12 October 1902, BP.

5. For complaints about Beveridge's tactics, see, for example, A. A. Armstrong to Charles W. Fairbanks, 30 December 1902, Fairbanks Papers (LL).

determining the policies of the Republic it shall be the people who shall be represented, and not merely square miles."[6]

New Mexico had a population of 195,000, but these were mostly Spanish-speaking Mexicans. More than 32 percent of the population could not read or write English or Spanish, and the aridity of the land made future population growth unlikely. Publicly—and even more bluntly privately—he made no secret of his animus against New Mexico's Spanish-speaking population. An Anglo-Saxon supremacist, he identified New Mexico with the Philippines. "Its enormous 'Mexican' preponderance in population, whose solidity fifty years of American influence has not changed," he told a Southern newspaper editor, "is the chief reason against the admission of that Territory."[7]

Perhaps Beveridge's most telling piece of ammunition was what he had learned of the forces behind the omnibus bill. Quay, he alerted his newspaper and magazine contacts, was acting in behalf of his long-time political lieutenant William H. Andrews (nicknamed "Bull"), who headed a syndicate of Pennsylvania industrialists and politicians with timber, mining, and railroad investments in New Mexico. Andrews hoped with the support of the political machine led by territorial governor Miguel A. Otero to tap the public treasury for a subsidy to finish his Santa Fe Central Railroad from Torrance northward to Santa Fe. The trouble was that federal law limited the amount of territorial indebtedness. Statehood would remove that stumbling block—and Quay was not the man to begrudge a friend a favor.[8]

But what disturbed him most was not Arizona's sparse population, not "Bull" Andrews's financial manipulations, nor even New Mexico's Spanish-speaking majority, but the fact that Arizona, Oklahoma, and the Indian Territory were strongly Democratic. While the Republicans had retained the upper hand in New Mexico throughout most of the years since the Civil War, the steady migration from Texas foreshadowed a Democratic majority within the near future. Beveridge feared that passage of the omnibus statehood bill would wipe out at a

---

6. U.S., Congress, Senate, Committee on Territories, *New Statehood Bill: Report to Accompany H.R. 12543*, 57th Cong., 2nd sess., 1902, S. Rept. 2206, pt. 1: 1–26, 29–31. *CR*, 57th Cong., 2nd sess., 1903, 36, pt. 2: 1122–23.

7. Beveridge to John Temple Graves, 18 February 1903, BP.

8. Beveridge to Frank Munsey, 4 December 1902, BP.

stroke the G.O.P. majority in the Senate. And partisan advantage was transmuted in his mind into national gain. "We are right in this matter," he assured *Indianapolis Journal* publisher Harry S. New, "—right from a party point of view and right from that higher point of view compared to which party interests are very small indeed."[9]

In dealing with Arizona and New Mexico, Beveridge could show weighty grounds apart from partisanship why admission should be denied. Oklahoma presented a more difficult question: it had a population of more than 400,000, largely native-born, and a flourishing agriculture, and its prospects for future growth were promising. Even Beveridge had to admit its qualifications for statehood. But Oklahoma could not be dealt with apart from the Indian Territory. There a tangled situation confronted Congress. Within the Indian Territory lived the Five Civilized Tribes—Cherokees, Seminoles, Creeks, Choctaws, and Chickasees. By 1895, however, roughly 250,000 whites—outnumbering the Indians by four to one—had moved into the Indian Territory. These newcomers had no legal right to their land, no voice in the tribal councils that governed the Indian Territory, no share in making the tribal laws under which they lived.

To remedy this situation, Congress had set up in 1893 the so-called Dawes Commission to arrange for the allotment of the lands belonging to the Five Tribes. Follow-up legislation provided for municipal incorporation, whittled down the authority of the tribal governments, and set 4 March 1906 as the date for their final termination. But what would take their place? The legislation establishing the Dawes Commission and the agreements made by the Commission with the Five Tribes had envisaged the Indian Territory's "ultimate" admission as a state. To forestall that danger, Beveridge wished to join the Indian Territory and Oklahoma without delay. The two, he explained in his majority report, supplemented one another. Oklahoma was largely agricultural and grazing country; the Indian Territory had rich timber and mineral resources. Combined, they would make a great state, "a noble addition to the Nation of which their people and the citizens of the whole Republic would be justly proud."[10]

Beveridge wanted to call a formal caucus to bind all Republican lawmakers to vote for the majority report. Though balking at this

9. Beveridge to Harry S. New, 19 December 1902, BP.
10. *New Statehood Bill,* 57th Cong., 2nd sess., 1902, S. Rept. 2206, pt. 1: 26–29.

departure from Senate tradition, the Republican leaders of the upper chamber—Nelson W. Aldrich of Rhode Island, William B. Allison of Iowa, Orville H. Platt of Connecticut, Mark Hanna of Ohio, and Eugene Hale of Maine—promised Beveridge their backing. The president's position was still in question. Theodore Roosevelt had recruited many of his "rough riders" from the Southwest, and while vice-president, had promised his former comrades-in-arms to support admission of the territories. But the Senate leaders induced the chief executive to exert his influence in behalf of the majority report. The information given him, Roosevelt replied to a plea from the Oklahoma delegate for his support of the omnibus bill, had "seriously shaken" him "as to the propriety of admitting New Mexico and Arizona as states at this time." Oklahoma, he declared, "should stand on its own merits, apart from the other two."[11]

Despite this formidable backing, Beveridge faced an uphill fight. Quay had lined up a majority of the upper chamber behind the omnibus bill: the solid Democratic minority hoped for six and perhaps eight new Democratic senators; the Rocky Mountain bloc—Republicans and Democrats alike—aspired to increase the area's bargaining power in national affairs; and a group of eastern and middle western Republicans with personal, political, and/or financial ties in the Southwest. These last included such party stalwarts as Boies Penrose of Pennsylvania, whose brother was part owner of a large Arizona mine; Stephen B. Elkins of West Virginia, a former New Mexico lawyer–land speculator and owner of vast tracts in New Mexico; and Joseph B. Foraker of Ohio, whose brother was a prominent New Mexico stockman and United States Marshal for the territory and an ardent statehood booster.

After counting heads, Beveridge saw that his only hope was to filibuster the bill to death. Quay threatened to block action on the appropriation bills unless the Hoosier allowed a vote on the omnibus bill. Although Beveridge remained adamant, the Senate leaders were reluctant to have the stalemate continue. The majority report proposed joining Oklahoma with the Indian Territory. Arizona had been part of New Mexico Territory until 1863. Why not reunite the two into a single new commonwealth? Quay, warned about losing his

---

11. Theodore Roosevelt to Dennis T. Flynn, 4 December 1902, Roosevelt Papers.

majority, was willing. Even if Arizona were joined with New Mexico, his friend Andrews could probably induce the new state to vote a subsidy for his railroad. The stumbling block was Beveridge. Through January and into late February, he continued to insist upon "no compromise."[12]

With the upper chamber facing a hopeless logjam as the filibuster continued, Beveridge reluctantly acquiesced. Whereupon Arizona's delegate Mark Smith, proclaiming that his people would rather remain a territory for fifty years than be joined with New Mexico, rallied the Democratic minority against the so-called joint statehood proposal. Faced with the threat of another filibuster, the Senate leaders decided to postpone action on the measure. Quay, exhausted from the fight, conceded on the floor of the Senate that the omnibus bill was dead. "I have won this fight," Beveridge exulted, "—the hardest and most notable one perhaps seen in the Senate for many a year." His victory "all the more notable because it seemed so hopeless," completed in Beveridge's own words, "up to to-day a record in the United States Senate unequalled in the attainment of a single Senator since that body was organized."[13]

With the 1904 presidential elections looming up, Beveridge—seconded by the Senate leaders—wanted to postpone action on "the whole wretched business" until after the campaign.[14] Quay, wanting no more delay, pushed for prompt approval of joint statehood. But Beveridge warned the president that wise politics dictated the postponement of all controversial and possibly divisive issues. Yielding to Beveridge's wishes, Roosevelt made no reference to the statehood question in his annual message to Congress. Although Quay tried to raise the matter in the Senate, continued Democratic hostility blocked action. And Quay's death on 28 May 1904 removed any further danger from that quarter.

While holding off action in the upper chamber, Beveridge arranged for the more disciplined House of Representatives to take the lead in preparing the way for prompt action after the election. The new Speaker of the House, Joseph G. Cannon of Illinois, reshuffled the membership of the House Committee on Territories to guarantee a

---

12. Beveridge to Shaw, 12 February 1903, BP.
13. Beveridge to Shaffer, 28 February 1903; to H. C. Pettit, 3 March 1903, BP.
14. Beveridge to William B. Allison, 7 September 1903, BP.

majority favorable to joint statehood. So successfully had Cannon done his work that a bill admitting Oklahoma with the Indian Territory as one state and Arizona with New Mexico as a second was rushed through the House in April 1904.

As soon as the "lame duck" session of Congress met in December, Beveridge reported the measure favorably from the Senate Committee on Territories. He was confident—as events proved, overconfident—about its passing the upper chamber. Within a few days, however, he saw that a bitter struggle lay ahead. Joint statehood roused fierce antagonisms. Territorial politicians saw their chances of governorships and senatorships reduced by half, corporate interests saw injury to their financial stakes in the territories, and the rival parties maneuvered for advantage in the unending game of politics. Their protests sounded outward from the territories to reverberate in the halls of Congress.

Joining Oklahoma with the Indian Territory into what Beveridge called Oklahoma the Great did not arouse the controversy that joining Arizona with New Mexico stirred. In Oklahoma, popular sentiment was favorable from the start. What hostility there was came from the territory's Republican politicians. Local G.O.P. leaders pleaded that the Republicans could retain control of Oklahoma, but that if Oklahoma were joined with the Indian Territory, the new state "would be as surely Democratic as Texas."[15] But Beveridge rejected their pleas as "kindergarten politics."[16] The influx of population from neighboring Texas would make Oklahoma Democratic whether or not it was joined with the Indian Territory. And with the national party leadership committed to joint statehood, the Oklahoma Republicans gave up the fight.

The Indian Territory presented more difficulties. The narrow ring of tribesmen who had dominated the tribal governments hoped to magnify their future political importance by the admission of the Indian Territory as a separate state. In July 1905, the chiefs, or their representatives, of four of the five tribes issued a call for a statehood convention to meet in August to show Congress the sentiment of the Indian Territory. The Indian chiefs and white speculators who dom-

15. J. W. Scothorn to Joseph B. Foraker, 9 December 1902, Foraker Papers (Cincinnati Historical Society).
16. Beveridge to Finley Peter Dunne, 11 January 1903, BP.

inated the proceedings drafted a constitution for a new state to be named Sequoyah after the legendary Indian chief, submitted the document for ratification by popular vote that fall, and asked Congress for admission.

Beveridge's warnings to Indian Territory leaders that continued separate statehood agitation would simply delay any action spurred a hastily organized boycott of the vote. And though the constitution was approved by 56,279 votes to 9,073, more than half of the voters had stayed away from the polls. The final blow to the Sequoyah movement came from Congress. Anticipating a state populated largely by whites from nearby southern states, the Democrats championed the cause of Indian rights, but few Republicans were found who would bolt the party leadership on this issue. Unable to win G.O.P. support, the Democrats concentrated their fire upon the Arizona–New Mexico half of the bill. "It is not with reference to Oklahoma and Indian Territory that we need help," Beveridge told a friendly newspaper publisher. That fight was "won." The difficulty was over "that part of the measure providing for one State to be formed of Arizona and New Mexico."[17]

Joint statehood aroused little enthusiasm in New Mexico. But the passage of the House bill split the territory's dominant political machine. Seeing no alternative, delegate Bernard S. Rodey came out in its favor. Governor Miguel A. Otero, however, remained bitterly hostile. The clash between the two men was aggravated by political rivalries within the territory. At the 1904 Republican territorial convention, the governor succeeded in blocking Rodey's renomination for delegate and pushed through the nomination of W. H. Andrews on a platform calling for separate statehood for New Mexico. The embittered Rodey ran as an independent on a joint statehood platform. Although Democrats contributed financially to his campaign to split the Republican vote, Rodey polled only 3,419 votes, while Andrews won with a plurality of more than 5,000 votes. The results, Republican territorial chairman Holm O. Bursum wrote Beveridge, proved that the people of New Mexico wanted "statehood within the present boundaries or nothing."[18]

Beveridge protested to the president about how Otero had been

---

17. Beveridge to Clarence P. Dodge, 30 November, 14 December 1905, BP.
18. Holm O. Bursum to Beveridge, 14 December 1904, BP.

"using the entire machinery of his office" to defeat administration policy.[19] Although he had been inclined to continue Otero in office for another four years, Roosevelt agreed not to reappoint the governor when his term expired in January 1906. Beveridge urged Rodey for the place. But the chief executive had promised Secretary of the Interior E. A. Hitchcock to appoint Herbert J. Hagerman, thirty-four-year-old son of one of New Mexico's leading railroad builders and landowners, who had been second secretary of the American Embassy in Saint Petersburg while Hitchcock had been ambassador. With Otero out—and with the new governor loyally cooperating with the administration—Andrews and his fellow New Mexico Republican leaders made their peace with the Indiana senator.

Arizona presented the most difficulties. Fear of "greaser" domination of the new state by New Mexico's large Spanish-speaking population roused strong feelings in that territory. The federal office holders, led by Governor Alexander Brodie and his successor Joseph H. Kibbey, vied with Mark Smith and the Democrats in denouncing the House bill. Powerful corporate interests joined in the attack. Arizona had fewer than thirty thousand voters, the bulk of whom were concentrated in a few mining centers, and over the years the Atchison, Topeka and Santa Fe and Southern Pacific railroads and the giant mining companies had controlled the legislature and kept their taxes low. Alarmed that their political influence would be diluted if Arizona were joined with New Mexico, spokesmen for the territory's mining and railroad corporations raised the cry that "union with the Territory of New Mexico would make property insecure and progress impossible in Arizona."[20]

So when Beveridge reported the House bill to the Senate, a powerful lobby swung into action. This lobby found an influential and resourceful champion in Ohio's Joseph B. Foraker. The Ohio lawmaker mobilized a powerful bloc of senators against joint statehood: the solid Democratic minority (except for one); the representatives, Republicans and Democrats, from the Rocky Mountain states; and G.O.P. lawmakers—such as Michigan's Russell A. Alger, a heavy investor in Arizona mining and railroad ventures—with interests,

---

19. Beveridge to Roosevelt, 28 September 1905, BP.
20. Donald D. Leopard, "Joint Statehood: 1906," M.A. Thesis, University of New Mexico (1958), pp. 9–10.

personal or political, in the territories; and a growing number of Republicans—such as California's Thomas R. Bard, whose support had been pivotal in blocking adoption of the omnibus bill—who balked at the injustice of forcing the unwilling Arizonans into statehood with New Mexico.

As the days passed, Beveridge saw his support dwindling. In desperation, he appealed to Roosevelt to whip dissenting senators into line. On the day before the vote, he took the floor in a last-ditch, two-and-a-half-hour appeal that brought repeated applause from the galleries. Neither territory alone was qualified for admission, he told the Senate—Arizona because its population was so sparse that its admission would "do violence to the principle of equal popular government on which this nation is founded"; New Mexico because "the great majority" of its people "are not of the blood and speech that is common to the rest of us." But to join the two *"Americanizes the whole mass of population within these Territories."* The result would be a great state, "not Arizona the little, but Arizona the great; not Arizona the provincial, but Arizona the national; not Arizona the creature of a politician's device, but Arizona the child of the nation's wisdom!"[21]

When the vote was taken on 7 February, the Oklahoma–Indian Territory half of the bill was approved by a wide margin. But sentiment had so shifted against the Arizona–New Mexico half that Beveridge beat a strategic retreat. To win over those senators reluctant to force an unwelcome government upon Arizona, he accepted an amendment requiring approval of the constitution of the new state by a majority in each territory. This compromise, however, failed to appease the bill's foes. The Senate approved, by a vote of 40 to 37, a second amendment providing for the immediate admission of New Mexico with its existing boundaries and leaving Arizona a territory until its population warranted statehood. In a tension-filled roll call, Beveridge's motion to reconsider was tabled by one vote—39 to 38.[22]

The House refused to concur in the Senate amendments. Although there was talk of a possible compromise on the basis of the first Senate amendment, which gave the Arizonans a veto over the new state's

21. *CR*, 58th Cong., 3rd sess., 1905, 39, pt. 2: 1924–38.
22. Ibid., pt. 2: 1970–2005.

constitution, the House conferees refused to budge, and Congress adjourned without further action. Beveridge was not unhappy over the deadlock. For the longer the struggle raged the more the fight had become for him a crusade for "the common good" against "selfish interests" and "personal and political ambitions." Vowing to renew the battle when Congress reconvened, he appealed to newspaper and magazine editors throughout the country for their support. "In favor of joint statehood for these Territories," he wrote Norman Hapgood of *Collier's*, "is nothing at all but great statesmanlike reasons. The 'interests' are all against us; the politicians are all against us; every corrupt influence is against us."[23]

In anticipation of the showdown, Beveridge arranged with the Speaker for swift action by the lower house. He persuaded the president to include in his annual message a strongly worded recommendation calling for "making the four Territories into two States."[24] Although Cannon railroaded the measure through the House, the Senate presented a more difficult hurdle. Frank M. Murphy, head of the Santa Fe, Prescott, and Phoenix Railroad and one of Arizona's leading mine owners, organized a powerful lobby made up of representatives of the territory's mining and railroad corporations to do battle against the House bill. And Ohio's Joseph B. Foraker continued to mastermind the fight on the Senate floor. The tide was running against Beveridge. The longer the struggle raged, the more people— in and out of the Senate—balked at forcing the Arizonans into statehood with New Mexico.

Further complicating the situation was the pending Philippine tariff bill. Rumors were in the air of a deal between the respective opponents of the Philippine tariff bill and the statehood bill. At the behest of the secretary of war, William Howard Taft, Roosevelt had promised to give the Philippine measure first priority. Although a backer of Philippine reciprocity, Beveridge appealed to Roosevelt to drop the Philippine bill until the statehood bill was out of the way, "or they'll trade our eyes out of our heads." "We can win," he pleaded, "if we adopt Napoleon's tactics of concentrating on ONE measure at a

23. Beveridge to Delavan Smith, 30 January 1905; to Norman Hapgood, 11 October 1905, BP.

24. Theodore Roosevelt, *State Papers as Governor and President, 1899–1909*, vol. 15 of *The Works of Theodore Roosevelt*, ed. Hermann Hagedorn, National Edition, 20 vols. (New York, 1926), p. 337.

time—not otherwise." Shaken by an informal poll showing a majority against the House bill, he begged the president to intervene with doubtful senators. "Four days remain for statehood," he appealed. "We can, must & will win. Four days—an age. If the (1) Speaker & House Organization, the (2) Senate leaders & Senate Organization (who are with us on *this* & the (3) President of the United States *combined* cant[*sic*] get the five men needed, we had all better go out of business."[25]

Bowing to Beveridge's wishes, Roosevelt agreed to postpone the Philippine tariff bill. And on 8 March, the day before the statehood vote, Beveridge made his own final appeal to the Senate. He directed his heaviest fire against the move to require approval of the measure by voters of each territory. The Constitution, he pointed out, had wisely made Congress the sole judge of the qualifications of new states because the founding fathers had recognized that the admission of a state involved the welfare of the entire nation. Giving each territory a veto power over the bill would allow "a majority *of a small minority living in a portion* of the proposed new state" to nullify the national interest as determined by Congress.[26]

But the next day the upper chamber approved by a lopsided 42–29 vote the amendment requiring a special referendum in the territories, with the "sole" question, "Shall Arizona and New Mexico be united to form one State?" A second amendment striking out all reference to Arizona and New Mexico was approved by a narrower 37–35 margin. The amended bill provided simply for the admission of Oklahoma joined with the Indian Territory.[27] When the House refused to concur in these Senate amendments, the bill went to conference. The Democrats protested Beveridge's heading the Senate conferees because he was out of sympathy with the will of the majority. But this move fizzled out when Beveridge assured the upper chamber that he would stand up for the Senate's wishes regardless of his personal views.

The conference was Beveridge's last chance of salvaging what he could from his defeat. After the Senate vote, he realized that he would have to agree to referendum in the territories. But to pose the question of Arizona–New Mexico statehood directly to the voters put the

---

25. Beveridge to Roosevelt [5 March 1906], Roosevelt Papers.
26. *CR*, 59th Cong., 1st sess., 1906, 40, pt. 4: 3515–37.
27. Ibid., pt. 4: 3591–97.

issue too baldly for his liking. Instead, he proposed first holding the convention to draft a constitution for the new state and then submitting the document for the approval of the voters in each territory. A negative vote in either would block ratification. This vote would take place at the same time as "the election of officers for a full State government, including members of the legislature and two Representatives in Congress."[28]

His hope was that if a satisfactory constitution were submitted, the Arizona voters would be more favorably disposed, and that the candidates for office would support ratification. Alarmed at this possibility, the Arizonans and their Senate champions resisted adoption of the conference report. Lacking the votes, Beveridge had to back down, withdraw his first report, and bring in a new report acceptable to the anti-jointure forces. The new report provided for holding the referendum at the regular territorial elections in November rather than at a special election. The voters would at that time select delegates to a constitutional convention, but the convention would meet only if both territories approved joint statehood.[29] With this final compromise, the focus of the struggle shifted from Washington to the Southwest.

New Mexico appeared safe. The dominant Republican machine led by "Bull" Andrews and Holm O. Bursum, the chairman of the territorial central committee, lined up in support of jointure. Many New Mexicans, such as former governor Le Baron Bradford Prince, had come to believe that statehood with Arizona was preferable to remaining a territory. Others, like Bursum, anticipating that Arizona would vote no, wished to curry favor with the administration by supporting the measure. "New Mexico will take care of herself," Andrews assured Beveridge. "The rub is in Arizona."[30]

The long delay in admission had converted many Arizonans to joint statehood as the only alternative to continued territorial status. By the end of 1905, joint statehood leagues had been established throughout the territory. Roosevelt wrote a public letter, which the pro-jointure forces reprinted and distributed, warning "the people

---

28. Ibid., pt. 8: 7736–40.
29. Ibid., pt. 9: 8333–37, 8390–403.
30. W. H. Andrews to Beveridge, 23 September 1906, BP.

of Arizona" that rejection of joint statehood would condemn the territory "to an indefinite continuance of a condition of tutelage." And Beveridge added his own warning. "If you people down there," he admonished pro-jointure leaders, "who are in favor of the great boon of statehood cannot place it before the voters in the proper light, why, of course, you can remain a territory for the next twenty-five years, for be sure that if you do not get in now you will not get in for a quarter of a century at least."[31]

But the pro-jointure forces faced an uphill fight in Arizona. The territory's powerful railroad and mining corporations along with the Arizona Cattle Growers' Association threw their influence against the measure. Nearly all the territory's newspapers were hostile. Governor Joseph H. Kibbey, as leader of the Republican party in the territory, arranged with the chairman of the Democratic territorial committee, E. E. Ellinwood, who was the attorney for the Copper Queen mining corporation, to hold the conventions of the two parties simultaneously and adopt resolutions urging a "no" vote. Furious over the governor's action, Beveridge appealed to the president to remove Kibbey for his disloyalty to administration policy. Roosevelt, however, refused. Believing the fight "well-nigh hopeless," he would not further risk his prestige in what he called "forcible-feeble action."[32]

In New Mexico, the Republican machine delivered the vote as promised, and joint statehood carried by a vote of 26,195 to 14,735. But Arizona rejected jointure by a five-to-one margin—16,265 votes to 3,141—and the candidate for territorial delegate of the pro-jointure Statehood Party polled only 508 votes out of the more than 23,000 cast. More than corporate influence and political manipulation was responsible for the outcome in Arizona. The vote reflected the antipathy felt by Arizona's Anglo-Americans toward New Mexico's Spanish-speaking Mexican population.

Beveridge, however, more than ever convinced of the righteousness of his cause, blamed "corrupt influences"—the mining companies, the railroads, the gamblers, the cattle barons, and the politicians—for the defeat of the measure. He even claimed that, given "the forces

---

31. Roosevelt to Mark A. Rodgers, 27 June 1906, in Morison, *The Letters of Theodore Roosevelt*, 5: 321–22. Beveridge to Charles F. Ainsworth, 26 June 1906, BP.

32. Roosevelt to Beveridge, 22 September 1906, BP.

arrayed against joint statehood in Arizona," the 20 percent favorable vote was "a decided victory." So far as he was concerned, the struggle was not over. He had become too personally involved to give up. "This is what happens in every great cause," he told Chief Forester Gifford Pinchot. "It always gets knocked out at the first. But also it always grows." Let Arizona remain a territory for a while. Then its people would have second thoughts about their mistake. "Arizona the great," he predicted, "will come in time."[33]

The statehood fight marked the first step in Beveridge's shift from standpattism to progressivism. The experience was disillusioning for Beveridge. Where in the statehood battle was that business statesmanship he was so fond of extolling as the remedy for the nation's problems? "I don't want anybody ever again to talk to me about the high moral tone of wealthy men when their pocketbook is touched," he said angrily of the Arizona lobby. And as he looked around, he saw the same pattern repeated. "The same influences that are trying to defeat this bill," he wrote Gifford Pinchot, were trying to defeat Pinchot's conservation program. "The whole network of graft and corruption is a network—and when one thread is touched the whole fiber responds."[34]

---

33. Beveridge to Shaw, 16 November 1906; to Bernard S. Rodey, 4 January 1907, BP. Beveridge to Gifford Pinchot, 12 November 1906. Pinchot Papers.

34. Beveridge to Shaw, 17 December 1905; to Pinchot, 15 November 1905, BP.

8

Beveridge Moves toward Progressivism

Disillusioned by the statehood fight, Beveridge wrote an article for the *Saturday Evening Post* in the fall of 1905, "Private Fortune a Public Trust." The article started out as a restatement of the traditional doctrine of stewardship: the duty of the rich man to devote his surplus wealth as "a sacred trust for the benefit of our common humanity." But then came a strikingly new note. If the masters of wealth failed to live up to this "Twentieth Century ideal of money"—"if they cling to the mediaeval doctrine that what a man shall do with his wealth is nobody's business but his own"—public sentiment will demand action by Congress, "and we shall have either the accumulation of great fortunes prevented by law or their management so directed by law that they shall serve the country from which they were drawn and the people from whose necessities they were made."[1]

He followed this article with a second, warning that "the rich man in public life" whose horizons were limited by his own self-interest was as dangerous to the body

---

1. *SEP*, 18 November 1905, pp. 4–5.

politic as the demagogue who incited the poor against the rich. Too many rich men, in politics and out, could not see beyond their own selfish interests to the public good—and Beveridge took the mining corporations and railroads of Arizona as his prime example. After sending the article to the magazine, he had second thoughts about the possible reaction of his fellow senators. His remarks, he told *Post* editor George H. Lorimer, hit "too squarely between the eyes" to be "practically wise." But Lorimer remonstrated that the article "says things which should be said by someone in the Senate."[2] After much reflection, Beveridge gave the go-ahead. The response was a flood of letters of congratulation, and cries of pain from politicians who felt attacked.

Beveridge saw alarming signs of a return to the strife-ridden 1890s. There was the rapid growth of the American Federation of Labor. By 1905, Indiana had 72,504 union members in 1,280 local unions, making it one of the leading states in union membership. Even more frightening was the sharp increase in the Socialist vote in the 1904 elections—in Indiana nearly four times the 1900 total. Settlement house workers were laying bare the poverty of factory laborers, the exploitation of women and children, and the social dynamite of the teeming slums.

Even middle-class America was growing restless. The muckrakers were filling popular magazines with exposés of the corrupt alliance between big business and the political bosses. The rapid tempo of trustification was arousing widespread anxieties and resentments. By 1906, insurgency was on the march across the middle border. "I have been carefully studying the present popular unrest and interviewing numbers of people about it," Beveridge wrote to his friend John C. Shaffer. "I am coming to the conclusion that it is not a passing whim, but a great and natural movement such as occurs in this country, as our early history shows, once about every forty years. It is not like the granger episode or like the Debs episode. The former of these affected only the farmers; the latter only the 'workingmen.' The present unrest, however, is quite as vigorous among the intellectuals,

---

2. Beveridge to George H. Lorimer, 23 November 1905; Lorimer to Beveridge, 27 November 1905, BP. The article appeared in *SEP*, 16 June 1906, pp. 3–4, 16.

college men, university people, etc., as it is among the common people."[3]

The Republican sweep in 1904 had reinforced the determination of party stalwarts to "stand pat." But the Hoosier had learned from his stumping that the vote represented no mandate for the G.O.P. as a party. The landslide was a personal tribute to Roosevelt as the champion of the "square deal." An astute and ambitious politician, he foresaw that an ostrich-like standpattism was self-defeating. Unless the Republican party faced the problems raised by industrialism with the same boldness that its founders had faced the slavery issue, Beveridge warned the Indiana G.O.P. state convention in the spring of 1906, disaster lay ahead. "We must turn to these new social and economic questions which have to do with the daily lives and happiness of human beings and which press for answer; questions that involve the righteousness of American business, a juster distribution of wealth by preventing dishonest accumulation of gain; questions that look to the physical, mental, moral upbuilding of all the workers in factory and on farm throughout the entire Republic; the control of great public businesses."[4]

Similar anxieties were pushing Theodore Roosevelt toward progressivism. Safely elected in his own right, Roosevelt was becoming more and more alarmed about the multiplying signs of unrest. The time had come, he told Congress in his annual message of December 1905, for positive action by the federal government against corporate wrongdoing, and he took the railroads as his first target. He recommended giving the Interstate Commerce Commission the authority, when a given rate was challenged, to determine the maximum reasonable rate. Modest as this proposal was, the president's recommendation struck at the most cherished right of private enterprise—the freedom to set prices.

In the battle that raged in the upper chamber, Beveridge played a secondary part. Not only was he deeply involved in the continuing statehood fight, but the long-drawn-out hearings before the Committee on Privileges and Elections in connection with the seating of Senator Reed Smoot of Utah were taking up much of his time. Despite loud demands from Indiana church groups for Smoot's expulsion because of his Mormonism, Beveridge had become convinced that

3. Beveridge to John C. Shaffer, 27 March 1906, BP.
4. *Indianapolis Star*, 12 April 1906.

the charges against him were without basis. The whole business, he confided to his old friend Judge John H. Baker, was "disgusting."[5] At the showdown within the committee on 1 June 1906, Beveridge voted for Smoot's seating. And when the question came before the full Senate the following session, the Indiana lawmaker came to Smoot's defense with an eloquent plea for religious tolerance.

Beveridge's support of Smoot raised no more than a passing flurry. But his stand on the railroad bill anticipated his later insurgency. For he rallied behind the president in the bitter fight underway over "broad" versus "narrow" court review of Interstate Commerce Commission rulings. Fighting to retain his leadership of the Senate, Rhode Island's Nelson W. Aldrich was irate at the desertion of a man picked for a place within the ruling circle of the chamber. For a moment, the normally cold Aldrich lost his temper during a debate in the Senate and threatened the Hoosier with revenge. "How hard," Beveridge wrote Roosevelt, "for the mere office hunting politician & the ordinary man over forty years of age, to realize that the world is moving onward—yes & *upward*—every minute."[6]

Although he thought the compromise leaving the court-review question in "purposeful obscurity" (John M. Blum's phrase) a triumph for the "railroad Senators," Beveridge hailed the Hepburn Act as a landmark in the extension of federal control over business, and admired Roosevelt's skill in forcing the bill through a reluctant Congress.[7] And before the end of the session, the Congress would approve an even more far-reaching extension of federal authority after a fight in which Beveridge would hold the center of the stage.

The stage was set by the timely publication on 15 February 1906 of Upton Sinclair's *The Jungle*. Charles Edward Russell's "The Story of the Greatest Trust in the World"—serialized first in *Everybody's* and then published as a book—had exposed in shocking detail the ruthlessness and greed of the meat packers. Indictments were pending against five meat-packing companies and seventeen of their officers for violation of the Sherman antitrust law. Starting in January 1905, the distinguished British medical journal *The Lancet* had run a series

5. Beveridge to John H. Baker, 17 March 1904, BP.
6. Beveridge to Theodore Roosevelt [9? April 1906], Roosevelt Papers.
7. Beveridge to Albert Shaw, 20 May 1906, BP.

of articles assailing the Chicago packing houses as unsanitary. And thanks to the work of Dr. Harvey W. Wiley, chief chemist of the Department of Agriculture, the country was increasingly interested in pure food. While Sinclair's appeal for socialism went unheeded, the disclosures about what he called "the condemned-meat industry" met a responsive public.

Attracted by the advance publicity, Beveridge purchased a copy of *The Jungle* as soon as the book was published. After reading the novel, he was so excited that he gave a copy to the president, who was sufficiently disturbed by it to send labor commissioner Charles P. Neill and New York lawyer and social worker James B. Reynolds to Chicago to make a full investigation. Beveridge saw the possibility of winning personal glory—and political advantage—by sponsoring the legislation to remedy the abuses spotlighted by *The Jungle*. The president was responsive to Beveridge's suggestion and put him in touch with Neill and Reynolds after their return from Chicago early in May with a blistering report on the packing houses.

At the same time—unknown to Beveridge—the legal staff of the Department of Agriculture was preparing its own meat inspection legislation. Beveridge learned of the department's bill accidentally when he met the secretary of agriculture, "Tama Jim" Wilson, at a dinner party. Not wanting anyone else to introduce a measure that he had been working on, he asked the president if he could sponsor the administration bill in the upper chamber. Roosevelt assented. But when the Secretary sent over the department's measure, Beveridge found it less carefully drawn than his own and "rejected it in toto excepting only the section on fees." In consultation with Wilson, A. D. Melvin (chief of the Bureau of Animal Industry), James R. Garfield (head of the Bureau of Corporations), Neill, and Reynolds, he rewrote and revised the measure. He confided to a friendly Chicago newspaper publisher in mid-May that he was drafting a bill that "will cause something of a sensation, especially, out in Chicago."[8]

On Monday, 21 May, three days after Senate passage of the Hepburn act, Beveridge introduced his meat inspection bill in the upper chamber. The bill provided for mandatory inspection of all cattle, sheep, swine, and goats whose meat was to be sold in interstate or foreign commerce and the destruction of any carcasses found

---

8. Beveridge to Shaffer, 11 May 1906; to Shaw, 1 July 1906, BP.

"unfit for human food"; required the inspection and dating of all meat products and canned meats and the destruction of "all such products" found "to be impure, unsound, composed of unhealthful ingredients, or which have been treated with or contain any dyes or deleterious chemicals of any kind"; and authorized the Department of Agriculture to regulate sanitary conditions in the packing houses. If the packers appealed any ruling by an inspector, the decision of the secretary of agriculture would be "final and conclusive." After 1 January 1907, "no person, firm, or corporation shall transport" across state lines any meat or meat product not "inspected, examined, and marked as 'inspected and passed,' in accordance with the terms of this act."[9]

He realized that all these safeguards could be nullified by an insufficient force of inspectors. After the popular excitement aroused by *The Jungle* had passed, the packers could stampede Congress into voting an inadequate appropriation with the ever-popular cry of economy. To avert that danger, his bill authorized the secretary of agriculture to charge the packers a fee for every animal inspected. The funds available for the inspection service would thus automatically keep pace with the future growth of the industry. Beveridge privately described his measure as "the most perfect meat inspection bill in the world—that looks like an extravagant statement, but it is true."[10]

The bill would remedy the abuses in the meat-packing industry. But no one could miss its wider bearings. A Hamiltonian, Beveridge in his most standpat days had upheld a broad constructionist interpretation of the powers of Congress. And given his increasing alarm at the popular unrest, he recognized that only the federal government could effectively deal with the problems accompanying the rise of big business. The Hepburn law was a major step forward in strengthening the power of the federal government to deal with business wrongdoing; Beveridge's meat inspection bill represented an even more far-reaching expansion of national authority. That measure, he wrote to Albert Shaw, was "THE MOST PRONOUNCED EXTENSION OF FEDERAL POWER IN EVERY DIRECTION EVER ENACTED, INCLUDING EVEN THE RATE BILL ITSELF."[11]

---

9. *CR*, 59th Cong., 1st sess., 1906, 40, pt. 8: 7127, 7420–21.
10. Beveridge to Henry W. Bennett, 28 May 1906, BP.
11. Beveridge to Shaw, 26 May 1906, BP.

The introduction of the bill aroused a flurry of excitement among the packers. The packers had forged a close-working partnership with the big livestock producers represented by the American National Livestock Association, and a flood of telegrams and letters came to the White House from cattlemen pleading against hasty action. Shocked at what his two investigators had found, Roosevelt demanded legislation to prevent the recurrence of those abuses. But he hoped to achieve this aim with a minimum of damage to the meat industry and the stock raisers. So he refused to commit himself when Beveridge asked him to send Congress a special message relaying the Neill-Reynolds report.

Beveridge was impatient, however, and forced the issue on 25 May by moving his bill as an amendment to the pending agricultural appropriation bill. He warned his colleagues that if a fight were made against the amendment, he would deliver a speech that would shock the country. Joining in the battle, Roosevelt repeated his warning that he would make public the Neill-Reynolds report unless satisfactory legislation was passed. To underline this threat, he had Neill summarize his findings to the representatives of the livestock interests, William E. Skinner and W. L. Carlisle, who had hastened to Washington, and to leading senators from the western cattle-raising states. After meeting with Neill, Skinner had a conference with Beveridge. When the latter refused to postpone his demand for a vote on his amendment, Skinner telephoned the packers for instructions. In panic, they agreed to offer no resistence. Thereupon the Senate passed the amendment without a dissenting vote.

Within hours, however, the packers recovered their nerve. Industry spokesmen joined in denying that anything was wrong in the packing houses and attacked the Beveridge amendment as hastily drawn, too rigid, and unconstitutional. The packers had powerful friends in James W. Wadsworth, chairman of the House Agriculture Committee and a wealthy stock-raiser from New York's Genesee Valley, and his second-in-command, William Lorimer, the notorious "blond boss" of Chicago and a long-time ally of the packers. The protests of the cattlemen that the packers would defray any fees by reducing the prices for livestock alarmed western members. Many lawmakers— east and west—shrank from such an extension of federal authority over private industry.

Roosevelt had hoped to wield the threat of publication of the Neill-

Reynolds report to force swift House approval of the Beveridge amendment. But the sensational write-ups filling the newspapers and magazines undercut this strategy. Brushing aside the chief executive's pleas, Wadsworth and Lorimer proceeded to pull the teeth of the Senate amendment. After consulting with Beveridge, secretary of agriculture Wilson, commissioner of corporations James R. Garfield, Neill, and Reynolds, the president transmitted to Congress the Neill-Reynolds report with an accompanying special message demanding adoption of Beveridge's amendment to halt the "traffic in diseased or spoiled meats." For a moment, Roosevelt had wavered on the fee question. But Beveridge and Wilson convinced him that without that provision the "whole purpose of the law can at any time be defeated through an insufficient appropriation."[12]

Despite the uproar that followed, Wadsworth and Lorimer refused to back down and formally reported the House committee substitute on 14 June. The more Roosevelt studied the committee bill the angrier he became. He complained that there was no provision for nighttime surveillance of the packing houses to prevent the illicit practices said to go on when the plants were shut. The dating of canned meats had been struck out. The civil service requirement in the appointment of new inspectors had been waived for the first year, thus leaving those appointments as the patronage of the packer-dominated congressmen from the packing-house districts. And the committee had replaced the fee provision with a permanent appropriation of one million dollars a year—a sum barely adequate for the first year of the inspection service.

What most upset the chief executive was the provision giving the packers the right to appeal to the federal courts. Not that he denied the right of judicial review. But this review should be limited to the strictly procedural question of whether or not the secretary of agriculture's method of reaching his decision had been fair, and should not include a judicial reappraisal of the facts. The broad court review provided for by the House committee bill, would, however, transfer the final word regarding federal inspection from the experts of the Department of the Agriculture to the judiciary, place before the

---

12. U.S., Congress, House, *Conditions in Chicago Stock Yards: Message from the President . . . Transmitting the Report of Mr. James Bronson Reynolds and Commissioner Charles P. Neill . . .* , 59th Cong., 1st sess., 1906, H. Doc. 873, pp. 1–3.

courts technical questions they were not qualified to give judgment on, and thus "nullify the major part of the good which can be expected from the enactment of this law."[13]

"You are wrong, 'very, very wrong,' in your estimate of the Committee's Bill," Wadsworth replied. He could not see how a provision guaranteeing the packers their constitutional right of appeal to the courts when their property rights were violated "can be justly or properly objected to." He objected most strongly to the charge that the substitute included no provision for nighttime surveillance of the packing houses. The committee's bill provided for inspection "during the nighttime as well as during the daytime" when slaughtering "is conducted during the nighttime." "Can the English language," the New York representative asked, "be made any plainer?"[14]

On rechecking the substitute, Roosevelt found the clause and, embarrassed, had to apologize. He blamed Beveridge for misinforming him, but the Hoosier stood his ground. The provision to which the congressman referred applied only to those times when slaughtering was going on. It was when the plants were shut that skullduggery was said to take place. His bill provided that the inspectors "shall have access during the nighttime as well as the daytime to every part" of the packing houses "without reference to whether or not any slaughtering or other work is being done therein." Roosevelt grudgingly admitted that his wording was "preferable."[15] Acceding to Beveridge's pleas, Roosevelt insisted upon closing any possible loophole in this question.

At a meeting on Friday morning, 15 June, a majority of the House Committee voted to stand pat, thus defying the president. This impasse placed Speaker of the House "Uncle Joe" Cannon in a difficult position. He found Roosevelt, who was himself worried about splitting the party, willing to meet the House committee halfway. After much discussion, a compromise was hammered out. The fee provision

13. Roosevelt to James W. Wadsworth, 15 June 1906, in Morison, *The Letters of Theodore Roosevelt*, 5: 298–99.

14. Wadsworth to Roosevelt, 15 June 1906, Roosevelt Papers. The provision in question is in U.S., Congress, House, Committee on Agriculture, *Amendments to Agricultural Appropriation Bill: Report to Accompany H.R. 18537*, 59th Cong., 1st sess., 1906, H. Rept. 4935 [pt. 1]: 3.

15. Beveridge's provision is in *CR*, 59th Cong., 1st sess., 1906, 40, pt. 8: 7420. For Roosevelt's conceding that his version was "preferable": Roosevelt to Beveridge, 16 June 1906, in Morison, *The Letters of Theodore Roosevelt*, 5: 300–301.

was dead; Wadsworth and Lorimer backed by the Speaker refused even to give the secretary of agriculture stand-by authority to levy fees if the congressional appropriation was insufficient. But the permanent appropriation was raised to three million dollars a year, which Roosevelt accepted as providing sufficient leeway for the future growth of the meat industry without yearly fights over the budget.

Under Roosevelt's prodding, the committee voted to eliminate the civil service waiver and add a provision explicitly giving the inspectors access to the packing houses "at all times, by day or night, whether the establishment be operated or not." Most important, Wadsworth agreed to drop its court review provision if the words in the Senate amendment making the judgment of the secretary of agriculture "final and conclusive" were struck out. Those words, Roosevelt conceded, might be taken to violate the Constitution by appearing to deny appeals of any kind to the courts. The chief executive had won his major points. Though disappointed by the committee's refusal to yield on the dating of canned meats, he was not willing to risk loss of face by insisting upon what he regarded as a minor detail. The committee reported the new bill, with the White House's blessing, on Tuesday, 19 June, and the House gave swift approval.[16]

Beveridge regarded the House action with mixed emotions. "In the main," he told a newspaper interviewer, he was "highly pleased" with the final bill. "I recognize in it nearly all of the provisions of my bill which were temporarily eliminated by the House committee. They have put back nearly all the teeth they pulled out." He was most gratified at the new provision for nighttime surveillance of the packing houses "whether the establishment be operated or not." The action of the House committee in adding that provision "makes me think that perhaps after all when it comes down to the last lingering analysis I may not have been so very wrong." But he was disappointed at the failure of the House bill to require the dating of canned meats. And he had pleaded with Roosevelt not to retreat on the fee question, since "the future is involved."[17]

Beveridge felt so strongly that he canceled his scheduled Fourth of July address on foreign policy before the American Chamber of

---

16. *CR* (House), 59th Cong., 1st sess., 1906, 40, pt. 9: 8720–29.
17. *Indianapolis Star,* 20 June 1906. Beveridge to Roosevelt [16? June 1906], Roosevelt Papers.

Commerce in Paris to remain in Washington and continue the fight when the agricultural appropriation bill came back to the Senate. Denouncing the packers, he insisted that the consumer had a right to know whether his canned meat was five years old or five days old. To conceal the age of the meat *"is a fraud* on the consumer." Even more important was adoption of his fee provision. Could Congress be depended on to vote sufficient funds after the present excitement had passed? The government seal of inspection would be worth millions of dollars in free advertising for the packers. *"Why should the people pay for the packers' inspection, instead of the packers paying for their own inspection?"*[18]

Senator Francis Warren of Wyoming, a leading sheep raiser and spokesman for the livestock interests in the upper chamber, replied that if the packers were forced to pay for inspection, they would defray the cost by reducing the price paid to the stock raiser and raising the price charged the consumer. Beveridge then asked why, if the packers could so easily shift the burden, they were so bitterly fighting the provision? At present, he contended, the packers paid the lowest and charged the highest the market allowed. The chairman of the Senate Committee on Agriculture, Redfield Proctor of Vermont, who though nearly crippled with rheumatism had returned to Washington to work for passage of effective meat inspection legislation, backed the Indiana senator. The Senate then voted overwhelmingly to disagree to the House substitute and stand by Beveridge's amendment.

But the House conferees continued to insist that canned meats could stay unspoiled for years. To put the date on American canned meats would only hurt their sale abroad in competition with the products of other countries that did not require dating. The House conferees were even more adamant against any provision for fees. Finally, on Friday, 29 June, with the session drawing rapidly to a close, Beveridge advised his colleagues to yield rather than to defeat the entire measure. "In all great reforms," he explained to the Senate, "—for this is one of the greatest of practical reforms which has been legislated upon by the American Congress in a quarter of a century— it is the duty of those who propose the reform to fight for every essential provision; but not to imperil the life of the measure itself."[19]

---

18. *CR*, 59th Cong., 1st sess., 1906, 40, pt. 9: 8763–67.
19. Ibid., pt. 10: 9657–58.

Approval by the Senate followed quickly. One 30 June, Roosevelt signed into law the agricultural appropriation bill with its meat inspection amendment and sent the pen to Beveridge in appreciation of his role in passing the legislation. "You were the man who first called my attention to the abuses in the packing houses," he told Beveridge. "You were the legislator who drafted the bill which in its substance now appears in the amendment to the agricultural bill, and which will enable us to put a complete stop to the wrongdoing complained of."[20]

Beveridge was determined to renew the fight for the two features rejected by the House conferees when Congress reconvened in December 1906. He even induced Roosevelt to urge their adoption in his annual message. When his bill was pigeonholed in the Senate Committee on Agriculture, he sought to get it moving again by tacking its provisions on as amendments to the new agricultural appropriation bill. The Senate agreed to his first amendment—to require the dating of canned meats—without debate. But his second amendment—the fee provision—aroused strong resistance. Senators from the western states protested that the packers would defray any fees paid by reducing the prices of livestock. Beveridge then charged the packers and the cattle barons with making a deal to strangle the inspection service.

But Senator Warren raised the point of order that the Hoosier's amendment involved general legislation that could not be offered as an amendment to an appropriation bill under the rules of the Senate. The chair upheld the point of order and ruled the amendment out of order. And when the House conferees refused to accept the dating of canned meats, their Senate counterparts gave way after a half-hearted struggle..

Disappointed but undaunted, Beveridge vowed to continue the fight at the next session. His suffering from a case of ptomaine poisoning after he had eaten spoiled canned meat reinforced his determination. No action, however, was taken by Congress. By 1908, the Department of Agriculture was assuring the country that the packing houses of the United States had attained a standard of cleanliness and

---

20. Roosevelt to Beveridge, 30 June 1906, in Morison, *The Letters of Theodore Roosevelt*, 5: 326–27.

hygiene unequaled anywhere in the world. Without an aroused public, Beveridge could not overcome congressional inertia and hostility.

But Beveridge, like Roosevelt, had achieved his primary aim. And the furor over the meat inspection law had spurred Congress into passing the long-delayed pure food and drug law. That, with the Hepburn Act, made three epoch-making pieces of legislation passed by the first session of the Fifty-Ninth Congress. Underlying all three, Beveridge explained to a G.O.P. rally that fall, was a single guiding principle "which our complex social and industrial order has developed"—that "when any business becomes so great that it affects the welfare of all the people, it must be regulated by the Government of all the people." This was not simply a political slogan, he told Albert Shaw, but "an accurate statement of principle."[21]

At the same time, the fight over the meat inspection law was another landmark in his political awakening. The experience reinforced his disillusionment with business statesmanship. More and more he complained—publicly as well as privately—that "every great measure for the people's good" was resisted "by some vast financial interest whose improper practices we were striving to end." Even more disheartening was the blindness and folly of so many of his fellow Republicans. Despite the popular uproar, he confessed to a friend, Congress would never have acted "if Roosevelt had not picked up his big stick and smashed the packers over the head with it and their agents in the House and Senate."[22]

After Congress had adjourned, Beveridge went off to New England for his vacation. While there, he continued sounding out public sentiment through correspondence and in talks with his fellow vacationers. He discovered a swelling undercurrent of unrest. On all sides, he reported to Albert Shaw, there was a growing demand for "a moral regeneration of American business." When "Uncle Joe" Cannon opened his campaign in Illinois with his famous "standpat" speech, Beveridge lamented that the Speaker "utterly fails to see the signs of the times." "The country is moving on so much faster than the politicians that most of the latter are like a bunch of belated

21. *Indianapolis Star*, 4 November 1906. Beveridge to Shaw, 5 November 1906, BP.

22. *Indianapolis Star*, 26 October 1906. Beveridge to Francis E. Baker, 1 August 1906, BP.

travellers who have come to catch a train and stand on a platform waiting for it when as a matter of fact the train has passed on a long while ago."[23]

Such tardiness was not for the Hoosier. On the stump that fall, he called for an inheritance tax, revision of the tariff, the direct primary, a national child labor law, and stricter government regulation of giant corporations. The applause of his audiences convinced him that he had struck a popular chord. The election results further showed how the wind was blowing. The Democrats made sharp gains in Indiana and throughout the country. The losers were Old Guard Republicans who had not stood by the president—including Congressman James W. Wadsworth. "You have no idea," Beveridge warned publisher Frank Munsey after his cross-country speech-making trip, "how profound, intense and permanent the feeling among the American people is that this great reform movement shall go on."[24]

---

23. Beveridge to Shaw, 10, 19 August 1906, BP.
24. Beveridge to Frank A. Munsey, 10 November 1906, BP.

9

Saving the Child

While campaigning in the fall of 1906, Beveridge found the loudest applause when he called for the adoption of a national child labor law. The ground for this response had been prepared by the activities of the National Child Labor Committee in publicizing the suffering of the nation's child workers. Growing support for the committee's work was coming from women's clubs throughout the country. The popular magazines had begun to take up the question. Mrs. John Van Vorst's "The Cry of the Children" in the *Saturday Evening Post* was followed Edwin Markham's emotional "The Hoe-Man in the Making" in William Randolph Hearst's *The Cosmopolitan.* John Spargo's *The Bitter Cry of the Children* shocked Americans with its exposé of how the United States "in its commercial madness devours its babes."[1]

From 1904 on, Roosevelt had prodded Congress to authorize an investigation by the Bureau of Labor. But his own soundings of public sentiment convinced Beveridge that another investigation, even by the Bureau of Labor, was "not enough." The public, he wrote the chief executive, "is

---

1. John Spargo, *The Bitter Cry of the Children* (New York, 1906), 147.

better informed on this question than you would believe. The magazines have been agitating this thing for four or five years you know." The time had come for action by Congress. "We can not," he told a rally in Indianapolis closing the 1906 G.O.P. campaign in the Hoosier state, "permit any man or corporation to stunt the bodies, minds and souls of American children and ruin the future of the American Republic."[2]

Beveridge's motives for championing this cause were mixed. He was outraged by the inhumanity of child labor. His own earlier drudgery in the fields and lumber camps paled beside the harsher plight of youthful toilers in crowded factories and sweatshops. His investigation, he reported to Albert Shaw, showed that child labor was "even a more serious evil than was supposed." There were tens of thousands of young men and women "whose bodies have been injured, minds have been stunted and whose very souls have been dulled." Nor were these ills limited to the present generation. Crippled in body and spirit, the victims of child labor "produce children who are more or less degenerate."[3]

Beveridge was an ambitious man, eager for the spotlight, his eye upon the presidency. Leadership of the fight against child labor promised the popular acclaim he longed for. And no Republican could wish the Democrats to gain the benefit of sponsoring so popular a measure. "I am holding my breath," he confided to Roosevelt's private secretary, "for fear of seeing an announcement any day that some Democratic congressman or senator will propose just such a law." Even more alarming was the danger that the archdemagogue of the day, William Randolph Hearst, "will beat us to it." His magazines, Beveridge warned, have been agitating the issue. "We have got to beat them to the goal and score a touchdown before they begin to play."[4]

But more than personal and partisan advantage moved him. As an American nationalist, the Hoosier senator feared for the republic's future unless action were taken. Let this country take heed from the example of Britain, he warned. The thousands of men found physically unfit during the Boer War showed how child labor had under-

---

2. Beveridge to Theodore Roosevelt, 16 October 1906, BP. *Indianapolis Star*, 4 November 1906.
3. Beveridge to Albert Shaw, 22 November 1906, BP.
4. Beveridge to William Loeb, Jr., 12 November 1906, BP.

mined British manhood. Most alarming was the threat that child labor presented to the safety and stability of American institutions. "When these children grow up and understand how they are ruined for life," he lamented to John C. Shaffer, "there is developed the classes which we all fear and have reason to fear."[5]

The states could not halt the cancer. The more progressive commonwealths remained at the mercy of the least advanced. As a Hamiltonian, Beveridge saw no constitutional barrier to action by Congress—and his own meat inspection amendment showed how to deal with the child labor problem. The bill he introduced when Congress met forbade any carrier from transporting in interstate commerce the products of any factory or mine which had not filed an affidavit that no children under fourteen years of age were employed. Stiff penalties were laid down for violation by the carrier or the filing of a false affidavit by the factory or mine. "There is no question whatever," he assured Roosevelt's secretary, "about the constitutionality of this law. Neither is there any question about its being practical. Neither is there any question about the fact that it is absolutely the only way we can reach this subject by national statute."[6]

Looking for support, Beveridge hoped to gain the backing of the National Child Labor Committee. After a lengthy discussion of the pros and cons of federal legislation, the committee's Board of Trustees, at their meeting of 23 November 1906, postponed action until 6 December, so that they could poll the committee members on the question. The discussion at the December meeting was heated. Beveridge appeared in person to explain and defend his bill. But several members were alarmed about the effect of endorsing the bill upon the committee's work in the South, where the gravest child labor abuses were found. Leading the attack, wealthy New York lawyer and philanthropist Robert W. de Forest challenged the effectiveness of the law without on-the-spot inspection of factories and mines, questioned its constitutionality, and warned that "our influence in the South would be seriously impaired by giving our official approval to a measure which many Southerners will think of the Force Bill variety."[7]

---

5. Beveridge to John C. Shaffer, 20 November 1906, BP.
6. Beveridge to Loeb, 12 November 1906, BP.
7. Robert W. de Forest to Paul M. Warburg, 6 December 1906, National Child Labor Committee (NCLC) Papers (LC).

Even before Beveridge raised the question, however, many members of the committee had grown disillusioned over the slowness of the progress at the state level. The Hoosier's bill crystallized this dissatisfaction. The majority of the trustees voted to endorse his bill, "believing that it will establish a National standard to correct the evils of child labor in their important National aspects . . . and will tend to establish equality of economic competition, without minimizing State responsibility."[8] Beveridge was the featured speaker at the committee's annual convention the following week, and the more than four thousand persons attending enthusiastically adopted a formal resolution of support by a viva voce vote. The committee even sent its director for Southern operations, Alexander J. McKelway, a Presbyterian minister turned newspaper editor, to Washington to lobby for the bill.

But the Indiana lawmaker failed to gain the hoped-for backing of organized labor. Reflecting the American Federation of Labor's long-standing mistrust of federal interference in labor matters, the federation's 1906 convention turned down a resolution in favor of a national labor law and came out for "the enactment of a law in the several states prohibiting the employment of children under sixteen years of age." The convention the following year reaffirmed the A.F. of L. commitment to state action, thus weakening Beveridge's hand. When he wrote Roosevelt that "organized labor is overwhelmingly for this bill—militantly for it," the chief executive retorted that he had spoken with top A.F. of L. leaders, and "not a single one of them would admit that he favored it."[9]

Even more disappointing was Roosevelt's refusal to give his support. In his annual message of December 1906, he limited his recommendations to urging a child labor law for the District of Columbia as a model for the states to follow. To save face, Beveridge told newspaper reporters that the president favored his bill but had learned about his plans too late to include the recommendation in his

8. Minutes of NCLC Board of Trustees, 6 December 1906, ibid.

9. *Report of Proceedings of the Twenty-sixth Annual Convention of American Federation of Labor . . . 1906* (Washington, 1907), pp. 138, 164; *Report of Proceedings of the Twenty-seventh Annual Convention of the American Federation of Labor . . . 1907* (Washington, 1907), pp. 28, 336–37. Beveridge to Roosevelt, 11 November 1907, BP. Roosevelt to Beveridge, 12 November 1907, in Morison, *The Letters of Theodore Roosevelt,* 5: 844.

message.[10] And he pleaded with the chief executive to send Congress a special message. After much soul searching, however, Roosevelt decided against supporting the bill. Organized labor was lukewarm if not hostile; the leaders of the child labor movement were split; he himself had doubts about the legislation's constitutionality; and he was unwilling to risk his prestige in losing the fight.

Although Congress, in January 1907, authorized the investigation by the Bureau of Labor, Beveridge dismissed the action as a meaningless sop to outraged public feeling. Nor could he arouse much enthusiasm for the proposed model child labor bill for the District of Columbia. Child labor in the District was hardly the problem that existed in more heavily industrialized areas. His strategy was to force the Senate to go on record, for or against his bill. He expected that few lawmakers in the showdown would dare vote against so popular a measure. To force a vote, Beveridge, on 23 January 1907, moved his own bill as an amendment to the pending District bill.

For three days, 23, 28, and 29 January, Beveridge held the floor in a brilliant speech in support of his bill. He read affidavit after affidavit showing the extent and inhumanity of child labor in the United States. "The evidence is before the Senate," he said, "of the slow murder of these children, not by tens or hundreds, but by the thousands. But let us not 'hasten' to their relief 'too fast.' Let us 'investigate.'" With industry grown nationwide, the states could not halt the disease. Unless his bill were adopted, children throughout the republic would continue to suffer from the backwardness of the least progressive states. "We all hear talk about the dangers of a certain 'lower class,'" he admonished. "Had we not better do something to stop the production of that 'lower class,' that 'dangerous class?'"[11]

From the jammed galleries came applause that repeatedly forced the presiding officer to gavel for silence. But a majority of the Democratic senators represented the rising industrial forces of the "New South" that depended so heavily upon poorly paid child labor. And even progressive-minded Southerners remained wedded to the traditional state's rights shibboleths of the Southland. Although many Northern manufacturers in states with child labor laws favored action by Congress to remove the advantages enjoyed by their Southern

---

10. *Indianapolis Star,* 7 December 1906.
11. *CR,* 59th Cong., 2nd sess., 1907, 41, pt. 2: 1552–57, 1792–826, 1867–83.

competitors, the Republican Senate leadership shrank from so bold and far-reaching an extension of federal authority over business. Few senators favored a national child labor law; fewer wished to go on record against so popular a measure. Thrown off balance by Beveridge's strategy of offering his bill as an amendment to the District of Columbia bill, the lawmakers shelved further discussion of the entire matter.

The House leadership displayed more shrewdness in sidetracking the identical measure introduced in the lower chamber by Representative Herbert Parsons of New York. The bill was referred to the House Judiciary Committee for a ruling on its constitutionality, and early in February the committee issued a report condemning the measure as an unconstitutional invasion of the powers reserved to the states. Assailing the committee as a self-appointed "junior supreme court," Beveridge denounced the report as "absurd." The purpose was to head off action on his bill "without giving the courts of the country a chance to pass on the questions at all." The same cry of state's rights was raised against every reform that threatened the ill-gotten profits of "some unrighteous financial interest."[12]

In reply, Beveridge drew up a lengthy brief upholding the constitutionality of the bill. The power to regulate commerce, he argued, involved the power to prohibit. Such was the generally understood meaning of the word "regulate" at the time the Constitution was adopted. There were currently on the statute books "no less than seventeen laws prohibiting various articles from interstate commerce." And the Supreme Court's decision in *Champion* v. *Ames* (1903—the famous "Lottery Case") had "absolutely settled" the authority of Congress "to exclude from interstate commerce any article, which in our judgement, is deleterious to the people of the United States." That power could be abused. But its possible abuse was no argument against its existence. "The power exists," he told Roosevelt; "—if it is abused, the remedy is in the hands of the people at the ballot-box."[13]

Vowing to renew the fight when Congress reconvened in December 1907, Beveridge was heartened by signs of increasing support in and

12. *Indianapolis Star*, 8 February 1907. Beveridge to Henry Beach Needham, 9 April 1908, BP.
13. Beveridge to Roosevelt, 22 October [1907]; to Miss Harriet Lake, 22 November 1907; to Mrs. W. S. Major, 21 March 1908, BP. *CR*, 59th Cong., 2nd sess., 1907, 41, pt. 2: 1869–83.

out of Congress. Resolutions in favor of the bill were beginning to flow in from women's clubs throughout the country. Democratic leader William Jennings Bryan announced his support. When he had introduced the bill, Beveridge confessed, he had thought that it would take at least five years to pass. The struggle in Britain had taken decades. But the awakening of the public had been so rapid "that I am now hopeful of getting it through the Senate this session of Congress and through both houses the following session."[14]

An unexpected setback followed, however. The resignation early in 1907 of Edgar Gardner Murphy in protest against the National Child Labor Committee's endorsement of the Hoosier's bill sparked renewed controversy within the committee. A former Episcopal minister in Montgomery, Alabama, and head of the Southern Education Board, Murphy had taken a leading part in the founding of the committee. But reflecting deep-seated Southern prejudices, he denounced federal interference in a sphere which he thought properly belonged to the states. Warning that its continued support of the measure would disrupt the organization, Robert W. de Forest moved at the 25 October 1907 meeting of the Board of Trustees "that this Committee withdraws its approval and endorsement of the . . . so-called Beveridge Bill." After a heated debate, the trustees decided to poll the full membership of the National Committee. "We have," NCLC executive secretary Samuel McCune Lindsay complained to Beveridge, "reactionaries in corporations not for profit as well as in corporations who figure now-a-days so largely in the newspapers."[15]

Upset by the news, Beveridge personally appealed to influential members of the committee for their backing. "This bill has caught on and is going to be a 'go,'" he protested to a leading social worker. "It would be absurd for the National Child Labor Committee to abandon it in the middle of the fight." But the members who replied to the poll voted eighteen to ten to withdraw the committee's endorsement. To soften the blow, the resolution was revised not to mention the Hoosier's bill by name. The board thereupon unanimously resolved that "the National Child Labor Committee will for the present take no further action with reference to National legislation" until the

---

14. Beveridge to Lake, 22 November 1907, BP.
15. Minutes of NCLC Board of Trustees, 25 October 1907, NCLC Papers. Samuel M. Lindsay to Beveridge, 8 November 1907, BP.

investigation underway by the Bureau of Labor was finished and shed more light on the question. "I don't like it," Samuel McCune Lindsay wrote Beveridge, "but . . . it was the best we could do."[16]

This setback was followed by another rebuff from the White House. Throughout the fall, Beveridge had bombarded the president with appeals that he come out in support of his bill. The measure, he told Roosevelt, was "a part of your national statesmanship. And it is in this national statesmanship that you are doing your greatest service to our country and upon that national statesmanship your name will live in history." The time was ripe. The newspaper and magazine exposures and the work of the National Child Labor Committee had touched the public conscience. "No legislation you could propose to Congress will be so righteous, or *anywhere near so popular as this measure.*"[17]

Beveridge's appeals failed to move Roosevelt. In his annual message of December 1907, Roosevelt urged the adoption of an inheritance and income tax, the national incorporation and regulation of interstate businesses, the fixing of railroad rates on the basis of physical valuation, the establishment of a postal savings bank, the limitation of labor injunctions, and the extension of workmen's compensation laws and of the eight hour day. But he refused to endorse the Indiana senator's national child labor bill. He questioned the extent of its popular support, remained dubious about its constitutionality, was skeptical of its effectiveness, and even challenged the facts and figures about child labor that Beveridge had presented. If the states refused to meet their responsibilities, the president warned, Congress would have to act. But before doing this, "it ought certainly to enact model laws on the subject for the Territories under its own immediate control."[18]

Though disappointed, Beveridge was not disheartened. The key, he believed, was publicity to awaken the nation's conscience, and he missed no opportunity to agitate the issue. When a young playwright sent him a play dealing with child labor, he sent the manuscript on to a producer he knew. He wrote the introduction when Mrs. Van

---

16. Beveridge to Lindsay, 5 November 1907; Lindsay to Beveridge, 27 November 1907, BP. Minutes of NCLC Board of Trustees, 26 November 1907, NCLC Papers.

17. Beveridge to Roosevelt, 11 November 1907, BP.

18. Roosevelt, *State Papers as Governor and President,* 438.

Vorst expanded her *Saturday Evening Post* articles into a book. He continued to bombard Roosevelt with pleas for his support. He appealed to labor leaders to have their unions come out in favor of his bill. He urged leaders of women's clubs throughout the country to flood Congress with resolutions of support. "In this effort to stop the murder and ruin of millions of American children, we must depend upon the humanity of the women of this country more than on all other forces put together."[19]

His strategy remained to force the Senate to go on record by presenting his bill as an amendment when the District of Columbia bill came up for a vote. Rumors of his plans alarmed the sponsors of the District bill, and the National Child Labor Committee appealed to him not to confuse the issue. At first he was adamant in dismissing the District bill as "a mere fake."[20] But Roosevelt joined in pleading with him to hold off. To offer his bill as an amendment, the chief executive warned, would frighten the Senate into reshelving the District bill. "The wise thing is to get what is imperatively needed and can be had, and not to throw it away in making what is certain to be an unsuccessful effort to get something else in addition."[21]

Under White House pressure, Beveridge agreed. But he made no secret of his feelings. He supported the District bill, he told the Senate, "not because it will effect anything of great consequence, but because it is a step, however short, in the right direction." The fight for a national law would continue. "Let no person deceive himself. This bill, applicable to the District of Columbia, where the evil does not really exist, will not assuage the wrath of the American people against what is the real infamy that has awakened the conscience of the nation; nor will it in the remotest degree quiet that conscience."[22]

As the price for his acquiescence, Beveridge obtained a promise from Senator Jonathan P. Dolliver of Iowa, the chairman of the Senate Committee on Education and Labor, that the committee would take up his own bill and make an early report to the upper chamber. Beveridge doubted if the committee would make a favorable report; but even if reported "without recommendation," the legislation would

---

19. Beveridge to Major, 21 March 1908, BP.
20. Beveridge to Owen R. Lovejoy, 14 March 1908, BP.
21. Roosevelt to Beveridge, 30 March 1908, in Morison, *The Letters of Theodore Roosevelt*, 6: 985.
22. *CR*, 60th Cong., 1st sess., 1908, 42, pt. 6: 5801.

go on the calendar for Senate action.[23] When no report was forth-coming, he bitterly assailed the Iowan. Unhappily there was nothing he could do. "We will have to wait a while," he confessed, "for more ammunition in the way of facts."[24]

Although the bill was dead for the present, Beveridge's agitation of the issue had spurred Congress into approving the investigation by the Bureau of Labor into the working conditions of women and children and adopting the District of Columbia child labor bill. His speech in the Senate and the publicity given his bill had awakened millions to the plight of the working child. In 1914, the National Child Labor Committee, disheartened by the slow gains made at the state level, reversed its former reversal and came out for a national child labor law. And when two years later Congress passed the Keating-Owen bill, the chief architect of the new law hailed Beveridge as "the pioneer in the field of federal regulation" of child labor.[25]

The fight over his child labor bill was another milestone in Beveridge's maturing progressivism. The opposition to the measure strengthened his alienation from the old guard in Congress. In their blindness, the reactionaries blundered toward socialism or worse. Writing to banker-philanthropist Isaac Seligman, Beveridge claimed:

> I am perhaps as active a defender of honestly-gotten wealth and of legitimate business as any man now vigorously in public life. I went to the Senate as a conservative and my public speeches show that I have stuck to that creed. But it is just such villainies as child labor defended by some apparently respectable people that in the public mind casts discredit upon all business both good and bad.[26]

---

23. Beveridge to Lake, 12 May 1908, BP.
24. Beveridge to Oliver P. Smith, 22 December 1908, BP.
25. A. J. McKelway, "Another Emancipation Proclamation: The Federal Child Labor Law," *American Review of Reviews* 54 (October 1916): 424.
26. Beveridge to Isaac N. Seligman, 13 November 1907, BP.

10

Tackling the Tariff

While fighting to save the child, Beveridge was tackling an even more explosive issue—the tariff. Protection was the very ark of the G.O.P. covenant; even sound money held a secondary place in the hearts of the Republican faithful. From his first days on the stump, Beveridge had extolled the protective tariff as the foundation stone of national prosperity. And throughout his first term in the Senate, he hailed the Dingley Act for restoring prosperity after the grim days of the 1890s. The "fatal figures of 1893," he warned his audiences during the 1904 campaign, should "be enough to warn us from tampering with our vast and intricate tariff system to which the vast business of the greatest business nation of the world is delicately adjusted."[1]

But the Hoosier was never the ultraprotectionist that so many of his fellow Republicans were. Anxious, to the point of obsession, about the dangers of overproduction, he favored reciprocity agreements to gain new markets abroad for American exports. The Dingley Act had authorized the chief executive to negotiate reciprocal trade agreements subject to the approval of both houses

---

1. *Indianapolis News,* 29 September 1904.

of Congress. But the lawmakers refused to approve all but one of the treaties negotiated. Beveridge was appalled by the shortsightedness of the "forces of irrational protectionism."Although he himself was "a protectionist of the radical type," he had no patience with those "protected interests which in their greed for the dollar of the immediate moment don't seem to be willing to take measures which alone can continue the markets now theirs."[2]

And by 1906, he was becoming increasingly apprehensive over the growing hostility toward the Dingley Act. The years after 1897 witnessed a steadily rising price level, and more and more people were blaming the trusts and the tariff for safeguarding the trusts from foreign competition. Taking the lead in the attack upon the Dingley Act were business interests adversely affected by the existing schedules. New England manufacturers demanded lower duties on Canadian raw materials. The shoe manufacturers accused the packers of taking advantage of the duty on hides to raise leather prices. The fabricators of finished iron and steel products assailed the United States Steel Corporation for selling iron and steel at lower prices abroad than at home. The American Newspaper Publishers' Association demanded free pulp and newsprint to break the grip of the International Paper Company.

At the same time, the renewed talk of foreign discrimination unless the United States reduced its tariffs alarmed American exporters. The growing agitation in Britain for imperial preference threatened loss of even the Canadian market. The National Association of Manufacturers at its May 1905 convention called for prompt action by Congress to place "the United States in a position . . . [to] protect our present markets against the rising tide of discrimination." And the narrowly averted tariff war with Germany which loomed up that summer sparked an angry demand throughout the farm belt for reciprocity agreements to save the European market for American foodstuffs. Representatives of the meat packers, millers, and farmer and livestock raisers' organizations met in Chicago in August and launched the American Reciprocal Tariff League, with Alvin H. Sanders, publisher of the *Breeders' Gazette,* as president, to push the fight for a "maximum and minimum" tariff for reciprocity purposes.[3]

---

2. Beveridge to R. E. C. Long, 29 October 1901, BP.
3. *Proceedings of the Tenth Annual Convention of the National Association of*

The complaints against the Dingley Act reverberated in Indiana. Hoosier farmers were up in arms over the threatened loss of the German market. The state's leading industries—meat packing, flour milling, foundry and machine shops, manufacturers of wagons and agricultural implements—were those businessmen most hostile to the existing tariff. A confidential report from a political lieutenant early in 1905 warned Beveridge of the "unmistakable demand" for tariff revision among the G.O.P. rank and file in the Hoosier state.[4] In a poll of the state's eleven Republican congressmen at the end of the year, all agreed that public opinion in Indiana strongly favored revision. When talking with vacationing Eastern businessmen at Rangely, Maine during the summer of 1906, Beveridge found even staunch protectionists dissatisfied with the Dingley schedules. He told Roosevelt that the country was "sick and tired of that false, reactionary and foolish motto: 'Let well enough alone.' "[5]

Blaming the sharp drop in the Republican vote in the September Maine election to discontent over the tariff, Beveridge came out while campaigning that fall for reductions in "two or three" schedules where "the conditions these schedules were made to fit have changed." The duty on steel billets, bars, plates, and rails should be lowered, while wood pulp, newsprint, lumber, and sugar should be placed on the free list. Beveridge reaffirmed his support for a tariff that would protect every American industry. But honest protection should do no more than equalize the difference between the cost of production at home and abroad. Excessive rates, he warned his listeners, were not simply "an economic error" but "a moral wrong" threatening "the whole protective system."[6]

"Tariff revision is always heartily and instantly cheered," he reported to the president, while in his talks "with our people before the meetings" he found "but one sentiment"—that "there must be some tariff changes."[7] The election returns gave further confirmation of the popular mood. The G.O.P. majority in the House of Representatives was cut in half, and such prominent standpatters as James T.

Manufacturers . . . 1905 (New York [1905]), p. 185. *Chicago Tribune,* 17–18 August 1905.

4. H. C. Pettit to Beveridge, 7 February 1905, BP.
5. Beveridge to Theodore Roosevelt, 21 August 1906, Roosevelt Papers.
6. *Indianapolis Star,* 18 October 1906.
7. Beveridge to Roosevelt, 1 October 1906, BP.

McCleary of Minnesota and John F. Lacey of Iowa went down to defeat. Even John Dalzell, Cannon's right-hand man on the House Rules Committee, won in his heavily industrialized Pittsburgh district by a few hundred votes contrasted with his former pluralities, which had run into the thousands. Most personally alarming to Beveridge were G.O.P. losses in Indiana.

His pleas for immediate revision, however, simply irritated the chief executive. From his first days in the White House, Roosevelt had trod softly on the tariff issue, aware of its explosive possibilities. The tariff, he insisted, was not a moral question, but a business proposition that should be decided on grounds of expediency. And expediency dictated his keeping his hands off. Though he personally favored revision, he told Beveridge, the party leaders in Congress balked at action before the presidential election in 1908. Consequently, he could do nothing. Premature action, he reminded the Hoosier in the manner of a schoolmaster drilling a dull pupil, could split the party.[8]

Though acquiescing in the decision to postpone revision until after the 1908 election, Beveridge wished for a bold stroke to neutralize unrest over the tariff. In his debate with Democratic leader William Jennings Bryan in *The Reader* magazine in the fall of 1907, he set forth his own three-pronged tariff program. First, the G.O.P. should formally pledge in its platform revision promptly following the election. Second, the party should promise adoption at that time of a maximum and a minimum tariff. As the maximum, he would retain the existing Dingley rates "or higher rates"; for the minimum, lower rates, but rates that would still "carefully protect all American industries." The lower rates would be granted those countries that "open their markets to us"; the higher rates would retaliate against those which refused.

Third—and most important—was the immediate establishment of a permanent, expert, nonpartisan tariff commission authorized to "do anything necessary to get the exact facts as to the cost of production, state of the market and all the other elements that enter into the making of every tariff schedule" for action by the new Congress. Beveridge had been much impressed with the work of the German tariff commission in framing a new tariff that succeeded in expanding

8. Roosevelt to Beveridge, 23 August 1906, BP.

German markets abroad while protecting its domestic producers. And he saw in the German example the answer to the Republican dilemma. Simply to promise revision, he warned Roosevelt, would not suffice. "The people are distrustful" of the old guard leaders in Congress "who want to keep these schedules exclusively in their own hands." But if the party could "go before the people" in the campaign, "saying not only that the tariff is to be revised, but also that we are already at work on it in the Republican way—the practical way—of getting the facts and arranging the classifications, we will take every whiff of wind out of the sails of the opposition on this issue."[9]

Even more appealing than this short-run political gain were the larger possibilities of the tariff commission as a bulwark of protectionism. As a staunch protectionist—and loyal party man—Beveridge was disgusted with repeated tariff upheavals "every ten or twelve years." To sit back and permit abuses to build up until the resulting popular discontent climaxed in "a general tariff smash-up" was "not good business, scientific nor good sense." His long-term goal was to have the tariff commission revise, within broad limits set by Congress, the schedules, one by one, as new conditions warranted. The tariff would thus be placed on a scientific and, more important, a permanent basis safeguarded from the ups and downs of politics. "An ideal commission and an absolute handling of the tariff question," the Hoosier confided to a fellow tariff commission advocate, "would be one that gave this tariff commission the power to alter rates from time to time.[10]

But given the political situation, he dared not publicly avow this long-range aim. Instead, the bill he introduced in the Senate in January 1908 provided for a purely fact-finding body. The commission would not fix rates or even recommend duties but would simply find "the facts which Congress, for want of time, can not ascertain." The bill, he confessed to sympathetic business leaders, did not "go as far" as he would have liked. But he thought a "conservative" measure was "as far as it is best to go at this time." Because of the hostility of G.O.P. leadership in Congress, "we have got to make it so that any

9. *The Reader* 10 (November 1907): 618–26; 11 (December 1907): 73–81. Beveridge to Roosevelt, 12 March 1908, Roosevelt Papers.

10. Beveridge to Scott Bone, 17 November 1906; to Curtis Guild, Jr., 1 June 1910, BP.

of their plausible arguments will fall flat at the beginning. Out of this conservative and most reasonable bill, to which nobody can object, we will be able to get a really scientific commission."[11]

The introduction of the Hoosier's bill crystallized the growing demand for a tariff commission spurred by the German example. The American Reciprocal Tariff League was pushing for "a permanent tariff commission" to recommend the "schedules and items to be considered in reciprocal concessions." Early in 1907 the National Convention for the Extension of Foreign Trade demanded "the establishment of a permanent nonpartisan advisory board or commission" to recommend "from time to time, such modifications in the customs duties . . . as may, in their judgment, be necessary." Later that year, the board of trustees of the Merchants' Association of New York went on record in support of "a permanent tariff commission" to "take the tariff out of politics and politics out of the tariff." Similar resolutions were adopted by the Baltimore Chamber of Commerce, the Merchants' Exchange of Saint Louis, the Chicago Board of Trade and the Massachusetts State Board of Trade.[12]

Leadership of the tariff commission agitation was taken by the National Association of Manufacturers under its president, Saint Louis stove manufacturer James W. Van Cleave, and the chairman of its Tariff and Reciprocity Committee, H. E. Miles, a farm implement manufacturer from Racine, Wisconsin. The association's 1907 convention approved a resolution calling for "a non-partisan Tariff Commission . . . to investigate thoroughly and scientifically the various schedules." The N.A.M. chieftains affirmed their continued devotion to "generous" protection for every American industry. Their target, Miles explained, was the "bastard" schedules benefiting politically influential interests at the expense of those "not active in Washington, but attending to their business in the accustomed ways." Although the commission would not fix rates, its findings "would be almost all controlling." The "over-protected industries," Van Cleave declared, "are as much afraid of an impartial expert investigation as the culprit is of the court."[13]

---

11. *Indianapolis News*, 9 January 1908. Beveridge to H. E. Miles, 6 January 1908; to James W. Van Cleave, 10 January 1908, BP.

12. *CR*, 60th Cong., 1st sess., 1908, 42, pt. 2: 1576–77.

13. *Proceedings of the Twelfth Annual Convention of the National Association of Manufacturers . . . 1907* (New York [1907]), pp. 39–40, 163–73, 209–15;

The Indiana lawmaker worked in close touch with the N.A.M. leaders in drafting his tariff commission bill. Their alliance was a shaky affair. When attacked for his ties with the militantly anti-union organization, Beveridge hastened to deny any sympathy with the association's labor baiting. The N.A.M. leaders had their own suspicions about Beveridge's soundness on labor questions. But these differences were subordinated to the larger task at hand. Association spokesmen endorsed his bill as "substantially our own Bill" and promised that "the National Association of Manufacturers will co-operate with you in every possible way." And Beveridge relied upon the association as "the most vigorous supporters of the tariff commission idea."[14]

All those interests dissatisfied with the Dingley Act rallied behind his tariff commission bill. Favorable resolutions were adopted by the American Meat Packers' Association, the American National Live Stock Association, and the National Millers' Federation. Milling companies forwarded petitions. The National Grange gave its backing. The shoe manufacturers declared that a full investigation would justify their demand for free hides. The fabricators of finished iron and steel products saw in the tariff commission a weapon against the United States Steel Corporation. The newspaper publishers' lobby working for free newsprint promised its support. Local businessmen's groups throughout the country—chambers of commerce, boards of trade, merchants' associations, and manufacturers' clubs—joined in the groundswell of support for the measure.

But the legislation faced an uphill battle in Congress. The G.O.P. leaders wanted no agitation of the tariff issue before the election. Nor did they welcome a bill that would limit their control over tariff making. If there was no more logrolling, how could the individual lawmaker safeguard those local interests upon whose support his re-

---

Proceedings of the Thirteenth Annual Convention of the National Association of Manufacturers . . . 1908 (New York [1908]), pp. 112–15. Miles to Van Cleave, 11 January 1908; to H. H. Lewis, 11 April 1908; Van Cleave to Earl A. Thissell, 12 October 1908, in U.S., Congress, Subcommittee of the Senate Committee on the Judiciary, *Maintenance of a Lobby to Influence Legislation: Appendix*, 63rd Cong., 1st sess. (4 vols., Washington, 1913–14), 2: 1274–75, 1542–43, 2175–76 (hereafter cited as *Maintenance of a Lobby: Appendix*).

14. Miles to American Industries, 10 January 1908, in *Maintenance of a Lobby: Appendix*, 2: 1270. Van Cleave to Beveridge, 9 January 1908; Beveridge to Henry Riesenberg, 2 February 1909, BP.

election depended? If the tariff was taken out of politics, who would contribute the funds required to lubricate the party machinery? The Democrats assailed the tariff commission proposal as a G.O.P. stratagem to remove the tariff as an issue in the upcoming campaign. And all those profiting under the Dingley Act rallied to the defense of the existing system. A tariff commission, warned the president of the ultraprotectionist American Protective Tariff League, "would be a constant menace to American industry." Its activities, a spokesman for the United States Potters' Association echoed, "would keep the business world in such a state of uncertainty as to stop all industrial activity in this country."[15]

After having dodged the tariff question throughout his presidency, Roosevelt had no wish to tackle the issue in his last days in the White House. He told the measure's supporters that he was "heart and soul" for a tariff commission. But he refused to include a favorable recommendation in his annual message, explaining that given the present temper of Congress his support would do more harm than good. Their only hope, the president advised, was to light a fire under Congress.[16] Taking the chief executive's advice, the N.A.M. arranged for a delegation of businessmen to visit Washington early in February 1908 for talks with congressional leaders. To gain the maximum publicity, the Hoosier scheduled a major address in the Senate to coincide with their visit, and the N.A.M. arranged to distribute reprints.

In his speech, Beveridge took pains to reassure the lawmakers that, under his bill, tariff making would remain exclusively in the hands of Congress. The commission would not be "allowed to fix duties or even to suggest any rate," but would act simply as the servant of Congress in gathering the data required. The difference in the cost of production in the United States and abroad was "a question of fact." But the House Ways and Means Committee and the Senate Finance Committee, "no matter how able, wise, and industrious," could not find out "the facts concerning thousands and thousands of articles." Too often the committees accepted at face value the figures given by interested manufacturers. "Would it not seem," he challenged, "that any business or any man who is against the plan of having experts with plenty

15. *American Economist*, 24 April 1908, pp. 193–94; 22 May 1908, p. 251.

16. A. B. Farquhar to Van Cleave, 7 December 1907, in *Maintenance of a Lobby: Appendix*, 1: 1194–95.

of time find out the facts, that he does not want the facts found out?"[17]

Although the visiting businessmen met with a chilly reception from House and Senate G.O.P. leaders, Beveridge was heartened by his private soundings among the lawmakers. Many senators, he reported to the N.A.M. leaders, had assured him of their support if the bill were reported to the floor. The key to success was for the business interests backing the tariff commission to keep up the pressure. And the bitter fight raging in the upper chamber over the Aldrich currency bill authorizing the banks to issue emergency currency on the backing of state, municipal, and railroad bonds played into his hands.

Aldrich wanted Beveridge's support and approached him through his long-time friend George W. Perkins. Beveridge demanded as the price for his backing that the Finance Committee report his tariff commission bill favorably and permit a vote in the Senate. But the most the Rhode Island lawmaker would concede was a resolution directing experts from the Treasury Department to begin compiling data for use by the new Congress in revising the tariff. Convinced that this compromise was the most he could secure, Beveridge favored acceptance. "Must make any arrangement we decide on before Aldrich's financial bill voted upon," he wired the N.A.M. leaders, "because after its passage he would make no compromise whatever."[18]

The N.A.M. leaders had their misgivings. The trouble with an investigation by government experts, Miles replied, was that Congress could too easily ignore their findings. If, however, the president were authorized to add three or four well-known outsiders, their report would carry more weight with Congress and the country at large. Beveridge succeeded in inducing the president to support his demand for adding outsiders to the departmental experts. But Aldrich remained adamant. In this impasse, Perkins interrupted his vacation, rushed to Washington, and arranged a deal between Beveridge, Roosevelt, and the Rhode Islander.

Aldrich dropped the most controversial feature of the currency bill—the railroad bond provision—to speed Senate action. Beveridge undertook to move the establishment of a monetary commission to make a thorough investigation of the nation's banking and currency system—which Aldrich hoped would supply the leverage required

---

17. *CR*, 60th Cong., 1st sess., 1908, 42, pt. 2: 1577–83.
18. Beveridge to Miles [12 March 1908] (telegram), BP.

for the adoption of his central bank scheme. In return, Aldrich promised adoption of a joint resolution providing that subcommittees of the House Ways and Means and the Senate Finance Committee should begin tariff hearings during the recess and authorizing the president to appoint government experts to assist in their investigations. "It is either this or nothing," Beveridge informed the N.A.M. leaders. "I think we had better do this than nothing."[19]

Beveridge carried out his part of the bargain. But the House G.O.P. leaders continued to balk at even departmental experts. Whereupon the angry Hoosier warned Roosevelt that unless the promised resolution were adopted, the tariff commission supporters would renew their agitation. To underline this threat, the N.A.M. started a drive to force the adoption of tariff commission planks by G.O.P. state conventions throughout the country. Anxious to prevent further disturbance before the election, Roosevelt intervened and, in private talks with House leaders and special message of 28 April, urged prompt approval of a resolution authorizing a preliminary tariff investigation by "the appropriate committee of the House of Representatives and Government experts in the Executive service."[20]

Beating a partial retreat, Sereno E. Payne of New York, the chairman of the House Ways and Means Committee, promised that the new tariff "will be a maximum and minimum tariff," and, on 16 May, presented a resolution—which the House approved—authorizing his committee to sit during the recess "to gather such information, through Government agents or otherwise, as to it may seem fit looking toward the preparation of a bill for the revision of the tariff." That same day, the Finance Committee reported and the Senate approved a resolution authorizing the Committee "to call to their assistance experts in the Executive Departments of the Government" and directing the Committee to "secure proof of the relative cost of production in this and in principal competing foreign countries" of articles covered by the tariff "upon which changes in rates of duty are desirable."[21]

Rejoicing that the upper chamber had "in substance" adopted the N.A.M.'s demand, Miles hailed the Senate resolution in his report to the N.A.M. convention the following month as "the first recognition

19. Beveridge to Miles, 16 March 1908, BP.
20. CR, 60th Cong., 1st sess., 1908, 42, pt. 6: 5327–29.
21. CR (House), 60th Cong., 1st sess., 1908, 42, pt. 7: 6430–34; ibid., p. 6382.

by either branch of Congress of the underlying principle of international costs as properly determining each particular rate." The
Senate action, Van Cleave affirmed, "is in effect what this Association
has been asking for." Alvin H. Sanders, president of the American
Reciprocal Tariff League, praised the resolution as "the thin edge of
the wedge" for a permanent tariff commission. Most exultant was
Beveridge. "At the beginning of the session," he boasted to a newspaper interviewer, "it did not look as if we should be able to obtain
a single concession from the standpat element, but as the session proceeded we were able to secure concession after concession until finally
we got an arrangement for an investigation of the tariff schedules by
the committees of Congress, thus paving the way for tariff revision
at an early date."[22]

And Beveridge moved to keep up the pressure upon the lawmakers.
When Henry Riesenberg, an Indianapolis cigar manufacturer and
president of the Indiana branch of the National Rivers and Harbors
Congress, suggested the establishment of a similar body to spearhead the fight for a tariff commission, Beveridge put him in touch
with the N.A.M. leaders. Van Cleave responded enthusiastically, and
the N.A.M. took the lead in arranging for a National Tariff Commission Convention to meet in Indianapolis in mid-February 1909. The
gathering was a huge success, with delegates in attendance representing 223 agricultural, civic, commercial, and industrial organizations.
Even president-elect William Howard Taft wrote the convention's
sponsors pledging his support for a permanent tariff commission.[23]

The convention voted to set up a new organization—tentatively
called the Committee of One Hundred—to carry on the fight. But
the N.A.M. leaders remained in firm command. Van Cleave was
named chairman of the Committee of One Hundred; the treasurer
was John Kirby, Jr., a member of the N.A.M. executive board and
presidential heir-apparent; and H. E. Miles was chairman of the
executive committee. Furious at the "superficial and unbusiness like
methods" of the House Ways and Means Committee in its preliminary
work on the new tariff bill, Van Cleave put the association's Washington lobbyists into action. While party leaders, Democrats and

---

22. *Proceedings of the Thirteenth Annual Convention of the National Association of Manufacturers . . . 1908*, pp. 193, 208–9. Alvin H. Sanders to Beveridge,
20 May 1908, BP. *Indianapolis Star*, 9 June 1908.

23. William H. Taft to Riesenberg, 5 January 1909, BP.

Republicans, were hostile, a canvass of members of Congress showed strong rank-and-file support for a tariff commission. "I am confident," the top N.A.M. lobbyist reported, "that we have got such a splendid line on both Members of the House and Senate that we can get a bill of this kind through at the extra session."[24]

24. [Van Cleave] to Sereno E. Payne, 24 November 1908; [M. M. Mulhall] to D. M. Parry, 9 February 1909, in *Maintenance of a Lobby: Appendix*, 3: 2396–97, 2650.

11

The Widening Split

By 1908, the Republican party was seriously divided. Attacks upon Roosevelt from business, which had begun with the struggle over the Hepburn railroad rate bill, reached their peak after the financial panic of 1907. Standpat Republicans blamed the chief executive for destroying business confidence. As the G.O.P. divided into a stubbornly standpat majority and growing progressive minority, Beveridge sided with the president. He admired the flamboyant, vigorous Teddy—"the elemental man with his vast vitality and fine fearlessness"—as a man after his own heart. And he realized the popularity of the "square deal." The chief, he wired Roosevelt's secretary after the 1906 election, "was never so strong in the hearts of the people."[1]

Beveridge had no personal quarrel with the American society of his time. He was impelled toward progressivism by his anxiety over the threat from below—the specter of social upheaval that had haunted him from the 1890s and was reawakened by the growing popular unrest he found beneath the surface of American life. The path of safety and sound policy lay between the extremes repre-

1. Beveridge to Theodore Roosevelt, 4 October 1905; to William Loeb, Jr., 7 November 1906 (telegram), BP.

sented by the reactionaries "who think every human advance revolutionary and wrong" and "the ultra-radicals." "Surely," he wrote in his magazine debate with William Jennings Bryan, "it is wise to consider the lessons of history. Nearly every great revolution, with its terror and bloodshed, could have been avoided had just demands been granted."[2]

Thus the federal government must step in to guard the public against business wrongdoing. Given the nationwide scope of modern day business, Beveridge explained, the states could no longer handle the problem. The time had come for national action. And, like Roosevelt, he saw publicity as the first step. His favored solution was adoption of a law requiring national incorporation of all firms doing a nationwide business. All such firms would have to file reports with the Bureau of Corporations giving full data about their assets, liabilities, and business activities. The threat of public disclosure, the Hoosier predicted, would deter most would-be wrongdoers. If not, the data compiled by the Bureau of Corporations would provide a "rational" and "scientific" basis for further action by Congress and the executive.

But he envisaged no sweeping assault upon business, big or small. He continued to warn against any moves against overcapitalization that would penalize the innocent purchasers of watered stock. He continued to balk at physical valuation of the railroads as the basis for rate fixing. He continued to distinguish "between the honest, high-motived and constructive present-day business man and the opposite kind who bring discredit upon all big business men." He continued to defend "the formation of giant corporations and trusts as the result of natural economic laws." Taking as a slogan "Regulation, not extermination," he called for amendment of the Sherman law to legalize "reasonable" combinations. And government ownership remained anathema.[3]

The federal government must similarly intervene to safeguard working men and women from the worst abuses of industrial life.

2. Beveridge to Frank P. Flint, 14 September 1908, BP. *The Reader* 11 (January 1908): 158.
3. Beveridge to W. I. Schaffer, 30 March 1907; to George W. Perkins, 26 October 1907; to W. C. Brown, 20 May 1907, BP. *The Reader* 9 (May 1907): 579. Beveridge, *The Meaning of the Times and Other Speeches* (Indianapolis, 1908), pp. 427–28.

The worker, Beveridge reminded his fellow comfortable, middle-class Americans, was "a human being, not a mere machine," who had "the right to get something out of life." And unless labor received its share of national prosperity, socialism would continue to pick up new recruits. "The nation," he proclaimed in his Lincoln's Birthday speech in 1908, "will tolerate no violence caused even by injustice, but the nation should permit no injustice that may cause violence."[4]

Beveridge did not favor a federal minimum-wage law or even a maximum-hour law for adult workers. But there were areas where Congress could—and should—act to provide a model for the states and private industry. He supported the bill introduced by Senator Robert M. La Follette prohibiting interstate railroads from keeping operating personnel on duty for more than sixteen continuous hours. He backed adoption of the Wisconsin lawmaker's Railroad Employees Compensation Act. He endorsed the A.F. of L. bill to extend the eight hour day for government employees to cover the employees of contractors and subcontractors doing work for the government.

His major legislative effort was his bid to amend the workmen's compensation law for federal employees, passed by the House in May 1908, to provide broader coverage, give more generous benefits, and do away with the common-law doctrine of "contributory negligence" as a bar to the recovery of damages. But when Roosevelt, alarmed by old guard warnings that a fight would jeopardize Senate approval of even the House bill, appealed to him to withdraw his substitute, Beveridge reluctantly acquiesced. Although he continued to think the House measure amounted to "very little," he told the chief executive, "I am with you so thoroughly in your general scheme of statesmanship that I have been willing to let the serious defects of this bill go."[5]

But what about the millions of workers not reached by this federal legislation? Beveridge accepted the fact that labor unions were their first line of defense. He was, he assured United Mine Workers president John Mitchell, "in the heartiest sympathy—a blood sympathy born of my own daily life—with those who are devotedly and honestly doing all in their power to uplift the condition of those who toil with

4. *The Reader* 10 (September 1907): 384. *The Indianapolis News,* 13 February 1908.

5. Beveridge to Roosevelt, 27 May 1908, BP.

their hands." But he continued to worry lest unions go too far, and so he tempered his approval of unions with pleas for "moderation and self-restraint" and warnings against violence and "extravagant and unreasonable demands."[6]

This ambivalence was reflected in his response to the leading demand of organized labor—the limitation of the use of injunctions in labor disputes. He was willing to require a hearing on making a temporary injunction permanent within seven days after its issuance. He was even prepared—though grudgingly so—to bar the issuance of a temporary injunction without first giving notice to the party enjoined. But he stood adamant against the A.F. of L. demand for a jury trial for violators, calling it "class" legislation.

Beveridge's injunction proposal failed to satisfy the A.F. of L. leaders, while the National Association of Manufacturers denounced the bill as a sellout to organized labor. These attacks from the two extremes strengthened Beveridge's conviction that his bill represented the square deal for all. "Don't be like the British Government were," he admonished a die-hard businessman, "when they refused some reasonable things asked for by the colonists and finally resisted them so long that the colonists revolted. My anti-injunction bill is not only just to labor but it is safety to capital in the end."[7]

He saw Roosevelt as a man who shared this larger aim of saving the masters of capital from their own short-sightedness—a fellow champion of the middle ground between "the dull reactionary" and "the excited extremist."[8] At meetings of the Republican steering committee, he bombarded party leaders with demands for action on the president's recommendations for an inheritance tax, national incorporation of interstate corporations, limitation of labor injunctions, and regulation of stock market speculation. He even backed Roosevelt's handling of the Negro troops in the Brownsville incident. And when hostile lawmakers assailed the chief executive on the floor of the Senate, Beveridge rose in his defense."[9]

---

6. Beveridge to John Mitchell, 8 October 1908, BP. *The Reader* 10 (September 1907): 381.

7. *The Reader* 10 (September 1907): 385–86. Beveridge to A. M. Glossbrenner, 19 February 1908, BP.

8. *Indianapolis Star,* 26 September 1908.

9. See, for examples, *CR,* 60th Cong., 1st sess., 1908, 42, pt. 4: 3370–76; 60th Cong., 2nd sess., 1909, 43, pt. 4: 3738–39.

His support for the president increasingly alienated the Hoosier from the old guard Senate leadership. By 1908, Orville H. Platt, whom Beveridge regarded as the wisest and most far-sighted of the Senate leaders, was dead; John C. Spooner had retired; and William B. Allison, perhaps the most sensitive of the Senate leaders to public opinion, was a dying man. After the Hepburn bill fight, a widening gulf divided Beveridge from men like Nelson Aldrich and Eugene Hale who remained blind to the popular anxieties and resentments that were pushing him toward progressivism. When in December 1907 he applied for a vacancy on the Senate Finance Committee, Aldrich turned him down because of his advocacy of a tariff commission.

The smoldering antagonisms within the G.O.P. burst into flame over Roosevelt's request in his message of December 1907 that Congress authorize four new battleships. From 1901 to 1905, the chief executive had urged rapid naval expansion. Then, in December 1905, he informed Congress that for the immediate future he would ask for no more than a single new battleship a year to replace worn-out units. But the crisis with Japan growing out of the anti-Japanese agitation in the Pacific Coast, the revolution in battleship design heralded by the completion in December 1906 of H.M.S. *Dreadnought,* which rendered all previous battleships obsolete, and the failure of the Hague Conference in the fall of 1907 to halt the spiraling naval arms race led Roosevelt to resume his naval expansion program lest the United States fall behind its rivals. And to rally popular support for increased naval appropriations, he hit upon the spectacular tactic of sending the American battle fleet, in December 1907, on a voyage around the world.

But his four-battleship request was coldly received in Congress. There was, in and out of Congress, a growing "peace bloc" hostile to increased military appropriations. Many lawmakers were alarmed over the prospective budgetary deficit resulting from depressed economic conditions. Those—and they were numerous—who refused to face up to the country's new global responsibilities outside of the Western Hemisphere questioned the desirability of a large offensive navy. Conservatives, more and more disturbed at the administration's domestic reform policies, saw in the naval program a safe issue on which to defy and embarrass the President. And even former supporters of naval expansion such as Senator Eugene Hale of Maine, the powerful chairman of the Senate Naval Affairs Committee, were opposed to the chief executive's proposed changes in naval administration, the promotion system, and battleship design and resented his freewheeling, personal brand of diplomacy. Rejecting the four-battleship proposal by an overwhelming 199–83 margin, the House of Representatives voted to authorize only two new battleships.

When the naval appropriation bill came before the Senate, Beveridge took over leadership of the four-battleship forces. Although Senator Samuel Piles of Washington was picked to present the four-battleship amendment in order to dramatize the Pacific Coast demand for a larger navy against the Japanese threat, Beveridge led the bitter fight that followed. He canvassed the Senate to win over doubtful members, kept the White House in touch, took the brunt of the old guard attacks, and acted as spokesman for the president in defense of his naval program.

More than loyalty to the chief executive animated Beveridge. Even before the Russo-Japanese war, he had looked upon Japan as this country's most dangerous rival in the Far East—the cockpit of future world rivalries—and had repeatedly warned that in a world where steam and electricity had so narrowed distances, the United States could no longer afford the luxury of unpreparedness. Unless Congress approved the four battleships Roosevelt had requested, he told the upper chamber, the United States would become a third-rate power unable to uphold the Monroe Doctrine in the Western Hemisphere or the Open Door in the Far East. Unpreparedness was a standing invitation for the Japanese to begin war; strengthening the navy would deter any possible aggressors. "*This is not a war measure,*" he pleaded. "Senators, THIS IS A PEACE MEASURE."[10]

The old guard replied with a bitter personal attack. Eugene Hale reminded the chamber that the Hoosier had predicted before the Russo-Japanese war that "no nation could stand in the East before Russia." Why should the Senate heed the warnings of so dubious a prophet? Rhode Island's Nelson W. Aldrich took up the attack in a rare public speech. The United States, Aldrich told the upper chamber, was protected against the danger of foreign attack by the two great oceans. He went on to belittle the danger of hostilities with Japan. The conclusion in late February 1908 of the so-called Gentle-

---

10. *CR*, 60th Cong., 1st sess., 1908, 42, pt. 6: 5165–75.

men's Agreement to end Japanese immigration to the United States belied the war scare raised by the supporters of the four-battleship amendment. And could anyone believe that two additional battleships would deter a would-be aggressor? The United States should not waste its resources to "prepare for possible conflicts which, in my judgment, will never occur except in the fancy or imagination of the Senator from Indiana." "Aldrich," Beveridge complained, "literally raged on the floor."[11]

But Beveridge replied with dignity, ignoring the personal assaults. A crisis, he reminded the lawmakers, often arises unexpectedly. The Mafia incident in New Orleans in the 1890s came without warning, yet it could have plunged this country into war with Italy. A similar outbreak on the Pacific Coast could at any moment lead to war with Japan. "If we build four ships," he told the chamber, "and it appears that we do not need them so rapidly, we need not build any next year, and no harm will be done; but if it should occur that we do need them, then no mistake has been made and a great disaster may be saved." Privately, he was not so restrained. "Aldrich, Hale and that crowd," he told an Indiana newspaper editor, "did everything in God's world that could be done or ever has been done to defeat us. The House organization, with Cannon at its head, did the same thing. Promises and pledges, threats against appropriation bills, trades and deals of all kinds . . . were made to Senators in order to get them to line up against the President's recommendation. The plain truth about it is that it was not a battleship fight at all but a fight against Theodore Roosevelt."[12]

When the four-battleship amendment came up for a vote, the upper chamber voted nay by fifty to twenty-three. But the Hoosier's fight had shaken the party leadership. Before the roll call, William B. Allison rose and, seconded by Hale, promised to continue in future years to provide two new battleships a year instead of only one. Even after this promise, a large bloc of Republicans—largely from the Pacific Coast and Mountain states, where alarm over "the yellow peril" was the strongest—bolted. "We got almost twenty more votes than we thought we would get when we started into the fight," Bev-

---

11. Ibid., pt. 6: 5212–18. Beveridge to Horace Ellis, 1 May 1908, BP.
12. *CR*, 60th Cong., 1st sess., 1908, 42, pt. 6: 5287–89. Beveridge to Walter Bradfute, 28 April 1908, BP.

eridge exulted. He regarded the promise of two new battleships a year in the future as a "moral victory." So did Roosevelt. "Beveridge," his secretary wrote Albert Shaw, "made a very game fight and the net result has been really a victory."[13]

The bitter words hurled across the Senate floor widened the breach between Beveridge and the Senate leaders he had so admired when a freshman lawmaker. Their hostility to the Hepburn Act, the meat inspection legislation, the child labor law, and the tariff commission revealed their blindness to the nation's domestic needs. Now the battle over the four battleships showed Aldrich, Hale, and their followers blind to this country's responsibilities as a world power. "For three years," Beveridge exclaimed, "I have been dead set against their views on public questions, and I am getting more against them every day. . . . If they keep on this way, there is danger that we will lose the State and the country."[14]

By 1908, the clash over national issues had begun to have repercussions upon Indiana politics. But this development came slowly. At the start of Beveridge's second term, the factional rivalry in Indiana was no more than a continuing struggle for place, perferment, and power. The nomination of Charles W. Fairbanks for the vice-presidency led, even before the election returns were in, to a scramble among eager aspirants for his seat in the Senate. The Fairbanks wing of the party lined up behind conservative Congressman James A. Hemenway of the First District. Rather than become involved in a possibly losing fight, Beveridge decided to make a deal with Hemenway. "Unless he turns out to be the most unlimited . . . liar that ever lived," he reported to Albert Shaw, "he will prove an extremely agreeable colleague."[15]

At first, affairs ran smoothly. When the patronage was reshuffled following the election, Beveridge retained Henry C. Pettit as United States Marshal. Out went A. E. Nowlin as the Collector of Internal Revenue for the Sixth (Lawrenceburg) District. In his place, Beveridge appointed Elam H. Neal of Jonesboro, the Eleventh District G.O.P. chairman. Joseph B. Kealing remained as United States Dis-

---

13. Beveridge to Charles W. Miller, 2 May 1908; to Bradfute, 28 April 1908, BP. Loeb to Albert Shaw, 29 April 1908, Shaw Papers.

14. Beveridge to Charles R. Lane, 30 April 1908, BP.

15. Beveridge to Shaw, 13 December 1904, BP.

trict Attorney. But Hemenway kept John R. Bonnell on as Collector
of Internal Revenue for the Seventh (Terre Haute) District. In January 1905, Beveridge had his long-time personal friend Henry W.
Bennett appointed postmaster of Indianapolis. At the same time he
induced the chief executive to name Leopold G. Rothschild Collector
of the Customs at Indianapolis when that post became vacant. When
he learned what had happened, Congressman Jesse Overstreet of Indianapolis protested that the collectorship was his patronage, not
the senator's. But Roosevelt went ahead and appointed Rothschild,
thus showing Hoosier politicians where the White House stood.

Even the newspaper situation was looking up. In June 1903, Muncie
traction magnate George F. McCulloch had launched the *Indianapolis
Star*. Despite McCulloch's past hostility, Beveridge regarded the new
paper as more favorable in its treatment of him than the *News* or the
Journal. A morning paper, the *Star* bought out the rival *Journal* in
June 1904. But the circulation war with the *Journal* had been expensive, and McCulloch wished to dispose of his newspaper interests—
which included the *Muncie Star* and *Terre Haute Star*—to devote
full time to his other business undertakings. Alarmed that Fairbanks
would buy this so-called Star League, Beveridge appealed to his
friend John C. Shaffer to purchase the newspapers. Shaffer lacked the
cash but was anxious to promote Beveridge's political fortunes, and
so he arranged with Daniel G. Reid, Indiana banker and organizer of
the "tinplate trust," to put up the bulk of the money and place the
Star League under his management.

Thus armed, Beveridge moved to take over the G.O.P. state organization. He had never trusted State Chairman James P. Goodrich, and
now slights, real or imagined, spurred him to action. And Fairbanks's
ambitions for the G.O.P. presidential nomination in 1908 further
inflamed hostilities. Beveridge had hopes of his own for the presidency, but to have a show for the nomination, he had to become
master in his own state. His appointees throughout the state were put
to work in behalf of his hand-picked candidate for state chairman; he
even interceded with the administration to halt enforcement of the
civil service regulations barring political activities by federal officeholders.

To keep the Seventh District in line, Beveridge made a deal with
Indianapolis mayor Charles A. Bookwalter. Under Bookwalter, Indianapolis suffered from the same ills that plagued so many cities at the

turn of the century: administrative mismanagement, police graft, and corrupt ties between the city administration and the public utilities, the liquor interests, and the underworld. A revolt of good-government Republicans led by the *Indianapolis News* had defeated Bookwalter for reelection in 1903. But he made a comeback two years later and returned to city hall. Bookwalter's hostility toward the *News* extended to Fairbanks. Capitalizing on this situation, Rothschild maintained close ties with Bookwalter, while Beveridge campaigned for him in 1903 and again in 1905. "With Bookwalter in the saddle," Beveridge was confident that the Seventh District would be "a cinch."[16]

At first, the tide appeared running his way. But the *News* strongly backed Goodrich. So did Governor J. Frank Hanly. The vice-president spent freely from his personal fortune. Hemenway went back on his promise to stay neutral. At the height of the struggle, Daniel G. Reid abruptly removed Shaffer as publisher of the Star League and threw the influence of the papers against Beveridge. The final—and perhaps decisive—blow was the most unexpected. From his base in Terre Haute, John R. Bonnell swung the Fifth Congressional District behind Goodrich. Beveridge was deeply hurt. "It is the first time in my life that I ever had a man whom I had signally favored betray me."[17]

Goodrich's reelection gave new life to the Fairbanks-for-president boom. Beveridge was in a dilemma. He continued to hope that he might win the prize, but if he could not, he hardly wanted the vice-president to do so. Factional strife in Indiana would dash Fairbanks's hopes. But after his defeat in the state chairmanship fight, Beveridge dared not make trouble: his factional rivals controlled the state party organization; the *Indianapolis News* was hostile; and, under its new management, the Star League was anti-Beveridge and even more anti-Roosevelt and an outspoken supporter of Fairbanks for president. Seeing no alternative, Beveridge announced his own support of Fairbanks.

After Roosevelt had picked secretary of war William Howard Taft for his successor, Beveridge did what he could behind the scenes to elect delegates to the national convention who, in case of a showdown, would switch to the rotund Ohioan. But he remained publicly

---

16. Beveridge to Miller, 8 December 1905, BP.
17. Beveridge to A. B. Anderson, 24 January 1906, BP.

loyal to Indiana's favorite son. When Roosevelt admirers belabored him for supporting a reactionary machine politician like the vice-president, he replied that the chief executive understood and approved. No public man, he reminded civil service reformer William Dudley Foulke, could accomplish much if a political maverick. Thus, "all of us find ourselves compelled, for what we think are the larger purposes, too often to support men that ought not to be supported for anything."[18]

At the same time, he worked to rebuild his political fences. As a first step, he came out during the 1906 campaign for adoption of a statewide direct primary for the nomination of all candidates from the county level to United States Senator. Confident of his popularity with the rank and file of the voters, Beveridge hoped that the direct primary would break the grip of his factional rivals upon the party machinery. And the reform fitted in with his maturing progressivism. The popular will, he told his audiences, could not prevail so long as a handful of political manipulators in the pay of the special interests controlled the machinery of the two parties and forced the voters to choose between Tweedledum and Tweedledee.[19]

Although staking his prestige upon adoption of the statewide direct primary, Beveridge could not bring many of even his closest supporters into line. The legislature voted to limit the direct primary to the nomination of city, township, and county officers, and members of the state legislature "when the same are to be elected exclusively from any such county." Even for those offices, the primary was mandatory only in the four counties having cities with a population of thirty-six thousand or over.[20] Beveridge denounced the new law as a fraud passed to quiet the popular demand for the direct primary without destroying machine rule, and he pledged to continue the fight.

But the next major party battle—the fight for the 1908 gubernatorial nomination—would take place under the old rules. Beveridge's candidate was long-time friend, former state attorney general Charles W. Miller. The Fairbanks-Hemenway-Goodrich faction put forward Congressman James E. Watson. From their college days, Beveridge and

---

18. Beveridge to William Dudley Foulke, 10 February 1908, Foulke Papers (ISL).

19. *Indianapolis Star*, 24 October, 4 November 1906.

20. *Laws of the State of Indiana . . . 1907* (Indianapolis, 1907), pp. 627–52.

Watson had been bitter rivals. Beveridge regarded Watson as his worst enemy in the state and feared that his election as governor would endanger his own reelection two years later. Growing differences over national issues reinforced their hostility. With Roosevelt's policies drawing the line of division within the G.O.P. more and more sharply, Fairbanks, Hemenway, and Watson were to be found on one side, and Beveridge on the other.

The political situation in the Hoosier state, however, was not that simple. Governor J. Frank Hanly had given the state four years of forward-looking administration. He had gained a deserved reputation as an uncompromising foe of the liquor traffic, vice, gambling, and political corruption; he had pushed through the General Assembly legislation establishing a strong and effective railroad commission, regulating trusts, outlawing "bucket shops," placing the state's charitable and correctional institutions on a nonpartisan basis, and setting up a legislative reference bureau; and he had urged adoption of a state inheritance tax, an antilobby law, and stricter regulation of insurance companies. But many of Beveridge's warmest local supporters had taken the wrong side on these measures. Miller himself had balked at the statewide feature of the direct primary bill.[21] And though the National Association of Manufacturers strongly backed—and organized labor opposed—Watson because of his antilabor record in Congress, one of Miller's business supporters, a man rated "dead right on labor matters" by a N.A.M. leader, assured doubters that Miller was as sound as his rival on that issue.[22]

This blurring of the lines of division in Indiana favored Watson.[23] His backers controlled the party machinery in most of the districts; he had the support of the state's leading newspapers; he had a lavish campaign fund—Beveridge charged that he spent between $125,000 and $200,000. Coming into the state convention the front runner by an easy lead, Watson picked up sufficient bandwagon votes from two local favorite-son candidates to win the nomination on the fifth ballot. His victory was so bitter a pill for the Beveridge people that many threatened to cut the ticket on election day. But Beveridge warned

---

21. James W. Noel to Beveridge, 10 January 1907, 4, 8 April, 5 September 1908; Leopold G. Rothschild to Beveridge [— February 1907], BP.

22. C. A. Carlisle to H. E. Miles, 22 January 1908; Miles to M. M. Mulhall, 27 January 1908, in *Maintenance of a Lobby: Appendix*, 2: 1325, 1337.

23. Beveridge to Miller, 5 April 1908, BP.

against such action. The stigma of party disloyalty could be fatal to his own political fortunes two years later. And the half of the state senate elected in 1908 would remain in the legislature when he came up for reelection.[24]

There followed another disappointment for Beveridge, which was at the same time a further illustration of the split in the G.O.P. The Hoosier had his heart set upon becoming temporary chairman of the Republican national convention. Roosevelt wrote Harry S. New of Indiana, the chairman of the Republican National Committee, urging Beveridge as his personal choice for the post. When Taft supporters on the committee protested that Beveridge was publicly committed to another candidate for the presidential nomination, Roosevelt had the secretary of war write his managers waiving any objection to the Hoosier. And New privately assured Beveridge of his backing. Beveridge was so confident of receiving the honor that he prepared his keynote address. But the standpat majority on the National Committee—with the connivance of New, who later claimed he was acting at Taft's secret request—refused to name so ardent a Roosevelt man and picked instead the safe and unimaginative Julius C. Burrows of Michigan.

When Beveridge arrived at the convention, he found a growing boom for his nomination for vice-presidency. The Taft managers pleaded with him to accept the nomination to head off the candidacy of Congressman James S. Sherman of New York, backed by the old guard. Though flattered by the request, Beveridge refused. Rather than become the capital's forgotten man, he would remain in the Senate and nurse his presidential ambitions. But his refusal did not end the matter. Many middle western delegates continued to plead with him to run with the secretary of war. Adamant, Beveridge replied that if his name were placed in nomination, he would rise from his seat and decline.[25]

Beveridge returned from the convention with mixed feelings. The platform was too much of "a half and half affair." He was "deeply humiliated" when the convention voted down Wisconsin senator Robert M. La Follette's proposed planks for publicity of campaign contributions, popular election of United States Senators, and physi-

---

24. See, for example, Beveridge to Charles F. Remy, 15 August 1908, BP.
25. Beveridge to John C. Shaffer [— July 1908], B.P.

cal valuation of railroads. He was disappointed at the convention's failure to endorse the tariff commission. Even the tariff plank adopted was a straddle promising revision of the tariff without specifying downward revision. And he regarded the vice-presidential nomination of "Sunny Jim" Sherman as "distinctly reactionary."[26]

Beveridge had not been personally close to the G.O.P. standard bearer. And he had misgivings—or so he later recalled—about the Ohioan's ability or desire to carry on the Roosevelt policies.[27] These misgivings were strengthened when he learned that Taft planned to name James A. Hemenway as his campaign manager for the Middle West. But Taft abandoned the idea when his top adviser, Frank H. Hitchcock, warned that Hemenway's old guard ties made his appointment unwise. Taking a leaf from Roosevelt's book, the nominee exercised flattery upon Beveridge and invited him to his vacation hideaway at Hot Springs, Virginia, to discuss campaign strategy. Beveridge came back fully won over. "He impressed me," he reported to John C. Shaffer, "as almost boyish in his simplicity and truthfulness and sincerity, and I must confess, to my surprise, that I liked him far better than I ever did before."[28]

By the fall of 1908, he had found new interests in life which tempered his political disappointments. In the years after the death of his wife he had been kept busy with Senate business, running errands for his constituents, and keeping in touch with the Indiana political situation. While Congress was in session, he had a bachelor apartment at the respectable though far from luxurious Portland on Fourteenth Street near Thomas Circle. In summer he went to the country and combined rest with work on his magazine articles and speeches. There remained, however, many a lonely hour.

During the winter of 1906-7, he was introduced to Catherine Eddy, of a socially prominent Chicago family. By spring they were engaged. "If ever in my life I believed that our dear Lord helped me—& I know he has & often—I firmly believe," he wrote John C. Shaffer, "He has brought this rare girl into my life."[29] They were married in August

---

26. Beveridge to Robert M. La Follette, 29 June 1908; to Scott Bone, 9 July 1908, BP. Beveridge to Lucius B. Swift, 29 July 1908, Swift Papers.

27. Beveridge to Shaffer, 31 May 1919; to Mark Sullivan, 12 August 1925, BP.

28. Beveridge to Shaffer [— July 1908], BP.

29. Beveridge to Shaffer [—— 1907], Shaffer Papers.

1907 at the American Embassy in Berlin, where the bride's brother, Spencer Eddy, was first secretary of the legation, and honeymooned in the Italian Dolomites. After his marriage, Beveridge built a roomy house in Indianapolis, at 4164 Washington Boulevard.[30] In August, 1908, Catherine gave birth to their first child, whom the proud father named Albert, Jr.

In his new happiness, Beveridge found more and more irksome the demands politics made upon his time and energies. He had spent so little time with Catherine since their marriage, he complained as the 1908 campaign approached, that she felt almost as if she were a widow. And for what? Did any one appreciate his efforts? In this mood, he even threatened to stay home during the campaign unless he was given a special train. But Republican National Chairman Frank H. Hitchcock soothed his ruffled feelings, and he gave himself unstintingly to the battle. He covered sixteen thousand miles—starting in Ohio and going on to Minnesota, the Dakotas, Montana, Washington, Oregon, California, Nevada, Colorado, Oklahoma, Nebraska, Kansas, Missouri, and then back to Chicago before finishing up the campaign in Indiana—and delivered almost four hundred speeches.

Beveridge was convinced that only a straightforward progressive campaign could win for the G.O.P. against Democratic nominee William Jennings Bryan. Thus, he coupled praise for the achievements of the administration with promises of further reform— a national child labor law, tariff revision, the establishment of a tariff commission, the direct primary, stricter regulation of corporations, and the limitation of labor injunctions. The issue, he told his audiences, was whether or not the historic movement for righteousness began by Theodore Roosevelt would continue. Bryan could not be trusted with the presidency. He was a dreamer, and his rash and poorly thought-out policies would demoralize business and plunge the nation into a depression. Elect Taft, he appealed, to "lead us safely and surely along the well-marked course we are following."[31]

---

30. For a description of the house, see *Indianapolis Star*, 2 April 1922. The property was valued for tax purposes in 1914 at $11,940 (*New York Times*, 11 February 1914) and in 1922, after the actual cash value system of assessment had been instituted, at $40,000, with his personal property valued at $14,700, (Charles R. Kellogg to Beveridge, 28 March 1923, BP).

31. *Indianapolis Star*, 6 September 1908.

But the G.O.P. was in trouble in the Hoosier state. The hard times following the panic of 1907 were being attributed to the incumbent Republicans. The party was badly factionalized. Progressive-minded voters were hostile to gubernatorial nominee James E. Watson because of his standpat record while House majority whip and right-hand man to Speaker "Uncle Joe" Cannon. Organized labor campaigned actively against Watson, with A. F. of L. President Samuel Gompers taking the stump in Indiana. In contrast, Democratic candidate Thomas R. Marshall appealed to progressive sentiment with a program calling for a new primary election law for the selection of all state and local candidates, direct election of United States senators, guaranty of bank reposits, limitations upon injunctions in labor disputes, strengthening of the employees' liability law, strong action against trusts, sharp reductions in the tariff, and economy in government.

The final blow to Republican chances was the revival of the prohibition issue. Under the existing law, the majority of voters in any ward or township could bar the sale of liquor. This arrangement allowed "wet" strongholds to exist in the middle of largely "dry" counties. The Anti-Saloon League demanded county local option. Prohibitionists estimated that under such a provision all of Indiana except for a handful of counties with large cities and/or a sizable foreign-born population would vote dry. An ardent temperance advocate, Governor J. Frank Hanly forced the G.O.P. state convention to adopt a county local option plank in its platform.

When the Democrats promised to retain the existing ward and township system, the state's powerful brewery interests threw their support behind the Democratic gubernatorial candidate. The Republican leaders hoped that the issue would win for the party more "dry" Democratic votes than lose "wet" Republican votes. But in September Hanly, against the wishes of party leaders, called the General Assembly into special session to adopt county local option. Trapped, the Republican majority had to agree. Passage of the law cost Watson his foremost campaign issue: "dry" Democrats were freed to vote their own party ticket, while the "wets" redoubled their activities for the Democratic nominee. And Hanly further muddied the waters by stumping for statewide prohibition.

Taft carried Indiana by more than ten thousand votes. But Marshall was elected governor by a plurality of nearly fifteen thousand. And though holdover senators gave the G.O.P. a slim lead in the upper house, the Democrats had a majority on joint ballot for the election of a United States senator. The prohibition issue had contributed to the Republican downfall. More, however, was involved. The hostility of organized labor had hurt. And revolt against standpattism was sweeping through the Middle West. The Republican defeat in Indiana reflected this wider discontent. The lesson was not lost upon Beveridge. "The movement which you have thus far so gloriously led," he wrote Roosevelt, "must go on—will go on, whether any of us want it or not."[32]

---

32. Beveridge to Roosevelt, 14 November 1908, BP.

12

The Payne-Aldrich Tariff Fight

The new president's inaugural address won Beveridge's enthusiastic applause. He was heartened by Taft's pledge to continue Roosevelt's fight for "the suppression of the lawlessness and abuses of power of the great combinations of capital." He was even more reassured by Taft's call for downward revision of the tariff. "President Taft's emphatic assertion of progressive policies is inspiring," Beveridge told a newspaper interviewer. "It shows . . . that he is faithful to the best interests of all the people."[1]

Beveridge entered Johns Hopkins Hospital for a hernia operation several days before the meeting of the special session of Congress called to revise the tariff. During his convalescence he was disturbed by the reports coming out of Washington. The first shock was Taft's refusal to support the party rebels in their fight with Speaker Joseph G. Cannon over the House rules. Then followed Taft's disappointing message of 16 March 1909, calling Congress into special session: there was no attempt to

1. William H. Taft, *Presidential Addresses and State Papers* (Garden City, N.Y., 1910), pp. 53–68. *Indianapolis Star*, 9 March 1909.

rally public sentiment; he failed even to specify downward revision; and tariff commission supporters were alarmed by his failure to include any recommendation for a tariff commission.

The bill reported by the House Ways and Means Committee had its shortcomings. The duty on hosiery was raised; the minimum duty on women's gloves was jumped from $1.75 a dozen to $4; the duties on mercerized cotton were raised; no significant reductions were made in the wool schedule; and the duty on refined sugar was cut by a meaningless five cents per hundred pounds. But coal, hides, and iron ore were placed on the free list. The rates on steel products were cut by as much as half; on pig iron from $7 to $2.50 a ton. The duty on lumber was reduced from $2 to $1 per thousand feet and on newsprint from $6 to $2 a ton. When the bill came before the House, petroleum and petroleum products were placed upon the free list.

All the insurgents in the House rules fight voted for the bill. The loudest grumblings came from standpatters unhappy over the reductions made. But a fight was looming in the Senate. Robert M. La Follette of Wisconsin protested that the measure did not fulfill the party's campaign pledges. Joseph L. Bristow dismissed the bill as "a fraud," "an outrage," "a graft, pure and simple."[2] Although Albert B. Cummins of Iowa at first reacted favorably, further study disillusioned him. His Hawkeye colleague Jonathan P. Dolliver remained noncommittal, but he had grown more and more restive under old guard rule and was spending much of his time over on the House side listening to the debate.

The amended and rewritten bill reported by Nelson W. Aldrich from his Senate Finance Committee on 12 April, fed the flames of revolt. To win the backing of the range senators, Aldrich placed a 15 percent duty upon hides. A new method of classifying cotton goods promised New England manufacturers a windfall. The duty on structural steel was increased approximately 100 percent over the 1897 rate. A duty of twenty-five cents a ton was imposed on iron ore and sixty cents per ton on coal; the duty on lumber was boosted to $1.50 a thousand feet and on newsprint to $4 a ton; and the Dingley rates on petroleum were restored. "The policy of protection," Bristow

---

2. Joseph L. Bristow to C. B. Kirtland, 20 March 1909; to Fred W. Trigg, 7 April 1909; to Harold T. Chase, 26 March 1909, Bristow Papers (Kansas State Historical Society).

complained, ". . . is being contorted into a synonym for graft and plunder."[3]

After Beveridge returned to Washington, he plunged into a detailed examination of the bill. The exertion so soon after his operation brought on a near physical collapse. But he was so dismayed at what he found that when the battle was joined in the upper chamber, he lined up with a bloc of nine fellow Republicans in revolt against the Senate leadership—La Follette, Bristow, Cummins, Dolliver, Moses Clapp and Knute Nelson of Minnesota, Coe Crawford of South Dakota, and Norris Brown and Elmer J. Burkett of Nebraska. The insurgents thought they could rely on the backing of the White House. The chief executive had called Dolliver in and urged him and Beveridge to take the lead in a fight to improve the bill and even talked of vetoing an unsatisfactory measure.

Acting as floor leader for the insurgent bloc, Beveridge labored behind the scenes to maintain a solid front. He made few speeches but, with interjections, reinforced the more detailed attack of a fellow insurgent. Assailing the steamroller tactics adopted by the Senate leaders to push the bill through without a full debate, he repeatedly needled Finance Committee members with demands for an explanation of the reasons for increases over the rates in the House bill. Under the withering insurgent attack, the Senate leaders began to lose their tempers—and their heads. "Aldrich and the old crowd are gone," Beveridge wrote his wife at the beginning of June. "He has lost his cunning. Thrice in two days he has gone all to pieces."[4]

Beveridge supported higher rates when the interests of his constituents were threatened or when he thought the duty required for "honest protection." He voted against placing agricultural implements on the free list. He balked at the free admission of shoes. He demanded more protection for Indiana's tinplate industry. "Our differences," he told the bill's supporters, "are not so very wide—sometimes an eighth of 1 per cent, sometimes a tenth of 1 per cent, and sometimes a fourth of 1 per cent; sometimes several per cent; sometimes more, sometimes less. The differences are as to the justice and wisdom of rates and not as to the principle of protection."

---

3. Bristow to C. M. Sheldon, 21 April 1909, ibid.
4. Beveridge to Mrs. Beveridge, 1 June 1909, in Bowers, *Beveridge and the Progressive Era*, p. 345.

But higher rates than were justified by "the difference between the cost of production here and abroad" were "extortion." Monopolies such as the National Cash Register Company took advantage of the excessive duties to raise their prices. The higher prices, he charged, were a "grievous" burden upon the little man making $500 to $1,000 a year with a wife and four or five children. The resentments thus aroused were threatening to destroy the protective system. When Aldrich denounced him as the leader of "the heterogenous combination" against the bill and read him out of the G.O.P., Beveridge, standing nearly face to face with the Rhode Island senator, answered that he, not Aldrich, was the real friend of protection and a true Republican.

The bitterest exchange came when Beveridge asked for more protection for Indiana's tinplate industry. Aldrich pointed out that the United States Steel Corporation produced 80 to 90 percent of tinplate made in the country and expressed shock, even indignation, at the Hoosier's wish to profit the steel trust. Beveridge answered that he was acting at the request of the tinplate workers. "When the Senator from Indiana wants to have something done," Aldrich replied, "it is always the workingmen, and not the employers or the manufacturers that will get the benefit of it. If he is opposed to a thing being done, it is the manufacturers who will get the benefit and not the employees." "And with the Senator from Rhode Island," Beveridge retorted amid laughter from the galleries, "it is always the manufacturers, and never the employees."[5]

As the debate went on, complaints were heard that the delay was upsetting business. Beveridge suspected that the flood of letters coming in demanding prompt action were inspired by the special interests to stampede the insurgents. He angrily denied that the insurgents were guilty of wasting time. And he vowed to continue his fight to improve the bill even at the risk of further delay. Unless the bill were made "right," he warned the former president of the National Association of Manufacturers, the country will face "another tariff flurry" in three or four years. "What I have been afraid of," he explained to John C. Shaffer, "is that the extortionists will succeed in getting

5. *CR*, 61st Cong., 1st sess., 1909, 44, pt. 2: 1886–87; pt. 3: 2356–63, 2552, 2882–94; pt. 4: 3494–97, 3655–56, 3798, 4182, 4280–83.

through so unjust a bill that people will tear it all to pieces in the next Presidential campaign."[6]

But the Hoosier fought a losing battle. He voted for free iron ore to break the United States Steel Company's stranglehold upon the domestic supply; the standpatters—joined by eighteen Democrats— imposed a duty of twenty-five cents a ton. He voted to reduce the duty on lumber to one dollar; the Senate approved a duty of $1.50. The sugar duties were adopted over his "no" vote. He voted for free hides; the Senate approved a duty of 15 percent. He accused the American Woolen Company of taking advantage of excessively high duties to exploit the consumer; but the reductions demanded by the insurgents were voted down. The bitterest fight came over the cotton schedule. Although paired and thus not voting, Beveridge took the floor to go on record against the Finance Committee rates.

Washington's summer heat sapped men's energies and frayed their nerves. Starting in June, the Senate began night sessions to speed action on the bill. The insurgents were thereby forced to stay up into the early hours of the morning studying the different schedules. "I'm tired of work," Beveridge wrote his wife on 1 June, "—so tired—you can't imagine how tired." "I am lonely and weary and disgusted, and worn out," he wrote a week later. "Worked and worried all last night," he reported in a third letter. ". . . I am very tired and almost at the limit of endurance."[7]

To meet the government's estimated one hundred million dollar deficit, the House bill had included a graduated inheritance tax. But the Senate Finance Committee struck out that provision. And with over thirty states having their own inheritance taxes, even the insurgents balked at adding a federal levy. Instead, an insurgent-Democratic coalition led by Cummins and Democratic leader Joseph W. Bailey of Texas put forward an amendment for a 2 percent tax upon all corporation and individual incomes above $5,000. The amendment's sponsors claimed the backing of nineteen Republicans and all the Democrats—a majority of the upper chamber.

---

6. Beveridge to D. M. Parry, 14 May 1909 (telegram); to John C. Shaffer, 21 May 1909, BP.

7. Beveridge to Mrs. Beveridge, 1, 28 June, 8 July 1909, in Bowers, *Beveridge and the Progressive Era*, p. 347.

Beveridge favored the inheritance tax. But he thought the income tax would stifle individual effort; he was doubtful about the possibility of collecting an income tax without a nationwide network of spies; and he shrank from the possible constitutional repercussions. "To pass an income tax precisely like the one that the Supreme Court declared unconstitutional," he explained to a constituent, "would be the hardest imaginable blow to the respect which the people ought to retain for the Courts." The Democrats' support for the income tax was "a purely political maneuver," and Beveridge lamented the mistake of his fellow insurgents in falling into the trap.[8]

Taft shared Beveridge's anxiety that adoption of an income tax would expose the Supreme Court "to very severe criticism whatever it does."[9] As an alternative source of revenue, he came out for a 2 percent excise tax on the net incomes of all corporations engaged in interstate commerce. Not only had the Supreme Court upheld a similar tax, but he thought the measure an adjunct to his larger program of corporate regulation because corporations would be forced to open their books for examination. Despite business protests, Taft exploited the threat of the Cummins-Bailey amendment to force the standpatters into approving the corporation tax and an income tax amendment to the Constitution. With the old guard whipped into line, he called in one after another of the Republican bolters and won their backing.

Beveridge was among the lawmakers invited to the White House. He was unhappy over the president's move. Indiana businessmen were up in arms against the corporation tax. And he agreed, he confided to Albert Shaw, that the levy "would work a grave injustice" because "it would lay the burden of taxation upon a corporation, while not laying the same burden upon a partnership doing the same business and perhaps even a larger business." If the chief executive had taken "a firm stand" and declared that the Supreme Court had decided the question, "there is no question but what the income tax could have been easily defeated" without substituting the corporation tax.[10] But he reluctantly acceded to Taft's pleas and promised to stand by the administration.

8. Beveridge to Charles F. Remy, 21 June 1909, BP. Beveridge to Albert Shaw [— May], 17 June 1909, Shaw Papers.
9. William H. Taft to Mrs. E. G. McCagg, 28 June 1909, Taft Papers.
10. Beveridge to Shaw, 17 June 1909, Shaw Papers.

At the showdown, on 2 July, he was paired in favor of the corporation tax, while Bristow, Clapp, Cummins, Dolliver, and La Follette voted no. Beveridge then joined the majority in voting down the Cummins-Bailey amendment—with only Bristow, Clapp, Cummins, La Follette, and William E. Borah of Idaho on the G.O.P. side voting yes. The constitutional amendment empowering the federal government to levy an income tax passed without a dissenting vote. Although he remained against imposing an income tax "unless it should be necessary" as an emergency measure, he voted for the constitutional amendment, he told an angry businessman, because "it is an outrage that the Government does not have the power to impose it in case of war or other like necessity."[11]

While examining the internal revenue sections of the measure, Beveridge discovered a loophole. In 1898, Congress had increased the taxes upon tobacco as a wartime emergency move. To make up for this increase, the law allowed the manufacturers to reduce the size of their packages without any reduction in price. The wartime taxes were removed in 1902; but the law expressly authorized continuance of the short-weight packages, and the manufacturers did not lower their prices. The resulting extra profit, Beveridge estimated, amounted to $184,000,000 over the eight years, with the bulk pocketed by the American Tobacco Company.

To give the government, rather than the tobacco trust, the benefit of this windfall, Beveridge offered an amendment increasing the tax upon cigarettes, cigars, snuff, and smoking tobacco. Tacked on was a provision barring the giving away of prize coupons, a device by which the American Tobacco Company had crushed its competitors. A similar provision in the Dingley Act, Beveridge informed the Senate, had been repealed at the same time Congress had removed the wartime tax. And this action had followed upon the heels of the launching of the American Tobacco Company with its millions of dollars of watered stock. "THAT VAST CAPITALIZATION," he thundered, "WAS DONE UPON THE ASSUMPTION THAT CONGRESS WOULD AFTERWARDS DO HERE EXACTLY WHAT CONGRESS DID DO HERE."[12]

The Hoosier lawmaker had such command of his facts and figures

---

11. Beveridge to Parry, 10 January 1910, BP.
12. *CR*, 61st Cong., 1st sess., 1909, 44, pt. 2: 2022–28; pt. 4: 3723–42.

that no one dared answer. Old guard Senator Elihu Root of New York even hastened over to congratulate him. Backed into a corner, Aldrich asked the Hoosier not to demand an immediate vote upon his amendment and promised that the Finance Committee would bring in its own report when the Senate reached the internal revenue sections of the bill. On 5 July, Senator Reed Smoot of Utah reported from the Finance Committee an amendment increasing the taxes on tobacco products. Included was a provision outlawing the giving away of prize coupons. A friendly newspaper correspondent called the Finance Committee action the "greatest concession yet granted to any senator" by the party leaders in the tariff fight.[13]

The House bill included a provision authorizing the president to impose across-the-board increases of 20 or in some instances 25 percent of the existing rates against countries that discriminated against the United States. The Senate Finance Committee increased the difference between the maximum and the minimum to 25 percent ad valorem—25 percent not of the minimum rates but of the value of the goods. Although welcoming the provision as an improvement over the Dingley law, Beveridge complained that the authority given the president was too narrowly limited. The chief executive had to impose the maximum or the minimum rates on "absolutely everything" and thus lacked the flexibility to make trades "on each and every article."[14]

Worse, the House bill contained no provision for Beveridge's pet reform—a permanent, nonpartisan, expert tariff commission. Beveridge reintroduced his tariff commission bill in the Senate and lined up the insurgents in its support. The National Association of Manufacturers redoubled its lobbying activities, even hiring Cannon's former right-hand man and Beveridge's long-time personal and political rival, former Congressman James E. Watson, to pull strings on Capital Hill.[15] Making a show of reasonableness, Aldrich assured the Indiana lawmaker that the Finance Committee would bring in an

---

13. *Indianapolis Star*, 6 July 1909.

14. Beveridge to Edward A. Rumely, 25 March 1910; to S. S. Strattan, Jr., 22 March 1910, BP.

15. When a congressional investigating committee in 1913 exposed Watson's lobbying for the tariff commission, Beveridge was badly embarrassed and denied any knowledge of his activities: Beveridge to John C. O'Laughlin, 30 August 1913, BP.

amendment that would satisfy the tariff commission backers. What he had in mind was the establishment of a bureau within the Department of Commerce. Beveridge rejected Aldrich's draft as "not as broad as I thought it should be."[16] He and the N.A.M. leaders insisted upon the addition of outside experts—preferably men of wide business experience—to give the report of the commission more weight with Congress.

When Aldrich gave way on this question, Beveridge drafted the following amendment to section 2—the maximum and minimum provision—of the tariff bill:

> To secure information to assist the President in the the discharge of the duties imposed upon him by this section, and information to aid Congress in tariff legislation and the officers of the Government in the administration of the customs laws, the President is hereby authorized to appoint such persons as may be required to make thorough investigations and examinations into the production, commerce and trade of the United States and foreign countries, and all conditions affecting the same. Said persons shall have the power to take testimony, administer oaths and compel the production of books and papers.[17]

Aldrich rejected this provision as too sweeping. He insisted upon substituting "employ" for "appoint." Beveridge balked. "Appointees" would have a fixed term of office; mere "employees" would be subject to dismissal at the will of the president. An even greater stumbling block was the Rhode Island senator's adamant refusal to accept the provision giving the commission authority to require sworn testimony and the production of records.

At this juncture, however, James W. Van Cleave, president of the National Association of Manufacturers, hastened to Washington to break the stalemate. He conferred with the chief executive, who assured him that the phraseology demanded by Aldrich gave him all the authority he required and promised to use that authority to the limit in establishing a tariff commission in fact as well as in name. Thinking "that one bird in the hand is better than ten in the bush," Van Cleave approved the watered-down draft.[18]

---

16. *CR*, 61st Cong., 1st sess., 1909, 44, pt. 5: 4861.
17. *SEP*, 24 September 1909, p. 9.
18. James W. Van Cleave to H. E. Miles, 3 May 1909, in *Maintenance of a Lobby: Appendix*, 3: 2846–49.

Beveridge thought that the N.A.M. chief had conceded too much, too soon. He was most unhappy about the failure to give the commission authority to examine witnesses under oath and require the production of books and papers. Even the N.A.M.'s top Washington lobbyist agreed that if Van Cleave had stood firm, a much better measure could have been achieved. But with his business support neutralized, the Hoosier had to go along. On 30 April, Aldrich presented his tariff commission amendment to the maximum-minimum section of the bill and took pains in the debate that followed to neutralize the insurgents by telling the Senate that Beveridge had given his approval.

To the last, Aldrich hoped to detach Beveridge from the insurgent bloc. But his concessions were too few and too late for the Hoosier. The bill before the Senate was not the honest revision that had been promised. And the reports from Indiana told of the popularity of Beveridge's stand with the voters from his state. On 11 June, he assured La Follette that he was "in the movement to stay." "If as many as ten senators from great, populous, strongly Republican sections vote against the bill on its passage in the Senate," he explained to *Review of Reviews* editor Albert Shaw, "I think there is no question but what the bill in conference will be shaved down to a point where we will have such a bill . . . that we can all go to the country upon as a redemption of our promises."[19]

When the bill came up for final vote on 8 July, the ten insurgents—Beveridge joined by Bristow, Brown, Burkett, Clapp, Crawford, Cummins, Dolliver, La Follette, and Nelson—voted no. Before the vote, the Indiana lawmaker rose to explain "the views of some of us." The gravest threat to protection, he reminded his fellow Republicans, was the "subtle but deadly peril of excess." The insurgents had fought to avert that danger and redeem the party's "sacred" pledge to the nation. "I want to preserve that historic American system so dear to our hearts; and we know that history tells us that the only danger to such a system is that it shall be made unjust. We know that history declares that the way to preserve a policy is to keep it just, and the way to preserve a party is to keep its faith."[20]

---

19. Belle C. and Fola La Follette, *Robert M. La Follette* (2 vols., New York, 1953), 1: 276. Beveridge to Shaw, 17 June 1909, Shaw Papers.

20. *CR*, 61st Cong., 1st sess., 1909, 44, pt. 4: 4314.

The last hope of honest revision was in the conference committee—
and the pivotal man was William Howard Taft. The insurgents, however, had become more and more disillusioned with the president.
His intervention in the income tax squabble resulted in a Pyrrhic
victory. Most disappointing was his failure to take a strong hand in
the fight for lower rates on the floor of the Senate. Beveridge retained
his faith in the chief executive longer than many of his fellow insurgents. But the president's continued inaction disillusioned even the
Hoosier. Taft was impossible, he wrote his wife at the end of June.
"When both Aldrich and I think so, it is so. The Administration is
doomed."[21]

Part of the difficulty with Taft was what his military aide called
his "phlegmatic temperament," his scruples about executive interference with the legislature, and his political ineptness. More important, the chief executive never thought the Finance Committee bill as
bad as the insurgents did. Much of the outcry against the measure,
he believed, came from the newspapers, aggrieved by the higher
Senate duties on newsprint and engaging in "the grossest misrepre-
sentation" to discredit the bill. And he hoped to work with party
leaders in the conference to gain free iron ore, hides, coal, and oil,
lower the duty on newsprint to three dollars, and reduce the tariff on
lumber "as low as we can make it." If successful, he told Beveridge, he
was "very hopeful" that "even those who voted against it in the
Senate, with one or two exceptions, will deem it their duty to vote for
the bill when it comes out of conference."[22]

But when the conferees met, Taft had to trim his demands to avert
a party revolt. In the give and take that followed, the duty on iron ore
was reduced from 25 to 15 cents a ton, on coal from 60 to 45 cents a
ton, on lumber from $2 to $1.25 per thousand feet, on newsprint from
$4 to $3.75 a ton; reductions were made in the duties on shoes and
boots; and petroleum was placed on the free list. Although the woolen
schedule could not be touched (so powerful was "the union of the
wool growers and the woolen manufacturers"[23]), Taft forced adoption
of free hides. He succeeded in knocking out the increased duty on

---

21. Beveridge to Mrs. Beveridge, 30 June 1909, in Bowers, *Beveridge and the Progressive Era*, p. 349.
22. Taft to Ernest M. Pollard, 13 July 1909, Taft Papers. Taft to Beveridge, 13 July 1909, BP.
23. Taft to Elbert F. Baldwin, 18 July 1909, Taft Papers.

gloves. And while Aldrich would permit no tampering with the increases over the Dingley rates upon the higher-priced cottons made
by New England mills, he allowed reductions on the cheaper grades
of cotton goods.

Although the insurgents had warned that lowering the duties upon
raw materials without reducing the tariff upon finished products
would benefit the eastern manufacturers rather than the consumer,
Taft remained optimistic about winning over a majority of the bolters.
La Follette was written off as a lost cause. So was Bristow. But the
chief executive still hoped that the two Iowa senators would vote for
the bill and was most optimistic about Beveridge's falling into line.
"I think," Taft wrote his wife, "the press on the whole will regard the
bill as improved by reason of my recommendations, advice, and influence, and I sincerely hope that it will break the bad effect on the
country which a misunderstanding of the Aldrich bill had had."[24]

Beveridge was in a quandary. He did not wish to break with the
president, but the bill reported from the conference was not the
honest revision he had fought for. The woolen schedule was "a perfect
outrage"; the reductions upon shoes and boots were "a fraud and a
pretence"; the cotton schedule was increased "all along the line," with
the highest increases upon those articles "most worn by the people";
the increased duties on silk, zinc, and linoleum added to the burdens
of the average consumer; the sugar tariff remained "a stench in everybody's nostrils"; there was "a tremendous increase" in the duty on
structural steel used for buildings and bridges; iron ore, lumber, wood
pulp, and paper should have been on the free list to save the country's
dwindling natural resources; and the conferees had reduced the new
taxes upon tobacco while striking out his anticoupon provision. "I've
made up my mind," Beveridge confided to his wife on 30 July, "to do
the right thing and leave the results to the people. If they don't see
it, they are not worth my slaving my life out for them in politics."[25]

On the following day, Beveridge joined Bristow, Clapp, Cummins,
Dolliver, La Follette, and Nelson in publicly announcing their decision to vote against the conference report. Shocked by the news, Taft

---

24. Taft to Mrs. Taft, 30 July 1909, ibid.
25. Beveridge to Shaw, 3 [—] August 1909, Shaw Papers. Beveridge to
Walter Bradfute, 18 February 1910; to Bennett Gordon, 12 March 1910, BP.
Beveridge to Lucius B. Swift, 17 March 1910, Swift Papers. Beveridge to Mrs.
Beveridge, 30 July 1909, in Bowers, *Beveridge and the Progressive Era,* p. 363.

had the postmaster general, Frank H. Hitchcock, make a personal—
and *"passionate"*—appeal to the Hoosier to return to the fold. Wavering, Beveridge attempted to induce his fellow insurgents to vote for
the conference report. Dolliver was the swing man. If the Iowan had
decided to vote for the bill, Beveridge probably would have followed
him. But Dolliver refused to do so.[26] Beveridge had to fish or cut bait.
And how could he without loss of face vote for the bill after his attacks
upon its shortcomings?

Perhaps decisive for Beveridge was what the conference had done
with the tariff commission provision. The House Republican conferees—backed by the Speaker—balked at accepting even a modified
tariff commission, while the Senate representatives headed by Aldrich
were no more than half-hearted in their support. Alarmed by reports
that the conferees planned to scuttle or emasculate the Senate-
approved provision, Beveridge appealed to the president to intervene.
But though Taft reaffirmed his support for a tariff commission, he was
surprisingly unconcerned about the details. The conference proceeded
to strike out, not only the words "information which will be useful to
Congress in tariff legislation," but the clause "to make thorough
investigations and examinations into the production, commerce, and
trade of the United States and foreign countries, and all conditions
affecting the same."[27]

Beveridge protested that what remained limited the function of
the so-called tariff board to ascertaining whether or not foreign countries were discriminating against the United States. Aldrich reassured
him that the provision "allows the President to employ whoever he
pleases without limit and to assign such duties to them as he sees fit,"
including investigation of the cost of production at home and abroad.
Taft, he told the upper chamber, agreed that the conference report
gave him sufficient authority. If so, Beveridge replied, "all that might
have been done under a tariff-commission bill can and will be done
under this provision." But if not—and he had his doubts—he would
renew the fight for his tariff commission bill at the next session of
Congress.[28]

His doubts were reinforced when Aldrich's top lieutenant, Eugene

---

26. Beveridge to Shaw, 3 August 1909, Shaw Papers.
27. *CR* (House), 61st Cong., 1st sess., 1909, 44, pt. 5: 4649.
28. *CR*, pt. 5: 4839, 4861–62.

Hale of Maine, powerful chairman of the Senate Appropriations Committee and one of the Senate conferees on the tariff bill, told the upper chamber that action of the conference in striking out the words "and information which shall be useful to Congress in tariff legislation" was "not done unadvisedly." The conference report, he explained, limited the tariff board "to an inquiry as to the discrimination that is made by other countries against the United States" and nothing more. "Language can not give a more restricted scope to the authority on the part of the President under this provision." The more Beveridge studied the wording the more convinced he became that the Maine lawmaker was "correct."[29]

To vote against the bill would be dangerous for Beveridge. His factional rivals would seize upon his insurgency to brand him a traitor to the G.O.P. And how would the White House react? But the pluses outweighed the minuses. The "people who wanted to knock would knock anyway," his most trusted political lieutenant reported from Indiana. The state "was overwhelmingly revision downward" and to backtrack would damage his standing with the people.[30] At the showdown on 5 August, the conference report was approved by a vote of forty-seven to thirty-one—but with Beveridge voting no. He left immediately for Dublin, New Hampshire, to rest. "Two nights sleep cleared my head & steadied my nerve," he wrote Shaw. "Glad I voted right—it was good conscience & good politics."[31]

The public response was heartening. Cummins reported that he found on his return to Iowa "a deep and pervading belief that we have stood for the right things." "Don't you worry," Dolliver assured Beveridge, "about what is going on in the Country. If we had had a direct line from the skies we could not have 'done a better job' for ourselves than when we stood for our own convictions against all comers including the big chief." The bulk of Indiana's Republican newspapers endorsed Beveridge's stand. Even the *Indianapolis News* hailed the insurgents for having "fought the people's battle right down to the finish." He found, Beveridge wrote Knute Nelson, that most of the businessmen he met while at Dublin were "for us, and this with all their might."[32]

29. Ibid., pp. 4866–70.
30. Leopold G. Rothschild to Beveridge, 3 August 1909, BP.
31. Beveridge to Shaw [8 August 1909], Shaw Papers.
32. Albert B. Cummins to Beveridge, 17 August 1909; Jonathan P. Dolliver to Beveridge, 14 September 1909; Beveridge to Knute Nelson, 6 September 1909, BP. *Indianapolis News,* 6 August 1909.

Beveridge hoped that his vote against the bill would involve no break with the President. Taft, he reported optimistically to Shaw, "is not, I think, going to make it a personal issue."[33] Even La Follette refrained from attacking Taft personally. The chief executive, however, had grown more and more disgusted with the insurgents, with what he regarded as their self-righteousness, egotism, and pettiness. Beveridge was the most irritating. "He tires me awfully," Taft confessed to his wife. "He attitudinizes so much, and is so self-centered and so self-absorbed."[34]

When signing the bill on 5 August, Taft tried to walk the tight rope of praising the measure without attacking the insurgents. Although not "a perfect bill or a complete compliance with the promises made," the measure, he declared, did represent "a sincere effort on the part of the Republican party to make a downward revision." Beveridge was quick to react. The president's statement, he exclaimed to Albert Shaw, "is an endorsement of us—or else a frightful blunder. Im [sic] thinking he'll need me more than I need him before we are through with it."[35]

So unstable a balance could not last, and the differences between Taft and the insurgents were spotlighted when the president undertook in mid-September a cross-country speaking tour. He started out at Boston with lavish praise for Aldrich—which raised insurgent tempers. The climax came on 17 September at Winona, Minnesota, the home of Representative James A. Tawney, the only one of the state's representatives to have voted for the tariff bill. He praised the Payne-Aldrich act as "the best tariff bill that the Republican party has ever passed, and therefore the best tariff bill that has been passed at all." He disclaimed any wish to criticize those who had voted against the bill. But as for himself—and in defense of the embattled Tawney—he believed that party solidarity was "much more important than the reduction of rates in one or two schedules of the tariff."[36]

The insurgents had been looking upon the chief executive with growing suspicion. But the Winona speech made the split irreparable. The chief executive "has made an issue in this state which we could

33. Beveridge to Shaw, 3 August 1909, Shaw Papers.
34. Taft to Mrs. Taft, 14 July 1909, Taft Papers.
35. Henry F. Pringle, *The Life and Times of William Howard Taft: A Biography* (2 vols., New York and Toronto, 1939), 1: 445. Beveridge to Shaw [8 August 1909], Shaw Papers.
36. Taft, *Presidential Addresses and State Papers*, pp. 209–30.

not ignore if we wanted to," said Cummins. ". . . We shall find out at the next State Convention whether the Republicans of Iowa support Dolliver and myself, or Aldrich and his crowd." "Poor Taft," Dolliver complained, "made a sad mess of it at Winona. I knew he was good natured but I never dreamed he was so dull. . . . It is like taking candy from children for Aldrich to confer with Taft." "It is hard to keep still on Taft," La Follette confided to his wife, "and I think . . . we have got to come out ultimately against him." The president, thundered Joseph Bristow, "seems to have surrendered absolutely to Aldrich. There is but one course for me to take, and that is to fight."[37]

The Winona speech crystallized the latent division within the G.OP. Indiana Republicans had to take sides. The *Noblesville Ledger* assailed the speech as "the unkindest cut of all." The *Fort Wayne Sentinel* praised the insurgents "for the manliness and courage of their conduct." The *Gary Times* declared that Beveridge had represented the majority of Indiana Republicans in his vote against the tariff. The *Richmond Palladium* denounced the chief executive for confusing "Republicanism" with "Aldrichism." The *Indianapolis News* warned that the president's attack upon the insurgents was straining the loyalty of "the people of the west."

But the president's remarks spurred a conservative reaction. The *Peru Journal* hailed "the wisdom and true party fealty" of the president and castigated Beveridge for joining with the Democrats in voting against a Republican tariff bill. The *Marion Chronicle* seconded the chief executive's praise of the Payne-Aldrich bill as the best tariff law ever enacted. The *Lafayette Journal* editorialized that the president's "sound sense should appeal to the whole nation" and declared that "those chautauqua statesmen fighting for advertising will confer a benefit on the country by stopping the agitation." And Beveridge's factional rivals within the party saw in the breach between him and the administration renewed hopes for their own political comeback.[38]

The widening party split alarmed Beveridge. Indiana was a close state, and Republican factionalism could tip the state to the Democrats. The chief executive had "made a serious mistake." Beveridge regretted that Taft had made such an "unfortunate impression in this

---

37. Cummins to Beveridge, 1 October 1909, BP. La Follette, *Robert M. La Follette*, 1: 282–83. Bristow to Beveridge, 20 September 1909, Bristow Papers.
38. *Indianapolis News*, 18 September 1909. *Indianapolis Star*, 24 September 1909.

State"—unfortunate, he hastened to add, "so far as he himself is concerned." The administration had started off on the wrong foot. Taft was in deep trouble, he told Albert Shaw, and the "next session will show where he will land."[39]

---

39. Beveridge to Bristow, 4 October 1909, BP. Beveridge to Shaw [20], 29 September 1909, Shaw Papers.

13

Insurgency

Despite the Winona speech, Beveridge returned to Washington in December 1909 hopeful that he could work in harmony with the chief executive. He had no quarrel with the legislative program laid down by the president in his cross-country tour: establishment of a postal-savings bank system; legislation to require prior notice before issuance of injunctions in labor disputes except "in rare and meritorious cases"; limitation of the Sherman law to only those combinations "entered into with actual intent to monopolize or suppress competition"; strengthening the rate-fixing authority of the Interstate Commerce Commission; and investigation by the new tariff board into "the cost of production abroad and here" to "accumulate data upon which a new and proper revision of the tariff might be had."[1]

But the tariff fight had poisoned the political atmosphere. After the Winona speech, the insurgents looked upon Taft with distrust and hostility. Their attacks upon the tariff aroused Taft's suspicions that their aim was to wreck his administration and defeat him in 1912. Exasperated by their "hysteria"

---

1. Taft, *Presidential Addresses and State Papers,* pp. 192, 201–8, 228–30, 233–42.

and "hypocrisy,"[2] the president drew closer to the old guard leaders in Congress. He privately encouraged an old guard counterattack in the insurgents' home states. Although denying any wish to punish the insurgents for voting against the Payne-Aldrich bill, he threatened to cut off the patronage of any lawmakers who continued to oppose administration measures. The resulting squabbles over patronage exacerbated the conflict within the G.O.P.

Beveridge was caught in the cross fire. The popular applause that greeted his vote against the Payne-Aldrich tariff showed that insurgency was popular.[3] Yet facing a tough fight for reelection in Indiana, he did wish to alienate G.O.P. regulars by warring with the president. His fellow insurgents came from one-party states. If they retained their grip upon the local party machinery, they were unbeatable. But even a small Republican defection could throw the Hoosier state to the Democrats. Though writing off Bristow, Cummins, La Follette, and even Clapp as irreconcilable, Taft retained hopes for Beveridge. "I believe," the chief executive noted, "Beveridge is anxious to help, . . . but he is so uncertain as to what he ought to do . . . with respect to its influence on the home election, that he is not very dependable."[4]

The first test came over statehood for Arizona and New Mexico. During the last years of the Roosevelt administration, Beveridge had stood as a rock against their admission as two states. Roosevelt, never as emotionally committed as the Indiana lawmaker to joint statehood, accepted Arizona's vote as final and came around to support of their prompt admission to boost G.O.P. popularity in the Southwest. At the 1908 Republican national convention, the delegates from the territories traded their votes on the injunction plank in return for adoption of a favorable statehood plank. In February 1909, the House of Representatives approved statehood by a voice vote. But the Hoosier took advantage of the extensive land frauds found in New Mexico to bury the measure in the Senate Committee on Territories.

Beveridge pleaded with the new chief executive not to push the statehood question. Arizona, he warned, was hopelessly Democratic,

---

2. William H. Taft to Guy W. Mallon, 13 January 1910; to Guild A. Copeland, 9 February 1910, Taft Papers.

3. See, for example, Beveridge to Henry Beach Needham, 2 October 1909, BP.

4. Taft to Lucius B. Swift, 19 February 1910, Swift Papers.

while New Mexico was doubtful. Four more Democratic senators could give the Democrats control of the upper chamber. Even if the new states returned Republicans, whoever was elected would represent the railroads and mining companies that dominated the territories and thus would be unlikely to sympathize with his legislative program. But Taft was adamant about fulfilling the statehood pledge in the G.O.P. platform. The House of Representatives swung into line and, on 17 January, passed a bill admitting the territories. Rather than buck the president, Beveridge went along. "I have given my word on this matter," he confided unhappily to John C. Shaffer, "and while I do not approve of the admission of these states at all, nevertheless my word once given is sacred."[5]

He would not, however, accept the bill passed by the House. That measure, he complained, was "unspeakably bad" in "certain particulars."[6] He added detailed safeguards to protect from land thieves the public lands given the new states for schools. And while working with Department of Interior experts on these safeguards, he came across a gigantic giveaway in the provision granting each of the new states three million acres of public lands for the payment of their existing county and territorial indebtedness. No other state had received such federal largess upon its admission. The most Beveridge would allow was the grant of one million acres apiece for the payment of country bonds issued to assist railroads—bonds that the courts had ruled illegal but which the railroad promoters had induced Congress to validate.

The House bill had provided that voting qualifications for the election of delegates to the constitutional conventions and ratification of the constitutions should be those prescribed by existing law for the election of the territorial legislature. But Arizona G.O.P. leaders protested to Washington that the Arizona legislature had passed, over the veto of the governor, an educational qualification framed to disenfranchise Spanish-speaking Republican voters. To remedy this "outrage done to the people of Arizona,"[7] Beveridge amended the bill to require that not only the election of delegates to the constitutional convention and the vote on ratification, but the election of new state officers, should be held under the former electoral law.

---

5. Beveridge to John C. Shaffer, 10 March 1910, BP.
6. Beveridge to Shaffer, 25 January 1910, BP.
7. Beveridge to Richard E. Sloan, 17 February 1910, BP.

At the same time, he strove to limit as much as possible the influence of New Mexico's large Spanish-speaking population. Although stipulating that the public schools "shall always be conducted in English," the House bill had provided that "nothing in this act shall preclude the teaching of other languages in said public schools." Beveridge had this provision struck out. And whereas the House bill had required all state officers to know English sufficiently well to perform their duties without the aid of an interpreter, the Senate committee extended this requirement to include members of the legislature. The purpose of these amendments, Beveridge frankly told the upper chamber, was to hasten the breakdown of "the curious continuance of the solidarity of the Spanish-speaking people" in New Mexico "which has been for a long time a serious problem before Congress and before the better people down there."[8]

The most controversial amendment involved the procedure for the admission of the new states. The House bill had included the standard provision for admission by proclamation of the chief executive upon popular ratification of their constitutions. But the Senate committee required submission of the ratified constitutions to the president and Congress for their approval. As a nationalist, Beveridge believed that the nation as a whole was as concerned as were the people of the territories that their constitutions be wisely drawn. And worried that the new states would vote Democratic, he wished to postpone their admission until after the 1910 elections. Thus amended, the bill was reported to the Senate on 14 March 1910. There remained much lingering opposition. The insurgents were lukewarm because they feared that the new states would send four more railroad senators to Washington, while the old guard was alarmed lest more western representatives, and probably Democrats at that, would weaken their shaky grip upon the upper chamber. But the Indiana lawmaker—faithful to his word—continued to push for action. The president threw his influence behind the measure. And the exigencies of politics played into the hands of the statehood backers. In a deal to line up Democratic votes in his battle with the insurgents over the pending railroad legislation, Senate leader Nelson W. Aldrich promised a vote on the statehood bill before the end of the session.[9]

8. *CR*, 61st Cong., 2nd sess., 1910, 45, pt. 8: 8227.
9. George E. Mowry, *Theodore Roosevelt and the Progressive Movement* (Madison, Wisc., 1946), pp. 101–2.

When the measure came before the Senate for debate on 16 June, the Democrats assailed the Senate committee amendments. Congress, Democratic lawmakers charged, had no right to prescribe qualifications for the election of state officers after adoption of the constitution. An even graver invasion of state's rights was the provision requiring submission of the new states' constitutions to Congress and the president for their approval. So long as the constitutions were, on their face, republican in form and not in conflict with the Constitution of the United States, the people of the new state—not Congress, nor the chief executive—were the judges of what constitution they should have. But with the adjournment of Congress rapidly approaching, the Democrats gave way rather than block passage of the bill. The motion to substitute the bill reported by the Senate committee for the House measure was carried by a vote of forty-two to nineteen. The vote on final passage was unanimous.

All that remained was House concurrence. Beveridge declared bluntly that he would not yield on his version of the bill and warned that the House must accept the Senate measure or delay the admission of the territories until the next session of Congress. Statehood boomers grew alarmed that a plot was afoot to defeat the legislation by a disagreement between the two houses. But Taft intervened and urged House leaders to accept the Senate bill. Unhappy with the Oklahoma constitution with its provisions for initiative and referendum, and alarmed at what he regarded as a rising tide of radicalism in the West, the chief executive welcomed the veto given him over the constitutions of the new states.[10] The House Republican leaders fell into line. So did the Democrats rather than see a deadlock. On 18 June, the House by a unanimous voice vote agreed to the Senate substitute. Two days later, Taft—with Beveridge present as his guest—signed the bill into law.

With the approval of the enabling act, the next step was the adoption of constitutions for the new states. The New Mexican constitution was a highly conservative document: the referendum provision was riddled with exemptions and limitations; there were no provisions for the initiative and recall; amendment of the constitution was made exceedingly difficult; and the corporation commission was left

<hr>

10. Taft to Joseph G. Cannon, 17 June 1909, Taft Papers. For Taft's unhappiness over the Oklahoma constitution, see Taft to Nelson W. Aldrich, 31 January 1909, Aldrich Papers (LC).

toothless. In contrast, Arizona—which Beveridge had feared under the thumb of corporate influences—had adopted a constitution providing for the initiative, referendum, and recall of all elective officers including judges. Taft, on 24 February 1911, formally approved the New Mexico constitution. The House gave its approval, but Beveridge prevented a report from the Senate Committee on Territories until midnight, 3 March. Even then, he yielded only to heavy administration pressure. And at that late hour, Democratic senator Robert Owen of Oklahoma was able to block favorable action by tying New Mexico's admission to approval of the controversial Arizona constitution. Thus, Beveridge ended his term in the Senate with the territories still territories.[11]

At the same time, Beveridge worked in harmony with the president in sponsoring the administration's Alaskan government bill. Alaskan resentment at the Roosevelt administration's conservation policies had spurred a growing demand for more home rule to facilitate the rapid exploitation of the territory's natural resources. For that reason, conservationists opposed an elective legislature for Alaska. Despite his bad press in the Ballinger-Pinchot controversy, Taft took the conservationist side. Mindful of his experiences in the Philippines, the chief executive favored placing the legislative authority in a commission appointed by the president. "Local self-government or home rule," he explained, would be unwise "in a country so large as Alaska, with a scattered nomadic population, intense local and sectional feeling," and inadequate communications.[12]

Beveridge gladly agreed to sponsor the administration's bill. Convinced that a popularly elected legislature for Alaska would be at the mercy of predatory interests seeking to exploit the territory's resources, he saw the bill as a way to strike a blow for conservation while cooperating with the White House on a measure "which is very dear to the President's heart." On 24 January, he reported the bill from the Committee on Territories and had the measure treated as unfinished business before the upper chamber. "While the bill will arouse

---

11. For the final action after Beveridge left the Senate, see Robert W. Larson, *New Mexico's Quest for Statehood, 1846–1912* (Albuquerque, N.M., 1968), pp. 292–301.

12. Taft, *Presidential Addresses and State Papers,* pp. 282–85.

considerable debate," he predicted, "it will not be one of the things which [will] involve any of the vicious fighting of the session."[13]

But the link-up of the question with the conservation issue sparked an attack on the measure by a bloc of western senators led by Idaho's William E. Borah. Borah denounced the Alaska government bill as another eastern-inspired scheme to block the rapid development of the west—an un-American attempt to deny self-government to the forty thousand American citizens living in Alaska. Southern Democrats, vigilant of state's rights, joined in assailing the legislation as a denial of the fundamental rights of American citizens. Alaska's delegates to Congress, James Wickersham, a vocal champion of home rule, capitalized on the suspicions roused by the Ballinger-Pinchot controversy to make sensational charges that the sponsors of the appointive commission plan were in league with the Guggenheims to exploit Alaska's coal lands.

Rising to the bill's defense, Beveridge declared that the president was "absolutely right about this bill"; pointed out that Taft's experience in the Philippines had made him the nation's foremost expert on the administration of noncontiguous territories; and reaffirmed his own support for the measure.[14] Taft was furious at the bill's opponents. The charges of Guggenheim influence, he complained to Borah, were manufactured "out of the air."[15] But rather than jeopardize the rest of his legislative program by a long and perhaps losing fight, he instructed Beveridge to allow the Alaskan government bill to be laid aside in favor of the postal-savings bank bill. Although disappointed at the chief executive's decision to abandon the measure at the first sign of the fight, the Hoosier acceded to his wishes.[16]

Yet despite Beveridge's wish to maintain harmony with the president, the rift between the two men widened as the session proceeded. When Taft dismissed Gifford Pinchot in January 1910, Beveridge instinctively sided with the chief forester. He had become friends with Pinchot during his first term in the Senate while chairman of the Committee on Forest Reservations and the Protection of Game, their relationship growing so close that Pinchot served as godfather

13. Beveridge to A. C. Bartlett, 7 January 1910, BP.
14. Beveridge to Shaffer, 25 January 1910, BP.
15. Taft to William E. Borah, 26 January 1910, Taft Papers.
16. Beveridge to Clarence F. Bicknell, 14 April 1910, BP.

for his daughter Abby, born in April 1910. In the years that followed, Beveridge became a champion of Pinchot's conservation policies in the upper chamber. As a Hamiltonian, he sympathized with the forester's dream of planned resource development to replace the wasteful methods of the past. And in his maturing progressivism, he shared Pinchot's alarm over the danger of a monopolization of the nation's natural resources by a selfish few.[17]

The next clash came over postal-savings bank legislation. The bill reported by Senator Thomas H. Carter of Montana from the Committee on Post-Offices and Post-Roads provided that the postal-savings bank funds should be deposited "as nearly as practicable" in local banks for local use. But protests from western bankers and businessmen against any legislation that would permit withdrawal of those funds from the local communities to New York or Chicago led Carter to accept—and the Senate to approve—an amendment sponsored by Albert B. Cummins of Iowa requiring the deposit of postal-savings bank funds in banks "doing business in the city, town, or village in which such post-office is situated." With this stumbling block removed, swift passage of the bill was anticipated.[18]

Then came a bombshell from the president. In his Lincoln Day speech before the New York City Republican club, Taft denounced the move to limit deposit of postal-savings bank funds and demanded authority to invest the money in government bonds. What if the local banks, whose doubtful soundness had spurred the demand for postal-savings banks, failed? The result would be "a financial disaster greater than any panic we have heretofore met." In line with the chief executive's wishes, Senator Reed Smoot of Utah presented an amendment permitting withdrawal of the funds from local banks and their investment in government bonds "when, in the judgment of the President, a war or any other exigency involving the credit of the Government so requires."[19]

Insurgent suspicions were aroused that the amendment was framed to smooth the path for Senator Nelson W. Aldrich's central bank scheme. A major stumbling block to Aldrich's plan was the more than

17. Beveridge to Albert Shaw, 15 November 1909, Shaw Papers.
18. CR, 61st Cong., 2nd sess., 1910, 45, pt. 2: 1283, 1326–27, 1430–33.
19. Taft, Presidential Addresses and State Papers, pp. 575–76. CR, 61st Cong., 2nd sess., 1910, 45, pt. 3: 2621.

seven hundred million dollars worth of 2 percent government bonds held by the national banks as backing for their national banknotes. These bonds could only be sold at a discount because later issues carried higher interest rates. But under this amendment Taft could use the postal savings bank funds to buy up these bonds. To tie the chief executive's hands, Cummins moved his own amendment to limit the president's authority to withdraw the postal-savings bank funds exclusively to time of war.

Beveridge personally favored the Rhode Island lawmaker's central banking plans. But the Smoot amendment occasioned a flood of protests from Indiana bankers and businessmen, including "the most conservative merchants of our state," against any removal of the postal-savings banks funds from the local banks and communities. "I have seldom seen them so worked up," Beveridge confessed, "as they were at the administration's proposition that the money collected by these savings banks should be used to relieve national banks of the two per cent. [bonds] which they hold." So, to the chief executive's disgust, Beveridge voted for the Iowa lawmaker's amendment.[20]

Although the amendment was defeated by a vote of forty to eighteen, the Republican defections alarmed the bill's floor manager. To bring the insurgents back into the fold, Carter "dictated and procured the introduction" of an amendment by William E. Borah prohibiting the investment of the funds in bonds bearing lower than 2¼ percent interest. Since the Borah amendment would frustrate the Aldrich central bank plot, the insurgents took the bait. All voted for the Borah amendment; all but La Follette voted for the Smoot amendment as amended by the Borah amendment; and all voted for the bill on its final passage through the Senate. "We succeeded," Beveridge reported to a small-town Indiana newspaper publisher, "in amending it so as to make it reasonably acceptable to the local merchants in all the towns and cities of the country. Having so amended it, every insurgent supported it."[21]

In the House, however, the administration forces succeeded in knocking out the Borah amendment and giving the president a free hand to invest the postal-savings banks funds in government bonds

---

20. Beveridge to Gifford Pinchot, 23 March 1910, BP.
21. Thomas H. Carter to Dr. O. M. Lanstrum, 9 March 1910, Carter Papers (LC). Beveridge to Rudolph G. Leeds, 10 March 1910, BP.

without any limitation upon the interest rate. When the measure was returned to the Senate, Taft actively pushed for acceptance of the House measure. Bristow, Cummins, and La Follette stood firm, but the chief executive called in what Bristow termed the "near-insurgents" and "made a personal matter of it." Beveridge was the swing man, and, nervous about the possible impact of his differences with the president upon his reelection, he went along with the chief executive. When the Hoosier gave way, all the waverers "tumbled over to his side."[22]

Taft's success with the postal-savings bank bill was another Pyrrhic victory. And the breach in the party was further widened by the administration's railroad bill. The insurgents distrusted Attorney General George W. Wickersham, the chief architect of the measure, as a corporation lawyer. Their apprehensions were heightened by newspaper reports telling of consultations between administration officials and railroad executives in drafting the bill. When the measure was reported from the Committee on Interstate Commerce early in March, Cummins and Minnesota's Moses Clapp issued a minority report denouncing the bill as "not an advance in the regulation of interstate commerce, but a long step backward." La Follette also assailed the measure as "the rankest, boldest betrayal of the public interest ever proposed in any legislative body."[23]

The lines were forming for another clash between the insurgents and the administration, and again Beveridge would have to take his stand. "The legislative developments down here," he wrote, "are not at all good." He had been ill with the grippe and then busy with the statehood fight, and so, he confessed, knew "little about the bill." But he did know that "a fierce and determined fight will be made" against the measure, and from what he could learn, "even from the most extreme reactionaries, there are provisions of it which are very bad indeed." His mind was still open, but he would, he pledged, "both fight and vote for what is the right thing."[24]

22. Joseph L. Bristow to William Allen White, 23 June 1910, White Papers (LC).

23. *CR*, 61st Cong., 2nd sess., 1910, 45, pt. 3: 2821–23. Robert M. La Follette, *La Follette's Autobiography* (paperback ed., Madison, Wisc., 1963), p. 180.

24. Beveridge to Leeds, 10 March 1910, BP. Beveridge to Shaw, 9 March 1910, Shaw Papers.

Cummins began the attack in mid-March with a four-day-long speech. He directed his heaviest fire against the six sections establishing a special "court of commerce" to hear all appeals from rulings of the Interstate Commerce Commission. The Iowa senator argued that there were not sufficient cases to justify a specialized tribunal, that such a court would be subject to tremendous pressure from the railroads, and that loose wording opened the door for "broad" review of commission decisions. Distrustful of the administration, he blasted the provision giving the Department of Justice exclusive responsibility for defending I.C.C. rulings in the courts and excluding the Commission or interested private parties from participating in the proceedings.

The Iowa lawmaker went on to assail section 7 suspending the antitrust laws and legalizing railroad agreements on rates and classifications because the bill did not require prior approval by the I.C.C. before the agreement went into effect. While praising section 10 for allowing the I.C.C. to investigate on its own initiative the reasonableness of a new rate rather than waiting for a complaint by a shipper, Cummins wished to authorize the commission to suspend any increase indefinitely, instead of for a mere sixty days, until its investigation was completed. He protested that sections 13, 14, and 15 legalized all existing capitalization, fictitious or not, under the cloak of preventing future issuance of watered stock. And he demanded action to bar the long- and short-haul discrimination from which many western communities suffered.

The Iowan's speech convinced Beveridge that the administration bill was "rotten."[25] Even many standpatters were so disturbed that Attorney General Wickersham hastened to amend the measure on "three or four points." He agreed to restore the requirement in the Hepburn bill for at least five days notice before issuance of an injunction against a commission ruling, to permit appeals to the Supreme Court from temporary injunctions granted by the commerce court, and to authorize the commerce court "in its discretion" to allow the participation of affected private parties. Although boggling at the requirement of I.C.C. approval before rate agreements under section 7 went into effect, he added a vaguely worded proviso making such agreements "subject to the approval of the Commission."[26]

---

25. Beveridge to Pinchot, 23 March 1910, BP.
26. George W. Wickersham to Taft, 19 March 1910, Taft Papers.

But these amendments failed to satisfy Beveridge and his fellow insurgents. The struggle that followed on the floor of the upper chamber made irreparable the breach between the insurgents and the president. The insurgents wrote the chief executive off as a traitor to the progressive movement. Taft replied by embarking upon an aggressive campaign to purge the leading trouble makers at the upcoming primaries. Speaking at Chicago's Hamilton Club on 9 April, Wickersham made support of the administration's railroad bill the test of party loyalty. "The time of running with the hare and hunting with the hounds is over," he warned, "and everyone must choose whether or not he is for the President and the Republican party."[27]

The speech, Beveridge complained bitterly, "was carefully prepared, read over and O.K.'d by the President" and "voices the real sentiments of the administration." This heavy-handed attempt to whip the insurgents into line, the Hoosier confided to Albert Shaw, "has made things much worse than ever." When La Follette replied with a blistering attack upon the administration for discontinuing the suit against the merger of the New Haven and the Boston & Maine railroads, Beveridge praised the Wisconsin lawmaker's speech as "the ablest thing he has ever done." "Political conditions here in Washington," he reported to his brother-in-law, "are in the utmost confusion. The administration's program seems to be going to pieces."[28]

Beveridge acted as parliamentary floor leader for the insurgents in their attack upon the railroad bill. He raised points of order, interjected embarrassing questions, highlighted the issues with his sharp comments, and exchanged angry words with old guard leaders. The disgusted Aldrich lumped him with La Follette, Bristow, Dolliver, Clapp, and Cummins as "irreconcilable progressives" whom he vowed to drive from the party. Taft joined in reading the insurgents out of the G.O.P. When he asked the party leaders to call a meeting of all Republican senators to discuss the railroad bill, he excluded the six troublemakers. "I give them up," the chief executive fumed.[29]

The first major test of strength came at the end of April over section 7. No antitrust admirer, Beveridge approved suspension of the Sherman Act as regards the railroads. But he demanded that any

---

27. Mowry, *Theodore Roosevelt and the Progressive Movement*, p. 100.

28. Beveridge to Shaw, 11, 14 April 1910, Shaw Papers. Beveridge to Spencer Eddy, 4 May 1910, BP.

29. *Indianapolis Star*, 6 May 1910. Taft to Aldrich, 12 May 1910, Aldrich Papers.

rate increase resulting from a railroad agreement made under section 7 must be approved by the I.C.C. before going into effect to protect shippers and the public. When a count of heads showed that the insurgents had the votes to pass such an amendment, Aldrich, to save face, made a deal with the Democrats to strike out the entire section. The price he paid was abandonment of his foot dragging on the statehood bill. "The reactionaries," Beveridge exclaimed angrily, ". . . seem determined to slaughter the entire railroad legislation merely because we had the votes to knock out of the bill an indefensible feature of it."[30]

The Hoosier spearheaded the attack upon the "inexcusable injustices" and "monstrous abuses" growing out of long- and short-haul discrimination.[31] This question was so explosive a political issue throughout the West that even so loyal an old guard lawmaker as Montana's Thomas H. Carter threatened to bolt unless western grievances were satisfied. Aldrich was forced to accept an insurgent-approved amendment presented by Senator Joseph M. Dixon of Montana prohibiting any railroad from charging more for a shorter than a longer haul when the shorter was included in the longer except in special cases where the I.C.C. found sufficiently dissimilar circumstances to justify a higher rate.

The administration forces rallied to defeat, by thirty-seven votes to twenty-eight, a Beveridge-supported move to eliminate the commerce court. La Follette's amendment for physical valuation of the railroads was voted down thirty to twenty-five. But the old guard had to yield point after point: telegraph and telephone lines were placed under I.C.C. supervision; permission was granted the commission or any interested party to take part in the defense of commission decisions before the courts, and the attorney general was barred from discontinuing any case over their objective; the loophole for possible "broad" review was eliminated; sections 13, 14, and 15 were struck out; and the insurgents took advantage of the uproar over the across-the-board rate increases announced in late May to amend the bill to place the burden of proof upon the railroads to justify any increases in rates and to authorize the I.C.C. to suspend the new rates for up to ten months pending a ruling upon their reasonableness.

---

30. Beveridge to Henry W. Bennett, 4 May 1910, BP.
31. *CR*, 61st Cong., 2nd sess., 1910, 45, pt. 6: 6207.

Although the insurgent-Democratic coalition in the House was not as successful as its Senate counterpart, the insurgents saved the Senate bill from mutilation in conference by threatening to keep Congress in session through the summer rather than yield their hard-won gains. When the bill came up for final passage on 17 June, all the insurgents, except La Follette, who abstained because of the defeat of physical evaluation, voted for its adoption. The measure did—as Beveridge boasted—represent a far-reaching step forward in federal regulation of the railroads. But the insurgents, not the administration, received the credit. "The influence of Taft," Joseph L. Bristow complained, "has been against us in every move we have made to improve the law." And the Kansas lawmaker could hardly restrain his anger at the chief executive's "hypocrisy" in talking progressivism but then selling out to the Old Guard.[32]

Another thing that came between the president and Beveridge was the fate of the latter's pet reform—the tariff commission. In line with his pledge to use to the utmost his authority under the Payne-Aldrich law, Taft appointed, in September 1909, a three-man Tariff Board, consisting of Alvin H. Sanders, editor of the *Breeders' Gazette* and chairman of the American Reciprocal Tariff League, James B. Reynolds, an assistant Secretary of the Treasury, and Henry C. Emery, professor of political economy at Yale University, and directed the board to draw up what he called in his Winona address "a small encyclopedia of the tariff" that would provide all necessary facts about "the operation of the tariff" including "the cost of production abroad and here."[33]

Although ultraprotectionists denounced the president for stirring up trouble, Beveridge indicted the existing board as "a fake if ever there was one" and renewed the fight for his own bill. The members of this "so-called tariff board," he explained, "are not officers of the Government. They are mere employees. They have no authority or higher legal standing than the President's clerk or stenographer." They could be discharged at will; the president could order them to stop work at any time; they could not compel the production of papers or require sworn testimony; and the scope of their activities was "confined to the maximum and minimum section of the bill." And

---

32. Joseph L. Bristow to Harold T. Chase, 13 June 1910, Bristow Papers.
33. Taft, *Presidential Addresses and State Papers,* pp. 228–29.

he lined up his fellow insurgents to renew the fight for his own tariff commission bill.[34]

After the passage of the Payne-Aldrich bill, the National Association of Manufacturers had withdrawn from active participation in the tariff commission movement because of the divisive effect the issue had had upon its membership. The leadership of the movement was taken over by the Committee of One Hundred—renamed the National Tariff Commission Association. The moving spirit of the new organization, the pugnacious H. E. Miles, undertook to build a backfire in the home districts of recalcitrant lawmakers. With popular resentment over the tariff kept aflame by the high cost of living, even conservatives began to look more favorably upon the tariff commission.

Worried about the upcoming elections, Taft pushed for a new and larger appropriation to continue the existing tariff board for another year. The Democrats attacked the board as a G.O.P. stratagem to remove the tariff as an issue in the forthcoming elections, while die-hard standpatters remained hostile. But the House G.O.P. leaders went along with the chief executive and put in the sundry civil appropriation bill a provision appropriating $250,000 to "enable the President to secure information to assist him in the discharge of the duties imposed upon him" by the maximum and minimum section of the Payne-Aldrich law, "including such investigations of the cost of production of commodities . . . as are authorized by said act."[35]

When the appropriation bill came before the Senate, Beveridge was in a quandary. His first impression was that the provision authorizing the existing tariff board to make "such investigations of the cost of production of commodities . . . as are authorized" by the Payne-Aldrich law was a farce. The Payne-Aldrich law, the Hoosier complained, "does not authorize them to make any investigations whatever." He suspected that the purpose of its sponsors was to undercut the demand for "any real, honest tariff commission legislation" by deceiving "the people into thinking they have a tariff commission."[36]

Eventually, however, he talked himself into believing that the

---

34. Beveridge to Curtis Guild, Jr., 18 November 1909, 22, 27 April 1910; to Robert A. Brown, 12 April 1910, BP.

35. *CR* (House), 61st Cong., 2nd sess., 1910, 45, pt. 7: 6804–16.

36. Beveridge to Guild, 1 June 1910, BP.

legislation "does add something" to the president's authority. The provision adopted by the House, he told the upper chamber, "practically restores what was stricken out by the conference committee last session" and was "the first fruit of the seed sown now almost three years ago for a tariff commission. . . . It is a recognition in formal written law of the beginning of this great business reform—a small beginning, it is true, but a real one."[37]

But he had no illusions about the shortcomings of the existing tariff board. Its members were still no more than "employees" of the president without fixed salaries or tenure; the chief executive could terminate the work at any time; they had no power to compel business firms to produce their books and records. And he blamed Taft for the failure of Congress to pass his own tariff commission bill. Had the chief executive "even lifted his finger" in its support, he complained to John C. Shaffer, his bill would have passed. "The plain truth is that since I wrote the Tariff Commission Bill three years ago and began the fight for it, Mr. Taft has given me no encouragement whatever."[38]

Midway through the session, Beveridge prepared to greet Roosevelt, on the latter's return from hunting lions in Africa, with a blistering indictment of Taft for betraying the "great historic movement" begun under Roosevelt to restore "common honesty" in politics and business. Public feeling against the administration was, he reported, "rapidly crystallizing into something like hatred." If Taft were renominated, he would drag the party down to defeat. He himself would not "lift a finger" in his support. When he thought, he told John C. Shaffer, of the miles he had traveled and the speeches he had delivered for Taft, "who not only does not appreciate it but who seems to have forgotten absolutely that I ever did anything at all for him," he was so angry that he could hardly contain his feelings.[39] So embittered had become their personal relations that, when Congress adjourned, Beveridge even refused to make the customary end-of-the season visit to the White House to pay his respects.

Taft returned Beveridge's hostility. The Hoosier's personality grated upon the chief executive. And he was infuriated when Bever-

---

37. *CR*, 61st Cong., 2nd sess., 1910, 45, pt. 7: 7799–813, 7864–67.
38. *SEP*, 24 September 1910, p. 57. Beveridge to Shaffer, 27 June 1910, BP.
39. Beveridge to Pinchot, 23, 24 March 1910; to Shaffer, 10 March 1910, BP.

idge joined in the attacks upon one after another of his legislative proposals. Beveridge, Taft complained bitterly to Nelson W. Aldrich early in March, "while apparently acting with the Administration, was organizing the insurgent element for its most effective operations." With members of his family, Taft was even blunter about the Hoosier. "I utterly despise him," he said, "as a demagogue and an opportunist of the worst type, and a man in whose veracity and reliability one can have but little confidence." When in May he wrote to Roosevelt lamenting the "hard time" he had had since entering the White House, he included Beveridge in his list of G.O.P. lawmakers who "have done all in their power to defeat us."[40]

Beveridge was alarmed by rumors that "the powers that prey" planned to knife him in the legislature even if the G.O.P. carried Indiana, as well as by reports from Washington of conferences between the chief executive and Hoosier old guard leaders. Fighting for his political life, he saw no alternative but to appeal to the voters on his record as an insurgent at the risk of a total break with the president. His determination to run a progressive campaign was strengthened by his continuing anxieties over the dangers to American institutions unless the reforms he advocated were adopted. "We have got to straighten out things in this country," he warned his cousin, a wealthy Ohio textile manufacturer,

> for not only business but the whole structure of our national society is going to be imperilled before many years to come. The people won't stand injustice—*they simply will not*. It is injustice that has caused every revolution in the history of the world. It is the wise man and the patriot who tries to correct it in political battles before it causes a worse kind of a battle.[41]

---

40. [Butt], *Taft and Roosevelt*, 1: 301. Taft to Hulbert Taft, 11 April 1910; to Theodore Roosevelt, 26 May 1910, Taft Papers.

41. Beveridge to E. L. McClain, 14, 18 March 1910, BP.

14

Defeat

The Democratic sweep of Indiana in 1908 left Beveridge the state's top-ranking Republican. Vice-president Charles W. Fairbanks, at the end of his term, left for a world tour. Congressman James E. Watson had gone down to defeat in the governorship race. The Democratic majority in the legislature on joint ballot elected Benjamin F. Shively to replace James A. Hemenway in the Senate. Democratic congressmen had been elected in all but two of Indiana's thirteen districts. Thus, the bulk of the federal patronage was in Beveridge's hands. "All of you boys," he instructed his political lieutenants, should "get it out quietly that I will be the sole and absolute distributor of patronage under Taft's administration."[1]

When United States District Attorney Joseph B. Kealing resigned rather than handle Roosevelt's prosecution of the *Indianapolis News* for criminal libel, Beveridge arranged for the appointment of his longtime friend Charles W. Miller. Although the Civil Service Commission had found Elam H. Neal, the Collector of Internal Revenue for the Sixth District, guilty of violating the

---

1. Beveridge to Leopold G. Rothschild, 22 December 1908, BP.

civil service law by his political activities and recommended a penalty of six months' suspension, Beveridge successfully interceded with the president to quash the matter.

Henry C. Pettit remained United States Marshal, while Leopold G. Rothschild continued as Collector of Customs at Indianapolis. But Beveridge replaced John Bonnell as Collector of Internal Revenue at Terre Haute with Charles G. Covert, the postmaster at Evansville, "thus attaching" Hemenway's former righthand man in the First Congressional District "to the cause of righteousness."[2] With 1910 a census year, he had the appointment of census supervisors throughout the state. And he had subject to his recommendation the approximately seven hundred postmasterships in the eleven Democratic congressional districts.

Alarmed by the chief executive's threat to cut off the patronage of the insurgents, Beveridge was upset when the president delayed sending to Congress a number of his postmastership recommendations. But Taft continued to hope for cooperation with Beveridge, and so when the latter made an angry protest to Postmaster General Frank H. Hitchcock, prompt White House action followed. His worsening relations with the chief executive during the second session of the Sixty-First Congress led to further trouble over the patronage. When he spoke to Taft toward the end of the session about an Indiana appointment, the president angrily declared that he would not honor his recommendations because he had tried to defeat the administration's measures. Beveridge's renewed protests to Hitchcock, however, smoothed over the matter. And there were no further patronage difficulties until after his defeat.

Armed with the patronage, Beveridge solidified his grip upon the party machinery. Hand-picked candidates for district chairman—such as young Will H. Hays in the Second District—were brought out in each district. In only two districts were there even contests, and every district convention endorsed Beveridge for reelection. There was talk of Harry S. New, the former G.O.P. national chairman, as the new state chairman. But New was reluctant to take on what he suspected would be a thankless job, and Beveridge had grown doubtful about his loyalty. The nod went to E. M. Lee,

---

2. Beveridge to Samuel G. Blythe, 23 July 1910, BP.

former mayor of Lawrenceburg, whose loyalty Beveridge regarded as "unquestioned." The state committee unanimously elected Lee and then named Beveridge's secretary, John F. Hayes, committee secretary.[3]

Despite his grip upon the party organization, Beveridge was disturbed by the newspaper situation. In 1908, Daniel G. Reid sold his interest in the Star League newspapers to John C. Shaffer. But Shaffer's ownership was disputed in a court battle by George F. McCulloch, who had retained ownership of the preferred stock. Beveridge was convinced that control of the papers in friendly hands was indispensable for his political future, not only in Indiana, but for his presidential aspirations. With Shaffer growing more and more unhappy over the long and costly litigation and talking of selling his holdings, Beveridge was desperately worried lest the papers fall into hostile hands. At Shaffer's behest, he even interceded with federal district judge Albert B. Anderson to ask for a speedy decision.

A more vexing—and immediate—difficulty was what to do about the county-option liquor law. Although the victorious Democrats were pledged to its repeal, the Republicans retained a narrow margin in the upper house of the legislature. Beveridge personally was afraid that repeal would stir up renewed prohibitionist agitation. But his advisers warned that failure to repeal would cost the party the votes of thousands of Republican "wets" and thus "mean the same thing over again that we just had" in the 1908 election. So Beveridge let his Indiana supporters push for repeal, while he himself remained above the battle.[4]

This strategy, however, backfired when the upper house of the legislature defeated repeal by a vote of twenty-six to twenty-three. The "wets" were furious—a leading brewer and behind-the-scenes power in the G.O.P. accusing Beveridge of double-dealing.[5] The "drys" were up in arms because his top lieutenants had supported

---

3. Beveridge to George A. H. Shideler, 9 February 1910, BP.
4. Rothschild to Beveridge, 10 February 1909; Beveridge to Rothschild, 12 February 1909, BP. For an example of his refusal to become involved on the ground that the issue was purely a state matter, see Beveridge to James Bingham, 1 March 1909, BP.
5. Rothschild to Beveridge, 2 March 1909, BP.

repeal. "Dry" hostility was fanned when the Republican state convention failed to endorse the county-option law in its platform.[6] And further aggravating his difficulties were the stories circulating about Beveridge's excessive drinking. Charles P. Taft's *Cincinnati Times-Star* even ran a cartoon with an unflattering picture of Beveridge and a whiskey bottle and the caption " 'Beverages' are the issues in Indiana."[7]

Beveridge's gravest handicap was the factional strife within the Indiana G.O.P. After the 1908 election, the Watson-Hemenway followers had complained bitterly about treachery within the ranks and threatened revenge. And they foresaw that if Beveridge won reelection, their own political futures were finished. The split between Beveridge and the president aggravated the situation. Rallying behind the chief executive, the old guard demanded endorsement of the Payne-Aldrich tariff in the state platform. "If we hope to have anything left of what we formerly stood for," Hemenway exhorted his followers, "the republican party has got to rally and not allow itself to be led any longer by populistic leaders."[8]

Hesitant voices were heard within Beveridge's own camp. But Beveridge would not permit any straddling. He was impressed with reports from Indiana telling of growing hostility toward the tariff because of the high cost of living. The upset victory in a special congressional election in late March 1910 of tariff reformer Eugene N. Foss running on the Democratic ticket in a strongly Republican Massachusetts district confirmed his belief about the popularity of his own stand. "I am profoundly convinced," he confided to a friend, "that we have got to strike straight out from the shoulder with the heaviest possible blows or we are lost. But if we do that we will win overwhelmingly."[9]

Beveridge instructed his political lieutenants that "every man—I mean literally every man" on the resolutions committee "shall be absolutely right" so that the 1910 Indiana state Republican convention would "pass off without a row."[10] As a further safeguard, Bever-

---

6. See, for example, Everett Reese to Beveridge, 26 June 1910, BP.

7. *American Review of Reviews* 41 (May 1910): 551.

8. James A. Hemenway to Lucius C. Embree, 23 February 1910, Embree Papers (ISL).

9. Beveridge to Albert B. Anderson, 25 March 1910, BP.

10. Beveridge to Henry W. Bennett, 6, 10 March 1910, BP.

idge had himself made temporary chairman and keynoter. The top old guard leaders—Fairbanks, Watson, Hemenway, and former state chairman James P. Goodrich—boycotted the convention in protest. Without leadership, the standpatters made no trouble.

The platform called for establishment of a permanent tariff commission, reciprocity, conservation, a national child labor law, ratification of the income tax amendment, enactment of "such limitation of the power of injunction as will not imperil the liberty of any man without notice and hearing," and increased pensions for old soldiers; but the Payne-Aldrich law was ignored. Taft was given a half-hearted endorsement: "We indorse his administration and pledge to him our support in any efforts to secure the enactment of progressive legislation." In contrast was the ringing praise for Beveridge, "and especially his record in the last session of Congress, which deserves the unqualified approval of all the people of the state."

The bulk of Beveridge's keynote speech consisted of an attack upon the Payne-Aldrich bill—an attack that was, he wired George H. Lorimer, "greeted with intense enthusiasm." He reaffirmed his support for "a protective tariff which covers the difference between the cost of production here and abroad." But at stake in the Payne-Aldrich fight was a moral question. "Extortion is not protection." "The coming battle," he told the assembled delegates, was not a party contest, but a struggle "between the rights of the people and the powers of pillage." And in that struggle, "the Republicans of Indiana stand for the people."[11]

His fellow insurgents in Washington hailed the Indiana convention as a blow "against the evil influences which are seeking to capture the government." The president was furious. He would not, Taft fumed to his brother, lift a finger to assist Beveridge's reelection. "I suppose I prefer a Republican to a Democrat; but he has attempted to kill my legislation in such a way in the Senate that I do not feel under any obligation to him. He has made his bed and must lie in it."[12] And when he canceled his scheduled visit to Indianapolis, friend and foe interpreted the action as a protest against what had happened at the state convention.

11. *Indianapolis Star,* 6 April 1906. Beverage to George H. Lorimer, 5 April 1910 (telegram), BP.

12. *Indianapolis News,* 6 April 1910. William H. Taft to Charles P. Taft, 19 April 1910, Taft Papers.

Outgunned at the state convention, the standpatters continued their fight at the district conventions and succeeded—to Beveridge's embarrassment and anger—in pushing through resolutions praising the Payne-Aldrich law in the First, Sixth, Eighth, Tenth, and Eleventh Districts. Even more disturbing were their behind-the-scenes efforts to nominate Republican candidates for the legislature who would knife Beveridge even if the G.O.P. captured the legislature. "He will learn," Joseph B. Kealing assured the chief executive's secretary, "that there are plenty of votes in the Legislature . . . who will not vote for him . . . because they do not believe he is a *republican any* more."[13]

Hearing of these underground activities, Beveridge directed his lieutenants to see that every Republican legislative candidate "should be put under a binding iron clad instruction not only to vote for me . . . but also that he shall not under any circumstances vote for anybody else." Despite reassuring reports from Indiana, Beveridge continued to worry about the back-stairs plotting of his factional rivals. "It is in the air," he reported to a friend, "that if I carry the legislature it is to be bought or otherwise influenced."[14]

At times, Beveridge talked of quitting "this rotten game" and retiring from politics "to write my articles and books" and "live my life in some decency and comfort."[15] More and more he resented having to spend so much time away from his family. Like most men who become fathers late in life, he doted upon his son and namesake. And in April 1910, his wife gave birth to a daughter, whom he named Abby.

But he was too ambitious a man and too much a fighter to give up without a struggle. The keystone of his strategy was to make up the loss of standpat Republican votes by picking up independent and Democratic support. Thus he instructed his campaign managers to make his own reelection, rather than the Republican party, the issue. And he vowed personally to go "right square down the line for progressive principles." Any backtracking would be "bad morals" and worse politics. He even directed the G.O.P. state committee not to allow the standpat leaders to take a "conspicuous" part in the cam-

---

13. Joseph B. Kealing to Charles D. Norton, 28 September 1910, Charles D. Hilles Papers (Yale University Library).

14. Beveridge to H. C. Pettit, 16 April 1910; to Mark Sullivan, 5 September 1910, BP.

15. Beveridge to Lorimer, 25 February 1910, BP.

paign. "Where we placate one standpat vote," he warned, "we will lose many, many independent and Democratic votes."[16]

Returning in September from his vacation in New Hampshire, Beveridge plunged into an exhausting campaign tour. His first week's schedule was typical. He opened the campaign on 27 September in Indianapolis. Between 28 September and 1 October he managed to address meetings in eight different towns: Attica, Lafayette, North Vernon, Greensburg, Vevay, Batesville, Scottsburg, and Columbus, in addition to performing the campaign rituals of shaking hands, conferring with local party workers, and kissing babies. Midway through the campaign his voice had become husky, almost breaking under the strain. By election day he had spoken in nearly all of Indiana's 92 counties and had delivered 125 speeches before a total audience of more than 150,000.

He extolled the achievements of "progressive Republicanism" over the past ten years: the Department of Commerce and Labor, the Hepburn Act, the pure food and drug bill, the meat inspection law, and the conservation of the nation's resources. But much remained to be done: the establishment of "a thorough going, permanent, nonpartisan tariff commission" to remove the tariff from politics; exemption of legitimate combinations from the Sherman antitrust law coupled with stricter federal regulation against wrongdoing; national incorporation of all business engaged in interstate commerce to stop overcapitalization; physical valuation of the railroads; and adoption of a leasing system for the remaining public domain.

He accused the Democratic party of being dominated by reactionary bosses under the thumb of "Wall street's masters," pleaded for an end of "unthinking partisanship," and warned that "the interests" were raising a vast "corruption fund" for his defeat. At stake in Indiana was the future of the great movement underway "for the betterment of man" against "the forces of organized greed." "The overthrow of the invisible government of mighty interests that the visible government of the people may endure is the issue of this campaign. And it is invisible government against which we war."

In a bid for labor votes, he called for an end to the abuse of injunc-

---

16. Beveridge to Albert B. Cummins, 9 September 1910; to John ·F. Hayes, 4 August 1910; to Charles F. Remy, 20 July 1910, BP.

tions in labor disputes by requiring notice and a prompt hearing; extension of the eight-hour-day law to cover government contractors; amendment of the Sherman act to exempt labor unions "from the operation of a law never meant for them"; and "the greatest of all human reforms"—legislation by Congress to wipe out the curse of child labor. "After all," he proclaimed, "what should be the purpose of all our laws? What is the reason for our republican form of government? Is it not that the human beings who make up the nation shall have larger opportunities for life, liberty, and the pursuit of happiness?"

He simultaneously reassured businessmen that these reforms would benefit, not injure, business. Stricter regulation of giant corporations was not only required "for justice to all the people," but was "essential to general business stability and security" by removing "the sense of injustice and the feeling of resentment among the people." A tariff commission would end the "business storms and earthquakes" accompanying repeated tariff upheavals. Justice to labor meant safety for capital. And he appealed to Hoosier businessmen to break the chains imposed by "your industrial overlords" and join in the battle to remedy "those business evils which unjustly build up dangerous fortunes of a few mighty business men at the expense of multitudes of smaller business men and to the injury of all the people."[17]

Beveridge appealed to progressive leaders throughout the country to take the stump in Indiana. Even before Roosevelt's return from Africa, he had bombarded the former chief executive with appeals that he campaign for him. The Hoosier's importunities annoyed Roosevelt. He grumbled about Beveridge's vanity, egotism, and publicity-seeking. Although more and more disillusioned with his old friend in the White House, Roosevelt wished to keep the insurgents at arm's distance in hopes of finding "a common ground upon which Insurgents and Regulars can stand."[18]

Swallowing his irritation, Roosevelt promised to speak in Indiana. Beveridge was overjoyed at the news. But he was disturbed by the announcement that Roosevelt would also speak in Massachusetts for Senator Henry Cabot Lodge. Even worse were the reports in the

---

17. *Indianapolis Star,* 28 September, 11, 19 October 1910. *Indianapolis News,* 27 October 1910.

18. Theodore Roosevelt to Nicholas Longworth, 11 July 1910, in Morison, *The Letters of Theodore Roosevelt,* 7: 98–102.

newspapers that the former president would remain neutral in the struggle between insurgents and old guard.

Visiting Indiana on 13 October, Roosevelt gave a major address at Indianapolis and then whistle-stopped across the state, lauding Beveridge as a man "who stood fearlessly for the right when it needed nerve to stand for the right."[19] But his balancing act between the old guard and the insurgents, his *Outlook* article defending the Payne-Aldrich bill, his praise for Taft in his keynote address before the New York G.O.P. convention, and his speaking for Lodge undermined his effectiveness. Democratic campaigners ridiculed Roosevelt for eulogizing Lodge, who had voted for the Payne-Aldrich tariff, while at the same time supporting Beveridge, who had voted against the bill.[20]

Next to Roosevelt, Beveridge counted most heavily upon Dolliver. But early in October the Iowan sadly reported that ill health would prevent his coming. Eight days later he was dead from a heart condition. Beveridge was shocked by the news of the loss of his "dear friend and faithful comrade" and arranged to take off from campaigning to attend the funeral. But Cummins telegraphed him not to leave because "it would be an irretrievable disaster if after losing Dolliver by death we should lose you by defeat." Sorrowfully, Beveridge complied, but on the day of the funeral, he devoted his speeches to eulogies of Dolliver, who, he declared, "died a martyr to the cause of the people."[21]

Moses E. Clapp was the first of the Senate insurgents to visit Indiana in Beveridge's support. He was followed by Albert B. Cummins. Even though Dolliver's death placed on him an extra burden in his home state of Iowa, Cummins took the stump in Indiana for a week. Many of Beveridge's advisers in the state thought La Follette and Bristow too radical for Indiana voters. But the senator overruled their objections. Although La Follette could not come because of illness, Bristow stumped the entire state and coupled philippics against the Payne-Aldrich tariff with praise for Beveridge as a "senator who has ably and courageously done his duty."[22]

---

19. *Indianapolis News,* 13 October 1910.
20. See, for example, *Indianapolis Star,* 23 October 1910.
21. Cummins to Beveridge, 18 October [1910] (telegram), BP. *Indianapolis Star,* 16, 21 October 1910.
22. *Indianapolis News,* 4 October 1910.

Judge Ben Lindsey of the Denver Juvenile Court issued a public statement urging Beveridge's reelection. William Allen White wrote an article—which Beveridge thought "struck with the hammer of Thor"—for the *American Magazine,* extolling the Hoosier lawmaker as the champion of "the rights of men" against the "predatory interests." Gifford Pinchot contributed a thousand dollars to his campaign and took the stump in Indiana. Former secretary of the interior James R. Garfield toured the Hoosier state warning that Beveridge's defeat would deal the progressive movement "a backset from which it will not recover for years to come."[23]

But Beveridge faced an uphill battle. The Democratic triumph in Maine in September 1910 was symptomatic of Democratic progress throughout the country. Insurgency in Indiana lacked the deep-rooted popular support found in the states farther west. The old guard leaders—Fairbanks, Hemenway, Watson, Durbin, Goodrich, and Hanly—sat out the campaign, while complaining to Washington that the state committee refused to schedule proadministration speakers. When they did put in a token appearance, they undercut Beveridge by praising the Payne-Aldrich tariff, defending the president, and attacking the insurgents. And in crucial Marion County, where nine legislative seats were at stake, Joseph B. Kealing knifed the G.O.P. ticket.

At the same time, the Democrats succeeded in neutralizing Beveridge's appeals to progressive-minded Democratic voters. Democratic governor Thomas Marshall had come out in favor of the establishment of a state board of accounts to audit the financial records of state and local officials, for a new primary election law to include the nomination of candidates for the United States Senate, and for improvements in the state regulation of railroads, insurance companies, and other corporations. To avoid a recurrence of the cries of fraud, bribery, and double-dealing following the selection of Benjamin F. Shively by a secret Democratic legislative caucus after the 1908 election, Marshall pushed through the state convention formal designation of John W. Kern as the party's nominee for senator. Kern was highly popular with the Democratic rank and file. While a state senator in the 1890s, he had been active in behalf of union-backed

23. [William Allen White], "In the Interpreter's House," *American Magazine* 70 (October 1910): 854–56. Beveridge to William Allen White, 22 September 1910, White Papers. *Indianapolis News,* 19 October 1910.

legislation. Although personally opposed to free silver, he had stood by his party in 1896 and had become a personal friend of William Jennings Bryan.

Forcing the battle, Kern boldly challenged Beveridge's own progressivism. He reminded his audiences that Beveridge had voted for the ship subsidy bill with its payoff to J. P. Morgan's shipping trust. That he had voted against the income tax amendment to the Payne-Aldrich tariff. That he was against the major reform demanded by organized labor—trial by jury for violations of injunctions in labor disputes. That he had for years gone around the country defending the trusts. That he had found no fault with the Dingley tariff until popular feeling had grown too strong to resist, and that he had then experienced "a regular St. Paulian conversion." That he continued to defend the protective tariff—the mother of trusts. The people of Indiana, the Democratic nominee admonished, should not be misled by a man "whose theatrical battles against the great interests have not been surpassed since the bloodless struggles between Don Quixote and the windmills."[24]

These attacks placed Beveridge on the defensive. He explained at length that he had opposed the income tax rider to the Payne-Aldrich bill not because he was against the income tax but because as a believer in "the method of orderly liberty" he did not wish to bring the courts into disrespect, and he announced his support for the pending constitutional amendment. He reversed his former stand and expressed approval of "a jury trial as to the facts in alleged violations of injunctions by laboring men." He admitted his mistake in voting for the ship subsidy and pledged himself to vote against the measure in the future. He defended the protective tariff as the bulwark of national prosperity and stigmatized the Democrats as free traders who would destroy American living standards.[25]

Kern pressed his attack with biting wit. After Beveridge had recanted his vote for the ship subsidy bill, Kern boasted how he had labored for weeks "to wring this confession and expression of contrition from the reluctant lips of the man whose sermons on civic righteousness have so entranced his audiences throughout the state." When ex-Congressman Fred Landis hailed Beveridge as the cham-

---

24. *Indianapolis Star*, 29 October, 1 November 1910.
25. Ibid., 19 October 1910. *Indianapolis News*, 27 October 1910.

pion of the little people of the country—"Mary of the vine-clad cottage"—Kern replied that the price of everything Mary wore and even the lumber for her vine-clad cottage was increased by the protective tariff which Beveridge defended. And William Jennings Bryan, stumping for the Democratic nominee, assured his Indiana admirers that Beveridge "does not stand for any important reform that Mr. Kern has not stood for longer and fought harder for."[26]

Looming over the contest was the struggle underway between the "wets" and the "drys." Beveridge anxiously strove to soft-pedal the liquor question as no more than a minor issue in the larger battle "to destroy wicked and corrupt practices throughout the Nation."[27] But the Democrats would not let the G.O.P. off the hook. The party's state platform called for a return to the township-option system, and Governor Marshall made attacks upon the county-option law the highlight of his campaign speeches. The Democratic appeal to the so-called "liberal" vote struck a popular note among Indiana's large German population.

Although Beveridge continued to the last to predict a popular arising that would carry the G.O.P. to victory, the Democrats won majorities in both houses of the legislature, thus assuring that a Democrat would replace Beveridge in the Senate. Observers differed in their analyses of the results. Old guard hostility hurt, although Beveridge personally downgraded its significance. He himself felt the liquor issue "the chief element" in his defeat. But the liquor question was not the full story. There was a strong Democratic tide throughout the country fed by popular resentment—"Hatred is a better word," according to Beveridge—against the Payne-Aldrich tariff because of the high cost of living.[28] Perhaps most important was his failure— thanks to Kern's nomination and campaign—to attract progressive-minded Democratic votes.

Beveridge maintained a brave face. "Fortunes of war," he told reporters; "it is all right; twelve years hard work; clean record; I am content." Contrasted with the Democratic gains throughout the

---

26. *Indianapolis Star,* 15, 29 October 1910. *Indianapolis News,* 14 October 1910.

27. Beveridge to Reese, 2 July 1910, BP.

28. Beveridge to Lorimer, 17 November 1910, BP. In his subsequent bitterness, Beveridge would put more emphasis upon the importance of old guard treachery in his defeat: Beveridge to Walter Bradfute, 11 March 1914, BP.

country, he explained to his friends, the Republican showing in Indiana—historically a "doubtful" state—was remarkable. So close were many of the legislative races that fewer than a thousand votes rightly distributed would have given the Republicans a majority in the legislature. And he took pride in having made "a clean fight" against "admitted evils and for absolutely necessary constructive reforms." The seeds thus sown "will yield their sure and abundant harvest, and that speedily." "Even now," he boasted to William Allen White, "the Dems. are not crowing—while our fellows are acting, talking and FEELING like the real victors."[29]

His spirits were buoyed by the letters of regret pouring in. His old college chum, novelist David Graham Phillips, assured him that his defeat was but a temporary setback. "The people have to go where you are leading, and they have to have you at the head of the procession." Roosevelt praised him for having fought "the straightest of all the fights for progress." Gifford Pinchot hailed the results as "a moral victory." "Though defeated temporarily," Robert M. LaFollette editorialized in his magazine, "he comes out of the campaign true to his faith, with unsullied record, and practically victorious. . . . He is sure to come back." Even Billy Sunday sent his regrets. "Do not feel blue," the evangelist wrote, "—your time will come. Merit can no more be hid than sunshine."[30]

From a personal standpoint, he claimed he was "not in the least cast down." After twelve years on a treadmill, he found the opportunity for a year or two of rest, unhurried reading, and recharging his batteries "positively welcome." His wife was "delighted beyond measure" that he could spend more time with his family. Even politically, his defeat was not without its advantages. "I am out of the awful and even ridiculous skirmish that is bound to come almost immediately. And yet I can speak my mind whenever it is absolutely necessary." "The matter is not finished," he confided to Shaffer, "—indeed the blindest ought to see that it only has begun."[31]

---

29. *Indianapolis Star*, 10 November 1910. Beveridge to Gilson Gardner, 17 November 1910; to Roosevelt, 17 November 1910, BP. Beveridge to White, 18 November 1910, White Papers.

30. David Graham Phillips to Beveridge [— November 1910]; Roosevelt to Beveridge, 11 November 1910; Billy Sunday to Beveridge, 11 November 1910; Gifford Pinchot to Beveridge, 15 November 1910, BP. *La Follette's Weekly Magazine*, 19 November 1910, p. 3.

31. Beveridge to Shaffer, 17 November 1910, BP.

15

Lame Duck Senator

Beveridge returned to Washington for the lame duck session of Congress determined to carry on the fight for the reforms he had preached in his election campaign. The most important of these was his bill for "a permanent, genuine, nonpartisan tariff commission."[1] As a Republican, he wished to remove the tariff from politics. As a protectionist, he saw the tariff commission as security against any tampering with protection by the new Democratic majority in the House. And, he warned, the time was now or never. At the last session, the Democrats had voted against even the $250,000 appropriation to continue the existing tariff board.

His agitation of the issue had begun to pay dividends. During 1910, one state Republican convention after another—including the one in that bastion of standpattism, Massachusetts—had adopted tariff commission planks. Looking upon the lame duck session as their last chance, the leaders of the National Tariff Commission Association arranged for a steady fire of resolutions demanding establishment of a permanent commission. To bring pressure on the law-

1. *CR*, 61st Cong., 3rd sess., 1910–11, 46, pt. 1: 202–03.

makers, the association held its annual convention in Washington in January 1911 with more than five hundred delegates in attendance representing over a hundred agricultural, industrial, and commercial organizations.

The Republican defeat in the fall elections had converted many formerly hostile businessmen and politicians. The tariff commission would blunt the tariff as an issue in the 1912 elections while safeguarding against Democratic-insurgent tinkering with the present schedules in the new Congress. When Beveridge demanded prompt action on his bill, even Aldrich acknowledged that the issue "has got to be met in some form or other" and promised action before the end of the session. Throwing his weight into the scales, Taft prodded G.O.P. congressional leaders for legislation to make the existing tariff board "permanent." Beveridge was full of praise for the chief executive's "admirable" stand.[2]

The House leaders balked, but Taft, accusing them of a lack of "responsibility in respect to the party's future," called in the G.O.P. members of the House Ways and Means Committee for a stiff talking to.[3] His prodding—coupled with their own anxieties over the political future—brought the congressional leaders into line. On 24 January, chairman Sereno E. Payne reported the administration's bill for "a permanent tariff board" from the Ways and Means Committee. Although many Democrats assailed the tariff board as "a Trojan horse," a Republican trick "to harass, to delay, to prevent Democratic tariff reform," the bill passed the House on 30 January by 186 votes to 93.[4]

But the House action was overshadowed for Beveridge by a personal tragedy. His dearest and most faithful of friends, David Graham Phillips, was shot on 23 January by a mentally deranged violinist. Beveridge took the first train to New York to be at his friend's bedside. Assured that Phillips would recover, he returned to Washington, only to receive the news that Phillips had died. He took the next train back to New York and sorrowfully took charge of the

2. Ibid., pt. 1: 203. William H. Taft to Nelson W. Aldrich, 14 January 1911 (enclosing a copy of his speech before the National Tariff Commission Association Convention, Washington, D.C., 12 January 1911), Aldrich Papers. Beveridge to Taft, 14 January 1911, BP.

3. Taft to Aldrich, 14 January 1911, Aldrich Papers.

4. U.S., Congress, House, Committee on Ways and Means, *Tariff Board: Report to Accompany H.R. 32010*, 61st Cong., 3rd sess., 1911, H. Rept. 1979, pp. 1–2. *CR* (House), 61st Cong., 3rd sess., 1911, 46, pt. 2: 1671–710.

funeral arrangements. The death of "dear old Phillips" was a bitter personal blow. "He chummed with me in college," mourned Beveridge, "nursed me through a sickness and has been the only person who has unfalteringly believed in me in season and out of season all my life."[5]

He came back from the funeral the more determined to push forward as Phillips would have wished. The Republican members of the Senate Finance Committee were lukewarm, if not hostile, toward the tariff board bill, and with Aldrich away ill, party discipline was breaking down. Alarmed by rumors of a Democratic filibuster, Beveridge urgently warned the president that "not a moment is to be lost in reporting it."[6] The administration's new strong man, W. Murray Crane of Massachusetts, whipped the reluctant G.O.P. members into line. On 9 February, Henry Cabot Lodge reported the bill from the Finance Committee with two minor amendments: the first requiring Senate confirmation of presidential appointees to the board; the second directing the board to include "the cost of transportation from the place or places of production to the principal areas of consumption" in estimating the cost of production of articles covered by the tariff.[7]

But the Democrats threatened a filibuster to block a vote. The legislative situation played into their hands. Unlike the House rules, the Senate rules permitted unlimited debate; it was the short session of Congress; there was a backlog of appropriation bills awaiting action; the Lorimer case was before the upper chamber; the constitutional amendment for direct election of Senators was pending; the debate over Canadian reciprocity was raging; and the Republican leadership was unenthusiastic about the bill. In face of the Democratic filibuster threat, the president backed down and agreed to settle for adoption of a $400,000 appropriation to continue the existing tariff board for another year.

With the end of his term approaching, however, Beveridge was not willing to watch the demise of a measure for which he had so long fought. A bitter struggle was raging in the Senate over the seating of Senator William Lorimer of Illinois. Confident of a majority, the old

5. Beveridge to Charles E. Coffin, 6 February 1911, BP.
6. Beveridge to Taft [1 February 1911], Taft Papers.
7. *CR*, 61st Cong., 3rd sess., 1911, 46, pt. 3: 2425.

guard was pushing for a prompt vote. But the insurgents were blocking action in hopes of rallying public feeling against Lorimer. Given
this impasse, Beveridge struck a deal with the old guard. The
insurgents would permit a vote on Lorimer. In return, party leaders
agreed that Lodge would surrender floor management of the tariff
board bill, that Beveridge would take charge of the measure, that
the bill would be made the unfinished business before the Senate,
and that the chamber would sit "all night & every night" to break any
Democratic filibuster.[8]

The Democrats, however, would not permit a vote on the bill until
8:30 A.M. on 4 March, three and a half hours before Congress was to
adjourn. Although the Senate approved the measure by a fifty-six to
twenty vote, the Democrats in the House took advantage—with the
connivance of the G.O.P. leadership, progressives charged—of the
log jam in the closing hours of the session to block action by the lower
chamber. Beveridge was bitterly disappointed: after making the deal
on the Lorimer vote, he was outfoxed and the tariff board bill killed.

The outcome of the fight over Canadian reciprocity was another
disappointment for the Indiana lawmaker. The long quiescent Canadian reciprocity issue had been revived by a narrowly averted tariff
war with America's northern neighbor following adoption of the
Payne-Aldrich law. Although the administration succeeded in working out a temporary settlement, the narrowly averted clash converted
Beveridge into a champion of reciprocity with Canada. He even took
up the issue in his senatorial campaign. Reciprocity with Canada, he
told his audiences, "would mean millions of dollars of profit every
year to Indiana's factories." History, he exclaimed, has few examples
of "a policy so blind, so foolish and so ruinous as that so-called
statesmanship which, instead of fostering a purchasing market in
Canada, is making Canada a manufacturing competitor."[9]

The reciprocity agreement reached in January 1911, made only
limited reductions on American manufactured goods. The Canadians
reaped the major benefit, as nearly all Canadian natural products
were given free access to the American market. But President Taft
was delighted with what he regarded as a brilliant political stroke

8. "Memo on the Tariff Commission Bill" [28 February 1911], Box 326, BP.
9. *Indianapolis Star,* 11 October 1910.

that would neutralize popular discontent over the cost of living while discomfiting the insurgents—those "valiant 'defenders of God's patient poor,'" as he called them.[10] One after another of the insurgents and even "near-insurgents"—Bristow, Clapp, Cummins, La Follette, Nelson, William E. Borah of Idaho, Jonathan Bourne, Jr., of Oregon, Joseph M. Dixon of Montana, and Coe I. Crawford of South Dakota —assailed the reciprocity agreement as sellout of the farmer for the profit of the Eastern manufacturer.

Beveridge alone of the G.O.P. senators who had voted against the Payne-Aldrich bill supported Canadian reciprocity. In the heyday of his imperialism, the Hoosier had looked forward to the time when the stars and stripes would extend over our northern neighbor. Though disclaiming any annexationist ambitions, he may have in his heart of hearts looked upon reciprocity as a step toward fulfillment of that long-standing dream. A more immediate benefit was the opening of a badly wanted new market for America's surplus manufactured goods. He defended reciprocity as a conservation measure that would safeguard American forests and natural resources from exhaustion. And, most important, he told the upper chamber, reciprocity would lower the high cost of living that was rousing so much discontent. At stake was the larger welfare of the mass of the American people. "Let no small and temporary motives of local and unwise selfishness," he pleaded with his fellow lawmakers, "prevent the beginning of this noble policy."[11]

Throwing all his influence behind the agreement, even calling Congress back into special session, Taft picked up sufficient Democratic votes to carry the day. But Canadian voters in the general election of 21 September 1911 repudiated the government of prime minister Wilfred Laurier and the reciprocity agreement. Opponents of reciprocity north of the border had successfully aroused their countrymen's nationalist sensibilities by picturing reciprocity as an annexationist plot. Unfortunate utterances upon the American side lent substance to this propaganda. Perhaps most damaging was Taft's famous slip in his message of 26 January conveying the agreement to Congress, that the Canadian people had come "to the parting of the ways."[12]

---

10. Taft to Aldrich, 29 January 1911, Aldrich Papers.
11. *CR*, 61st Cong., 3rd sess., 1911, 46, pt. 3: 2181–85.
12. L. Ethan Ellis, *Reciprocity 1911: A Study in Canadian-American Relations* (New Haven, Toronto, and London, 1939), p. 114.

Beveridge was disappointed though not surprised by the result. After leaving the Senate in March 1911, he had undertaken to prepare a series of magazine articles on Canada. As a result of his trips to the north and interviews with Canadians prominent in all walks of life, he learned at first hand the strength of the protected interests in Canada, how the opponents of reciprocity were exploiting the annexation bogey to win popular support, and how the administration had fallen into the trap. When the Laurier government was defeated, he blamed Taft's "frightful blunder" in making his "parting of the ways" speech as "the final influence that beat Reciprocity in Canada—the decisive influence." Taft, he said, "is under some fell decree of fate to make blunders."[13]

The last battle of his Senate career had a happier outcome. This was his fight to unseat William Lorimer—the notorious "blond boss" of Chicago—as senator from Illinois. The background was the long bitter factional struggle within Illinois Republicanism. Although incumbent senator Albert J. Hopkins had won a plurality in the August 1908 preferential primary, the result was not binding on the legislature, and Lorimer was determined to block his reelection. The result was a legislative deadlock lasting five months. Not until 26 May 1909, on the ninety-fifth joint ballot, did a bipartisan majority of fifty-three Democrats and fifty-five Republicans break the impasse by electing Lorimer. Rumors circulated at the time that the lavish expenditure of money had greased the way for Lorimer's election. The storm broke publicly on 30 April 1910, when the *Chicago Tribune* published a sworn statement by Democratic legislator Charles A. White that he and other Democratic members of the legislature had been bribed to vote for Lorimer.

White related that he had been paid $1,000 by Lee O'Neil Browne, a downstate Democratic leader, to vote for Lorimer, and that in July one of Browne's lieutenants, Robert E. Wilson, had met with him and two other Democratic legislators who had voted for Lorimer, Michael Link and H. J. C. Beckemeyer, in a Saint Louis hotel and paid each $900 as their share of the slush fund—"jack pot"—used to influence legislation in the legislature. Link and Beckemeyer admitted to having been bribed. A third Democratic legislator, state senator Daniel W. Holtslaw, confessed that he had been paid $2,500 by fellow

13. Beveridge to Albert Shaw, 22 September [1911], Shaw Papers.

Democratic senator John Broderick to vote for Lorimer. The case became a national scandal. During the 1910 campaign, Theodore Roosevelt warned the Hamilton Club of Chicago that he would not be its banquet guest if Lorimer attended. Lorimer's invitation was withdrawn. And running for reelection in Indiana, Beveridge watched nervously lest the old guard pull "the Lorimer plan" and knife him in the legislature if the G.O.P. won a majority.[14]

At Lorimer's request, the Senate Committee on Elections and Privileges undertook an investigation. The report submitted by the committee majority to the Senate on 21 December 1900, upheld Lorimer's title to his seat. Under the existing precedents, the report explained, there were two grounds for declaring the election of a senator invalid. The first was that the person elected had himself "participated in one or more acts of bribery or attempted bribery, or sanctioned or encouraged the same"; the second was that "by bribery or corrupt practices enough votes were obtained for him to change the result of the election."

Neither was the case in Lorimer's election, the majority concluded. There was no evidence presented "which would tend in the remotest degree to implicate Senator Lorimer in any personal act of bribery or attempted bribery." As for the four self-confessed bribe takers, the bulk of the majority report was devoted to an attempt to discredit their testimony. But even if the four had been bribed, the report concluded, Lorimer still had a valid majority. The committee majority explicitly rejected the argument that the three bribe givers were as guilty as the bribe takers and that their votes were therefore invalid. Even if they had bribed others, a committee member told the Senate, there was no evidence that they had been bribed themselves to vote for Lorimer.[15]

Beveridge had refused to sign the majority report. When the committee had met in executive session of 20 December, he had protested that he had not had sufficient time to study the testimony in the case. After the committee majority went ahead and made its report, he demanded that the report lie on the table until he could go over the evidence. He made a thorough examination of the conflicting

---

14. Beveridge to William Dudley Foulke, 15 February 1910, Foulke Papers (ISL).

15. CR, 61st Cong., 3rd sess., 1910–11, 46, pt. 1: 547–52; pt. 2: 1415–25.

testimony and the available precedents governing corrupt elections in
the United States and abroad—"an amount of work," he wrote
George H. Lorimer, "which if I were in the law, I would not do for
less than a hundred thousand dollars."[16]

On 9 January, he roused a storm in the upper chamber by submitting a minority report holding Lorimer's election "invalid under
any possible view of the law." The majority report had exonerated
the three accused bribe givers on the ground that that had denied
the accusation. What did the majority expect the accused men to do?
replied Beveridge. "Did the majority expect everybody concerned
with these corrupt proceedings to confess?" Given the difficulty of
proving bribery, the accepted principle of law was "that bribery may
be and often must be proved by circumstantial evidence." And that
evidence was "overwhelming and conclusive." That made "at least
seven tainted votes"—the three bribe givers being "as guilty as the
four bribe takers."

Since there were 202 votes cast, with Lorimer having 108, if these
seven votes were subtracted from his total, his vote was 101—less
than a majority. And the evidence, Beveridge argued, convicted three
more legislators, of whom two had denied the charges, and the third
had died, "of having shared the plunder at the same time and places—
from the same hands and for the same consideration as their fellow
members who repeatedly testified to having received it." Beveridge
concluded by questioning whether "a seasoned politician" of Lorimer's experience had remained ignorant of what was transpiring. On
the contrary, the record showed intimate collaboration between Lorimer and "the chief instrument of bribery," Lee O'Neil Browne. Thus
Lorimer's election was invalid "even under the precedents which the
majority cite."

But the Hoosier lawmaker wished to go farther; he asked the
Senate to adopt a new and more stringent rule making a single act of
bribery invalidate the whole election. The defenders of the existing
precedents argued that such a rule would be unfair to a personally
honest candidate with an honest majority whose overzealous friends
had without his knowledge bribed some legislators. That danger,
Beveridge replied, was minor compared to the danger to free institutions from corrupt elections. If some votes were corrupt, was it not

---

16. Beveridge to George H. Lorimer, 24 December 1910, Lorimer Papers.

reasonable to assume others equally tainted whose existence could not be proved? Since expulsion would require a two-thirds vote, Beveridge moved a resolution, which required only a majority, declaring that William Lorimer "was not duly and legally elected to a seat in the Senate of the United States."[17]

Praise poured in to the Indiana lawmaker. "The whole country is with you in your minority report," Albert Shaw told him. Roosevelt had been convinced of Lorimer's guilt even before Beveridge submitted his report. But he praised the report as "conclusive" and urged his two old friends, Henry Cabot Lodge and Elihu Root, to vote against Lorimer. Taft helped line up a "good many of the regular Republicans on the side of . . . decency and honesty in politics."[18]

At first, Beveridge was confident of winning and pushed for a swift vote. But a powerful bipartisan coalition rallied behind Lorimer. Many Southern Democrats led by Senator Joseph W. Bailey of Texas balked at any federal interference with the electoral process. G.O.P. regulars looked upon the Illinois lawmaker as one of their own. Who could trust the word of self-confessed bribe takers, asked Republican Senator Jacob H. Gallinger of New Hampshire? Democratic Senator Thomas H. Paynter of Kentucky charged that White was a frustrated blackmailer; that Holtslaw had been induced to confess in return for the dropping of an indictment for perjury in another case; that the confessions of Link and Beckemeyer had been extorted by third degree methods. Bailey even claimed that the deposit slip showing that Holtslaw had banked the bribe money was a forgery. The case against Lorimer, declared Michigan's Julius C. Burrows, was a "conspiracy" by the *Chicago Tribune* to destroy its long-time political foe.

In reply, Beveridge summed up his indictment against "the sitting Member" from Illinois in a brilliant, three-day-long speech that was repeatedly interrupted by applause from the galleries. He ridiculed the charges of a "conspiracy" to frame Lorimer. "If so," he retorted, "that 'conspiracy' included reputable lawyers, State's attorneys, sheriffs, judges on the bench—everybody, nearly, it would appear." The evidence of large-scale bribery was "abundant and conclusive." He acknowledged that there was no evidence directly linking Lorimer

---

17. *CR*, 61st Cong., 3rd sess., 1910–11, 46, pt. 1: 654–57.
18. Shaw to Beveridge, 18 January 1911, BP. Theodore Roosevelt to Henry Cabot Lodge, 31 January 1911, in Morison, *The Letters of Theodore Roosevelt*, 7: 216–19. Taft to Roosevelt, 6 January 1911, Taft Papers.

with the bribery. But the common law regarded as an agent "*anyone who has a color for acting in behalf of the candidate.*" Since the evidence was overwhelming that Browne had been working closely with Lorimer to line up votes for his election, that fact "fixes the agency."

Lorimer's defenders had argued that even if there were seven, or as many as ten, tainted votes, Lorimer still had a valid majority; that those votes were null and void and should be subtracted from the total number of votes, thus leaving 192 legal votes cast and Lorimer with 98 untainted votes. Beveridge replied that nothing could be more unreasonable or dangerous. If that interpretation of the law were accepted, all a corrupt aspirant would have to do would be to bribe enough voters to reduce the total to a level where his honest votes constituted a majority. Corruption of the election process, he warned his fellow lawmakers, threatened the foundations of representative government. Men everywhere were asking, "What is going to become of the American experiment for liberty? Is it to succeed or is it to fail?" That was the question before the Senate. "*American institutions are on trial.*"[19]

The fight was the more bitter because of its link with the struggle underway over the pending constitutional amendment for popular election of United States Senators. Beveridge himself underlined the tie in his answer to a tirade by New York's Elihu Root blaming the downfall of the city-states of antiquity upon an excess of democracy. The extent of the country, the Hoosier replied, the size of the population, the intelligence and increased leisure of the average voter, and improved communications made a Greek-style demagogue impossible in the United States. The framers of the Constitution had designed the Senate as the bulwark of property rights against the masses. But property was not threatened in America. "Property needs no special representation in government. All that property needs is honesty on the part of its owners."

Suppose, Beveridge asked, the legislature picked someone the people did not want for senator? "Such things," he reminded the chamber with the Lorimer case in mind, "have occurred." That the agent—the legislature—should override the will of the principal—the people—was absurd. In state after state, however, the legislature

---

19. *CR*, 61st Cong., 3rd sess., 1911, 46, pt. 4: 3260–306.

was under the thumb of the local party boss. Even where boss rule was not present, the members of the state legislature—as in his own defeat—were elected on local issues having nothing to do with the larger questions before the Senate. The popular election of senators was part of the worldwide movement to make the government more representative of—and responsive to—the popular will. "We who in modern history began the march should continue to lead that historic progress."[20]

But the old guard succeeded in exploiting Southern anxieties over possible federal interference to defeat the constitutional amendment for popular election of senators. To win Democratic support, the insurgents had cooperated with Southern Democrats in the Senate Judiciary Committee to add to the joint resolution for popular elections the provision that the "times, places, and manner of holding elections for Senators shall be as prescribed in each State by the legislature thereof."[21] But when the resolution came before the upper chamber, old guard senator George Sutherland of Utah moved an amendment upholding federal control over senatorial elections. Given his nationalism, Beveridge joined with the G.O.P. regulars to pass the Sutherland amendment. Thereupon, enough Southern Democrats joined with the old guard to defeat the entire resolution.

This same bipartisan coalition lined up behind Lorimer. A head count by old guard leader W. Murray Crane in mid-February found a "safe" majority against unseating the Illinois lawmaker.[22] And with the tables reversed, the Lorimer supporters began pushing for a prompt vote on the Beveridge resolution while the insurgents sought to delay action until the next session when the progressive bloc in the Senate would be larger. But with the session rapidly drawing to a finish, Beveridge broke the impasse by his deal with the G.O.P. leadership on the tariff board bill. At the showdown on 1 March, his resolution to unseat Lorimer was defeated forty-six to forty—the lineup being nearly identical with the alignment on the constitutional amendment for popular election of senators. Beveridge could not hide his disappointment. But he remained confident that the battle

---

20. Ibid., pt. 3: 2251–59.
21. U.S., Congress, Senate, Committee on the Judiciary, *Election of Senators by Popular Vote: Report to Accompany S.J. Res. 134*, 61st Cong., 3rd sess., 1911, S. Rept. 961, p. 1.
22. W. Murray Crane to Aldrich, 17 February 1911, Aldrich Papers.

was not yet over. We have tried this case before the people of the country, he told a newspaper interviewer, and the people will render the final judgment.

That judgment vindicated the Hoosier. New evidence led to a reopening of the case, and in July 1912 the Senate voted fifty-five to twenty-eight to unseat Lorimer. And, perhaps more important, the continued agitation of the case spurred final congressional approval of the constitutional amendment for popular election of United States senators.

Although Beveridge supported Canadian reciprocity and Taft backed the unseating of Lorimer, the session brought no reconciliation between the president and the Indiana lawmaker. When the National Progressive Republican League was launched in January 1911 to spearhead the fight against Taft's renomination, Beveridge was a charter member. He brushed aside pleas from political lieutenants that he make peace with the White House. "Is it possible," he replied, "for us to equal in manipulation" the old guard leaders in Indiana? Moreover, public sentiment was with the progressives. "There can be no question that this movement is the great, growing and inevitably winning movement, and that speedily." To play up to the chief executive "would be to defeat the very end we have in view."[23]

While Beveridge was away in Washington, his rivals in Indiana were busily at work. "How the mighty are fallen!" exulted the editor of the *Noblesville Ledger* to Charles W. Fairbanks. "Especially the *little dictators* and *big demagogues*." There must be "a re-organization of our party on *safe* and *sane* lines. We want no more of the *personal ambition* and *self-glorification* business in Indiana." The anti-Beveridge forces were heartened by signs of presidential sympathy. "The President now is extremely friendly," ex-senator James A. Hemenway reported to a lieutenant. After 4 March, when Beveridge was out of the Senate, "there is no doubt but what our friends will have something to say" about the patronage in the state.[24]

The showdown was not long in coming. To solidify his grip upon the party machinery, Beveridge induced United States Marshal

---

23. Beveridge to John F. Hayes, 13 January 1911, BP.
24. Will H. Craig to Charles W. Fairbanks, 25 November, 1 December 1910, Fairbanks Paper (LL). James A. Hemenway to Lucius C. Embree, 7 December 1910, Embree Papers.

Henry C. Pettit to resign early in January and recommended the appointment of Republican state chairman Edwin M. Lee to the place. But his factional rivals rallied to block Lee's appointment. Hemenway told the president that the appointment would be "disastrous." Joseph B. Kealing warned that Lee was a Beveridge man first, last, and always and would, if he had "to choose between the President and Beveridge, follow the latter." The president would be making "a great mistake," another standpatter wrote, if he kept Beveridge's "departing influence alive by making any appointments at his special instance and request."[25]

Taft was in a quandary. He had, he explained to Fairbanks, "no confidence in Beveridge at all," personally or politically, and was not "in the slightest degree misled as to his continued hostility, whatever he may say."[26] But he had promised in the so-called "Norton letter" in September not to discriminate against the insurgents in patronage matters and was reluctant to go back on his word. Adding to his perplexity was conflicting advice within the administration's inner circle. In his dilemma, he turned to Harry S. New for advice. As Republican national committeeman from Indiana and the former Republican national chairman, New had become personally friendly with Taft. And the chief executive regarded him as neutral between the factions in Indiana.

From 1899 to 1904, New had managed to keep on friendly terms with Beveridge and Fairbanks. This political tight-rope act had won him election as G.O.P. national committeeman in 1900 and reelection four years later. But he blamed the vice-president for frustrating his ambition to go to the Senate in 1905 and lined up with Beveridge in the continuing factional struggle within the Indiana G.O.P. Privately, however, he never forgave Beveridge for not supporting his senatorial aspirations. His misgivings over Beveridge's growing progressivism widened the gap. In view of the confused political situation in the Hoosier state, the ambitious New saw the possibility of taking over the party leadership himself, backed by the federal patronage. When the chief executive asked his advice, he counseled against Lee's appointment.

25. Joseph B. Kealing to Hemenway, 20 January 1911 (telegram); to George W. Wickersham, 27 January 1911; J. H. Claypool to Taft, 26 January 1911, Taft Papers.
26. Taft to Fairbanks, 20 February 1911, ibid.

New's advice was decisive in deciding Taft against appointing Lee marshal. Still he was reluctant to make an open break with Beveridge. The president, a Fairbanks lieutenant reported, exaggerated Beveridge's popularity in the Hoosier state. And he felt that Lee deserved a reward for his labors as Republican state chairman. As a possible compromise, he suggested appointing Lee the Collector of Internal Revenue for the Sixth District—replacing Elam H. Neal, who was still under fire from the Civil Service Commission for his political activities and who had come to the parting of the ways with Beveridge—and "somebody with a leaning toward Fairbanks and the other side" as marshal.[27]

But Beveridge remained adamant about Lee's appointment as marshal. The issue had become too symbolically important for him to retreat. Fighting for his political life, he arranged for a petition signed by nearly all the Republican members of the state legislature and all the members of Republican state committee in support of Lee's appointment. He reminded the president of his promise not to discriminate against the insurgents in patronage members, assured him of his personal loyalty, and promised that his supporters would not trumpet Lee's appointment as a "Beveridge Triumph."[28]

Even louder protests came from the other side against removal of Neal. Surely, an old guard leader appealed, the president did not wish to assist Beveridge in punishing Neal for his "refusal to join in his crusade to discredit the administration." Ex-governor Winfield Durbin warned that Beveridge was and always would be "a disturber." "Would it be the part of political wisdom to rehabilitate him by giving him recognition in the distribution of patronage?" The collectorship, New advised, was "a much more important place politically" than the marshalship and Lee as collector would remain under Beveridge's "domination."[29]

In the face of these protests, Taft abandoned the idea of replacing Neal. But whom should he appoint as marshal? The Fairbanks-Hemenway-Kealing faction was pushing former Indiana secretary of state Fred A. Sims. But New was hoping to build his own personal machine and urged that "both factions be ignored and new blood

27. Taft to Addison C. Harris, 25 March 1911, ibid.
28. "Memo for Mr. Norton" from Gus J. K[arger], 7 February 1911, ibid.
29. George B. Lockwood to Taft, 25 March 1911; Winfield T. Durbin to Taft, 27 March 1911; Harry S. New to Taft, 26 March 1911, ibid.

selected" to build up "an entirely new organization." New's maneuvers brought heated protests from "the Fairbanks Organization."[30] To smooth over the friction between his would-be supporters in Indiana, Taft picked Edward H. Schmidt, a neutral figure acceptable to New and the Fairbanks-Hemenway-Kealing faction.

The turndown of Lee was the more galling for Beveridge because the loyalty of many of his followers ran no deeper than political expediency. When he tried to line up the Republican state legislators in the new legislature to support the Oregon system for the direct election of senators, his lieutenants reported that the proposal could not receive the approval of the G.O.P. caucus. His political weakness was further underlined when Taft reappointed old guardsman H. P. Loveland as postmaster at Peru despite Beveridge's warning that he would regard the action as a personal affront because of Loveland's activities against his reelection. Although Beveridge had his fellow insurgents in the Senate try to block Loveland's confirmation when Congress reconvened, the appointment went through. Forces loyal to the administration—and hostile to Beveridge—were in the saddle in Indiana.

---

30. New to Taft, 26 March 1911; "Memo for Mr. Hilles" from Gus J. K[arger], 6 April 1911, ibid.

16

Battling for the Lord at Armageddon

As 4 March 1911 approached, Beveridge had to decide what he would do after leaving the Senate. He could return to Indianapolis and reopen his law office. But the difficulties of starting practice from scratch did not appeal to him. He could, as many defeated lawmakers did, remain in Washington as a lawyer-lobbyist. But that would make a political comeback difficult, if not impossible, and he did not think his political career finished. So the law was out. Mrs. Beveridge had independent means. And he had found a ready market for his magazine articles. His minimum price for an article was $500, which he raised by the 1920s to $700. Through his writing, he could keep his name before the public and expound his views on current questions while retaining his freedom to continue politically active.

Because of the public interest in affairs north of the border spurred by the reciprocity fight, he undertook a series of articles on Canada, which he planned to expand into a full-length book. After the close of the session, he made two whirlwind trips to the north and found much to admire in the Dominion and much that his fellow countrymen could profit from. He applauded Canada's new antitrust law for preserving "industrial efficiency" while eliminating "financial piracy"; he praised her law for conciliation of industrial disputes as "the most notable and successful experiment ever tried in that perplexing field"; he hailed her immigration policies for maintaining "a homogeneous people"; he lauded the framers of the Canadian constitution for learning from the American experience "the disastrous results of the doctrine of States' rights"; and he extolled Canada's "system of responsible Parliamentary government by political parties."[1]

In late May, he sailed with his family to Europe for a badly needed rest. He rented a villa outside Lucerne, Switzerland, for the summer. The relaxation from the pace of his last years in the Senate was welcome. Catherine was "revelling in her most deserved holiday;" his two children were "blooming like flowers;" and he himself felt stronger "than for many, many years." But he kept a watchful eye upon political developments in the United States. Only his family kept him at Lucerne into the fall. "Lord! but I'm tired of Europe," he complained to a friend. "Never again for me—such an expedition as this."[2]

When Beveridge arrived back in the United States in October 1911, the political situation remained confused. After the mid-term election of 1910, Taft had launched a drive to maintain old guard supremacy within the G.O.P. and assure his own renomination. At Beveridge's return, the chief executive was in the middle of a seven-week cross-country tour to mend his political fences. In June 1911, Robert M. La Follette had formally announced his candidacy for the G.O.P. nomination. The head of the La Follette movement in Indiana was Rudolph Leeds, the young millionaire publisher of the *Indianapolis Sun* and the *Richmond Palladium*. But the Wisconsin senator's campaign was not making much headway either in Indiana or in the nation at large. Hanging over all political calculations was the question mark of Theodore Roosevelt. Would he support Taft for renomination? Would he back La Follette? Would he himself run?

Even before his return, Beveridge was bombarded by conflicting

---

1. *SEP*, 1 July 1911, p. 10; 23 September 1911, p. 26; 26 August 1911, p. 19. *American Review of Reviews* 44 (October 1911): 471, 476.
2. Beveridge to Lucius B. Swift, 4 July 1911, Swift Papers. Beveridge to George W. Perkins, 11 September [1911], Perkins Papers.

advice and pleas. Many of his long-time personal friends and supporters expected that Taft would win renomination and urged him to
make his peace with the chief executive. But no reconciliation was
possible. He was too bitter over the way the president had treated
him, and he was convinced that the administration's policies were a
disaster for the party and the country. The Canadian reciprocity
fiasco showed Taft at his blundering worst. Worse were the newspaper reports that the administration planned new and sweeping
antitrust prosecutions. "His insane policy of destroying great business
organizations instead of regulating and controlling them," Beveridge
raged, "is even worse than his other blunders. It will demoralize—
almost destroy—business for years."[3]

At the same time, he rebuffed with one excuse after another the
appeals of the La Follette managers that he come out for the Wisconsin senator. For he had dreams of his own as a possible dark-horse
candidate for the nomination. Reports indicated that the La Follette
campaign was lagging. He dismissed Taft as politically finished.
"Even the office-holders won't be for him—they want to hold their
offices & they know Taft would be defeated." Roosevelt was keeping
out of the tangle. "I think, George," he wrote Perkins from Switzerland, "that the great hour is almost here."[4]

After years of litigation, Shaffer won control of the Star League in
October 1911 and began featuring Beveridge as a presidential possibility in his newspapers. Another Beveridge-for-president booster was
Michigan's progressive governor, Chase S. Osborn. When the *New
York American* asked him whom he thought Roosevelt would support
for the presidential nomination, he answered: Beveridge. At the
beginning of January, he publicly called upon Taft and La Follette
to withdraw in favor of Beveridge or Roosevelt to heal the party's
wounds. The Michigan governor's statement, Beveridge reported to
his cousin, had made "a very deep impression" throughout the
country.[5]

Beveridge suffered, however, from lack of support in his home state.
His rebuff on the marshalship showed Hoosier politicians which way
the wind was blowing. All Indiana patronage was channeled through

---

3. Beveridge to Perkins, 24 September [1911], Perkins Papers.
4. Ibid.
5. Beveridge to E. L. McClain, 4 January 1911 [1912], BP.

Republican national committeeman Harry S. New. Jumping on the bandwagon, the Fairbanks-Hemenway-Kealing faction declared support of the president's renomination. Even state chairman E. M. Lee, continuing to angle for a federal job, was saying that Indiana would be solidly for Taft.

When his reward failed to materialize, Lee did a sudden turnabout. Announcing for reelection as state chairman, Lee declared that Taft could not carry Indiana, that the G.O.P. should not nominate a sure loser, and that the Hoosier state should send an uninstructed delegation to the 1912 national convention. Although denying any hand in Lee's statement, Beveridge hailed the state chairman as "about the bravest man I ever have heard of in politics." And he predicted an uprising of the rank and file against "the bosslets."[6]

But Lee's statement galvanized the administration forces into action. The State Committee hastened to deny that Lee was speaking for the committee. The Indiana Republican Editorial Association endorsed the president's renomination. When the hoped-for groundswell of support did not appear, Lee gave up his fight. The administration backers swept the district chairmanship races, and the new state committee selected old guardsman Fred A. Sims, the former secretary of state, as state chairman. The results, Taft's secretary and campaign manager boasted, showed the falsity of the talk that Indiana was hostile to the president.[7]

The final blow to Beveridge's hopes was the growing boom for Theodore Roosevelt. The Hoosier took no part in the first phases of the Roosevelt movement. When Michigan newspaper publisher Frank Knox appealed to him in mid-January to come out for the former chief executive, Beveridge made no reply. He even warned Roosevelt—or at least, later claimed he did, that, given Taft's grip upon the party machinery, Roosevelt could not win the nomination no matter what his popular support was. But when T. R. announced his candidacy on 25 February, Beveridge swung into line. The ties of personal loyalty to his old chief remained strong. Roosevelt stood for the same principles and purposes as he did. Beveridge was convinced that Taft could not possibly win—and he continued to think the worst about the Democrats. He was moved by his personal bitterness

---

6. Beveridge to Albert Shaw, 29 December 1911, Shaw Papers. Beveridge Gifford Pinchot, 20 December 1911, Pinchot Papers.

7. *Indianapolis News,* 1 February 1912.

toward the chief executive. And there were his own political ambitions. If his rivals maintained their grip upon the Indiana G.O.P., his hopes for a political comeback were dim.[8]

Taking the stump for Roosevelt, Beveridge denounced the administration's wild trust busting—symbolized by its suit against Beveridge's archetype of the "good" trust, the United States Steel Corporation—for paralyzing "honest business men" with uncertainty and fear. He praised T. R. as the "strong" chief executive required "to see that justice is done to all and denied to none" and extolled Roosevelt's record as champion of the public weal against "the powers of pillage"; but he soft-pedaled Roosevelt's demand in his Columbus speech for recall of state judicial decisions as a side issue. "As party men we want to win. As citizens we want the great forward movement in American life to go on. That is why we want, as our candidate for President, the leader of that movement and the man who surely can be elected, Theodore Roosevelt."[9]

Beveridge exuded confidence that a popular uprising would carry the state for T. R. But the Roosevelt forces faced formidable odds in Indiana. There was not sufficient time for them to make an extensive canvass or build an effective statewide organization. The administration cracked the patronage whip to keep the federal officeholders in line for the chief executive, and promises of appointments were freely made to gain the support of would-be officeholders. The *Indianapolis News* played up the prominence in the Roosevelt campaign of Beveridge's friend George W. Perkins to stigmatize T. R. as the trust-backed candidate. His advocacy of the recall of state judicial decisions alienated many lawyers and businessmen. Even Shaffer was so put off that the Star League newspapers joined in assailing Roosevelt as a threat to the American system of government.

Although there was much latent Roosevelt sentiment in the Hoosier state, the voters could not directly express their preferences. And the administration forces had the advantage of controlling the party machinery throughout most of the state. The county chairmen decided upon the method of electing the delegates to the district and state conventions that would choose the delegates to the national conven-

---

8. A former aide charged that Beveridge had appealed to him to support T. R. on the ground that Roosevelt's nomination meant "his political life or death": ibid., 2 October 1912.

9. *Indianapolis Star*, 14, 20 March 1912.

tion, selected the times and places of voting, and named the election officers and contest committees. That the Taft men would exploit their advantage to the fullest was shown in the first major test of strength—the election on 15 March of the delegates to the Seventh District convention. In voting marred by wholesale frauds and ballot-box thievery, the Marion County G.O.P. organization delivered 128 out of the 134 delegates for the president.

Nevertheless, the upsurge of Roosevelt sentiment nearly prevailed in the election of delegates to the state convention. While the state convention would name only the four delegates-at-large, the results would have far-reaching psychological impact in the country as a whole. The first returns showed a strong Roosevelt tide. Even the Taft managers for a time lost hope. The Roosevelt leaders were exultant. Beveridge reported to national headquarters that the Roosevelt ticket had carried at least eight and possibly as many as ten of the state's thirteen congressional districts. "We have won great victory for you," he wired T. R., "against tremendous odds and in spite of most shameful methods ever seen in this state. Work now ahead of us is to prevent their stealing them."[10]

As the later returns came in, the Taft managers regained their confidence and claimed a majority of from 150 to 200 out of the total of 1,439 delegates. But the vote was so close that the result depended upon the outcome of more than one hundred contests. Most were from Marion County, where the Roosevelt forces charged their ticket had been counted out. But the administration forces packed the credentials committee of the convention and seated the bulk of the pro-Taft claimants. A last-minute proposal by John C. Shaffer to split the delegates-at-large for the sake of party harmony was turned down by the president himself.[11] At the showdown, the convention voted to uphold the action of the credentials committee, the pro-Taft delegates placed on the temporary roll supplying the winning margin. After the convention had adjourned, a group of Roosevelt supporters met and named a rival delegation to the national convention.

The story was repeated at the district level. The Roosevelt forces captured the Sixth, Eighth, Ninth, Eleventh, and Twelfth Districts.

---

10. Beveridge to Theodore Roosevelt, 23 March 1912 (telegram), BP.
11. John C. Shaffer to William H. Taft, 25 March 1912 (telegram), Hilles Papers. Taft to Harry S. New, 25 March [1912] (telegram), New Papers (ISL).

The Taft people captured the Second, Fourth, Fifth, and Tenth Districts. Although the Roosevelt managers continued to cry about fraud and robbery in the Seventh District, no formal contest was filed before the G.O.P. National Committee because insufficient contests had been made at the time of the voting to give T. R. a majority in the district convention even if the Roosevelt challenges were upheld. In the First, Third, and Thirteenth Districts, however, the Roosevelt supporters bolted, held rump conventions, elected Roosevelt delegates, and filed contests before the National Committee.

Beveridge angrily charged that "every method known to politics," including "the corrupt use of money," "has been employed to change the will of the people as expressed at the polls." Although he had vowed not to campaign outside Indiana, he put aside the work of expanding his Canadian articles into a book and—at his own expense —undertook a cross-country speaking tour. He had come out in support of Roosevelt, he explained to Shaffer, "as a personal matter." But "the shameful things done" by the president's forces in Indiana "makes me feel, for the first time, like jumping into this fight with all my strength as a matter of principle. No cause should succeed which has to depend upon such outlaw methods."[12]

Sometimes he felt so disgusted that he talked of giving up politics. His campaign trip was physically exhausting. His giving up his magazine writing imposed a financial burden. He was unhappy over the long absences from his family. He resented the lack of appreciation for his work shown by the Roosevelt high command. But the growing possibility of a deadlock revived his hopes that the party might yet turn to him for the presidency.[13] And when that hope faded, he was receptive to the talk of himself for the vice-presidency.[14] In a last-minute switch—which the Taft backers blamed upon Beveridge— John C. Shaffer threw the support of his newspapers to Roosevelt and called for Beveridge as his running mate.[15]

But the G.O.P. National Committee awarded 235 of the 254 contested seats, including all the Indiana delegates, to Taft. At the convention, the administration steamroller achieved the chief execu-

---

12. Beveridge to Joseph M. Dixon [24 March 1912] (telegram); to John A. Kautz, 29 March 1912; to Shaffer, 28 March 1912, BP.
13. Beveridge to Chase S. Osborn, 13 April 1912, BP.
14. Beveridge to Shaw, 25 May 1912, Shaw Papers.
15. *Indianapolis Star*, 16 June 1912.

tive's renomination on the first ballot. Roosevelt's decision to lead a third party faced Beveridge with the most agonizing decision of his political life. He privately remonstrated with Roosevelt against running and stayed away from the meeting of Roosevelt delegates on the night of 22 June that launched the new party. When Roosevelt manager Senator Joseph M. Dixon of Montana asked him to sign the call for the new party's national convention, he held back. "After patient and careful thought," he wired Shaffer, "I have decided not to sign call or do or say anything whatever at present."[16]

He could not support Taft—that was "unthinkable" after the "thefts & frauds" at Chicago. Nor would he support any Democrat. But his first instinct was against following Roosevelt into the third party. Many of his most devoted personal friends and supporters in Indiana urged him not to leave the G.O.P. The emotional tug of party loyalty remained strong. "I simply cannot get myself up to joining the call for T. R.'s party," he confided to Albert Shaw early in July. "An unseen hand seems to hold me back." He had his doubts about the long-term future for the new party. He wished to be in a position to remake and rehabilitate the G.O.P. after the defeat he saw ahead. To bolt would destroy all possibility of reforming the Republican party from within. "T. R.'s party is too personal to last. We cannot hazard *all* on one campaign."[17]

Within the month, however, he had joined the new party. A complex of factors underlay his decision. There were the ties of friendship, not simply with T. R., but with George W. Perkins, who had become a leading figure in the Roosevelt camp. John C. Shaffer, having switched before the convention to support Roosevelt's nomination, had resolved to throw his lot in with the new party at least at the national level. There was his committment to the principles and policies for which the new party would stand. He had no doubt that Taft had stolen the nomination. The Indiana Bull Moose managers, anxious for his support, played upon his vanity with appeals that he alone could lead the party to victory in the Hoosier state.

And there was the question of his own political future. Albert B. Cummins of Iowa or Joseph L. Bristow of Kansas, who controlled the Republican party machinery in their states, could afford to remain

---

16. Beveridge to Shaffer [4 July 1912] (telegram), BP.
17. Beveridge to Shaw [6], 9 July [1912], Shaw Papers.

within the G.O.P. even while supporting Roosevelt for the presidency. But Beveridge was in a different position. Whatever he did, there would be a Progressive party in Indiana. That party would draw off a large part of his following in the Republican party. Thus even if the G.O.P. lost badly, his chances of recapturing control were dim. At the same time, if the new party were successful, he would be out in the cold. Seeing no alternative, he publicly announced his adherence to the Bull Moose standard on 25 July.

There was much talk of Beveridge's nomination as Roosevelt's running mate. But the state Progressive party convention was scheduled to meet before the national convention, and the demand by Indiana Bull Moosers that he run for governor was so strong that he had to accept. The platform called for the adoption of a far-reaching list of reforms: the initiative, referendum, direct primary, and recall "applied to all elective, executive, administrative and legislative officers"; a presidential preference primary; ratification of the proposed constitutional amendment for the popular election of United States Senators; corrupt-practices legislation; women's suffrage; a state civil-service law; a state inheritance tax; a public utilities commission; prohibition of the issuance of watered stock; free school books; improved vocational education; home rule and the commission form of government for Indiana's cities; better roads for Hoosier farmers; a minimum wage law for women; stricter child labor laws; a workman's compensation law; and a federal "industrial commission" modeled upon the Interstate Commerce Commission to regulate "corporations doing an interstate business." The liquor plank endorsed county local option as "a temporary relief" but declared that the "permanent solution" was the adoption of the initiative and referendum to allow the people to decide. "If I am elected Governor," Beveridge promised the cheering delegates, "no boss will stand between me and the people. . . . No agent of any machine, no lobbyist or any corporation, no anti-public influence will have any back door or front door entrance to the state house."[18]

The Roosevelt high command had asked Beveridge to deliver the keynote address at the national convention. But when he learned that T. R. was planning to address the gathering the same day, he protested that Roosevelt's "Confession of Faith" would overshadow

18. *Indianapolis Star*, 2 August 1912.

his own effort. Roosevelt's top campaign advisers, however, persuaded him to delay the speech until the second day of the convention in response to his formal nomination. Given the limelight, Beveridge aroused the assembled delegates to fervent applause with his first words. "We stand," he proclaimed, "for a nobler America. . . . We stand for a broader liberty, a fuller justice. We stand for social brotherhood as against savage individualism. We stand for an intelligent co-operation instead of a reckless competition. . . . We stand for a representative government that represents the people. We battle for the actual rights of man." The Progressive party "comes from the grass roots. It has grown from the soil of the people's hard necessities."

Its first target was to break the grip of "the invisible government" of the "corrupt boss" and "special interests," to "make sure the rule of the people" through the initiative, referendum, direct primary, recall, and popular election of United States Senators. Its second goal to maintain and foster prosperity, which required adoption of a "genuine, permanent, nonpartisan tariff commission" to "take the tariff out of politics" and the replacing of the Sherman Act with up-to-date legislation that would strike at the "evils of big business" rather than at "big business itself." The third major problem facing the American people was "a more just distribution" of that prosperity. The Progressive party, he told the delegates, took as its motto "Pass prosperity around," and thus demanded a national child labor law, a minimum wage law for women, provision for care of the aged, and even protection of male workers from "excessive toil" to save the nation's human resources "from the spoilers."[19]

With Beveridge continuing on as permanent chairman, the convention proceeded to nominate Roosevelt and California's Hiram Johnson for president and vice-president by acclamation. Behind the scenes, however, a bitter struggle was taking place over the new party's stand on the trust question. The resolutions committee approved a plank calling for "strengthening" the Sherman Act. After having assailed the law as out of date, ineffective, and even reactionary, Beveridge joined his friend George W. Perkins in protesting. He felt so strongly that in the midst of a wild demonstration on the floor of the convention he alternated between leading the cheering

---

19. Ibid., 6 August 1912.

and telephoning Roosevelt threatening to quit the party and urging
T. R. to do the same. Roosevelt quieted the Hoosier by having the
paragraph dealing with the Sherman law stricken from the platform
—but the question would continue to haunt the party.

After the convention, Beveridge went off to Seal Harbor, Maine,
for a rest. He returned to Indiana the last week of August to push
forward with the task of building the new party upon lasting foundations. The touchiest problem facing the new party was the question
of running full congressional, judicial, legislative, and county tickets.
Many Roosevelt men who had won the Republican nomination in
their localities wished to limit the new party to the presidential and
statewide races. Beveridge would not hear of this strategy. Having
broken with the party of his fathers, he called for a war to the finish
against the G.O.P. Let those on the Republican ticket "who really
are progressives at heart," he demanded, do "what others are doing all
over the country—resign from the Republican ticket and take places
on our ticket. It is just as illogical for a Progressive to be on a Republican ticket as it is for a Republican to be on a Democratic
ticket."[20]

The campaign was bitterly fought. G.O.P. leaders struggled to
rally the party faithful. To undercut the Bull Moose appeal, the state
platform took over many of the third party's leading planks. Republican endorsement of county local option won the party the support
of the Indiana Anti-Saloon League, and G.O.P. campaigners blamed
Beveridge for blocking adoption of such a plank two years before.
Republican speakers and newspapers, led by the *Indianapolis News,*
denounced T. R. as a would-be dictator trying to set himself above
the laws and the Constitution, stigmatized the third party leaders as
disappointed office-seekers, warned of the "deadly parallel" between
the Bull Moose and the Socialist platforms, and exploited George W.
Perkins's prominence as chairman of the Progressive National Executive Committee to tar the new party—and Beveridge personally,
because of his friendship with the financier—as trust-backed and
trust-dominated.

Stories about Beveridge's excessive drinking were revived. And
Indiana G.O.P. leaders leaked to the Senate committee investigating
campaign contributions that Beveridge had received in 1904 a large

---

20. Beveridge to Pemberton Pleasants, 15 September 1912, BP.

contribution from Perkins for his reelection campaign. The *Indianapolis News*, continuing its vendetta against Beveridge, gave the story front-page treatment. But this attempt to smear Beveridge failed. The witnesses before the committee testified that Beveridge had received $30,000 from Perkins, $25,000 from his cousin, wealthy Greenfield, Ohio, textile manufacturer E. L. McClain, and $2,500 from Gifford Pinchot, but that he had returned the money. Although committee chairman Moses Clapp wired him that his appearance was unnecessary in view of the testimony, Beveridge insisted upon coming and personally giving the lie to his accusers. The high point was when he quoted, at the demand of the committee, Perkins's reply: "An honest man is the noblest work of God."[21]

Although the bulk of the state's Republican newspapers remained with the G.O.P., the Indiana Progressive Press Association boasted a membership of over fifty papers, and the Star League did "heroic work" for the Bull Moosers.[22] Beveridge criss-crossed the state, covering a hundred to two hundred miles a day by automobile over poor roads, stopping by the wayside to dictate his speeches to an accompanying stenographer, delivering an average of two full-dress speeches plus three or four impromptu crossroads talks a day, shaking the hands of hundreds of wellwishers, and exhorting local party workers to "organize, organize, organize and then organize some more."[23]

When Roosevelt was shot by a fanatic in Milwaukee on 14 October, Beveridge rushed to his bedside in Chicago, put himself at the disposal of the National Committee for the rest of the campaign, and then went straight to Louisville to deliver Roosevelt's message to the American people that the fight must—and would—go on. After party leaders decided that Hiram Johnson as the vice-presidential nominee should fill the rest of Roosevelt's schedule, Beveridge resumed his Indiana speechmaking and kept up the fight right until the election. And amid the near-religious enthusiasm of his coworkers, he exuded confidence about carrying the state. "But whatever the outcome," he wired T. R. on the eve of the balloting, "I want to say to you in

21. U.S., Congress, Senate, *Campaign Contributions: Testimony before a Subcommittee of the Committee on Privileges and Elections . . .* , 62nd Cong., 3rd sess. (2 vols., Washington, 1913), 2: 1248.

22. Beveridge to Pinchot, 22 December 1913, BP.

23. *Indianapolis Star,* 5 September 1912.

advance that it has not only been a privilege but a joy to serve in such a cause as ours and under such a leader as you."[24]

Beveridge appealed to progressive-minded voters regardless of party affiliation to join in breaking the grip of the "bipartisan boss system." He pledged to enact into law the reforms in the Progressive state platform. He even came out, in response to questions from his audiences, in favor of minimum wage legislation for men. Dismissing the G.O.P. as hopelessly reactionary, he directed his sharpest fire against the Democrats. He assailed their gubernatorial nominee Samuel M. Ralston as the puppet of Tom Taggart's Indiana Democratic "machine." At first, he characterized Democratic presidential nominee Woodrow Wilson as a well-meaning, but inexperienced, man who would be helpless against his party's old guard. But as the campaign went on, he switched to a stronger line. Alarmed by the New Jersey governor's progressive appeal, he blasted Wilson as a fake reformer who lacked "a single constructive plan for ending the crying evils that oppress the people."[25]

At the same time, he took pains to reassure businessmen about the new party's soundness. Recall of judges or judicial decisions was silently buried. He promised that the Progressive program of trust regulation would free legitimate business from "the dead hand of uncertainty and fear." He denounced the Democratic attacks upon big business as "a campaign trick to excite the prejudices of the unthinking." He reaffirmed his support for "honest protection." He defended the social legislation demanded by the Progressives as "a measure of safety to society." He vowed to stand as firmly against spoliation of the rich by the poor as against unjust wealth. And he warned that Wilson's lack of experience, free-trade views, and hostility toward big business made him a threat to the nation's continued prosperity.[26]

But he failed to win over the bitterly hostile old-guard Republicans. Nor was he successful in making the inroads into Democratic support that he had hoped for. Despite his bid for labor backing, the annual convention of the Indiana Federation of Labor adopted a resolution presented by the representatives of the cigar makers' union assailing

---

24. Beveridge to Roosevelt, 4 November 1912 (telegram), BP.
25. *Indianapolis Star*, 12 September, 5, 22 October 1912. *Indianapolis News*, 2 November 1912.
26. *Indianapolis Star*, 8, 19 September, 15 October 1912.

Beveridge for failing to stop use of his name and picture to advertise a non-union-made cigar. Most union leaders in Indiana and throughout the country supported the Democratic ticket because of its anti-injunction plank. Democratic campaigners in the Hoosier state—led by Wilson, William Jennings Bryan, and Senator John W. Kern—kept reform-minded Democrats in line by affirming their own progressivism, lambasting the progressives for wanting to legalize "monopoly," and promising that a Democratic victory would mean "a new freedom for America."[27]

With the G.O.P. split, the Democrats carried the state with a plurality of more than one hundred thousand votes. But the Progressives in Indiana, as in the country at large, came in second, leaving the Republicans in third place. Beveridge led his G.O.P. rival, former governor Winfield T. Durbin, by more than thirteen thousand votes and even ran four thousand votes ahead of T. R. Although chagrined Republican leaders rationalized that thousands of G.O.P. voters had supported the Democratic ticket to insure Roosevelt's defeat, Beveridge hailed the results as "a great moral victory" heralding the long-needed realignment of parties, with the Progressives becoming the nation's liberal party and the Democrats the reactionary party. "I feel mighty good about the outcome," he wrote Gifford Pinchot. "We have done a big thing—we have founded a party which will endure."[28]

---

27. Ibid., 4 October 1912.
28. Ibid., 11 November 1912. Beveridge to Pinchot, 25 November 1912, BP.

17

From Politics to History

After the election, Beveridge turned to fulfill another dream. From his days as a law student, he had worshiped Chief Justice John Marshall as the patron saint of American nationalism and had nursed the ambition to do his biography. In 1908, he approached the editors of *Century Magazine* about the possibility of his writing a life of Marshall for serialization in the magazine. He envisaged at the time a brief interpretative sketch focusing upon Marshall's years as chief justice, along the lines of Frederick Oliver's popular biography of Alexander Hamilton. But his duties in the Senate, his losing bid for reelection, the fight over the 1912 Republican nomination, and the launching of the Progressive party kept him from going ahead until December 1912.

Once at work, he realized that the job was bigger than he had anticipated. Finding that almost no scholarly research had been done on Marshall's life before his appointment to the Supreme Court, he decided to write a full-scale biography and set about searching through local records for data on the Marshall family, tracking down his descendants to locate the chief justice's scattered papers, and personally going over the ground where Marshall had grown up. He ransacked book-

stores to build up his personal library. His researches carried him to
the Library of Congress, the Virginia State Library, the Boston and
New York public libraries, the Massachusetts Historical Society, the
Pennsylvania Historical Society, and the Virginia Historical Society.
He spent freely to hire research assistants.

For expert advice, he sought the acquaintanceship of the leading
historians of the Marshall era—Charles H. Ambler of Randolph-
Macon, author of *Sectionalism in Virginia from 1776 to 1861;* William
E. Dodd of the University of Chicago; Charles A. Beard of Columbia
University, author of the controversial *An Economic Interpretation
of the Constitution;* Clarence W. Alvord of the University of Illinois,
then at work on his massive study of the *Mississippi Valley in British
Politics;* J. Franklin Jameson, head of the Department of Historical
Research of the Carnegie Institution of Washington; Edward Channing of Harvard University; and Worthington C. Ford, director of
the Massachusetts Historical Society. Flattered by his interest and
caught up by his enthusiasm, these scholars gave freely of their time
in answering his questions, giving him advice and suggestions on his
research, and reading the manuscript.

Beveridge was lavish in his praise for their own work; he did what
he could do to advance their academic careers by taking advantage
of his magazine and newspaper contacts to write favorable reviews
of their work; he even put in a good word in their behalf with influential friends when they sought new jobs. Many became lasting personal
friends. Despite their political differences, he extolled William E.
Dodd as "all wool and a yard wide and everything else that is gen-
uinely and soundly attractive." He looked forward with relish to his
visits with Charles A. Beard—"the very best fellow that ever passed
under the arch of immortality." When Beard resigned from Columbia
in protest against the firing of anti-war professors, Beveridge hastened
to offer his assistance in finding him another job. Worthington C.
Ford became a close friend. "The more I know him," Beveridge confided, "the bigger he grows—and the dearer to me."[1]

He began writing during the summer of 1913 while at Dublin,
New Hampshire. Archibald Cary Coolidge arranged for him to have
free access to the nearby Harvard University Library. He did not
find the writing easy. He could not simply dictate at high speed to a

---

1. Beveridge to Claude G. Bowers, 11 October 1921; to Nathaniel W. Stephenson, 6 October 1925; to Gen. Morris Schaff, 19 December, 1925, BP.

stenographer as he did when turning out his speeches and *Saturday Evening Post* articles. If he were to produce a work that would be "the last word on the subject," he would have to write and rewrite, polish and repolish, check and recheck his facts.[2] And his labors were repeatedly interrupted by his Progressive party activities. By putting in ten to twelve hours a day, however, he succeeded in finishing the first volume—carrying the story up to the ratification of the federal constitution—by the summer of 1914.

Beveridge aimed to humanize Marshall, to make him a living, breathing man instead of the "legal Buddha" of popular mythology. He showed Marshall's humorous, playful, even devil-may-care side, his fondness for a sociable drink, a game of quoits, and the whist table. He referred to a newly discovered account book to reveal Marshall's income and expenditures while a young lawyer in Richmond. He quoted extensively from Marshall's letters to his wife to illustrate his life-long devotion to his "Polly." At times, he would allow his imagination to run too freely. Thus, for example, he described the Marshall family moving to their new Blue Ridge home—young John riding in the wagon, "a sturdy, red-cheeked boy . . . with alert but quiet interest showing from his brilliant black eyes," while his father walked alongside, his face radiating "grave but kindly command" with "the brooding thoughtfulness and fearless light of his striking eyes."[3]

As he worked away, the biography took on massive proportions. Anxious for the approval of the professional historians, Beveridge footnoted lavishly. The first twenty pages had sixty-six footnotes, many containing several citations. And to place Marshall in the larger context of his time and place, he devoted fourteen pages to a picture of Virginia society during Marshall's youth and twenty-seven more to the experience of Washington's army at Valley Forge, two full chapters to the state of the country between the winning of independence and the framing of the constitution and a third to the fight over ratification outside of Virginia, and more than 130 pages to the debate over ratification in Virginia convention. Many of his readers thought Marshall overshadowed by the mass of detail. But

---

2. Beveridge to J. R. Blocher, 11 September 1913, BP.
3. Beveridge, "Some New Marshall Sources," *Annual Report of the American Historical Association . . . 1915* (Washington, 1917), p. 203. Beveridge, *The Life of John Marshall* (4 vols., Boston and New York, 1916–19), 1: 36 (hereafter cited as *Marshall*).

the average reader, Beveridge explained in his preface, could not understand Marshall and his historical significance without this background.

The focus of the first volume was upon the forces and influences that made Marshall "the master-builder of American Nationality." Beveridge showed how Marshall's father, a champion in the Virginia legislature of the rights of the colonists, instilled in him a feeling of American patriotism. How his service in the Revolutionary army taught him "the danger of provincialism," "the value of Nationality," and "the necessity of efficient government." How his firsthand acquaintance while in the Virginia legislature with the turbulence, changeableness, excessive individualism, lack of any sense of civic responsibility, and antagonism toward repayment of debts, public and private, displayed by the masses in the years after the Revolution tempered his former enthusiasm for democracy and strengthened his support for a strong government to safeguard property and maintain law and order. By the time of the fight over ratification of the Constitution, Marshall had formulated "the elements of most of his immortal Nationalist opinions."[4]

Contrasting with his worship of Marshall was Beveridge's hostility toward Thomas Jefferson. Jefferson admirer William E. Dodd found this antipathy strange coming from a progressive. But the Hoosier denied any conflict. Progressivism stood for the expansion of the power of the federal government to deal with the problems of an industrialized society, and thus was but another forward step in the advance of "the idea of Nationality" that was Marshall's "contribution to our life." He conceded that running through Jefferson's "curious career" was "the unbroken & golden thread of fundamental democracy." But "did not Jefferson's democracy take the form not only of State rights but, deeper than that, of the most extreme individualism? And . . . was not this form of Jeffersonian democracy even more inconsistent and hostile with the democracy of our day than was any position taken by the nationalists of that day, if as I understand it, the very basis of true democracy today demands the social idea rather than the savage individualistic idea?"[5]

---

4. *Marshall,* 1: 9, 79, 145, 454.

5. Beveridge to William E. Dodd, 10 May (2 letters), 19 June 1913, Dodd Papers (LC). For an elaboration of his argument regarding the relationship

Beveridge granted that the self-interest of the "commercial and financial interests" was "the most effective force" in the adoption of the Constitution, that the battle over ratification was "partly an economic class struggle," and even that Marshall's own growing prosperity and business connections strengthened his support for a strong government. But he held that the conflict was, "in another and a larger phase," a struggle between "those who thought nationally and those who thought provincially," between those who stood for unrestrained 'liberty' and "those to whom such 'liberty' meant tumult and social chaos." Marshall, by temperament and experience, would have taken the constitutionalist side even without the influence of his financial ties. And though the Constitution did represent a "conservative reaction," Beveridge told Dodd, its framers built more solidly than they realized. "For, today, democracy can be made fruitful only through national action. Only thus can malign & non-public forces be mastered. And these evil interests now hide behind state rights. Thus providence, events, what you will, has made the forces which Marshall vitalized the agencies for the working out of the principles Jefferson advocated."[6]

While more and more caught up in his work on Marshall, Beveridge remained politically active. He addressed—at his own expense—Progressive party rallies throughout the country. He lobbied in Washington to make the Progressive delegation vote as a bloc on major legislation. He expounded the party's aims and principles in magazine articles. He spurred party workers in Indiana to strengthen their organization for the next trial of strength at the municipal elections in the fall of 1913 and contributed generously from his own pocket to finance the work. In his letters, speeches, and articles, he repeated the same message—that the Progressive party was not a temporary flurry and that the time had come for a permanent reorganization of parties along liberal and conservative lines. "If we stand firmly," he explained to Minnesota's Moses Clapp, "and show the people that win or lose, sink or swim, live or die, survive or perish, we stand and fight for our cause, the people with ever-increasing rapidity will come

between the Progressive Party program and "John Marshall's principle of nationality," see *Indianapolis Star*, 25 January 1914.

6. *Marshall*, 1: 242, 370–71. Beveridge to Dodd, 10 May, 19 June 1913, Dodd Papers.

to believe that at last here is a party which . . . is in dead earnest. When that moment arrives, the people will come to us in a great wave."[7]

But the Progressive showing in the 1912 elections had been due more to Roosevelt's—and in Indiana, Beveridge's—personal following than to the new party's own strength. Its congressional and local candidates in the Hoosier state ran far behind the presidential and gubernatorial nominees. Only one Progressive was elected to the state legislature. And despite arm twisting from the state headquarters, the new party failed even to run local tickets in many counties. This weakness at the grassroots was an almost fatal handicap for a party that had no patronage with which to reward its faithful, that lacked any long-established voter loyalties, and that was short of money. A warning sign of trouble was the return to the G.O.P. of Beveridge's friend and party financial angel, millionaire newspaper publisher Frank A. Munsey, and his call in the February 1913 issue of his magazine for amalgamation between the Progressive and Republican parties.

Even more disappointing was the failure of the bulk of the Republican insurgents who had remained with the G.O.P. in 1912 to rally to the new party after the election. At first, Beveridge was more puzzled than angered by the continued refusal of such former comrades-in-arms as Albert B. Cummins and Joseph L. Bristow to leave the Republican party. How could anyone be so foolish as to hope to reform the G.O.P. from within? But he was dismayed to find the Iowa lawmaker taking the stump for the G.O.P. candidate while he campaigned for the Progressive in the special election in the Third Maine Congressional District in September 1913. And when Republican progressives failed to leave their party even after the G.O.P. National Committee in December 1913 turned down their demand for a special national convention to reform the party's rules and procedures, Beveridge grew more and more bitter toward those "fair-haired boys of opportunism."[8]

The 1913 elections exposed the new party's weakness. Despite Beveridge's campaigning, the Republicans recaptured the seat in the Maine special election from the Democrats, while the Progressives

---

7. Beveridge to Moses Clapp, 27 June 1913, BP.
8. Beveridge to John T. McCutcheon, 2 January 1913 [1914], BP.

came in third, with a fall off of more than 50 percent from Roosevelt's 1912 vote. The municipal elections in Indiana revealed the same trend. The Democrats won in fifty cities, the Republicans in twenty-two, nonpartisan citizens' tickets in twelve, while the Progressives captured but five. The worst disappointment came in Indianapolis. Although the Progressives, spearheaded by the *Star*, mounted a strenuous campaign for their mayoral nominee, a well-known and popular physician and former city councilman, Dr. William H. Johnson, he ran third, behind the Republican candidate—to the jubilation of Hoosier G.O.P. leaders.

Aggravating the situation was the split within the Bull Moose ranks over the role of George W. Perkins and the trust question. Those Progressives committed to a restoration of competition blamed Perkins for elimination of the Sherman law plank from the platform, and complained that the New York financier's prominence in the new party was alienating millions of farmers and laborers. Perkins's high-handedness in making decisions without consultation added to his unpopularity. After the 1912 election, a powerful group of party leaders, headed by Amos and Gifford Pinchot, National Committee chairman Joseph M. Dixon, and John Parker of Louisiana, demanded restoration of the missing plank and the reduction of Perkins's influence within the party. At the party conference in December 1912, Roosevelt acceded to the restoration of the Sherman Act plank but he was adamant against the removal of Perkins as chairman of the Executive Committee.

Even Beveridge resented what he thought was Perkins's "dictatorial" manner and worried about the political wisdom of his prominence in the Bull Moose ranks.[9] But loyalty to friends was a gospel with the Hoosier, and he shared Perkins's hostility toward the Sherman law. So he rushed to the financier's defense in the party's inner circle. The conflict within the party became public in May 1914, when Amos Pinchot sent members of the National Committee a letter, some of which was leaked to the newspapers, denouncing Perkins and demanding his resignation. Beveridge was so furious that he wrote Amos a blistering letter, which on second thought he decided

---

9. Beveridge to George W. Perkins [—— 1912], Perkins Papers. Amos R. E. Pinchot, *History of the Progressive Party, 1912–1916*, ed. Helene M. Hooker (New York, 1958), p. 166.

against sending. When Gifford Pinchot sided with his brother, Beveridge cut off further communication with him. This public washing of the party's dirty linen, the Hoosier fumed, "amounts to treason in the ranks."[10]

Most disheartening to Beveridge was Roosevelt's failure to repudiate the "insidious" stories spread by the Republicans that he was planning to return to the G.O.P. Alarmed by the impact of such talk upon the morale of party workers, Beveridge warned that the "time has come when our great leader must sound a battle-cry such as even he never before has sent forth" to "reassure those who have rallied to his colors from Maine to California," and he pleaded with Roosevelt to announce publicly that he would not accept the Republican nomination in 1916. "The one thing we cannot and must not permit is any suspicion of our political and moral integrity, or of that of our great Leader." But T. R. refused. "There is ample time for many changes during the next three years," he told William Allen White, "and we must not tie ourselves down to any course so far in advance."[11]

Having burned his political bridges, Beveridge put the best possible face upon the party's setbacks in the 1913 elections, exhorted Progressives, in and out of Indiana, to rally their forces for the 1914 elections, and blasted talk of a return to the G.O.P. "How can men amalgamate," he exclaimed, "when they do not believe and want the same things, but believe in and want exactly opposite things."[12] Because of his work on the Marshall biography, Beveridge tried feverishly to discourage suggestions that he run again for the United States Senate. But he reluctantly gave in to the demands of party workers that he head the ticket. "Under the circumstances," he confided to Illinois Progressive leader Raymond Robins, "any other course would not only have injured the party but would have been tinged with dishonor."[13]

Temporarily putting aside his research and writing, Beveridge

---

10. Beveridge to Perkins, 19 June 1914, BP.
11. Beveridge to John C. O'Laughlin, 10 September 1913; to O. K. Davis, 10 September 1913; to Perkins, 23 September 1913, BP. Theodore Roosevelt to William Allen White, 8 October 1913, in Morison, *The Letters of Theodore Roosevelt,* 7: 752–53.
12. Beveridge to Lee Brock, 5 December 1913, BP.
13. Beveridge to Raymond Robins, 20 April 1914, BP.

traveled across the state spurring organizational work and exerting his influence to block fusion with the Republicans on local tickets. The Hoosier Progressives responded with a final effort to keep the party afloat. Although state chairman E. M. Lee had to step down for business reasons, his successor, Edward C. Toner, the editor of the *Anderson Herald,* vowed to keep up the fight without any trimming. Arrangements were quickly made to have a precinct committeeman for each of the state's precincts and full county and township tickets throughout the state.

Then came a bombshell from New York. Beveridge had hoped that Roosevelt would give the Progressives throughout the country a boost by running for governor of the Empire State. But T. R. refused, declared that victory could be won only by joining with the progressive-minded Republicans, and proposed that the Progressives nominate Harvey D. Hinman, a Hughes Republican, who looked to be the probable Republican nominee. Although the attempted fusion fell through, the news stunned Beveridge. Roosevelt's action, he complained bitterly, had demoralized party workers and frightened off would-be new supporters. "For fifteen years, in season and out of season, in sunshine and in storm, I have fought under Colonel Roosevelt's banner; never once faltering. . . . Why is it that I now am thrown down in this fashion?"[14]

Beveridge, however, pushed forward with his campaign. He continued to exhort party workers to keep up their efforts. He threw himself into an exhausting speaking tour of the state, averaging upwards of twenty speeches a week. He himself paid for the printing and distribution of campaign literature. T. R. acceded to his demand that he come and speak in Indiana to make up for the Hinman blunder—although Beveridge continued to grumble that Roosevelt was not giving sufficient time to the Hoosier state. The Star League newspapers went all out in support of Beveridge. And he kept up to the last a brave front, boasting of the crowds at his meetings and reporting large-scale crossovers from both old parties.

Beveridge branded as lies Republican propaganda that the Progressives were coming back, warned that the G.O.P. remained under the thumb of the reactionary standpat bosses and "corrupt interests," reminded voters how the old guard leaders still in the saddle had

---

14. Beveridge to Perkins, 25 July 1914, BP.

stolen the 1912 nomination, and denounced the Republicans as extortionists, not protectionists. He assailed Democratic incumbent Benjamin F. Shively as a do-nothing senator, blasted Tom Taggart's "Indiana Democratic Tammany Hall," and appealed to the voters to overthrow the bipartisan "boss system."[15]

But he directed his bitterest attacks upon Democratic misrule in the nation's capital. Repeal of the exemption from tolls of American coastwise shipping through "an American canal, built by the money of the American people, through American soil, owned by the American Nation," was wrong "legally, morally, economically, politically, and patriotically," a "*wickedly* wrong," even treasonable, a sellout to Britain. He was furious at the administration's treaty of apology and indemnity with Colombia over T. R.'s actions during the Panama revolution. The United States, he told the Progressive state convention, would not regain for years "the national prestige" and "standing abroad" lost by the administration's "vaudeville diplomacy."[16]

Even worse was Wilson's Mexican policy. The first mistake was the president's refusal to recognize the Huerta regime. What Mexico required, Beveridge insisted, was a strong man along the lines of the exiled Porfirio Díaz, whom he had extolled in the *Saturday Evening Post* as one of the foremost statesmen of the day. Nothing "except sheer force" was possible in dealing with "her millions of Indians and half-breeds." Unless Huerta could maintain "a strong and honest government," the United States would have to step in and do the job.[17] And he blamed the disorder and lawlessness in Mexico with its destruction of millions of dollars of property and loss of American lives upon the chief executive's efforts to topple Huerta.

In April 1914, the two countries came to the brink of war over the arrest of American sailors at Tampico, the American demand for a twenty-one gun salute in apology, and the occupation of Vera Cruz to prevent the landing of munitions for the Huerta forces. But rather than intervening militarily to "settle things" south of the Rio Grande "for all time to come," Washington backtracked and accepted mediation by Argentina, Brazil, and Chile. Beveridge could hardly contain

---

15. *Indianapolis Star,* 17, 24 October 1914.
16. Beveridge to W. C. Bobbs, 22 March 1914, BP. Beveridge to John C. Shaffer, 17 March [1914], Shaffer Papers. *Indianapolis Star,* 19 April 1914.
17. Beveridge to Shaffer, 11 August 1913, BP. For his praise of Díaz, see Beveridge, "Great Men of Our Day—Diaz," *SEP,* 11 August 1900, pp. 2–3.

his fury at this latest national humiliation. "It destroys, at a stroke," he raged, "our historic position as the dominant power on this hemisphere."[18]

But he made his leading issue in the campaign the administration's responsibility for the business downturn in the United States after the outbreak of the European war. He assailed the Underwood tariff for demoralizing business, reducing wages, and sacrificing the farmer. He accused the Clayton law of worsening the confusion paralyzing "legitimate" business. Although he reaffirmed his support for the party's social justice planks, he warned that reform must await the return of prosperity. Abandoned was his 1912 slogan "Pass prosperity around"; his new battle cry was "I call the business men of Indiana to the colors of permanent prosperity." And he toured the state calling for governmental economy, extolling the protective tariff, and pledging to "take the shackles from the hands of honest business men."[19]

Despite Beveridge's activity, the Progressives waged a losing fight. Wilson's success in pushing through his New Freedom program had dashed Beveridge's hopes for any exodus of reform-minded Democrats into the new party, and it had even attracted the support of many Progressives. Even in Indiana, the Democrats had stolen much of the Progressives' thunder. The Democratic-controlled legislature had established a public service commission with broad supervisory powers over the state's railroads, telephone companies, public utilities, and elevators and warehouses, ratified the constitutional amendment for popular election of senators, passed an anti-loan-shark law, provided for vocational education, instituted a tax-supported county-agent system, enacted a comprehensive housing law prescribing minimum building and maintenance regulations, adopted an inheritance tax, and submitted the holding of a new state constitutional convention to the voters, while the party's 1914 state platform declared for a statewide primary, a workmen's compensation law, and good-roads legislation.

At the same time, the Republicans, under the leadership of their astute and vigorous new state chairman, Will H. Hays, were making strenuous—and not unsuccessful—efforts to woo the Progressives

---

18. Beveridge to Shaffer [— April 1914], Shaffer Papers. *Indianapolis Star*, 19 May 1914.

19. *Indianapolis Star*, 13, 25 October 1914.

back with the assurance that the G.O.P. had cleaned its house. The party's senatorial nominee, former lieutenant governor Hugh T. Miller, was not tarred by the factional warfare of the past decade. The state convention pledged a reform of party rules and procedures to guarantee that "party programs, party platforms and party candidates shall be expressive only of the majority sentiment within the party, free from dictation or duress on the part of party management." Returning Progressives were assured against discrimination in party affairs. The platform took over many of the Progressive's social justice demands: stricter factory and mine inspection, a stronger state child labor law, legislation to provide better conditions and shorter hours for women wage earners, and a workmen's compensation law.[20]

Beveridge's attacks on the administration played into the hands of the Republicans. Their speakers traveled up and down the state making the same denunciation of the Democrats as Beveridge was making for having plunged the country into hard times, extolling the protective tariff as the bedrock of national prosperity, and appealing to Progressive voters to return to the G.O.P. as the most effective way of rebuking Wilson and his works. The election results showed the appeal of the G.O.P. strategy. Although ill health prevented him from making an active canvass, Miller led Beveridge by more than two to one, losing to Shively by only forty-five thousand votes. Beveridge's total skidded to 108,581, while the rest of the Progressive ticket lagged even farther behind. State after state reported the same results. The election, Beveridge lamented, had put the old guard back "in the saddle with feet thrust through the stirrups."[21]

Surveying the wreckage, Beveridge placed part of the blame for the Progressive debacle upon the economic hard times and the resulting popular determination to punish the Democrats by voting Republican. But he thought the most important single factor was the Hinman affair. If the commander-in-chief appeared ready to desert, why should the privates keep on fighting? If amalgamation was in the cards, why should dissatisfied old-party members throw in with a lost cause? Although no public break took place, the Hoosier could never feel the same about his former hero. When he heard that T. R. was not going to attend the party's postelection conference at Chicago,

20. Ibid., 24 April 1914.
21. Beveridge to E. L. McClain, 20 November 1914, BP.

he could not hide his bitterness. "If we had made a great showing," he exclaimed, ". . . he could not have been kept away from such a conference if he had been chained to a Baldwin locomotive going the other way." The time "when leadership really is needed and is indispensable is in the hour of defeat."[22]

---

22. Beveridge to White, 21 November 1914; to Perkins, 19 November 1914, BP. After the final collapse of the Progressive Party, Beveridge would insist that T. R.'s action in the Hinman matter had dealt the party a blow from which it never recovered. He even wrote an article for *SEP*, "The Launching and Wrecking of the Progressive Party," stressing this point, but decided upon second thought not to publish it. A copy of the article with the accompanying correspondence between Beveridge and George H. Lorimer is in the "G. H. Lorimer 1916" file, Box 206, BP.

18

The Death of the Progressive Party

After the 1914 election, Beveridge went to Europe to report on the war for *Collier's*. He retained his youthful enthusiasm for things military. He wished to see at first hand what the conflagration across the seas was about. And he welcomed the money *Colliers* editor Mark Sullivan offered—$6,500 for six articles, with an option for three more for $2,500—after the expenses of politics and the Marshall biography. He left for New York in mid-December accompanied by Paxton Hibben, a young writer and former Progressive candidate for Congress from Indianapolis, as secretary-interpreter. His aim, he explained to Sullivan, was "to give a picture of PEOPLES when at war."[1]

First he visited Germany. Anxious for a favorable press in the United States, the German authorities gave him their full co-operation. He had interviews with shipping magnate Albert Ballin, industrialist Walter Rathenau, theologian Adolf von Harnack, Social Democratic leader Albert Südekum, Tirpitz, Hindenburg, and Chancellor Beth-

---

1. Beveridge to Mark Sullivan, 8 December 1914, BP.

mann-Hollweg. He even had a two hour talk with the kaiser, who impressed Beveridge as "hard as nails, extremely intelligent, and well-informed, and with a steadiness that was amazing."[2] The Germans arranged for visits to the eastern and western fronts. The high point of the trip came when Beveridge found himself in the middle of "a real battle" between the Russians and Germans. ". . . shells tearing up the earth, men killed, the wounded, the prisoners, the earthquake of artillery, etc.," he wrote his wife. "It was splendid!"[3]

After completing his German articles in Switzerland, he went on to France. Although President Poincaré and the foreign minister, Delcassé, refused to speak for ascription, he had lengthy talks with former foreign minister Gabriel Hanotaux, philosopher Henri Bergson, Socialist leader Gustave Hervé, and industrialist Eugène Schneider. His visit to England was most disappointing. Foreign minister Sir Edward Grey would not be quoted by name, while prime minister Asquith kept their meeting to trivialities. But he did have interviews with Conservative leaders Sir Gilbert Parker and Lord Newton, former ambassador to the United States Lord Bryce, Charles Trevelyan, head of the New Union of Democratic Control, and George Bernard Shaw.

The trip, however, proved neither financially profitable nor politically advantageous. The task took longer than he had anticipated; he had difficulties with *Collier's* over their editing and delays in publishing the articles; and when Sullivan refused to take more than eight articles, Beveridge had to sell the overflow to Albert Shaw's *Review of Reviews* for only three hundred dollars apiece. He expanded the articles into a book, *What Is Back of the War*, published in the fall of 1915 by his friend and political supporter W. C. Bobbs. He took a personal hand in promoting the work—he even became aggrieved at George Perkins when Perkins refused to give him the Progressive party's mailing list for Bobbs-Merrill to use in advertising. But the sales were disappointing.

Beveridge grasped more fully than many of his contemporaries that the long-range significance of the conflict was the tremendous expansion of "collectivism" that could never be reversed after the

---

2. Beveridge to William E. Dodd, 4 February 1916, BP.
3. Bowers, *Beveridge and the Progressive Era*, pp. 469–70.

war's end.[4] But the articles and book were marred by his strong pro-German, anti-British animus. He had long suffered from a Fourth-of-July type of Anglophobia, while he admired Germany for its discipline, efficiency, martial spirit, and advanced social and economic legislation. After the outbreak of hostilities, he did not hide the fact that his sympathies lay with Germany. The United States minister to the Netherlands, Henry Van Dyke, who was sailing on the same boat with Beveridge to Europe, found him filled "up so tight with the Teutonic virus that there is not room in him for any thing else. . . . It is a kind of obsession,—makes one think of the Middle Ages and the necromancers."[5]

Despite his protestations of impartiality, Beveridge took pains to absolve the Germans from the atrocity stories circulating in the pro-Allied newspapers. He painted glowing pictures of wartime conditions in Germany: the plentiful supplies of food, the ample supply of manpower, the resourcefulness and efficiency shown in the mobilization of the nation's resources, and, most striking, the solidarity, determination, and patriotism that animated the German people of all walks of life. Although he found French spirits and resolve high, his treatment of the French scene lacked the enthusiastic and laudatory tone of his writing on Germany. The articles on Britain presented a gloomy report of deep-seated divisions, business selfishness, labor strife, and growing defeatism. And he insisted privately that he had deliberately understated the gravity of the British situation. "If I told the raw truth, people would be sure to say that I am not impartial."[6]

German-American organizations and spokesmen hailed the work. But pro-Allied enthusiasts were loud in their denunciations. T. R. fumed that the *Collier's* articles were "pro-German and anti-Ally." The *Literary Digest* called the book "a better (because more skilful) contribution to the German propaganda than any other that has yet

---

4. *SEP*, 19 June 1915, p. 23.

5. Henry Van Dyke to John H. Finley, 21 December 1914, Finley Papers (New York Public Library). I am indebted to Professor Marvin Gittleman of Brooklyn Polytechnic Institute for this reference. For Beveridge's long-standing admiration for Germany, see: Beveridge to H. M. Miller, 10 November 1911, BP. Beveridge, "Permanent Prosperity," *SEP*, 31 October 1914, p. 15. *Indianapolis Star*, 13 October 1914.

6. Beveridge to Albert Shaw, 6 May 1915, BP.

been made." Even Shaffer warned him against becoming "*too* Pro German." The pro-Allied *New York Evening Telegram* and *New York Herald* went so far as to link his name with a vast German conspiracy in the United States.[7]

The more he was attacked the more disgusted Beveridge became with the way the American people had been "saturated" with pro-Allied "falsehoods." And he accused the same big businessmen and financiers who fought reform at home of pushing for American involvement to save their millions of dollars of loans to the Allies. Although favoring universal military training as a nationalizing force, he was put off by the pro-Allied sympathies of the leading preparedness advocates. In a *Saturday Evening Post* article titled "Preparedness for Peace," he appealed to the American people to avoid foreign entanglements and devote their energies to putting their own house in shape. *Post* editor George H. Lorimer turned down another, stronger, plea for neutrality on the ground that the article was a pro-German, anti-Allied tract. "Why is it," Beveridge complained, "that if anybody today asserts that we ought to keep absolutely neutral and show favor to neither side, that such a person is at once denounced as pro-German; whereas those who want us to abandon neutrality are held up as the only true Americans?"[8]

Deepening Beveridge's gloom was the rapid break-up of the Progressive party. The 1914 elections had accelerated the return of party members to the Republicans. In June 1915, state chairman Edward C. Toner publicly called for disbanding the party, and when the Progressive state committee refused by a nine-to-three vote, he resigned, rejoined the G.O.P., and appealed to party members to follow. Roosevelt himself had concluded that the Progressive party was dead. As he became more and more wrapped up in the preparedness movement, he shunted to the background the New Nationalism and began a rapprochement with the old guard politicians and big businessmen he had once so loudly denounced. "The party," Beveridge complained to George W. Perkins, "is disintegrating . . . because the feeling has

7. Theodore Roosevelt to Gifford Pinchot, 29 March 1915, Roosevelt Papers. *Literary Digest*, 23 October 1915, p. 912. John C. Shaffer to Beveridge, 14 July 1915; Beveridge to Shaw, 20 August 1915, BP.

8. Beveridge to Eli Lilly, 24 July 1915; to Shaffer, 6 March 1916 (two letters), BP.

been growing among our people for more than a year that T. R. is flirting with the Republicans."[9]

Despite the party's setbacks, Beveridge appealed to Progressives, in and out of Indiana, to rally their forces and keep "fighting harder than ever for the things we stand for."[10] But he himself abandoned active leadership of party affairs in the Hoosier state and devoted his energies to finishing the second volume of the Marshall biography. When Indiana Progressive leaders appealed to him to permit the placing of his name in the state's newly adopted presidential preference primary to give the party faithful a psychological boost, he flatly refused. "I have given," he replied angrily, "more than almost any other man in the country . . . for the party; and all the thanks I get is that I must now drop the work of my life which I have three times dropped already in this cause, to once more do a thing which, this time, there is absolutely no need whatever of doing."[11]

While Beveridge was in Europe, his wife had purchased a house at Beverly Farms on the Massachusetts North Shore that they had admired the previous summer. He would rise early, go for a brisk hour's walk accompanied by his collie, and then write in his study until four o'clock, when he would take a break and another walk before returning to his labors. In hot weather he worked in the open on a platform built at the edge of the woods. After dinner, he would spend an hour or so in the drawing room with his wife, who would read to him aloud what he had written so that he could catch any rough passages missed by the eye. Returning to the study, he would continue writing until midnight or later.

Surrounded by his notes and source materials, he would write in pencil and have his stenographer make a typed copy. Then followed the job of revision, polishing, and condensing. By the end of the summer of 1915, he had the second volume in shape to send out to historians for their criticism. He stayed on at Beverly Farms through the following winter to be near the libraries of the Boston area, while he revised the manuscript according to the suggestions of his readers. The task, he confided to a friend, "is far and away the hardest, most

9. Beveridge to George W. Perkins, 6 May 1915, BP.
10. Beveridge to James B. Harper, 20 November 1914, BP.
11. Beveridge to E. M. Lee, 25 December 1915, BP.

painstaking, and exacting labor I ever undertook . . . . The modern method of writing definitive history does not permit the making of a single mistake nor pardon it if made."[12]

Perhaps the most helpful of his readers was the dean of American historians, J. Franklin Jameson. Albert Shaw had put him in touch with Jameson. Jameson had looked upon the senatorial Beveridge as a "glorified sophomore" too fond of hearing his own voice, and he was at first skeptical about his capabilities as a historian. But he did send Beveridge lengthy suggestions for further research. When he read the manuscript of the first volume, he found the work much better than he had expected. Though there was "an awful lot of sophomore rhetoric in it," Jameson confided to Worthington C. Ford, Beveridge had "brought together a good deal of interesting material; and during the process has learned more history than he started out with."[13]

Caught up by Beveridge's own enthusiasm, Jameson went over the manuscript page by page, pointing out factual errors and advising on style. He had two major criticisms—"too much use of the superlative" and so much background material that Marshall himself tended to become lost. Beveridge had the highest regard, even awe, for Jameson; he was, he told Shaw, "a superb man" with a "brain of light and heart of gold and his feet on the solid earth every minute of the time!" But he did not slavishly follow Jameson's advice. While he pruned the more long-winded passages and toned down his adjectives, he remained convinced that the average reader's "lamentable ignorance" of American history justified his broad life-and-times approach, and that to sell, the book must have "dramatic" flair.[14]

The work of revision dragged on until the spring of 1916. There was the last-minute search for any sources he may have missed. He wrote a a new chapter on the impact of the French Revolution upon

---

12. Beveridge to Albert B. Cummins, 21 October 1915, BP.

13. J. Franklin Jameson to Waldo G. Leland, 16 December 1907, in Elizabeth Donnan and Leo F. Stock, eds., *An Historian's World: Selections from the Correspondence of J. Franklin Jameson* (Philadelphia, 1956), pp. 114–15. Jameson to Worthington C. Ford, 1 September 1914, in Donnan and Stock, eds., "Senator Beveridge, J. Franklin Jameson, and John Marshall," *MVHR* 25 (December 1948): 464.

14. Jameson to Beveridge, 31 August 1914, in Donnan and Stock, "Senator Beveridge, J. Franklin Jameson, and John Marshall," pp. 469–73. Beveridge to Lindsay Swift, 23 March 1916, BP. For Beveridge's regard for Jameson, see Beveridge to Shaw, 31 December 1924, BP.

the United States to introduce volume two. There were vexing problems of style. Clarence W. Alvord criticized his excessive quotation, while Worthington C. Ford argued against his cutting down the excerpts from the more important Marshall letters and documents. There was the tiresome job of verifying facts and footnotes. To guard against slips, he hired H. J. Eckenrode, the author of *The Revolution in Virginia* who was eking out a living as archivist of the Virginia State Library, and Lindsay Swift, editor of the Boston Public Library, to go over the final draft of the manuscript "with the professional microscope."[15] As a double check, he kept Swift on to assist in the proof-reading.

Because of the sparseness of the Marshall papers, Beveridge had to rely largely upon later recollections and Marshall's own *Life of George Washington* in tracing the views and activities of the future chief justice during the first half of the 1790s. But he found more abundant materials when he came to deal with his role in the mission to France of 1797 and the XYZ affair, his election to Congress in 1799, and his service in the House and as secretary of state. And he succeeded in painting a graphic picture of Marshall as his contemporaries saw him—a man of "extraordinary ability," "uprightness," and "charm," yet a man whose playfulness, good nature, and indolence hid the "masterfulness," "commanding will," and "unyielding purpose" he would reveal on the bench.[16]

The major focus of both volumes was upon the interaction between Marshall and his times—how the political battles of the decade following the adoption of the Constitution shaped the conflicting philosophies of Marshall and "his great ultimate antagonist," Thomas Jefferson. Beveridge accepted the economic basis of party division as laid down by Charles A. Beard's *Economic Origins of Jeffersonian Democracy*—the debtors and the poor, on the Republican side, versus the creditors, the mercantile and financial interests, on the side of the Federalists. But he saw the real issue—underlying the conflicts over Hamilton's fiscal policies, over foreign policy, and over taxes—as a struggle between "Nationalism" and "localism."[17]

Nothwithstanding his professed espousal of scientific history, Bev-

---

15. Beveridge to Edward Channing, 3 February 1916, BP.
16. *Marshall*, 2: 563.
17. Ibid., 2: 42–44.

eridge could not hide his biases. He painted Thomas Jefferson as the archvillain of the story—a shifty, devious, small-minded, vindictive, and hypocritical politician whose state's rights doctrines sowed the seeds of secession and Civil War. He even stretched the evidence to present Jefferson in the worst possible light.[18] In contrast, he defended Hamilton's fiscal program as indispensable for the nation's well-being. And he found grounds for Marshall's suspicions about popular majorities in the shallowness, lack of restraint, and susceptibility to demagogic appeals shown by the masses during the 1790s.

Beveridge's sympathy for Marshall was strengthened by his personal disillusionment with democracy. His complaints about the lack of public recognition for his own achievements took on a new stridency. He castigated the low quality of leadership and lack of statesmanship he found in American public life; he blasted the public at large as too lazy, ill-informed, and juvenile to think seriously about the country's problems, too readily swayed by "silly catch-words" and "shallow artifices."[19]

A subtheme running through the book, intertwined with the larger issue of nationalism versus localism, was the struggle to maintain American neutrality in the conflict between Britain and France. Beveridge's account of that struggle read like a tract for his own time. He showed how Jefferson's pro-French sympathies threatened to involve the United States in a disastrous war; he hailed Washington for saving the nation from that fate; and he extolled Marshall as the American nationalist par excellence, who stood up against France and Britain as the champion of purely American rights and interests. To underline the moral of his story, Beveridge headed his chapters with such quotations from Marshall as "To lend money to a belligerent power is to relinquish our neutrality," "Separated far from Europe, we mean not to mingle in her quarrels," and "A fraudulent neutrality is no neutrality at all."[20]

Though unhappy with Beveridge's anti-Jefferson bias, William E. Dodd was sufficiently impressed to recommend its publication by Houghton Mifflin in his capacity as the firm's adviser on American

---

18. On his twisting the evidence, see Irving Brant, "John Marshall and the Lawyers and Politicians," in W. Melville Jones, ed., *Chief Justice John Marshall: A Reappraisal* (Ithaca, N.Y., 1956), p. 47.

19. Beveridge to Dodd, 4 February 1916, BP.

20. *Marshall*, 2: 257, 290.

history. Ferris Greenslet, the head of the prestigious Boston publishing house, was dubious, and Dodd's flippant description of the book as "interesting, if untrue" did not reassure him.[21] But when Worthington C. Ford seconded the recommendation, Greenslet asked Beveridge to submit the manuscript to Houghton Mifflin. After reading the work, he saw he had a winner. The terms agreed upon, Beveridge reported happily, were the best he had received: he would pay half the cost of publication, including advertising, and divide with the publisher half the profits. Putting the book at the top of its fall 1916 list, Houghton Mifflin rushed the volumes through for November 1916 publication.

Beveridge anxiously awaited the popular and scholarly reaction. The scattered critical or even lukewarm comments riled the author, but these discordant notes were submerged in the chorus of praise that greeted the volumes. Theodore Roosevelt declared in *The Outlook* that the Hoosier had produced a work that belongs "among the very few books of American political biography which stand in the first rank." The reviewer for the *New York Times* called the volumes "an important and interesting contribution to American biography" written with "notable literary skill." Henry Cabot Lodge wrote Beveridge a five-page letter of congratulations. President Nicholas Murray Butler of Columbia University—who had formerly thought him, Beveridge noted, "as just the last word in shallow-minded, uninformed demagogy"—hailed the biography as "one of the most illuminating and scholarly contributions to American history that has yet been made by any one."[22]

Even the professional historians were highly favorable. John H. Latané of Johns Hopkins wrote Beveridge that he had succeeded for the first time in making Marshall come alive as "a very real personality." Charles A. Beard called the volumes "among the very first biographies of American statesmen." Clarence H. Gaines of the University of Florida hailed the work as "a powerful piece of historical writing" whose "rigor of research" and "precision of judgment" fulfilled "the exacting standards that the modern scientific historians have set up." Princeton political scientist Edward S. Corwin, review-

---

21. Dodd to Ferris Greenslet, 6 August 1915, Dodd Papers.
22. Theodore Roosevelt, "Beveridge's Life of Marshall: A Review," *The Outlook*, 18 July 1917, pp. 448–49. *New York Times*, 14 January 1917. Nicholas Murray Butler to Beveridge, 19 February 1918; Beveridge to Ford, 9 February 1917, BP. Beveridge to Shaw, 25 February 1918, Shaw Papers.

ing the volumes for the *Mississippi Valley Historical Review*, complained about the excessive detail, quotation, and striving after "oratorical effect," but praised the work as "conceived and executed on a broad scale, with fine enthusiasm for the subject and admirable devotion to the truth." John Spencer Bassett of Smith, while taking Beveridge to task for his anti-Jefferson bias, applauded his industry, high degree of accuracy, and "remarkable power of visualization" in presenting Marshall as "a very human man."[23]

Nearly as gratifying as the favorable reviews and letters of congratulation was the book's sale. Despite its price—eight dollars for the two volumes—the first two impressions totaling 2,500 copies were sold out before publication. Even the publisher was surprised by the work's success. By March 1919, more than 4,000 sets had been sold, with Beveridge's share of the profits amounting to nearly $4,400. The reception given the work, the author replied to an enthusiastic reader, had given him the courage and strength to undertake the final two volumes dealing with Marshall's years on the Supreme Court. "It will take continuous effort, to the exclusion of absolutely all other activities, for at least two years and I fear three years, to accomplish this. But I shall keep at it until they are done."[24]

The success of the Marshall biography helped salve Beveridge's bitterness over the fate of the Progressive party. His refusal to take active leadership in Indiana accelerated the party's disintegration in that state. In a desperate bid to pick up prohibitionist support, the state committee made a deal with former governor J. Frank Hanly: he was willing to become the Progressive gubernatorial candidate if the party would go on record for statewide and national prohibition and drop its referendum, initiative, and recall planks. Beveridge was shocked. Had the state committee forgotten Hanly's bitter attacks upon the party, T. R., and himself in the 1912 campaign? Disgust over the Hanly deal speeded the exodus of the rank-and-file members of the party. At the last minute, Hanly let the Progressives down by refusing the nomination.

Beveridge protested that Roosevelt's plan to hold the party's na-

23. John H. Latané to Beveridge, 10 October 1917. Charles A. Beard to Beveridge, 19 November 1916, BP. Clarence H. Gaines, "John Marshall and the Spirit of America," *North American Review* 205 (February 1917): 287–92. *MVHR* 4 (June 1917): 116–18. *AHR* 22 (April 1917): 666–69.

24. Beveridge to J. H. Wilson, 10 March 1917, J. H. Wilson Papers (LC).

tional convention simultaneously with the G.O.P. gathering smacked of unconditional surrender. He dismissed as wishful thinking the possibility of Roosevelt's winning the G.O.P. nomination. The unrepentant old guard would never accept him, while his reputation as a war-hawk had lost him much of his popular support. The Hoosier wanted the Progressives to hold their convention before the Republicans and put their own ticket in the field. Only then would the G.O.P. leaders "see that we mean business, are not bluffing, and might make such terms with us concerning principles and candidates as would enable the two parties to make a united fight."[25]

But T. R. was determined to defeat Wilson at any price. The Progressive national committee at its meeting in January 1916 voted to hold the party convention at the same time as that of the Republicans. The bulk of the statement issued by the committee consisted of an attack upon the Wilson administration for its failure to uphold the "national honor" and an appeal to the Republicans in the name of patriotism to join in choosing "the same standard bearer and the same principles."[26] Beveridge washed his hands of any further participation in party affairs. Pleading the pressure of his work on Marshall, he turned down the temporary chairmanship of the national convention and refused even to go to Chicago.

Roosevelt's action in declining the Progressive nomination and pushing through the National Committee a resolution backing G.O.P. nominee Charles Evans Hughes faced the Hoosier with a painful dilemma. "What has become of that great and inspiring movement to organize American liberalism into a great political party?" he asked a fellow Progressive leader. "Have you seen anything of it any place? And what has happened to our wonderful national platform of four years ago?" Abandoned in the name of Americanism, preparedness, and the protective tariff. All his sacrifices and labor had been made in vain. "History," he exclaimed to George H. Lorimer, "has not one single example of a party or a movement which was used so coldbloodedly and wrecked so cynically and selfishly as the Progressive party has been used and wrecked."[27]

---

25. Beveridge to John C. Shaffer, 23 December 1915, BP.
26. *Indianapolis Star*, 12 January 1916.
27. Beveridge to E. A. Van Valkenburg, 16 June 1916; to George H. Lorimer, 24 June 1916, BP.

To return to the G.O.P. was agonizing for Beveridge. The party—in Indiana and throughout the country—remained under the thumb of the old guard. James P. Goodrich was the party's gubernatorial candidate, while Harry S. New had narrowly edged out James E. Watson in the newly adopted primary for the senatorial nomination. When Senator Benjamin F. Shively died in March, Beveridge had a fleeting hope that the Republican leaders could be induced to proffer him the nomination for the vacant seat as a step toward party reunification. But the Republican state convention proceeded to name Watson for the short term. And his long-time rival Charles W. Fairbanks was the Republican vice-presidential nominee. If Beveridge rejoined the G.O.P., he would have to support men whom he had denounced as not fit to hold public office.

The alternatives, however, were even worse. The struggle by a band of "lost ditchers" to keep the Progressive party alive was doomed to failure.[28] Many Progressives, in and out of Indiana, rallied to Wilson. Beveridge privately admitted that the Wilson administration had carried out many of the reforms for which he had fought, such as a national child labor law, a federal trade commission, and a tariff commission. But he could not overcome his lifelong antipathy toward the Democracy. The Democrats remained the party of "localism," free trade, and hostility to big business, whereas the war and the heightened foreign competition that would follow required a strong national government to "deal with all things that help or hurt the entire people," amendment of the Sherman law "upon the principle that business combination is not only natural and inevitable but necessary and beneficial," and a high protective tariff to safeguard against postwar foreign dumping.[29]

Nor could he swallow Wilsonian foreign policy. A die-hard imperialist, he raged against the administration-backed Jones bill granting the Philippines greater autonomy and promising independence by 4 March 1921. Given his long-standing anxiety over the yellow peril, he accused the administration of not taking a sufficiently firm stand against the Japanese threat to American interests and trade in the Far East. He was even more bitter against Wilson's Mexican

28. For Beveridge's aloofness from these efforts, see: James B. Wilson to Beveridge, 8 July 1916; Beveridge to Wilson, 12 July 1916, BP.

29. *Indianapolis Star*, 6 October 1916. Beveridge to Charles G. Dawes, 19 August 1916, BP.

policy. He felt that the continued turmoil south of the Rio Grande demanded full-scale American intervention to set up a Platt Amendment–style protectorate or even annexation. But the administration stumbled from blunder to blunder: the failure of the State Department's pro-Villa policy followed by the administration's backing down and recognizing Carranza, the Pershing punitive expedition followed by Wilson's failure to take strong action after the clash between Mexican forces and American troops at Carrizal in June 1916.

Perhaps his greatest fear was that the administration's policy toward German submarine warfare might drag the United States into a disastrous war. He was appalled by the chief executive's response to the sinking of the *Lusitania*. The ship was carrying munitions, and the passengers had been amply warned of the dangers but had knowingly taken the risk. The effect of the *Lusitania* notes, Beveridge complained, was to commit the United States to guaranteeing the safety of belligerent ships so long as one American passenger was on board. That blunder was aggravated by the president's "absurd" turnabout on the status of armed merchant men. Thus the "fool-hardiness" of a single American citizen in sailing on an armed belligerent merchant ship "would involve this nation of an hundred millions of people, in a war where scores of thousands of lives and billions of money would be lost to vindicate this right."[30]

Although he talked of sitting out the 1916 campaign,[31] Beveridge was too young and ambitious to give up politics. And with the majority of the Indiana Progressives, led by the Star League, following T. R. back into the Republican party, he had scant hope for a political comeback unless he joined them. George W. Perkins, who was acting as the go-between for the returning Progressives, arranged for Hughes to invite Beveridge for a private talk and ask him personally to take part in the campaign. After their talk, Beveridge announced his support for the G.O.P. standard-bearer. He was full of praise for the New Yorker as "calm, grave, farseeing," and was even convinced— rightly or wrongly—that if Hughes won, he would be in line for appointment as secretary of war.[32]

30. Beveridge to Shaffer, 6 March 1916, BP.
31. See, for example, Beveridge to Isaac Strauss, 17 June 1916, BP.
32. Beveridge to Mrs. Orville H. Platt, 29 July 1916, Platt Papers. *Re* the secretaryship of war, see: Beveridge to Dodd, 10 May 1918; Dodd to Walter Clark, 9 May 1919; to Desha Breckinridge, 26 August 1920, Dodd Papers.

Despite his return to the G.O.P., Beveridge remained pessimistic about the outcome of the election. His own political soundings revealed that Wilson had stronger popular support than most Republican strategists thought. Business was booming; farm prices were high; labor was fully employed at good wages; Wilson had skillfully neutralized the preparedness issue; the Democratic claim that Wilson had kept us out of the war had struck a responsive popular chord; the Democrats had enacted many of the reforms demanded by the Progressives; many former Progressives would not vote for the Republican ticket regardless of what Roosevelt said or did; and the Republicans lacked a winning issue.

At the beginning of September a new issue arose: Wilson's action in forcing through Congress the Adamson act granting railroad workers an eight hour day to head off a threatened nationwide strike by the railroad brotherhoods. Beveridge made the administration's "cowardice" a highlight of his campaign speeches. He was not against the eight hour day, he assured his listeners. Nor was he against higher wages for the railroad workers. But the issue was whether a handful of willful men could "exact special privileges by force." The administration's "cowering submission" was an invitation to lawlessness and anarchy.[33]

He had at first balked at speaking in Indiana. To speak for men who had for years fought him and all he stood for would be personally stultifying and would disillusion many admirers. But he yielded to the appeals of party strategists and closed the campaign in Indianapolis—although, to save face, he confined himself to national issues and failed even to mention the Republican senatorial and gubernatorial nominees. Disappointed but not surprised by Hughes's defeat, Beveridge boasted that his last-minute appearance had saved the day for the G.O.P. in the Hoosier state. Most gratifying were the enthusiastic receptions given him wherever he spoke and the flattering talk he heard about himself as presidential timber. The old magic was still there, he rejoiced. He still retained "the confidence and the friendship of the masses of the people."[34]

33. *Indianapolis Star*, 26 September, 6 October 1916.
34. Beveridge to E. L. McClain, 14 November 1916, BP.

19

Chief Justice John Marshall

Returning to his work on the Marshall biography, Beveridge pushed forward with the research on and writing of volumes three and four covering Marshall's years as chief justice. Minor illnesses, speech and magazine commitments, the loss of his secretary to the army and the need to break in a new man, his speaking for the Fourth Liberty Loan drive in Indiana in the fall of 1918, and his campaigning in the 1918 congressional elections delayed his progress. But he managed by working late into the night to finish volume three by the spring of 1918. He stayed in Boston over the winter of 1918–19 to be near the libraries there and wrote volume four while revising volume three in line with the suggestions of his readers. "How happy I shall be," he confessed to a friend, ". . . when I get the old boy happily buried. It is an awful job—so incessant, so continuous, so intricate. Untangling a mass of data and then telling the story so that it is clear enough for the reader to understand and entertaining enough to hold his attention is about the hardest task I ever tackled."[1]

He sent copies of his chapters dealing

---

1. Beveridge to F. H. Bigelow, 29 August 1918, BP.

with Marshall's major decisions to distinguished lawyers and jurists for their comments. He kept up a voluminous correspondence with historian friends, seeking their advice and hoping for their approval. Among these were Max Farrand of Yale, author of *The Framing of the Constitution*, Harvard historian Samuel Eliot Morison, Harold Laski, then teaching political science at Harvard, fellow Hoosier and former Progressive James A. Woodburn of Indiana University, and Princeton political scientist and constitutional law expert Edward S. Corwin. H. J. Eckenrode and Lindsay Swift remained on the payroll as expert consultants to go over the successive drafts word by word.

Anxious to make the work the "definitive biography" that would "stand for all time," he welcomed, even demanded, frank criticism. When Max Farrand—whom Beveridge regarded as "the most important and most helpful" of his new advisers—complained that in his chapter on *Marbury* v. *Madison* he had not presented "clearly" and "unmistakably" what Marshall had decided, why he had acted as he did, and what the significance of the decision was, Beveridge thanked him for "just the kind of straight talk I like." He rewrote the chapter twice and sent the new drafts back to the Yale scholar for his approval. Farrand found the second draft "a great improvement" and the third "pretty close to being the last word on the subject." Only then was Beveridge satisfied.[2]

His own political experience gave him an insight into the politics of Marshall's time that no academic historian could have. On the other hand, he was dealing with questions that remained hotly disputed. And his readers complained about too much background detail, repetitiousness, and excessive quotation from the arguments of rival counsel and Marshall's own decisions. These shortcomings were aggravated by his continued broad life-and-times approach. For example, he devoted a full chapter to the "financial and moral chaos" afflicting the country in the misnamed "Era of Good Feelings" as background for Marshall's decisions in the Dartmouth College case and *M'Culloch* v. *Maryland*. He was at his most overextended in dealing with the Aaron Burr treason case, which took up four long chapters.

2. Beveridge to John C. Shaffer, 8 April 1919; to Herschel Lutes, 9 April 1919; to Max Farrand, 19 September 1918; Farrand to Beveridge, 13 September 1918, 14 January, 7 February 1919, BP.

He continued to denigrate Jefferson. He was "absolutely certain" that Jefferson was from the start "determined to overthrow the Judiciary, or rather that he was determined to get it in his power." And he was not sure but that Jefferson did not have all his steps plotted out even while protesting that he had not.[3] In contrast was his treatment of Marshall's decision in *Marbury* v. *Madison.* He grudgingly accepted Corwin's argument in *The Doctrine of Judicial Review* that Marshall was wrong, and knew he was wrong, in holding section 13 of the Judiciary Act of 1789 unconstitutional—although Beveridge could not bring himself to say more in the text than that Marshall had seized upon a "pretext" that "had been unheard of and unsuspected hitherto." But this action heightened, rather than diminished, his respect for Marshall's statesmanship. The dangers presented by the Jeffersonian doctrines of nullification, unrestrained majority rule, and denial of the authority of the federal courts to declare laws of Congress unconstitutional made "vital the assertion of judicial supremacy over legislation at that particular point in American history." Thus, he lavished praise upon the chief justice for his "courage," "statesmanlike foresight," and "perfectly calculated audacity" in pulling off his bold coup.[4]

Beveridge revealed his animus against Jefferson most strikingly in his treatment of the Burr affair. He followed Walter F. McCaleb's *The Aaron Burr Conspiracy* (1903) in exonerating Burr of any treasonable purposes, explained that his aim was to invade Mexico if and when war broke out with Spain, and pictured the former vice-president as the victim of a Jeffersonian plot. Even if Burr had contemplated treason—which he personally doubted—Beveridge insisted that no evidence had been presented at the trial or since that he had committed any "overt act." Samuel Eliot Morison protested that Beveridge had not proved to his satisfaction that Jefferson's prosecution of Burr had been inspired by "mere vindictiveness." Could not have Jefferson been "sincerely convinced" that Burr was a traitor? "Or will you not admit that T. J. could be sincere?" Beveridge's answer was no. In the Burr case, Jefferson was moved by "his abnormal and almost insane love of popularity, his sensitiveness to criticism and dread of being made ridiculous, his implacable hatred

---

3. Beveridge to Edward S. Corwin, 25 February 1918, BP.
4. *Marshall*, 3: 132–33. Beveridge to Philander C. Knox, 7 January 1919, BP.

of anybody who antagonized him. When Jefferson set his teeth in anybody's leg he never let go."[5]

By the same token, Beveridge defended Marshall's role in the trial. Edward S. Corwin argued that Marshall, in his eagerness to free Burr and thus spite Jefferson, had resorted to a highly strained interpretation of the constitutional provision regarding treason that contradicted his earlier opinion in the case involving two of Burr's aides, Bollmann and Swartwout. Burr's lawyers had argued that even if the assemblage of a military force at Blennerhasset's Island had constituted an act of treason, Burr could not be convicted on that score since he was in Kentucky at the time. The prosecution relied upon the common law doctrine that "in treason all are principals." And Corwin took the prosecution's side, arguing that if the "overt act" of the assemblage were proved, "when by further evidence any particular individual is connected with the treasonable combination which brought about the overt act, that act, assuming the Common Law doctrine, becomes his act, and he is accordingly responsible for it at the place where it occurred."[6]

Beveridge, on the other hand, denied that Marshall was motivated by hostility toward Jefferson in laying down his narrow definition of treason, found his opinion consistent with his ruling in the case of Bollmann and Swartwout, and hailed his repudiation of the common law doctrine of "constructive treason" as a landmark in the protection of civil liberties. He insisted—as Marshall had in his opinion—that the constitutional provision of treason required that if Burr were guilty through "procurement" of the treasonable assemblage, "then that procurement must be proved by two witnesses, that being his overt act." If not, he contended, "our constitutional provision dont [sic] amount to a hill of beans." Since the prosecution had not produced the required two witnesses to testify that Burr had procured the treasonable assemblage, Marshall's opinion was "absolutely right." But shaken when Corwin, who had become his major authority on constitutional questions, continued to maintain his position, Beveridge conceded in his text that Marshall experienced "great embarrassment" in reconciling his "careless language" in the Bollmann-

---

5. Samuel Eliot Morison to Beveridge, 2 August 1918; Beveridge to Morison, 6 August 1918; to I. J. Cox, 5 February 1919, BP.

6. For Corwin's argument, see Edward S. Corwin, *John Marshall and the Constitution* (New Haven, 1919), pp. 93–113.

Swartwout case with his opinion in the Burr trial. Thus he left the question of the soundness of Marshall's ruling more ambiguous than he personally believed and more ambiguous than the evidence justified.[7]

Beveridge was distressed to find that Marshall had opposed the War of 1812 and had continued in his opposition even after hostilities were underway. "Its [sic] 'sure hell' searching for the truth & *finding* it," he wrote William E. Dodd. He even privately condemned Marshall's encouragement of the peace faction in its efforts to end the war as "not only morally but legally seditious." But in the text he sympathized with Marshall's disgust over Jefferson's "feeble" and "futile" retaliatory measures, belabored the Madison administration's truckling and partiality toward France, and took pains to show how Marshall deplored all talk of secession and rebuked resistance by a state to national authority.[8]

His admiration for the chief justice was strengthened by his reaction toward current political developments. For he saw the years after 1916 as another time of national danger similar to that facing Marshall after Jefferson's election. As a patriot, he rallied to the colors as soon as the decision for war was made. He sent telegrams to Indiana Governor James P. Goodrich and the White House offering his services in any capacity; he contributed to the multitude of fundraising drives underway, even borrowing money to buy more Liberty Bonds; he joined many of the patriotic organizations that sprang up; he appealed for "national unity" against the foe; and he called in his speeches for no peace short of unconditional surrender.[9]

But he could not wholeheartedly identify with the war spirit. He grumbled about the burden of the contributions he was asked to make, the rising prices, and the increased taxes; he reported finding growing popular dissatisfaction with the war; he bewailed the diffi-

---

7. Beveridge to Corwin, 22 March, 10 May 1918, Corwin Papers (Princeton University Library). *Marshall*, 3: 350, 496. For a recent defense of Marshall's opinion, see Robert Faulkner, "John Marshall and the Burr Trial," *Journal of American History* 53 (September 1966): 247–58.

8. Beveridge to William E. Dodd, 19 July 1918, Dodd Papers. Beveridge to James A. Woodburn, 10 January 1919, Woodburn Papers (LL). *Marshall*, 4: 8, 12.

9. *Indianapolis Star*, 31 May 1918.

culties that would face the country in the aftermath of the conflict. And he privately lamented that British propaganda had gulled this country into pulling the Allies' chestnuts out of the fire. "Personally," he confided to friends, "I would be willing to have an army of five million men raised and the greatest navy in the world built to uphold and defend American rights and interests"; but to see billions of dollars "squandered" and "scores of thousands of our men killed in order that England can control the Balkans and Asia Minor" made him "physically ill."[10]

Aggravating his depression was the spirit of vigilantism abroad in the land. The Chicago Public Library took his book *What Is Back of the War* off its shelves as pro-German, and the War Department barred the volume from training camp libraries. His failure to take an active part in the Liberty Loan drives until the Fourth Campaign in the fall of 1918 brought down much abuse upon him. His readers even warned him to tone down his account in the Marshall biography of British actions before and during the war of 1812. This wartime hysteria reinforced his sympathy for Marshall's distrust of popular majorities. The present situation, he admonished Jefferson admirer William E. Dodd, gave ample testimony of "how the multitude will (or can be made to) run this way & that like sheep—& devour like wolves. . . . Nothing can be more fanatical and tyranical *[sic]* than a mob."[11]

With peace, an even more dangerous threat to the nation's future safety and well-being appeared. Long before Wilson returned from Versailles, the Hoosier's sensitive nationalism had bristled at the propaganda put out by the League to Enforce Peace in behalf of United States membership in "a league of nations" to prevent future wars. Beveridge's suspicions were reinforced when Wilson, in his 27 May 1916 speech before the league's first national assembly, came out for American participation in such an "association of nations."[12] Beveridge in his campaign speeches that fall assailed the chief executive's plan for an "international alliance" as a "nest of serpent's eggs"

10. Beveridge to W. C. Bobbs, 18 June 1917; to E. L. McClain, 31 July 1917, BP.

11. Beveridge to Dodd, 21 June 1918, Dodd Papers.

12. Ruhl H. Bartlett, *The League to Enforce Peace* (Chapel Hill, N.C., 1944), pp. 40, 55.

that would involve the country in a "jungle of foreign troubles" and called for preservation of the nation's traditional policy of no entangling alliances.[13]

After American entry into the conflict, Wilson made the establishment of "a general association of nations . . . for the purpose of affording mutual guarantees of political independence and territorial integrity" the keystone of his peace program.[14] Alarmed by the favorable popular response, Beveridge raged at the "old male 'grannies' who over their afternoon tea are planning to denationalize America and denationalize the country's manhood." He interrupted his labors on the Marshall to deliver speeches and turn out articles denouncing "mongrel internationalism," and bombarded Republican leaders with pleas that the G.O.P. take as its battle-cry "Get Out of Europe and Stay Out."[15]

A multitude of reasons made Beveridge an irreconcilable on the League of Nations. There was his partisan Republicanism. If Wilson could pose as the savior of mankind from future wars, he, or his hand-picked successor, would win handily in 1920. There was his lifelong Anglophobia. For he saw the league as another British plot to trick their American cousins into guaranteeing and protecting British interests. There was his anxiety to prevent divisions within the United States along nationality lines. Would not membership in the league exacerbate the alarming hyphenism the war had awakened? And to fulfill his dream "to clean up & straighten out Mexico," the United States must retain "a free hand."[16]

What most spurred his hostility to the league was his own high-flying American nationalism. "I am not for America," he explained to publisher Ferris Greenslet, "but 'fer' America, as we say in the corn-fed West—'fer' America first, last and all the time; 'fer' America only, solely and exclusively." But membership in the league would take "out of our hands" the settlement of such "purely American questions" as relations with the Philippines, Cuba, the Panama Canal, the Monroe Doctrine, immigration policy, and even the

---

13. *Indianapolis Star,* 6 October 1916.
14. Thomas A. Bailey, *Woodrow Wilson and the Lost Peace* (New York, 1944), p. 334.
15. Beveridge to Theodore Roosevelt, 19 August 1918; to Will H. Hays, 19 April 1918, BP. *Indianapolis Star,* 31 May 1918.
16. Beveridge to Roosevelt, 5 October 1918, BP.

protective tariff; would take from Congress its constitutional power of declaring war and give that power of life and death over millions of American young men to foreign powers; and thus would mean "the end, historically speaking, of the American Nation as a separate, sovereign and independent power in the world."[17]

At the same time, he warned that Wilson's dream for the United States to act as world policeman would lead to endless trouble. In most instances, how could anyone determine which was the aggressor and which not? The futile American expeditionary force in Russia was but a foretaste of the foreign conflicts in which this country would become involved if a member of the league. Let us take advantage of our geographical blessings to remain aloof from the storms besetting the old world, he pleaded. "We are now in a perfectly wonderful position of power—we sit on the throne of the world—the world's greatest oceans on either side of us. Why surrender such a position which nature and providence has given us?"[18]

The news of details of the peace terms reinforced his anxieties about the league. The treaty was not the peace without victory that Wilson had promised but was as "sordid and disgraceful" a dividing up the "spoils" as history had recorded. Yet under article 10 of the covenant, "we are to underwrite these settlements and uphold them with our blood and money for all time to come." Beveridge saw the same handful of "international bankers" who had pushed this country into the war to save their loans to the Allies as the moving force behind the pro-league propaganda in the United States. The league, he fumed, was simply "a scheme to put the resources of this country back of the mountains of billions of British, French and Italian war bonds in which certain financiers . . . have invested enormously."[19]

The Hoosier bombarded the Senate foes of the treaty with advice on strategy, pleas to stand firm, and assurances of popular support. Hostility toward the league made for strange bedfellows. Whereas before he could not find words sufficient to denounce William E. Borah as a fake progressive, he could not now praise too highly the Idaho lawmaker. He found unsuspected qualities of courage, ability,

---

17. Beveridge to Ferris Greenslet, 10 April 1919; to Shaffer, 5 October 1918; to Albert B. Cummins, 20 February 1919, BP.

18. Beveridge to Chase S. Osborn, 4 February 1918, BP.

19. Beveridge to George Harvey, 22 April 1919; to Harry S. New, 15 September 1919; to Shaffer, 25 March 1919, BP.

and patriotism in old guardsman Frank Brandegee of Connecticut, while he extolled Philander C. Knox, from Boss Penrose's Pennsylvania fiefdom, as "one of the greatest, if not indeed the very greatest American statesmen of our times."[20] He was full of praise for Harry S. New when the Indiana lawmaker came out as a strong reservationist. The exigencies of the situation even overcame his long-time jealousy and dislike of Foreign Relations Committee chairman Henry Cabot Lodge.

Beveridge was impatient, however, with Lodge's more conciliatory —and more devious—approach. As the debate went on, he fussed about the willingness of the "concessionists" to "concede our case away." He dismissed any and all reservations as worthless. Could Wilson—who would remain in the White House until 4 March 1921— be trusted to abide by any reservations? And who would interpret the reservations? "The League Government," he answered; and thus "all our so-called reservations will be construed away," just as in the United States John Marshall had whittled down state's rights. "The entire League Covenant must be defeated, root and branch."[21]

The treaty's foes appealed to him to go on a nationwide speaking tour to rally public sentiment against the league. He had at first to refuse because he had promised Houghton Mifflin to have volumes three and four of the Marshall biography ready for publication in the fall of 1919. Although he kept two stenographers busy taking dictation and checking references, he did not finish volume four until May, and there remained the task of revision, verification of citations, and reading the proofs. He felt so strongly, however, that the nation's future was at stake that he agreed to take off a week from his proof-reading to make a swing through the Middle West. But the Chicago race riot forced cancelation of his speech there, and when he found the meeting in Saint Paul "in very bad hands," he abandoned the trip and hastened back to Beverly Farms.[22]

He feared Wilson—whom he regarded as the "craftiest of politicians since Jefferson"—would accept the reservations and thus win over sufficient Republican votes to ratify this "betrayal of America."[23]

20. Beveridge to Mrs. Philander C. Knox, 13 October 1921 (telegram), BP.
21. Beveridge to William E. Borah, 13 March 1919; to Cummins, 1 August 1919; to Philander C. Knox, 13 June, 5 October 1919, BP.
22. Beveridge to Harvey, 31 July 1919, BP.
23. Beveridge to Hiram Johnson, 31 July 1919; to Borah, 31 July 1919, BP.

But the chief executive played into the irreconcilables' hands by refusing to make any compromises. When on 19 November 1919 the Democrats in the Senate followed the president's instructions and joined with the irreconcilables to defeat the treaty with the Lodge reservations, Beveridge hailed the vote as "the greatest victory for America" since the founding of the republic. And he told Lodge: "You have risen to heights of statesmanship as lofty as, in the history of this country, ever has been reached by any man and you have shown, as a political general, a skill, wisdom, courage and patience that has few parallels."[24]

Looking back at John Marshall, Beveridge could but contrast Marshall's labors in upbuilding "the American Nation" with those "internationalists" who "propose to abolish the whole thing and go in for the 'brotherhood of man and federation of the world,' and all that sort of thing." He looked upon the biography not as simply a historical exercise but a tract for his own time that would reveal "the fundamentals upon which our Nation rests and must continue to rest if it is to endure." The most important of these was exclusive and undivided Americanism. "Marshall gets more reactionary as he grows older," the Hoosier wrote William E. Dodd. "But he had *one* GREAT idea—holding the Nation together. . . . Nationalism is our one and only hope."[25]

Thus Beveridge reduced the complex issues facing the court and country in the years after the War of 1812 into a struggle between nationalism and localism—with slavery, free trade, state banking, and debtor's relief laws aligned with localism, while slavery restriction, national banking, a protective tariff, and security of contract were marshaled behind the banner of nationalism. Marshall's decisions in *M'Culloch* v. *Maryland* (1819) and *Osborn* v. *Bank of the United States* (1824), upholding the constitutionality of the Bank of the United States, and *Cohens* v. *Virginia* (1821), affirming the supremacy of the Supreme Court over state tribunals, were presented as the great chief justice's answer to "that defiance of the National Govern-

---

24. Beveridge to Knox, 22 November 1919; to Henry Cabot Lodge, 21 November 1919, BP.

25. Beveridge to Clarence W. Alvord, 27 December 1918; to H. O. Fairchild, 21 February 1920, BP. Beveridge to Dodd, 7 July 1918, Dodd Papers.

ment and to the threats of disunion then growing ever bolder and more vociferous."[26]

Beveridge's admiration for Marshall extended to the chief justice's bias in favor of vested property rights. Did Marshall, in his decision in *Fletcher* v. *Peck* (1810), stretch the meaning of the contract clause to include legislative grants? Did he not stretch that meaning even more in the Dartmouth College case (1819), when he held a corporate charter a contract? Marshall's actions, Beveridge answered, were justified, or to be more accurate, were demanded, by "the mania for contract breaking" sweeping the country at the time. American business could not have progressed without the stability and protection given by those decisions. But did not those decisions leave the people at the mercy of a corrupt legislature? "If citizens will not select honest and able men as their public agents," Beveridge maintained, "they must suffer the consequences of their indifference to their own affairs."[27]

Perhaps the most troublesome and difficult section was that dealing with the case of *Fairfax's Devisee* v. *Hunter's Leasee* (1813). Gustavus Myers, in his debunking *History of the Supreme Court*, had asserted that Marshall had had a personal financial stake in the litigation. When his own researches appeared to confirm that Marshall was up "to some crooked work," Beveridge was tempted to relegate the case to a footnote or even "leave it out altogether."[28] But, strongly admonished by his readers to tell the full story and let the blame fall where it would, and retaining his faith in Marshall's honesty, he continued digging through the records. He was jubilant when he found conclusive evidence vindicating Marshall. Although he did not refer to the Myers work, even in his bibliography, he took pains to underline that Marshall's brother, not Marshall himself, had purchased from the Fairfax estate the disputed lands, that Marshall had "no personal interest whatever" in the litigation, and that he had "leaned backward" in refusing to sit during the arguments or participate in the discussions and conclusions of his fellow justices. "It would have been nothing short of tragic," Beveridge confided to Max Farrand, "had it turned out that the character of this great man had

26. *Marshall*, 4: 343.
27. Beveridge to Lodge, 28 December 1918, BP. *Marshall*, 3: 594.
28. Beveridge to Corwin, 12 March 1919; to Alvord, 28 March 1919, BP.

a rotten spot in it. Now that I am drawing my last volume to a close and get Marshall's proportions more accurately, and am better able to judge him truly, it is a joy that he grows upon me all the time in bigness, purity and strength."[29]

After reviewing Marshall's great decisions, Beveridge went on to present him as "the Supreme Conservative" in the Virginia Constitutional Convention of 1829–30, resisting with considerable success the rising tide of democracy. Although failing to point out how Marshall aided in the defeat of gradual abolition at a time when Virginia's action would have had far-reaching repercussions throughout the upper South, he did show how Marshall played a leading role in preserving the predominance of the slaveholding areas in the legislature and in maintaining the principle of property qualification as against manhood suffrage. By present-day standards, Beveridge admitted, Marshall's stand smacks of "cold reaction." But "had the convention reached any other conclusion than that to which Marshall gently guided it," the state would have been torn by dissension and even bloody strife. And if Virginia split asunder, he concluded triumphantly, "the growing sentiment for disunion would have received a powerful impulse."[30]

The final chapter was a moving portrayal of the aged chief justice saddened by the death of his beloved wife, his own health worsening, more and more despondent over the excesses of democracy in the age of Jackson, Georgia's successful defiance of the Supreme Court over its Indian policies, the swing away from his constitutional principles by his fellow justices, and the growing aggressiveness of disunionist sentiments. After several futile attempts, Beveridge decided against writing a final judgment or appraisal. "Try hard as I could," he explained to Max Farrand, "it was impossible to say anything that had not already been said in the four volumes."[31]

As his publisher's deadline approached, Beveridge toiled away at high speed and under tremendous pressure. He was the more anxious to finish because he had in the back of his mind the idea of trying

---

29. *Marshall,* 4: 150–51, 153–54. Beveridge to Farrand, 26 April 1919, BP.

30. *Marshall,* 4: 507–8. For criticism of Beveridge's account of Marshall's role in the Virginia constitutional convention, see Tracy E. Strevey, "Albert J. Beveridge," in William T. Hutchinson, ed., *The Marcus W. Jernegan Essays in American Historiography* (Chicago, 1937), p. 390.

31. Beveridge to Farrand, 15 September 1919, BP.

for a political comeback. Unfortunately, Lindsay Swift, who was going over the proofs as they came in, complained about the hundreds of errors that had crept in. Beveridge thought that Swift was simply overtired and exaggerating. But he acceded to Swift's plea that he hire a second man to assist in proofreading, looking up doubtful points, and preparing the bibliography. Finally, on 19 September, Beveridge returned the last of the proofs to the publishers.

To tap all possible markets, Houghton Mifflin put out a special autograph edition, a regular edition for sale through bookstores, and an edition for sale through subscription agents. Beveridge bombarded Houghton Mifflin with suggestions for promotion, including asking members of the Supreme Court for their endorsement and submitting the work for the Nobel Prize. He traveled around the country giving talks before bar association meetings on John Marshall and the development of the Constitution. He arranged through his friends in the magazine and newspaper world for favorable reviews. The curtailment of his magazine writing while finishing the Marshall plus the expenses of research had left him short of money. Besides, he looked upon publicity for the Marshall as a major asset in his hoped-for political comeback.

Like most authors, Beveridge complained to his publishers that they were not sufficiently advertising the work, that they were failing to keep the book stores adequately stocked, that they were pushing the subscription edition—from which he made less money—at the expense of trade sales. But these passing misunderstandings were smoothed away by the book's success. Despite its price, the Marshall even hit the best seller lists in many cities. Beveridge's half-share of the profits for the first six months of 1920 amounted to $5,940; for the first six months of 1921, $6,125. And the sales kept up steadily. As late as 1925, his proceeds for the first six months came to $1,741.

The second two volumes received a more mixed reception among professional historians than the first two volumes had. J. Franklin Jameson praised his grasp of "Marshall the politician and of the political implications of his work." But he privately felt that the Hoosier was "a little sophomoric in mind," "not very deep," and "not quite enough of a lawyer to deal in a really masterly manner with the legal aspects of Marshall's decisions." William E. Dodd had grown more and more unhappy over Beveridge's taking "sides." While acknowledging Beveridge's "industry," "faculty of clear statement," and skill in portraying Marshall's personal character, John Spencer Bassett in the *American Historical Review* found that the work "fails in the detachment that is the finest quality of the historian."[32]

The author was badly upset by an unsigned review in the *New York Evening Sun* contrasting his work unfavorably with Edward S. Corwin's brief *John Marshall and the Constitution* in the Yale Chronicles of America series. The reviewer blasted Beveridge for coloring "the events of the past to suit his own preconceived ideas and prejudices," most strikingly in his treatment of the Burr trial. When Beveridge learned that the author of the review was Thomas Jefferson Wertenbaker, then an instructor at Princeton, he suspected that Corwin had inspired his young colleague's attack. Although Corwin denied any hand in the review, and himself wrote a favorable appraisal of the volumes for the *Mississippi Valley Historical Review*, Beveridge's suspicions remained.[33]

He was even more distressed when University of Chicago constitutional historian Andrew McLaughlin lambasted his anti-Jefferson bias and his weakness in dealing with the legal side of Marshall's decisions in a review in the *Journal* of the American Bar Association. Although he had praised McLaughlin as "a darned good man and sound scholar," Beveridge was so stung by the review that he dashed off an angry letter to McLaughlin's University of Chicago colleague William E. Dodd, charging McLaughlin with not having read the volumes, "at least with any sort of care"; with the academician's jealousy of any non-Ph.D. writing a scholarly work, and a popular one at that; and even with "personal animosity." "I'll bet you," he raged, ". . . that McLaughlin's 'review' hurts him a lot more than me."[34]

But even among the scholars, the preponderance of comment was highly favorable. Clarence W. Alvord assured him that he had written "a great study." Charles A. Beard wrote that the volumes would be read "long after the Senator from Indiana or even Indiana is forgotten." Worthington C. Ford hailed the work as "a permanently

---

32. J. Franklin Jameson to James Bryce, 5 April 1920, in Leo F. Stock, ed., "Some Bryce-Jameson Correspondence," *AHR* 50 (January 1945): 289–91. Dodd to Beveridge, 15 June [1918], BP. *AHR* 25 (April 1920): 515–17.

33. *New York Evening Sun*, 20 December 1919. Corwin's own review appeared in *MVHR* 6 (March 1920): 581–84.

34. Beveridge to Dodd, 20 May, 1, 17 June 1921, Dodd Papers. For the review, see Andrew C. McLaughlin, "The Life of John Marshall," American Bar Association *Journal* 7 (May 1921): 231–33.

useful contribution to history"; Samuel Eliot Morison declared in the *Atlantic Monthly* that the volumes "will rank with the best historical biographies of American statesmen." Constitutional law expert Robert E. Cushman, then teaching political science at the University of Minnesota, praised the volumes as a work of "astonishingly accurate and exhaustive historical research," written "in a style so graceful and entertaining that the reader's interest will not lag through the two thousand five hundred odd pages," "a model to which the future writers of biographies may well repair."[35]

The most enthusiastic praise came from the legal fraternity. A professor of constitutional law at the University of Pennsylvania praised Beveridge's success in giving Marshall's decisions "their true place in the early history of our institutions." A federal court of appeals judge said the book "ought to be in the hands of every lover of his country, to guide him in solving some of the vital questions of the present day." Justice Oliver Wendell Holmes congratulated him on his depiction of "the Milieu and antecedents of Marshall's opinions." Leading constitutional lawyer Louis Marshall wrote him that he had "enabled us to appreciate better than ever before, . . . [Marshall's] wonderful contribution to American life—the idea that we are a Nation." The distinguished Thomas Reed Powell of Harvard Law School, in his review in *The Nation*, called the work a "really great biography."[36]

The lay public joined in the applause. The reviewer for the *New York Times* said "the story is told with such clearness and brilliancy that the biography has all the color, quality and interest of a great historical romance." The literary editor of the *New York Tribune* thought the volumes "peculiarly timely" in view of current attacks of the courts as the bulwarks of "ordered government." Columbia University president Nicholas Murray Butler hailed Beveridge's "literally stupendous contribution to American history and to American gov-

---

35. Alvord to Beveridge, 1 July 1919; Charles A. Beard to Beveridge, 29 November 1919; Worthington C. Ford to Beveridge, 3 June 1920, BP. Samuel Eliot Morison, "The Education of John Marshall," *Atlantic Monthly* 126 (July 1920): 45. Robert E. Cushman, "Marshall and the Constitution," *Minnesota Law Review* 5 (December 1920): 2–3.

36. Henry Wolf Bickle to Beveridge, 26 August 1920; William W. Morrow to Beveridge, 27 July 1920; Oliver Wendell Holmes, Jr., to Beveridge, 14 February 1920; Louis Marshall to Beveridge, 31 March 1920, BP. *The Nation*, 10 April 1920, pp. 478–79.

ernment." The chancellor of the University of Pittsburgh called the work, with its praise of Marshall, "a genuine contribution to the well-being and stability of the Nation at this particular period of our political and social development." General Leonard Wood applauded the volumes as "one of the most valuable and instructive works . . . ever produced in this country."[37]

Along with the praise came new honors: the 1920 Pulitzer Prize for biography; honorary degrees from Lafayette College, the University of Pennsylvania, and Brown University; election to membership in the American Antiquarian Society, the National Institute of Arts and Letters, and the American Academy of Arts and Letters. The Roosevelt Memorial Association awarded him its gold medal for "an eminent contribution to literature in the field of biography."[38] Leading universities vied to have him speak. The reception given *The Life of John Marshall*, Beveridge rejoiced, "goes far to reward me for the years of grinding toil I put into the production of it. I am more than ever convinced of the ancient truism that the extent of anybody's success depends upon the heart beats and life blood that one is willing to pay for it."[39]

---

37. *New York Times*, 25 January 1920. *Indianapolis Star*, 10 December 1919. Nicholas Murray Butler to Beveridge, 29 November 1919; S. B. McCormick to Beveridge, 5 January 1920; Leonard Wood to Beveridge, 13 December 1920, BP.
38. *New York Times*, 3 May 1926.
39. Beveridge to Richard W. Child, 23 February 1920, BP.

20

Trying for a Political Comeback

While finishing the biography, Beveridge was anticipating a political comeback. In 1920 his bitter personal and political rival, James E. Watson, was coming up for reelection to the Senate. Beveridge asked his friends to begin lining up support for a possible primary fight; he had his publisher flood the state with publicity for the Marshall book; and he himself returned to Indiana as soon as the book was off his hands to sound out the situation while speaking over the state for the Roosevelt Memorial Fund.

The long-standing factional rivalry between Watson, on the one hand, and Governor James P. Goodrich and former state chairman Will H. Hays, the newly elected Republican national chairman, on the other, worked to his advantage. Despite his past ties, Goodrich had proved a surprisingly progressive-minded chief executive, urging revision of Indiana's long out-of-date constitution, a state income tax, woman's suffrage, an item veto in appropriation bills, the short ballot, and simplification of the amending procedure. As Republican state chairman, Hays had successfully harmonized returning Bull Moosers back into the G.O.P. fold. And he owed his election as Republican National Chairman in February 1918 in large part to the support for former Progressives. Anxious for Beveridge's support, Goodrich and Hays played up to him, urged him to try for the G.O.P. senatorial nomination, and even humored his presidential ambitions.

As the filing deadline for the 1920 primary election approached, however, Beveridge began to have second thoughts about running. Watson would be a tough man to defeat. He retained in the back of his mind doubts about the trustworthiness of the Hays-Goodrich people, and these doubts were reinforced when Hays abandoned his plans to run for governor and decided to remain as G.O.P. national chairman without even telling Beveridge in advance. Beveridge was worried about the expense of a primary battle. His wife was against his running, while he himself had doubts if he should give up his newly won reputation as a historian to return to the political wars. And his pro-German reputation remained a handicap.

But what most cooled his interest in the Senate race was his re-awakened hopes for the presidency. T.R. had been the odds-on favorite to win the G.O.P. nomination in 1920. Even old guard leaders had rallied behind the former chief executive as the party's strongest vote-getter. Despite Beveridge's resentment about the death of the Progressive party, Roosevelt's praise for the first two volumes of the Marshall biography and their shared antagonism to Wilsonian "internationalism" had brought a rapprochement.[1] And Beveridge was deeply saddened by Roosevelt's death on 6 January 1919.

With Roosevelt gone, four major contenders entered the lists for the Republican presidential nomination—General Leonard Wood, the heir to much of the Roosevelt personal following, Senator Hiram Johnson of California, leader of the party's progressive wing and darling of the irreconcilables on the League of Nations, Governor Frank Lowden of Illinois, and Senator Warren G. Harding of Ohio, while a host of possible dark horses stood by. Given the confused political situation, Beveridge—encouraged by the ever hopeful John C. Shaffer—had visions of himself as a dark horse nominee. Publishers Frank Munsey and George Harvey promised their support as would-be king makers. The strategy was to slip Beveridge in as

---

1. Beveridge to Theodore Roosevelt, 5 October 1918, BP.

temporary chairman of the Republican National Convention in the hope that his keynote speech would stampede the convention. To lay the ground, Beveridge arranged for a series of major speeches to bring his name and views before the country.

At a time when such action took courage, Beveridge spoke out against the Red Scare sweeping over the country. He assailed, in his speeches and articles, the mob spirit that would deny the advocates of unpopular doctrines a hearing, blasted Attorney General A. Mitchell Palmer for his "astounding and highly advertised crusade against that free speech and free assemblage guaranteed by our Constitution," and warned that such "lawless" suppression of free speech "destroys the very foundations upon which the American nation rests."[2] As chairman of the Subcommittee on Law and Order of the Advisory Committee on Policies and Platform of the Republican National Committee, he put his signature on a report prepared by Dean Harlan Fiske Stone of Columbia Law School against a peacetime sedition law.

Though alarmed by the dangers of radicalism, he saw repression as worse than futile. As a matter of "good policy alone," he admonished supporters of a peacetime sedition law, the wisest course was "to let silly theorists and wildeyed visionaries blow off steam." But freedom of speech was more than a question of expediency for Beveridge. Despite his own fits of depression over the wisdom of popular majorities, he remained too much within the American mainstream to abandon his faith in "the good sense and upright character" of "the great body of the people." He took as his guide the "clear and present danger" rule laid down by his friend Justice Oliver Wendell Holmes, Jr., in *Schenck v. United States*. When Edward S. Corwin protested that the most vicious provocation to violence may be camouflaged in the most innocent-sounding language, Beveridge replied that this was "one of the perils incident to free institutions."[3]

The high point of his defense of civil liberties was his speech "The Assault upon American Fundamentals" before the annual meeting of

---

2. *Collier's*, 12 June 1920, p. 8. *Indianapolis Star*, 30 January 1920.
3. Beveridge to William Fortune, 6 August 1920; to Augustus Mason, 5 August 1920; to Edward S. Corwin, 3 March 1920, BP.

the American Bar Association in August 1920. He had a research assistant look up the growing body of state sedition laws; Zachariah Chaffee, Jr., of Harvard Law School sent him the proofs of his forthcoming book *Free Speech in the United States;* officials of the newly founded American Civil Liberties Union supplied information from its files; Charles Evans Hughes provided details about the expulsion of the legally elected Socialist members of the New York legislature. Beveridge was so shocked at what he found that he disregarded the advice of business friends to tread softly and he delivered a blistering, fully documented attack upon federal and state violations of the "American fundamentals guaranteed in our National Bill of Rights," which drew enthusiastic applause from even the largely conservative Bar Association delegates.[4]

Except for his defense of free speech, Beveridge's views should have pleased the most die-hard old guardsman. For a time after the break-up of the Progressive party, he remained faithful to its spirit: demanding a wartime excess profits tax, urging government recognition and support of collective bargaining between labor and management, and upholding the duty of the government to safeguard the health and welfare of the less fortunate members of society.[5] By the end of the war, however, he was convinced that the death of the Progressive party had destroyed the possibility of an effective liberal movement in United States for many years. His devotion to John Marshall had imbued him with the great chief justice's bias in favor of property rights against fickle majorities. And he was moved by alarm over the Bolshevik Revolution and its worldwide thrust.

But what had happened was not so much that Beveridge had swung to the right as that he was standing pat while the world moved into what he regarded as new and dangerous paths. He was never temperamentally a radical or even a reformer. He was a worshiper of order, efficiency, and material progress. In the heyday of progressivism, he had hewed to his vision of the neutral state, above the clashing groups in society, devoted to the public good. The major threat to that public good in the years after the turn of the

---

4. Beveridge, *The Assault upon American Fundamentals,* p. 4.
5. Beveridge, "The School and the Nation," *National Education Association of the United States: Addresses and Proceedings . . . 1917* (Washington, 1917), p. 685. *Indianapolis Star,* 15 April 1917, 23 February, 31 May 1918.

century had come from unrestrained wealth, and thus he called for strengthening the national government to prevent corporate wrong-doing and a large measure of social justice legislation to blunt the dangers of social upheaval from below. But he was never against big business, simply its abuses. And by 1919 he rejoiced that "those evil days are gone forever": that the "fundamental reforms so indispensable to promotion of the general welfare, so necessary to the prevention of a social, industrial and political cataclysm . . . are accepted by everybody as permanent, wise and righteous."[6]

Rather, the trouble was that regulation of business had gone too far. Reacting against the unprecedented centralization, bureaucratization, restraints upon men's activities, and high taxes accompanying the war, Beveridge criticized the extravagance and inefficiency of the government's wartime operation of the railroads, the proposals for postwar government ownership of the railroads and the merchant marine, and the growth of an "arrogant and insolent bureaucracy." And when the recession that settled over the country from the Armistice to the middle of 1919 reminded Beveridge of the grim days of the 1890s, he blamed governmental harassment and excessive taxes for paralyzing business activity. The return of prosperity, he warned, required a halt to bureaucratic interference with business, governmental economy, elimination of the wartime excess profits tax, restoration of the railroads to private hands, "a greater degree of protection . . . than ever before," a subsidy for the merchant marine, government encouragement and protection of American overseas trade and investment, repeal of the Sherman Act, and a return of hard work and thrift.[7]

If lawless capital were no longer a threat, there was another and more dangerous brand of "special privilege" menacing republican institutions. Even in the heyday of his progressivism, Beveridge had remained ambivalent toward labor unions. The passage of the Adamson Act followed by the labor turmoil at the war's end—the Boston police strike, the Seattle general strike, the strikes by the anthracite coal miners and the steel workers—transformed this ambivalence into distrust and anxiety. "Just as yesterday the question was whether

6. *Indianapolis Star*, 25 October 1919.
7. Beveridge to Henry M. Leland, 17 February 1920, BP. *Indianapolis Star*, 30 January 1920.

financial plunderers should exploit the nation, so today," he proclaimed in his speech celebrating the 299th anniversary of the landing of the Pilgrims in December 1919, "the question is whether labor bandits shall hold up the republic." He placed the major blame for the high cost of living upon extortionate wage increases won by the unions, denied any right to strike against the public interest, and called upon the government of all the people to stand firm against "labor autocrats."[8]

He kept up his fire against the League of Nations. He warned against the "alien propaganda" flooding the country "to weaken and destroy the very foundation of American nationalism." He urged the Senate irreconcilables to stand fast against efforts to "browbeat or seduce our men into accepting some sort of a 'compromise.'" He blasted talk of a possible alliance with Britain and France as contrary to America's traditional policy of neutrality. He found new arguments against American entanglement in European affairs in John Maynard Keynes's devastating attack upon the peace treaty, *The Economic Consequences of the Peace*. Even after the second—and final—vote on the treaty in March 1920, he continued to worry about a plot to sneak the United States into the league through the back door via the "Root World Court–League scheme" and exhorted Republican leaders to take up boldly Wilson's challenge to make the 1920 election a referendum on the league.[9]

While Beveridge was speaking out on the issues, John C. Shaffer was working to snare for him the temporary chairmanship of the national convention. Republican national chairman Will H. Hays promised his support. Hays had made his own deal with Watson, whereby Watson would abandon his bid to take over the state organization if allowed a clear field for his renomination, and thus Hays wanted Beveridge out of the Senate race. Watson, anxious to forestall a primary fight, pledged to arrange for Beveridge's selection as one of the four delegates-at-large from Indiana and back him for the temporary chairmanship. In return, Beveridge publicly announced that he would not run for the Senate for the sake of party harmony.

---

8. *Indianapolis Star*, 31 October 1916, 23 December 1919, 30 January 1920.
9. Ibid., 23 December 1919. Beveridge to Albert B. Cummins, 24 November 1919; to George Wharton Pepper, 18 September 1920, BP.

"The stars in their courses," he exulted to Shaffer, "are fighting for us."[10]

Because of his dark-horse ambitions, Beveridge remained aloof from the battle underway in Indiana between the leading presidential aspirants. After a bitterly fought campaign, Wood won a plurality in the Indiana presidential preference primary. But Johnson had run a surprisingly strong second. Lowden was third, while Harding—despite the public support of Senator Harry S. New and the behind-the-scenes backing of Watson—came in a poor fourth. After much debate, the Republican state convention voted to instruct the Indiana delegates-at-large to support Wood as long as he had a chance for the nomination. And party leaders grudgingly, in face of Shaffer's threatened retaliation by his newspapers, carried through with the bargain to select Beveridge as one of the "Big Four" delegates-at-large.

As convention time approached with none of the candidates having a decisive lead, Beveridge continued to hope against hope that the presidential lightning might yet strike him if he could sweep the delegates off their feet by his keynote address. But Hays failed to carry through with his promised support for the temporary chairmanship. Beveridge's hopes were dashed when the committee on convention arrangements at its meeting on 10 May chose Henry Cabot Lodge to deliver the keynote. As a sop to Beveridge, the story was leaked to the newspapers that he would be chosen the permanent chairman. Grasping at this straw, Beveridge appealed to friendly newspapermen to run stories and editorials boosting him for the permanent chairmanship, sought to line up support among the convention delegates, and even arranged for a public relations man to plant favorable stories about him as a possible dark-horse candidate for president.

Old guard leaders, however, had not forgiven his bolt in 1912. Supporters of the League of Nations and even mild reservationists balked at him as an irreconcilable. Rival presidential aspirants jockeyed for position. And Watson, despite his pledges, knifed his fellow Hoosier by making his own bid for the chairmanship of convention's all-important resolutions committee. The final blow came from his former Progressive party comrade-in-arms, Hiram Johnson. In a bow toward the progressive, anti-league wing of the party, the senatorial

10. Beveridge to John C. Shaffer, 16 February 1920, BP.

leaders managing the convention arrangements were willing to allow Johnson to name the permanent chairman. Johnson, perhaps suspicious when the Wood backers came out for Beveridge for the place, insisted upon William E. Borah. But the Idaho lawmaker refused to because of his involvement in the campaign-funds investigation underway. When the convention met, the committee on permanent arrangements voted to keep Lodge on as permanent chairman.

After this fiasco, Beveridge resolved to challege Harry S. New for the 1922 senatorial nomination. Hiram Johnson's showing in the presidential primaries had shown him the continuing strength of progressive sentiment and the popular appeal of the Californian's stand against the league. And he saw no alternative to his making the fight if he were to have any political future. Not simply was Watson untrustworthy and unscrupulous, but Beveridge was disillusioned and disgusted with Hays and Goodrich. "I have about definitely made up my mind," he alerted his Indiana friends, "to 'go to it' after the election is over, in the same systematic and thorough way that I did when I was in the Senate. There is no use to depend upon any of that crowd any longer."[11]

To support Harding was distasteful for Beveridge. He was put off by the Ohioan's past ties with the old guard, doubted if he was the strong man required to deal with the difficult times ahead, and distrusted him as a straddler on the league. Although "tremendously pleased" with Harding's stand against the league in his acceptance speech, he was furious at Harding's backtracking and endorsing American membership in "a world court," which, he said, would nullify "practically all" of what had been won in the defeat of the covenant.[12]

To support Watson for reelection was even more repugnant to Beveridge. But he realized that he could not afford to sulk in his tent if he were to run for the Senate two years later. After much haggling over scheduling, accommodations, and publicity, he made another extensive speaking tour, in and out of Indiana. He was so heartsick over what was happening, however, that for the first time he de-

---

11. Beveridge to Charles W. Miller, 3 July 1920, BP.
12. Beveridge to Halbert P. Gardner, 28 July 1920; to William E. Borah, 21 September 1920, BP. For Harding's endorsement of American membership in "a world court," see Wesley M. Bagby, *The Road to Normalcy: The Presidential Campaign and Election of 1920* (Baltimore, 1962), p. 136.

manded reimbursement for his expenses—although he took pains to hide the fact by having the G.O.P. National Committee send the check to his secretary rather than to himself.[13]

From the start of the campaign, he had no doubt that the accumulated grievances against the "ins" assured a "historic" Republican triumph.[14] Nevertheless, even he was surprised by the G.O.P. landslide that fall. And he foresaw difficulties ahead despite, or rather because of, the magnitude of the victory. The Republican majority, he realized, was "made up of inharmonious, and, I fear, irreconcilable elements." There were old-line reactionaries who had learned nothing and forgotten nothing at one extreme; at the other, radicals bitter over the war and the Red Scare. There were the different nationality groups—the Irish-Americans, the Italian-Americans, and the German-Americans—up in arms against the Versailles Treaty. Worse, he lamented, "the people have been led by a horde of uninformed stump speakers to expect that when we take charge everything will be all right," while, "as a matter of fact, no human power can untangle the muddle of economic conditions in which we are enmeshed" before the next election.[15]

After the 1920 election, Beveridge put his drive for the senatorial nomination two years later into high gear. He criss-crossed Indiana speaking before local civic, business, and church groups, women's clubs, bar associations, and American Legion posts. He saw that his Marshall book was well publicized in the state. Alarmed by moves underway to repeal or water-down the direct primary law, he took the lead in rallying public sentiment to block that move. A nucleus of long-time personal friends—A. M. Glossbrenner, Charles W. Miller, W. C. Bobbs, Leopold G. Rothschild, Willitts A. Bastian, former Seventh District Progressive party chairman, and Clarence R. Martin, former Marion County Progressive party chairman, undertook the "practical" work of building a political organization from the ground up.[16]

There was talk that Beveridge was slated to receive a high post

---

13. Beveridge to E. L. McClain, 25 September 1920; J. R. Blocher to Beveridge, 4 November 1920, BP.

14. Beveridge to Cummins, 28 July 1920, BP.

15. Beveridge to William R. Thayer, 16 November 1920; to William Heyburn, 9 November 1920, BP.

16. Beveridge to Ernest Bross, 17 June 1921, BP.

under the new administration as a move toward reconciling former
Progressives. But the only position that he wanted was the secretaryship of state, and he had no illusions about his chances. When
Harding offered him the ambassadorship to Japan, he turned the job
down as an expensive dead-end. The chief executive, anxious to
smooth the way for the renomination of his long-time personal friend
and political supporter, Harry S. New, approached him again, this
time with the ambassadorship to Germany. Again Beveridge declined.
"I shall either go to the Senate," he informed his Indiana supporters,
"or cut out all public activities absolutely and forever, and devote my
life to literature."[17]

Despite favorable reports from his Indiana lieutenants, Beveridge
began to have second thoughts about entering the 1922 primary contest against incumbent Harry S. New for the G.O.P. senatorial nomination. A proud man, he would rather not run than suffer another
defeat. New was a colorless, negative personality, and no match for
Beveridge as a campaigner. But he did have the strong backing of
the existing Republican state organization. And where would the
administration stand in the primary fight? Even if he won the primary,
what about the general election? The continuing postwar depression
was producing a reaction against the G.O.P. that would make victory
in 1922 doubtful. Democratic gains in the Indiana municipal elections
of November 1921 showed how the wind was blowing. Perhaps he
should retire gracefully from politics and devote his remaining years
to scholarship. He had won an assured reputation as a historian, and
the scholarly life had its attractions for a man of his advancing years
contrasted with the turmoil and frustrations of politics.

He had fallen in love with Beverly Farms and more and more
looked upon the North Shore village rather than Indianapolis as his
home. He kept a watchful eye for undesirable businesses that might
impair its beauty and reduce property values. He was elected a cor-
responding member of the Massachusetts Historical Society, was
nominated for membership in the Union League Club of Boston,
and became a life member of the Essex Institute. There he found a
new circle of friends—such as the distinguished Boston lawyer Arthur
Lord, Harold J. Coolidge of the Boston Coolidges, "Jimmie" Williams,
editor of the *Boston Transcript,* William R. Thayer, the popular biog-

---

17. Beveridge to Clarence R. Martin, 9 September 1921, BP.

rapher of Cavour and John Hay, Justice Oliver Wendell Holmes, Jr., literary critic Barrett Wendell, Harvard historians Edward Channing and Samuel Eliot Morison, Felix Frankfurter of Harvard Law School, and Worthington C. Ford. And these men urged him to devote his remaining years to history.

He had decided that if he did not run, his next project would be a multivolume biography of Abraham Lincoln. At first, he had inclined toward following the Marshall biography with a life of the elder William Pitt. But he was too much of an Anglophobe to feel comfortable with the great English nationalist; he doubted sales potentialities of such a book in the United States; and a quick check revealed that several "very well done" studies had been recently published in Britain. After further thought, he decided on Lincoln. Even a hasty look convinced him that most of the vast amount that had been written about Lincoln was "trash." The Houghton Mifflin people were enthusiastic about the sales possibilities of a Lincoln biography. Above all, Beveridge saw Lincoln as the statesman who had taken up and brought to fulfillment Marshall's nationalist philosophy.[18]

When the time came, however, the pull of political ambition remained too strong. Convinced by the reports from Indiana of a groundswell of popular support in his favor, Beveridge decided to go ahead with the race. His supporters began organizing Beveridge-for-senator clubs throughout the state. Discreet inquiries at the White House reassured him that while Harding personally favored New's reelection, he would remain neutral in the primary. His formal announcement was stage-managed for maximum effect. The Beveridge-for-senator clubs were instructed to send representatives to a rally at Beveridge's home in Indianapolis on 16 February, to ask him to run. Continuing to play the reluctant candidate to the last, he replied that their "spontaneous" and "voluntary" appeal constituted "a mandate which no man can ignore."[19]

No substantive policy differences divided Beveridge and his rival. New was a stalwart champion of the Harding administration's foreign policy, while Beveridge was privately hostile. He distrusted secretary

---

18. Beveridge to Worthington C. Ford, 9 November 1920, BP.
19. *Indianapolis Star,* 17 February 1922.

of state Charles Evans Hughes as pro-league. He was angered by the administration-backed treaty indemnifying "the Colombian black mailers" over the Panama affair. He suspected the Washington Disarmament Conference and its Four-Power Treaty as a British-inspired scheme to inveigle the United States into an Anglo-Japanese-American "understanding"—what he sarcastically called a junior League of Nations.[20] But he dared not speak out publicly lest he be stigmatized as a party bolter. Despite repeated challenges by his rival's backers that he state where he stood on the Washington Conference— which they hailed as the foremost achievement of the Harding administration—Beveridge remained silent.

Although the newly launched Conference for Progressive Political Action denounced New for his support of legislation "for the benefit of special interests,"[21] Beveridge's stand proved no more satisfactory to the reform-minded. The coming of the depression in the summer of 1920 had reinforced his fears about radicalism, even Bolshevism, in the United States, unless conditions improved. And his alarm over the radical threat reinforced his hostility toward "lawless" unionism. His stand, he confessed to friends, "will be attacked by the demagogues in and out of Congress—those professional guardians of the poor, shifty politicians who never did anything for the poor but raise particular hell with business. But I don't care a whoop how much they attack; the truth has got to be told."[22]

The first requisite for restoring prosperity, he told his audiences, was to reduce "excessive" railroad rates—which in turn required the rollback of the "inflated" wage increases extorted during wartime by the railroad brotherhoods. The second was to replace the investment-paralyzing personal and corporate taxes with a nationwide sales tax. The third was to encourage further business rationalization and efficiency through repeal of the "absurd and noxious" Sherman and Clayton acts. And he filled his speeches with blasts against union "despotism," "bureaucratic restrictions" upon business, "class legislation," and "demagogues" who wanted soak-the-rich income taxes. Business leaders, in and out of Indiana, responded with high praise

---

20. Beveridge to A. M. Glossbrenner, 31 August 1921; to Frank Brandegee, 1 October 1921, BP.
21. W. H. Johnston to ——, 18 April 1922 ,BP.
22. Beveridge to Warren G. Harding, 10 July 1920; to McClain, 29 October 1921, BP.

for his "courage" in calling "the people of the country back from their wanderings."[23]

But New was taking the same line. Thus the race came down to a personality contest. Pleading the duty of Senate business, New made few speeches in Indiana and relied on the backing of the party organization. In contrast, Beveridge undertook a strenuous campaign tour across the length and breadth of the state. He reminded the voters of his past record of constructive achievement while in the upper chamber, characterized his rival as a do-nothing senator, and plugged away with the slogan "Beveridge in May means victory in November."[24] While the *Indianapolis News* and the bulk of the state's Republican newspapers favored New, the Star League newspapers went all out for Beveridge, giving his speeches front-page coverage and bestowing lavish praise in the news and editorial columns.

Beveridge made the "leading issue" in the contest rival's "prodigious" campaign spending.[25] He sincerely felt that the excessive use of money in political campaigns was threatening public confidence in representative government; but at the same time he was hoping to capitalize on the popular restiveness that had fatally damaged the Lowden and Wood presidential candidacies in 1920 and had nearly cost Truman Newberry of Michigan his seat in the Senate. To avoid stirring up party regulars, Beveridge did not frontally attack New for his vote to seat the Michigan lawmaker. His strategy was to remind his audiences of his own fight against Senator William Lorimer. And he challenged New to agree with him to limit campaign expenditures. When New, as expected, refused, Beveridge sought to dramatize his own position by issuing weekly public statements of his expenditures.

What made the contest so bitter was the legacy of 1912. New based his campaign upon an appeal to party regularity as the champion of the administration. His supporters extolled him as Harding's right-hand man in the upper chamber, appealed for his renomination as a vote of confidence in the president, and publicly and privately assailed Beveridge as a party wrecker. Beveridge took advantage of these attacks to rally former Bull Moose party voters with the cry of

23. *Indianapolis Star,* 18 November 1921, 7, 30 April 1922. Darwin P. Kingsley to Beveridge, 5 May 1922, BP.
24. For slogan, see pamphlet *Beveridge for Senator* (copy in ISL).
25. *Indianapolis Star,* 22 April 1922.

discrimination against ex-Progressives in Indiana. At the same time, he denounced those who would imperil party success by reawakening past divisions, played up the fact that the president was keeping hands off the primary fight, and pledged himself to party regularity except "on matters of fundamental principle."[26]

The old stories about his drinking were brought up. The New people raised the cry that he had been pro-German and a wartime slacker, charges that struck a sensitive nerve with Beveridge. But the fading of wartime passions, his speech-making before American Legion posts and personal ties with influential Legion leaders, and his strong advocacy of a veterans' bonus while New had voted to kill the measure in the Senate succeeded in neutralizing his rival's appeal to the ex-servicemen's vote. The war issue may have even won votes for Beveridge. For the attacks upon his patriotism solidified the state's large German population behind him. A German-American leader estimated that 90 percent of the Republicans of German extraction marked their ballots for him.[27]

When the votes were counted, Beveridge defeated New by 206,165 to 184,505 votes. He won thirty-two of the forty-two counties where Roosevelt had run ahead of Taft in 1912, and probably the bulk of his vote across the state came from ex-Bull Moosers. But even in former standpat bastions, he benefited from voter dissatisfaction against the "ins" resulting from continuing hard times and high taxes. Thus, he ran strongly in rural districts where the farmers remained hard hit by low prices, picked up the votes of the striking miners in the coal mining districts, and carried heavily industrialized Lake County, where the workers were suffering from wage cuts and unemployment. His personal appeal, reputation as a pioneer in the fight against child labor, and long-time advocacy of women's suffrage gave him an edge among the newly enfranchised women voters.

But perhaps the decisive factor was the weakening of the solid organizational backing upon which New had relied. Factional rivalry in Marion County between former Indianapolis mayor Charles W. Jewett and county treasurer Ralph A. Lemke, who were backing New, and newly elected mayor Lew Shank, who jumped on the Beveridge bandwagon, sharply reduced New's majority there. And

---

26. Ibid., 10 March 1922.
27. Rev. G. E. Hiller to Beveridge, 5 May 1922, BP.

James E. Watson took advantage of his colleague's difficulties to launch a bid to take over the state organization. Although Watson publicly announced his support for New, he refused to take the stump on his behalf, and many of his followers worked for Beveridge. There is even evidence of a deal whereby the Beveridge people backed the Watson forces in the state chairmanship fight in return for support in the senate race.[28]

The Indiana primary made front-page news throughout the country. Democratic National Committee chairman Cordell Hull called Beveridge's victory "a plain and emphatic repudiation of the Harding Administration." *The Nation* hailed the vote as signifying "a revulsion of feeling against the present Administration."[29] Former Bull Moosers hailed Beveridge's nomination as proof of a rebirth of progressivism within the G.O.P., and his more enthusiastic boosters began talking of him as a possible contender for the G.O.P. presidential nomination in 1924. Such talk disturbed Beveridge. Foreseeing a tough fight ahead unless he could heal the party wounds left by the primary fight, he hastened to deny that his nomination represented more than a personal triumph, affirmed his loyal support of the Harding administration, and soft-pedaled talk of his presidential aspirations. His new campaign motto was "Normal Times and Sound Government."[30]

Though New was so bitter that he refused to congratulate Beveridge or pledge his support in the election, Republican leaders throughout the state swung into line in the name of party unity. The G.O.P. National Committee pledged its full assistance. Harding called upon all loyal Republicans to support the party's nominee and even personally invited Beveridge to open the Ohio campaign. On the surface, harmony prevailed between Beveridge and Watson. Watson assured the nominee of his fullest backing; Beveridge insisted upon Watson's delivering the keynote address at the Republican state convention; and Republican newspapers even ran fanciful stories about the lifelong friendship between the two men.

In his campaigning in the fall of 1922, Beveridge extolled the Harding administration for its steps toward cutting taxes, reducing

---

28. Haven McClure to Charles E. Hansell, 6 May 1922, BP. For New's bitterness over Watson's double-crossing him, see C. H. Stratton to Will H. Hays, 11 May 1922, Hays Papers (ISL).

29. *New York Times*, 4 May 1922. *The Nation*, 17 May 1922, p. 586.

30. *Beveridge for United States Senator* (pamphlet in ISL).

the national debt, and saving the farmers from bankruptcy. He defended the Forney-McCumber tariff—the highest in the nation's history—as "honest and necessary to the restoration and preservation of American prosperity." He denounced proposals to abolish or modify the authority of the courts to declare laws unconstitutional as "a blow at the very heart of the American constitutional system." He repeated his demands for further government economy, a halt to "socialistic" interference with business, and a nationwide sales tax to replace the present "crushing" and "confiscatory" personal and corporate taxes. He upheld the action taken by the administration to break the railroad shopmen's strike, called for repeal of the Adamson law, and blasted union "bosses" and labor "terrorism."[31]

The Democrats had nominated the popular Samuel M. Ralston, whom even Beveridge praised as "a darn nice man, and straight and clean."[32] As governor from 1913 to 1916, Ralston had won a reputation as a middle-of-the-road progressive and champion of governmental economy. He had the full backing of the state party organization headed by Tom Taggart, and the Democratic National Committee, hoping to pick up a Senate seat in Indiana, provided financial assistance. The publisher of the *Indianapolis News* promised him "fair and friendly" treatment. Looking to capitalize on the G.O.P. bloodletting, the Democratic state convention followed his advice to avoid "extreme platform declarations" that would frighten off possible Republican bolters. The explosive prohibition issue was silently buried. Ralston was personally a "dry," and the Democratic "wets," scenting victory, abandoned their demand for a plank calling for modification of the Volstead Act.[33]

Although Beveridge tried desperately to revive the League of Nations as an issue, Ralston refused to jump at the bait. Affirming his own support for the Washington Conference, he challenged Beveridge to say where he stood. When Beveridge called for payment of the Allied war debt in full, Ralston joined in with the same demand. Making his fight on domestic issues, Ralston assailed the Fordney-McCumber tariff as a sellout to the "special interests," denounced the

---

31. *Indianapolis Star*, 17, 27 September, 4, 25 October 1922.
32. Beveridge to Gifford Pinchot, 26 May 1922, BP.
33. Delavan Smith to Samuel M. Ralston, 15 May 1922; Ralston to William A. McInerny, 11 May 1922, Ralston Papers (LL). For the action of the Democratic state convention, see *Indianapolis Star*, 2 June 1922.

sales tax as a soak-the-poor "relic of the Middle Ages," and defended the eight hour day for railroad workers. Ralston's most telling campaign tactic was to contrast his own record while in the State House for governmental economy and reducing taxes with the increased expenditures and higher levies under his Republican successors—an appeal that struck a responsive chord with Hoosier voters.[34]

At the start of the campaign, Beveridge expressed confidence about the result. As election day neared, however, the tide was running against him. As the G.O.P. nominee, he suffered from the widespread popular dissatisfaction against the "ins"—what correspondent Mark Sullivan called "a mood of angry sullenness, of discontent with what is happening in the world"—from which he had profited in the primary.[35] While business had started to pick up, agriculture remained in the doldrums. Organized labor had been antagonized by the action of Republican governor Warren T. McCray in sending state troops into the coal mining region during the miners' strike that summer to guard the mines while coal was being mined for state institutions. The Harding administration's breaking of the railroad shopmen's strike in September further inflamed labor hostility against the Republicans. Farm groups and journals condemned Beveridge's sales tax proposal, denounced high property taxes, and warned that the new tariff would mean higher prices for manufactured goods.

Aggravating the trend against the G.O.P. were Beveridge's personal liabilities. His pro-German reputation cost him the votes of pro-Allied enthusiasts. Supporters of the League of Nations were hostile. Die-hard standpatters continued to look upon him as a dangerous radical. Harry S. New sat out the campaign, putting in but a single token appearance at a small town in which he praised the administration but failed to mention Beveridge. He even secretly fed the Democratic campaign managers with ammunition against Beveridge, while his more bitter supporters vowed revenge come November. In many counties, the local G.O.P. organization was lukewarm. And though actively campaigning for Beveridge, Senator James E. Watson wielded his knife behind the scenes to kill off another Republican rival.

And organized labor rallied its forces against Beveridge. A.F. of L.

---

34. *Indianapolis Star,* 21 September, 27 October 1922.
35. Ibid., 29 October 1922.

president Samuel Gompers made his defeat a major labor goal. The leaders of the railroad brotherhoods endorsed Ralston; the brotherhood-sponsored and -financed Indiana branch of the Progressive Political Action Committee campaigned actively for the Democratic nominee; and the brotherhoods' weekly newspaper *Labor* denounced Beveridge as a "political turn-coat," "one of the worst reactionaries in American public life," and "an open and avowed enemy of the workers."[36] Worried Republican politicians appealed to Beveridge to lessen his labor baiting, but he refused. As the campaign reached its climax, he launched more and more bitter attacks upon the "so-called 'labor leaders'" who were plotting to "sovietize American business," stir up "class hatred," and "mangle the American constitution."[37]

In the background a new and incalculable force was emerging. By the fall of 1922, the Ku Klux Klan boasted a large and growing Indiana membership. Beveridge had long assailed hyphenism in the name of "one hundred percent Americanism."[38] Yet he simultaneously denounced those who would divide the American people by setting religion against religion, race against race. He had only scorn for "the Chinese state of mind" of the nativist zealots. He joined in a protest against the growing anti-Semitism. He was disgusted by the anti-Catholic propaganda flooding the Hoosier state. He even came out publicly—partly from a wish to pick up Negro votes, partly because of his deep-seated belief in the maintenance of "law and order" —in favor of the pending federal antilynching bill.[39]

But with the Klan a force in the Hoosier state, Beveridge remained silent instead of speaking out against it. His silence, however, failed to appease the Klan. He roused Klan antagonism when he spoke for the reelection of Republican congressman Milt Kraus, a Jew, in the Eleventh District. And when Governor Henry Allen of Kansas, speaking in his behalf at Richmond, lashed out in a bitter attack upon the hooded order, Klansmen throughout the state were indignant. Stories circulated that Beveridge himself had assailed the Klan, that his wife

---

36. *Labor*, 27 May, 14 October ("Special Indiana Edition"), 4 November 1922.
37. *Indianapolis Star*, 27 October 1922.
38. Ibid., 25 October 1919.
39. Beveridge to Felix Frankfurter, 30 July 1921; to John Spargo, 8 December 1920; to Monsignor Francis Gavisk, 28 February 1922; to Edgar G. Brown, 5 August 1922, BP.

was a Catholic, and even that he was a Catholic. Although Beveridge angrily denied the stories, rumor outran his rebuttals.[40]

Running twenty-five thousand votes behind the G.O.P. nominee for secretary of state, Beveridge lost to Ralston, 558,169 votes to 524,558. The return of traditionally Democratic German and Irish voters who had bolted in 1920, the nationwide trend against the administration, Ralston's popularity, Klan hostility, the continuing low farm prices, and resentment against higher state taxes had their share in his defeat. Opposition from within his own party hurt badly. Thus he lost Marion County by more than six thousand votes, while G.O.P. Congressman Merrill Moores won reelection by eighty-five hundred votes. But probably decisive was Beveridge's alienation of many former supporters. He carried Wayne County—the banner Progressive county, which had gone Republican two years before by more than four thousand votes—by less than three hundred votes. And the labor vote swung heavily behind his Democratic rival. Ralston carried all of the state's major industrial, railroad, and mining centers, except the long-time Republican stronghold of Lake County, and even there, he sharply reduced the G.O.P. margin.

Beveridge maintained a brave front. He had run, he rationalized to his friends, not from personal ambition, but from a sense of duty, and now could go ahead with what he most wanted to do, write his life of Lincoln. As in 1910, he took solace in having made a brave fight for what was "fundamentally sound and right, both in economics and government." He even boasted that he personally was stronger in Indiana and throughout the country than ever before. "Now that it's all over," he wrote Mrs. Orville H. Platt, "I am glad I lost. Economic conditions through the country & the political situation in Washington are such that I would have been powerless to have accomplished anything. . . . Now, with prestige higher than ever & free from embarassments [sic] I may be of some real use to Republic. So I see God's hand in it."[41]

---

40. See, for example, Beveridge to Charles Carter, 23 October 1922, BP.
41. Beveridge to T. H. Adams, 2 December 1922, BP. Beveridge to Mrs. Orville H. Platt, 30 November 1924 [1922], Platt Papers.

21

The Beginnings of Lincoln

Now Beveridge was free to start his work on Lincoln. He made repeated trips through the "Lincoln country" of Kentucky, Indiana, and Illinois. He went through the manuscript collections at the Library of Congress. He made extensive use of the newspaper collections at the American Antiquarian Society, "the greatest treasure house of first-hand material that I have yet found or heard of."[1] Although he did more of his own research than he had done on the Marshall book, he continued to rely upon paid and unpaid research assistance to fill in the gaps. As the years of research went on, the expenses became a serious drain upon his purse.

His reputation as the biographer of John Marshall opened most doors. Local newspaper editors, lawyers, and Lincoln buffs gladly looked up and copied records for him without pay. He induced Jesse W. Weik, the editor of the *DePauw Alumnal Register,* who was the long-time friend of Lincoln's law partner William H. Herndon and co-author of *Herndon's Lincoln,* to lend him Herndon's large collection of Lincolniana in

---

1. Beveridge to Mrs. Jessie P. Weber, 21 April 1923; to William E. Connelley, 15 December 1925, BP.

return for Beveridge's recommendation that Houghton Mifflin publish Weik's book *The Real Lincoln.*

Professor Theodore C. Pease, director of the Illinois Historical Survey, permitted him to take to Indianapolis the thirty filing cases of material copied from the newspapers of Lincoln's day collected by the survey. Lincolniana collector Oliver R. Barrett let him go through his collection, sent him copies of unpublished Lincoln letters that he owned, and assisted him in tracking down additional Lincoln materials. Mrs. Eugene Hale, the widow of the former senator from Maine and the daughter of Republican Senator Zachariah Chandler of Michigan, brought her father's papers to Washington for Beveridge to examine. The grandsons of former Supreme Court justice David Davis and Congressman Elihu B. Washburne made available their grandfathers' papers.

A serious disappointment was the adamant refusal by Robert Todd Lincoln to allow him to see the collection of his father's papers that he had deposited in the Library of Congress on the ground that the papers contained material reflecting adversely upon the fathers of personal friends still living. And on the same day he wrote Beveridge his refusal, he signed a deed of gift to the library stipulating that the collection remain closed until twenty-one years after his death. Although Beveridge had mutual friends intercede with the old man, Robert Todd Lincoln would not relent. Furious at the shortsighted descendants of famous men who "wished the world to think of their ancestors as little tin Gods on wheels," Beveridge imagined that Lincoln was secreting dark family skeletons. He was so "desolated," he complained to Worthington C. Ford, that he was tempted to give up the task. "I wish to make this book definitive and do not care to waste several years of my life writing something that will be merely a stopgap."[2]

He compared notes with fellow Lincoln students. A few—such as Paul M. Angle, then executive secretary of the Lincoln Centennial Association, upon whom he came to depend heavily for advice and assistance—were trained scholars. Most were amateurs, like the Reverend Louis A. Warren, a small-town Kentucky minister, whose *Lincoln's Parentage and Childhood* would be published in 1926, and

---

2. Beveridge to Joseph C. Sibley, 28 February 1923; to Worthington C. Ford, 14 February 1923, BP.

the Reverend William E. Barton, minister of the First Congregational Church of Oak Park, Illinois and author of *The Paternity of Abraham Lincoln* (1920) and *The Soul of Abraham Lincoln* (1920). Beveridge had his doubts about the soundness of Warren's researches into Thomas Lincoln's Kentucky years and rechecked the sources himself. But he was pleasantly surprised by Barton and followed his work on the Lincoln genealogy—including Nancy Hanks's illegitimacy—in his own book. And though he privately thought Barton's two-volume *The Life of Abraham Lincoln* "badly jumbled," "turgid," and filled with unsupported statements, he generously arranged with his friend W. C. Bobbs for Bobbs-Merrill to publish the work.[3]

By this time, Beveridge had his writing technique perfected. Working upon one chapter at a time, he would finish his research, arrange his notes, immerse himself in his materials, and write a rough draft "as fast as pen will go." After his secretary had typed up this draft, he revised the manuscript "three or four" times to remove the "obvious errors of proportion and crudities of statement." Next came the task of verifying his facts, correcting mistakes, and adding the supporting references. He maintained his lavish scale of documentation, "to inspire in the readers a feeling of confidence," as he explained to his publisher. Thus his first twenty pages contained ninety-five footnotes, many occupying half a page. Last came "the hardest work of all"—condensing and more condensing. When finished, he would have the chapter mimeographed to send out for suggestions and criticisms. And then would follow another round of revision, polishing, and condensation.[4]

For scholarly advice and reading of the manuscript, he continued to rely upon his personal friends among the professional historians. Many were holdovers from the Marshall work—Worthington C. Ford, J. Franklin Jameson, Samuel Eliot Morison, Clarence W. Alvord, Edward Channing, Charles A. Beard, and H. J. Eckenrode. Unhappy over Beveridge's politics, William E. Dodd begged off reading the manuscript because of the pressure of his own work. But his place was more than filled by new recruits—Ulrich B. Phillips of the University of Michigan, the author of *American Negro Slavery*,

---

3. Beveridge to W. C. Bobbs, 15 November 1924; to Claude G. Bowers, 24 March 1925, BP.

4. *SEP*, 13 October 1926, p. 186. Beveridge to Ferris Greenslet, 21 October 1924, BP.

Arthur C. Cole of Ohio State, author of the *Whig Party in the South,* Theodore Pease of Illinois, John T. Morse, Jr., the editor of Houghton Mifflin's American Statesmen series, Nathaniel W. Stephenson, the editor of the Yale University Press Chronicles of America series, Frank Owsley of Vanderbilt, C. S. Boucher of the University of Chicago, author of *The Nullification Controversy,* Frank Hodder of the University of Kansas, and William E. Connelley, secretary of the Kansas Historical Society.

Grateful for their assistance, Beveridge did what he could to reciprocate. When Mrs. John D. Rockefeller, Jr., approached him to suggest a historian to write an authorized biography of her father, Senator Nelson W. Aldrich, he recommended Stephenson. He prevailed upon Worthington C. Ford to give Eckenrode a boost by favorably reviewing his book on Jefferson Davis. He himself wrote a highly laudatory review of Stephenson's brief *Lincoln: An Account of His Personal Life.* At Morison's request, he interceded with his friend George Harvey, then American ambassador to the Court of Saint James, to have the youthful Harvard historian appointed the first Harmsworth Professor of American history at Oxford University. He pulled what strings he could to have Arthur C. Cole named Morison's successor as Harmsworth Professor. But with Harvey no longer ambassador, his efforts were unsuccessful.

He did what he could to encourage beginners. Thus he took under his wing the young Indiana newspaperman and aspiring historian Claude G. Bowers. Although Bowers was a steadfast Jeffersonian and Democrat, he had long admired Beveridge personally and found in his *Life of John Marshall* an inspiration for his own historical ambitions. Flattered by the younger man's frank admiration, Beveridge wrote a friendly newspaper publisher recommending Bowers for an editorial position, discussed frankly with him the political situation, encouraged him to give up the "trivial and uncertain" game of politics and devote himself to history, gave him advice on his writing, recommended that Houghton Mifflin publish his *Party Battles of the Jackson Period,* and boosted his *Jefferson and Hamilton* in a review.[5]

Beveridge became increasingly active in the affairs of the American Historical Association. He attended its annual meetings whenever he

---

5. Beveridge to Bowers, 5 January 1920, BP.

could, renewing old friendships and making new ones. He was much in demand as a speaker at those sessions. In 1924, he was named a member of the association's committee on endowment, and the following year, became a member of the executive committee and chairman of the committee on endowment. Despite his exhausting and expensive labors on the Lincoln, he threw himself into the task of raising a hoped-for one million dollar endowment. He took an active hand in setting up state and local fund-raising committees, appealed to wealthy personal friends and acquaintances for contributions, and arranged through his newspaper and magazine contacts for publicity. And after his death, his widow gave $50,000 in his memory "as his tribute to the association and historical research."[6]

At the same time, he sought the advice of friends outside the historical profession where he thought their expertise would be valuable. Justice Oliver Wendell Holmes read the entire manuscript with a sharp eye. Beveridge sent copies of his chapters on Lincoln's legal career to eminent lawyers such as Felix Frankfurter and Dean Henry M. Bates of Michigan Law School for their suggestions. He consulted Ellery Sedgwick, the editor of the *Atlantic Monthly*, on questions of style. He asked an experienced Indiana politician for his appraisal of Lincoln's explanation of his defeat for the Senate in 1855 based upon his own firsthand knowledge of the political game. He had Jacob M. Dickinson of Tennessee, a Confederate veteran and former secretary of war in Taft's cabinet, read and criticize the manuscrip from the Southern point of view.

The more research he did the more disgusted he became with the "slush and rot" that had been—and was being—written about Lincoln. Nicolay and Hay had much "invaluable material," but their volumes were marred by poor writing, insufficient research, and lack of impartiality. He thought Jesse M. Weik's *The Real Lincoln* (1922) an invaluable "source book." His highest praise went to the much maligned William H. Herndon. Herndon had his faults; not all his conclusions were sound, and his fancy took over when, under the influence of transcendentalism and mysticism, he undertook to explore "souls." But Beveridge found him a "truthful, honest and thor-

---

6. *Annual Reports of the American Historical Association . . . 1927 and 1928* (Washington, 1929), p. 48.

ough man" who had "to an uncommon degree, the scholar's mind and habit of thought" and who was "absolutely trustworthy where he makes a statement of fact as such."[7]

The rest was largely "rubbish." Charnwood's brief one-volume life was "spotted with errors of fact so plain that they are glaring." Ida Tarbell's two-volume life (1900) was a mid-Victorian effort "to fumigate" Lincoln. Henry B. Rankin's *Personal Recollections of Abraham Lincoln* (1916) and *Intimate Character Sketches of Abraham Lincoln* (1924) were an "utterly untrustworthy" attempt to make Lincoln into "an impossible and unhuman angel who could not possibly make a mistake and who was without any human weakness whatever." He was extremely disappointed with Carl Sandburg's first two volumes (1926) because of their lack of adequate documentation, high-blown flowery style, and "incredible mistakes of fact." Not only had the "last word" on Lincoln not been written, he complained, but "the first word has not been penned."[8]

As he dug deeper into the Lincoln "morass," he found the task more difficult and demanding than the Marshall book because of the legends that had grown up about the martyred president. The mass of conflicting and contradictory data had to be weighed and resolved. Aggravating his difficulties in separating the wheat from the chaff was the continuing legacy of Victorian prudery. Thus Oliver R. Barrett boggled at permitting him to quote from a letter in his collection that Lincoln had written to Herndon, who had written something about "kissing the girls," advising his partner to "go it while you're young." "I am doubtful," he lamented to Worthington C. Ford, "whether the Mid-Victorians will permit any truthful and scholarly life of Lincoln to be written."[9]

He searched through forgotten court records to trace Thomas Lincoln's wanderings. He punctured such familiar legends as young

---

7. Beveridge to Ford, 28 December 1922; to James Ford Rhodes, 6 January 1923; to Jesse W. Weik, 10 May 1923; to C. H. Rammelkamp, 27 April 1923; to Paul M. Angle, 14 October 1926, BP.

8. Beveridge to Irwin Kirkwood, 7 February 1923; to Ford, 30 January 1923; to Charles A. Beard, 26 July 1924; to Nathaniel W. Stephenson, 18 December 1925; to Edward Weeks, 12 February 1926; to Clarence W. Alvord, 14 March 1925, BP.

9. Beveridge to Ford, 23 May 1923, 13 March 1924, BP. Lincoln's letter to Herndon is quoted in Beveridge, *Abraham Lincoln, 1809–1858* (2 vols., New York and Boston, 1928), 1: 451 (hereafter cited as *Lincoln*).

Abe's reading by firelight. He had a Washington lawyer friend look up in the Post Office Department records about his time as postmaster at New Salem. He pulled strings to have the War Department records checked about Lincoln's service in the Black Hawk War. His major source for Lincoln's earlier years was the material Herndon had collected after Lincoln's death. The trouble was that these accounts were often unreliable and contradictory. Beveridge's solution was to present, in the text or the footnotes, the conflicting evidence. Thus. for example, he coupled Nathaniel Grigsby's recollection that Lincoln read the Bible "a great deal" with the contradictory testimony of Dennis Hanks that he did not read it "half as much as [is] said."[10]

But his excessive reliance upon the Herndon-Weik papers led him astray at times. He accepted Herndon's account of the Ann Rutledge romance, although he did quote the contradictory testimony and admitted that "the nature and course" of Lincoln's courtship of Ann were "misty" and that "no positive and definite engagement resulted." Privately, he came to have even stronger reservations about the "whole Ann Rutledge myth," confessing to Paul M. Angle that "there was nothing in the story—at least very little." And when he read the manuscript of Angle's article "Lincoln's First Love?" he rejoiced that "at last this absurd myth . . . is to be exploded." Unfortunately, however, he died before he could revise his text accordingly.[11]

Similarly, his picture of Thomas Lincoln as an improvident, rather shiftless ne'er-do-well and rover was overdrawn, and his account of the Kentucky phase of Lincoln's life was too drab. He repeated uncritically the folklore about Lincoln the omnivorous reader. He took from Herndon "that fatal first of January" legend: that Lincoln had run away from his scheduled marriage to Mary Todd on 1 January 1841, leaving her at the altar. He accepted at face value the stories that Lincoln was so wrought up, even "crazy for a week or so," that his friends worried about his committing suicide—although he did concede in a footnote, after consulting with a leading psychiatrist, that there was "no proof that Lincoln was even temporarily insane."[12] And he followed Herndon in exaggerating Mary Todd Lincoln's ill temper and the unhappiness of Lincoln's home life.

10. *Lincoln*, 1: 72.
11. Ibid., 1: 149. Beveridge to Angle, 14, 25 October 1926, BP.
12. *Lincoln*, 1: 315.

Although vowing to give "the facts, the exact facts and all the facts,"[13] Beveridge was too much a man of his time to carry out such a program to the full. He did face up boldly to the hotly controverted question of Lincoln's religious beliefs with the blunt affirmation that the young Lincoln "rejected orthodox Christianity."[14] But he treaded more softly in dealing with the even more explosive matter of Lincoln's paternity. He personally shared Herndon's doubts about Lincoln's legitimacy. Writing to William E. Barton, he stressed how Judge David B. Davis had told Orville H. Browning that the suppressed first chapter of Ward Hill Lamon's *The Life of Abraham Lincoln* had contained "indubitable evidence" of Lincoln's own illegitimacy, and how another long-time Lincoln friend, Leonard Swett, had confided much the same to *Chicago Tribune* editor Horace White.[15] Yet—perhaps convinced by Barton's counterarguments or perhaps nervous about the public reaction—he skirted that touchy question in the text.

Nor was he immune to the legacy of Victorian prudery that rested so heavily upon his generation. Although he retold the story of Lincoln's arranging "a confusion of brides and grooms" after the Grigsby boys' wedding and then writing a "scurrilous description" of the mix-up in "The Chronicles of Reuben," he gave little prominence to the more glaring examples of Lincoln's youthful vulgarity. Thus, he simply described "some" of Lincoln's boyhood pranks as "unpleasing in the extreme." He had first written "nasty," but then substituted the milder expression. And even "nasty," he acknowledged, did not adequately describe one "so-called joke," which was "filthy in the extreme. I cannot write it; but it relates to defecation and Lincoln used the short word of four letters." Several of the reminiscences in the Weik collection, he confessed, contain material "which positively cannot be published or even so much as hinted at."[16]

Although he rarely went to bed before two or three o'clock in the morning and got up at six the following day, it was not until October

---

13. Beveridge to H. J. Eckenrode, 3 July 1923, BP.

14. *Lincoln,* 1: 301.

15. Beveridge to William E. Barton, 4 August 1924, Barton Papers (University of Chicago Library).

16. *Lincoln,* 1: 30, 92. Beveridge to William H. Townsend, 11 November 1924, BP.

1924 that Beveridge finished the first three chapters taking Lincoln up to his election to the legislature in 1833. Age and overwork were beginning to take their toll. He suffered through much of the first half of 1923 with a badly infected tooth and a grippe that in his run-down state he found difficult to throw off. He spent that summer in Switzerland resting. The vacation temporarily revived him. The following spring, however, he was plagued by a recurrence of the grippe and trouble with his sinuses. In September he had to take off a couple of weeks on a trip with his wife through the Maine woods.

Further delaying his progress was his continued involvement in public affairs. He kept up with his speechmaking in and out of Indiana. After his return from Switzerland, he spend most of the winter of 1923–24 turning out for the *Saturday Evening Post* a series of articles on the issues of the day—foreign affairs, the judiciary, the railroads, bureaucracy, and the presidency. "I hope," he confided to John C. Shaffer, "to be able to shape the Republican platform by these articles." To maximize his gains, political and financial, he brought the articles together in book form under the title *The State of the Nation*, which Bobbs-Merrill published in the spring of 1924. Sales, however, were "disappointing."[17]

He had grown more and more gloomy about the dangers facing the nation. The continuing turmoil across the ocean reinforced his hostility to any American political entanglement with the Old World. The impact of the League of Nations issue upon the different ethnic groups in America—even though successfully exploited by the G.O.P. in the 1920 election—illustrated anew the dangers to American unity from involvement in European affairs. Despite the defeat of the league covenant, Beveridge saw many snares ahead. Foreign propaganda was flooding the country and had even infected the school books in their accounts of the Revolution and War of 1812. The "international bankers" were trying to unload new foreign bonds on American purchasers and thus tie the United States "to the fortunes of the debtor nations more strongly than any possible alliance could chain us."[18]

He saw the same "fair-haired boys of Wall Street" behind the

---

17. Beveridge to John C. Shaffer, 17 September 1923; Bobbs to Beveridge, 21 November 1924, BP.

18. Beveridge to Samuel Eliot Morison, 9 January 1923; to Philander C. Knox, 22 June 1921, BP.

propaganda for the cancelation of the Allied war debts owed the United States government. Their purpose, he charged, was to safeguard the payment of the billions of dollars of privately-held debts at the expense of the American taxpayer. Strenuously opposed to any forgiveness or scaling down of the debt, Beveridge demanded that Britain and France turn over their West Indian possessions, "which geographically and by nature are American anyway," as down payment.[19]

He was becoming more and more distrustful of the Harding administration's foreign policies. He had privately stated during the 1922 campaign that popular suspicions that secretary of state Charles Evans Hughes was contemplating further involvement in European affairs was costing the Republican party—and himself—thousands of votes. He had assailed the secretary's suggestion in his speech before the American Historical Association in December 1922, for American participation in a commission of experts to study the reparations problem, as a dangerous step toward "getting mired up to our necks in the European slough of despair." His worst anxieties were realized when Harding on 24 February 1923, recommended United States adherence to the World Court. Here was the feared "back door" to the League of Nations—and Beveridge exhorted the irreconcilables in the upper chamber to stand fast.[20]

To join the World Court, he warned, would be politically disastrous for the G.O.P., since its winning issue in 1920 had been nationalism versus internationalism. The court was simply another scheme—like the league—to uphold the status quo. But could the status quo be maintained? Should the United States even try? His answer was a loud no. The treaty of Versailles was "the last word in folly, shortsightedness, passion and injustice." There could be no lasting peace in Europe so long as that arrangement stood. And he returned from his European trip convinced that another war was "certain to come within fifteen years and perhaps even ten years." Thus he balked even at the proposal that the United States enter into an international agreement to outlaw war. The "only one course of safety for us," he

---

19. Beveridge to Morison, 9 January 1923; to Halbert P. Gardner, 28 February 1923, BP.

20. Beveridge to William E. Borah, 1 November 1923; to Bert M. Fernald, 25 June 1923, BP.

pleaded, was "to keep out—keep clear out—of any political connection whatever with Europe at least for the next quarter of a century."[21]

At the same time, he was increasingly concerned about the threat from radicalism within the United States. The 1922 election results— the smashing triumph of Robert M. La Follette in Wisconsin, the election of Smith Brookhart in Iowa, Farmer-Laborite Henrik Shipstead in Minnesota, and Non-Partisan League leader Lynn Frazier in North Dakota, the Democratic victories in Washington, Montana, Kansas, and New York, Henry Cabot Lodge's near-defeat in Massachusetts, and his own loss in Indiana—showed a dangerous ferment at work. He feared that results would embolden the radicals to push forward with their program of soak-the-rich taxes and more government regulation. The resulting stifling of business would lead to another depression. And such depression would in turn lead to a further growth of radicalism.

In his speeches, articles, and personal letters, he denounced "the extravaganza of government control now being perpetrated upon the American people," the bureaucratic strait-jacketing of initiative and enterprise contrary to "economic law," the "excessive" and "confiscatory" taxes, the proliferation of the government "bureaucracy," and the ever swelling flood of "oppressive and autocratic laws" forced upon the statute books by "selfish minorities." Whereas in his progressive days he had called for establishment of an industrial commission with far-reaching supervisory powers, now he extolled the honesty and public spirit of the nation's business leaders, blasted the Federal Trade Commission for its "meddlesome" and "incessant" interference with business, and called for business "self-regulation" through national trade associations—"the normal and wholesome regulative force . . . of American industry and trade."[22]

He no longer paid even lip service to the social reforms he had preached in former years. After the Supreme Court had struck down the federal child-labor tax, he had considered coming out in his 1922 senatorial campaign in favor of readoption of the Keating-Owen law and asking the Court to reconsider its previous decision in *Hammer* v. *Dagenhart*. But he was so aroused over the railroad shopmen's strike

21. Beveridge to Frank A. Munsey, 27 April 1923; to Albert B. Cummins, 18 September 1923, BP.

22. Beveridge to George H. Lorimer, 15 January 1923, BP. *Indianapolis Star,* 19 June 1923. *SEP,* 15 March 1924, pp. 33, 189, 193, 197.

that he never followed through and instead made attacks upon union bossism his leading campaign issue. When an official of the National Child Labor Committee asked him to write an article in support of the child labor amendment approved by Congress in June 1924, he declined with the excuse that he was too busy. He refused even to endorse publicly its ratification, raising the specter that the amend-might open the door to barring the "wholesome outdoor occupation of children" on farms.[23]

He was disturbed by the growing number of attacks upon the Supreme Court—"the king-bolt of our whole system"—spurred by its five-to-four decisions striking down the Keating-Owen child labor law and the Washington, D.C., minimum wage law for women. He suggested that the Court undercut the radical assault upon judicial review by adopting on its own initiative the "very moderate" procedural rule that at least six of the nine judges concur in declaring laws of Congress unconstitutional. But he stood adamant against any action by Congress to limit the Court's jurisdiction and authority. Even worse was Robert M. LaFollette's proposed constitutional amendment to permit Congress to overrule the court by a two-thirds majority. Beveridge feared that the Wisconsin senator would poll an "enormous" protest vote in the 1924 presidential race.[24]

He was dismayed by the scandals of the Harding administration— the frauds in the Veterans' Bureau, the rumors of graft and corruption in the Justice Department, and Teapot Dome. He was perhaps even more shocked by the conviction of a leading official of the Anti-Saloon League—the self-proclaimed defender of American morality–for forgery and graft. Unless all those guilty of wrongdoing were rooted out, he warned, the public at large would come to believe that nobody could be trusted. And when that happened, the American system of popular government could not long survive. "The supreme need of the hour is to re-establish the confidence of the people in the rectitude of our law-makers and those who conduct our government."[25]

Although most observers thought his political career finished, old dreams died hard. In 1926 there would be another opportunity to try for the Senate—and to even scores with James E. Watson. He

---

23. Beveridge to Dan C. Flanagan, 16 February 1925, BP.

24. Beveridge to Tiffany Blake, 18 December 1923; to Clarence R. Martin, 19 July 1924, BP.

25. Beveridge to Irwin Kirkwood, 18 February 1924, BP.

had his 1922 campaign manager Clarence R. Martin keep in touch with his primary supporters for the next round. He helped rally supporters of the direct primary to block its repeal. He acquiesced in the demand for his Indiana backers that he withdraw his signature from a petition calling for the release of wartime political prisoners to avoid the possible adverse political repercussions.

He still dreamed that he might yet become president. He never had much liking or respect for Harding, and his dislike for the chief executive was heightened by his appointment of Harry S. New—who he believed had betrayed him in the Senate race—as Postmaster General. He thought that Harding was steadily losing strength and deluded himself that if the anti-Harding sentiment continued to grow, the G.O.P. might turn to him. Harding's sudden death in August 1923, the breaking of the Teapot Dome scandal, and the resulting uncertainty and confusion fed his hopes. Thus, as he had done four years before, he kept hands off in the scramble underway among the rival aspirants for delegate support at the G.O.P. national convention.

Working in his favor was the local political situation. The indictment of Governor Warren T. McCray in 1923–24, first for embezzlement and then for using the mails to defraud, and his subsequent conviction on the second charge, had dealt the Indiana G.O.P. a grave blow. The Klan was casting its lengthening shadow over the state, with a bitter struggle for power raging between former Indiana Grand Dragon D. C. Stephenson and Walter F. Bossert, the representative of the Atlanta national headquarters and Imperial Wizard Hiram Wesley Evans. And this struggle had become intertwined with the battle underway for control of the G.O.P. state organization between the Watson following and the New-Goodrich-Hays faction, Bossert lining up with the anti-Watson forces while Stephenson threw his support to the senator. Taking advantage of this tangle, John C. Shaffer traded the backing of his Star League newspapers in a bid to line up a delegation to the G.O.P. national convention, including Beveridge himself as one of the delegates-at-large, that would swing to Beveridge if the convention deadlocked.

Coolidge's skillful handling of the political situation, however, clinched his own nomination long before the G.O.P. convention met. With Coolidge's selection assured, interest focused upon the possible vice-presidential nominee, and there was growing talk around the country of Beveridge for the number two spot. Although Coolidge publicly kept his hands off the vice-presidential scramble, the newspapers reported that the chief executive preferred a member of the G.O.P.'s progressive wing as his running mate to undercut the appeal of La Follette's third-party candidacy. When Beveridge and his wife stayed at the White House while in Washington in May, the rumors multiplied that Coolidge favored the Hoosier for the vice-presidential nomination.

On the one hand, Beveridge continued to look upon the vice-presidency as a political dead-end. On the other, he was so bogged down in his work on the Lincoln that he was receptive to a face-saving way out of what appeared more and more an impossible task. Although he would not seek the place, he confided to his cousin, if the nomination came to him, "I shall take it and do my best."[26] After a behind-the-scenes hassle, the state convention doubled the number of delegates-at-large to make room for all the aspirants for that honor. But Watson maintained his grip upon the G.O.P. organization. Not only did he have the backing of D. C. Stephenson and his Klan following, but he reportedly made a deal with Imperial Wizard Hiram Wesley Evans to call off Bossert in return for his supporting the seating of the challenged Klan-backed senator Earl B. Mayfield of Texas. And he pushed through the state convention a resolution indorsing himself as Indiana's candidate for the vice-presidency. Although admirers continued to boom Beveridge for the place, the Watson candidacy was a fatal handicap, and the nomination went to Chicago banker-politician Charles G. Dawes.

Beveridge was tempted to sit out the campaign. He had scant respect for Coolidge personally; he was alienated by the chief executive's support for United States adherence to the World Court; he was disappointed over the failure of Congress to pass the constructive legislation, such as the sales tax, that country required; he was unhappy over the Klan's control of the G.O.P. in the Hoosier state; he suspected that Republican gubernatorial nominee Ed Jackson was owned "body and soul" by Watson; he remained bitter over his betrayal in 1922; he was peeved at the failure of the Republican campaign managers to play up to him; and he was busy with the Lincoln.[27]

---

26. Beveridge to E. L. McClain, 19 May 1924, BP.
27. Beveridge to Bobbs, 27 September 1924, BP.

At the same time, he realized that if he were going to challenge Watson for the senatorial nomination in 1926, he could not afford to sulk in his tent. So he agreed to take the stump, but, despite a plea from the chief executive himself, exclusively in Indiana. He attacked Democratic candidate John W. Davis for his proposal to amend the Constitution to require simply a majority vote for ratification of treaties; he denounced La Follette's plank for government ownership of the railroads; he defended the Supreme Court. He could not, however, find many favorable things to say about the G.O.P. standard-bearer. "For the next few years," he told his audiences half-apologetically, "we want no flashes of genius, no daring experiments, no brilliant adventures." What the United States required was "prudence, moderation and simplicity in the conduct of public affairs." Thus Coolidge was "exactly the kind of a man the country needs in the White House at this particular time."[28]

Beveridge was more positive in his praise of Republican gubernatorial nominee, Ed Jackson, for his stand against any move to repeal the direct primary. When a disappointed admirer regretted his speaking for the Klan-backed Jackson, he lamely pretended ignorance of the situation because of his absorption in his work on the Lincoln. He thus stayed regular, even though his heart was not in the task. And he took solace in the applause of his crowds. "Never in all my life," he reported to John C. Shaffer, "did I have such big and friendly meetings."[29]

As soon as the 1924 campaign was over, Beveridge returned to Beverly Farms and buckled down to work on Lincoln's years in the legislature. He spent hours gathering background data on Vandalia and Springfield of Lincoln's day—the condition of the streets, the appearance of the houses, how the members of legislature and townspeople dressed and talked, so that his readers could "see those places and the people" as Lincoln had. He went through the local newspapers for those years. But his major source was the eight large volumes of the *Journal of the Illinois Legislature*. As he read with a magnifying glass the thousands of badly printed, fading pages which no one before had consulted, what he found was "not only vital but dramatic." For all the issues that would continue to face the country

---

28. *Indianapolis Star*, 30 October 1924.
29. Beveridge to Shaffer, 11 November 1924, BP.

through the 1840s and 1850s—internal improvements, banking, temperance legislation, and slavery—had come before the legislature during Lincoln's ten years there.[30]

Although he had expected to summarize the legislative years in a few pages, he ended up by writing two lengthy chapters that constituted what a distinguished Lincoln scholar has called his "most original work." But his study of those years simply increased Beveridge's perplexity over Lincoln's "inexplicable character." He found Lincoln a skillful and calculating politician who "subordinated everything" to moving the state capital to Springfield and keeping it there; a staunch defender of the State Bank at Springfield, and "of vested interests and the conduct of business, unmolested as far as possible, by legislative or any kind of governmental interference"; a major architect of the ruinous internal improvements program that reduced the state to bankruptcy; and a highly partisan Whig.[31]

In these chapters, Beveridge succeeded in clearing away long-standing myths. He showed that while Lincoln was personally a nondrinker, he was not the temperance reformer of prohibitionist mythology. Beveridge was so nervous about possible attacks from the prohibitionists that he even requested a leading Boston lawyer to verify Lincoln's votes on the temperance legislation that came before the legislature. Nor did he find Lincoln the antislavery champion of Republican legend. Thus, Lincoln protested against a resolution denouncing the abolitionists; but agreed that their agitation was worsening the lot of the slaves. He affirmed the injustice of slavery; but maintained that Congress could and should not interfere with slavery in the South. He spoke out in behalf of law and order; but, because of Elijah Lovejoy's unpopularity in Springfield, made no more than a passing reference to the violence at Alton.

Beveridge saw the years between his running away from his marriage to Mary Todd and his election to Congress in 1846 as Lincoln's "Years of Discipline." The Mary Todd affair gave him a badly needed lesson in humility, while his subsequent marriage to the lady provided a lifelong tutelage in patience. He thoroughly reexamined Lincoln's

---

30. Beveridge to Weber, 10 May 1923; to Beard, 10 March 1925, BP.

31. *Lincoln*, 1: 144, 195, 236. For the appraisal of Beveridge's chapters on Lincoln's years in the legislature, see Benjamin P. Thomas, *Portrait for Posterity: Lincoln and His Biographers* (New Brunswick, N.J., 1947), p. 254.

near duel with Democratic state auditor James Shields in 1842, even
checking out their respective heights and arm lengths to show how
Lincoln had laid down conditions for the duel to gain the maximum
advantage from his longer reach. But he pictured Shields more favorably than Herndon had done and concluded that the episode taught
Lincoln the importance of consideration for others. Next to his marriage, the most important step Lincoln took in those years was his law
partnership with William H. Herndon. The deeper Beveridge went
into the Lincoln story, the larger Herndon loomed in his estimation as
"the carburetor in the great man's career."[32]

As with the legislative years, Beveridge had expected to summarize
Lincoln's term in Congress in a few paragraphs. When he found, to
his surprise, that no previous biographer had even looked at the
Congressional Globe, he felt impelled to devote two more lengthy
chapters to those two years. But he continued to find scant evidence
of the great Lincoln of the future. He remained the supercautious,
even shifty, politician. "If only I could run into one little thing which
Lincoln did or said during this period which was perfectly clear and
free from mystery," he complained. ". . . But he managed to throw a
cloud about nearly everything." Even when Lincoln presented his bill
for the abolition of slavery in the District of Columbia, "he left
everybody in the dark by three or four cryptic sentences which he
made to the House after he finished reading the bill."[33]

What most annoyed Beveridge as a lifelong American expansionist
was Lincoln's attacks on the Polk Administration—attacks that came
"perilously near pettifogging." His readers protested that he had not
dealt justly with the Mexican side of his account of the conflict, that
he had pictured Lincoln as simply a "cheap politician" who resorted
"to *sophistries* in order to find a political issue," and even that he
appeared "hostile to Lincoln—as if you definitely disliked him."
Beveridge replied that Justin Smith's *The War with Mexico* (1919)
had demolished the "old Whig-Abolition-Republican" slave-power
conspiracy theory of the war, that the United States was justified
"after years and years of pinching and biting by the Mexicans" in
giving them "a good swift kick," and that humanity would have been

32. Beveridge to Weik, 1 June 1925, BP.
33. Beveridge to Dr. Charles L. Nichols, 20 May 1925, BP.

the gainer had the United States taken all of Mexico. As for Lincoln, there was no question, he told Morison, but that he had been motivated "purely" by political expediency in his attacks upon the war.[34]

Beveridge devoted the final two chapters of the first two volumes to Lincoln's activities as a lawyer. Although none of the cases in which Lincoln was involved, he admitted, deserved more than a few lines, he spent long hours and many pages to clear away "for good and all" the "incredible quantity of sheer rot and imagination" that had been written about that phase of Lincoln's life. Thus, for example, he disposed of the legend that Lincoln had substituted a false almanac in the "Duff" Armstrong murder trial, deflated the significance of the almanac in Armstrong's acquittal, and showed how Lincoln's brilliant appeal to the jury's sympathies was the decisive factor in the acquittal. And he took pains, perhaps even to the extent of not giving Lincoln his due, to show that Lincoln was "no knight-errant of the law" doing battle for the poor and afflicted, but that he took "what came to him," "did his best for his client," and charged "normal" fees.[35]

Beveridge did not finish those chapters until the fall of 1925 and he estimated that he would require twelve to eighteen months more of full-time labor to write the second volume, plus another year for the final revisions. Many times he was so discouraged by "the magnitude and complexity" of the task that he talked of "throwing up the sponge." Although his "Scotch tenacity" kept him at his labors, he grew more and more troubled as he went more deeply into Lincoln's career on how to reconcile the unsuccessful Illinois politician and middling lawyer, secretive, reserved, infinitely cautious, sloppy, and lazy, with the Lincoln of the 1860s. "The Lincoln of Illinois," he lamented to his publisher, "could not by any possibility, have been the Lincoln of the Second Inaugural or the Gettysburg speech. They

---

34. *Lincoln*, 1: 425. Beard to Beveridge, 25 August [1925]; Frank Owsley to Beveridge, 14 April 1925 [1926]; Greenslet to Beveridge, 4 August 1925; Beveridge to Morison, 6 January, 28 June 1925; to Beard, 15 September 1925, BP. For a criticism of Beveridge's view that Lincoln was being a shifty politician in his attacks upon the Mexican War, see Townsend to Theodore C. Pease, 26 September 1932, Beveridge file, Illinois Historical Survey Records (University of Illinois Library, Urbana-Champaign).

35. Beveridge to Chester I. Long, 31 October 1925; to Henry M. Bates, 9 January 1926, BP. *Lincoln*, 1: 547, 554. For criticism that Beveridge failed to credit sufficiently Lincoln's high ethical standards as a lawyer, see J. G. Randall and Richard N. Current, *Lincoln the President* (4 vols., New York, 1945–55), 1: 38.

can exalt him all they like, but the cold fact is that not one faint glimmer appears in his whole life at least before his Cooper Union speech, which so much as suggests the glorious radiance of his last two years."[36]

36. Beveridge to John A. Scott, 12 December 1924; to Felix Frankfurter, 20 November 1924; to John T. Morse, Jr., 13 October 1925; to Greenslet, 2 February 1924, BP.

22

The Final Years

The time was fast approaching when Beveridge would have to decide about trying for the 1926 G.O.P. senatorial nomination. He was a proud man, and wanted vindication after his defeat in 1922. He was bitter toward James E. Watson for has past treacheries, and to defeat him in the primary would be sweet revenge. His difficulties with the Lincoln biography made a political comeback appear more attractive. The Indiana political situation looked favorable, as the leaders of the former New-Goodrich-Hays faction—the party "outs"—promised their support. And by temperament a man of action, Beveridge ached to return to the firing line and do battle against the dangers facing the republic.

The dangers loomed more and more threatening. Although fellow irreconcilable William E. Borah of Idaho, now chairman of the Senate Foreign Relations Committee, was leading the fight against United States adherence to the World Court, how long could he hold the fort? The Supreme Court remained under attack. Even worse was Vice-President Charles G. Dawes's proposal for majority cloture in the Senate, which Beveridge thought the "most dangerous" attempt yet made "to mangle our institutions."

While Dawes's target was the troublesome progressive Republicans in the upper chamber, the more farsighted Hoosier feared the result "in case the radicals should get in control of the government" in the near future. "Within the last few years," he wrote, "more serious proposals have been made to modify fundamental American institutions than . . . during any one period in our history."[1]

In Indiana, Beveridge continued to keep a watchful eye for any move to repeal the direct primary. Heartened by the reports coming in from the Hoosier state, he encouraged his Indiana supporters to go ahead with their work, laying down, as conditions for his running, first, an ironclad guarantee from the New-Goodrich-Hays people that they would not turn around and knife him in the November election; and second, that he would make no public announcement until after the nominating petitions had been circulated and had received enough signatures—a minimum of 10,000 and preferably 50,000—to show the country that there was a "genuine, honest and strong demand on the part of the public."[2]

At the same time, there were strong countervailing forces at work. There was the problem of money for another primary campaign, and the handicap of Watson's personal following and grip upon the party machinery. Beveridge had come to realize that his dream of winning the presidency would not materialize. He was reluctant to give up the life he was leading at Beverly Farms. There he was near the libraries he needed for his work on Lincoln; there he could relax from his labors by taking off for a swim or a round of golf and could make trips through the Maine woods or down to New York to see a show; there he had his family and new circle of friends. These friends urged him to keep out of politics and finish the Lincoln biography. And his wife was strongly against his returning to politics.

In late August, he wrote A. M. Glossbrenner, who was in charge of matters in Indiana, that he had decided not to run. The decisive influence, he explained, was the problem of what to do about Lincoln. The first volume could not be published alone. If he stopped now, he would delay, perhaps permanently, finishing the work. If he could win the nomination without having to campaign, he could finish

---

1. Beveridge to John C. Shaffer, 4 May 1925; to Joy E. Morgan, 20 May 1925, BP.
2. Beveridge to A. M. Glossbrenner, 6 August 1925, BP.

volume two before the fall of 1926. But that was "impossible." "Had
the present political situation," he told Glossbrenner, "existed two
years earlier, or even one year earlier; or had that situation presented
itself two years hence, or even one year hence, I could, perhaps, have
done or could do now what I am asked to do and what I earnestly
wish I could do."[3]

His friends in Indiana pleaded with him to reconsider, assured
him that he could win handily without taking an active role in the
campaign, and gave encouraging reports about the groundswell of
popular support. Beveridge weakened in his resolve not to run. If his
supporters went ahead and circulated nominating petitions, he wrote
Glossbrenner on 10 October, "and put me in anyway, without my con-
sent or even knowledge," then he would accept and make the race.
But he laid down stiff conditions: he wanted assurances that he
would not have to do more than deliver a few speeches so that he
could finish the second volume of the Lincoln work before the fall
campaign; that the petition drive would have to show a strong public
sentiment in his favor; and that he would not have to put up any of
his own money.[4]

At this juncture, the situation was transformed by the death of
Samuel Ralston on 14 October 1925. Beveridge's friends, headed by
John C. Shaffer and his Star League newspapers, pressured Governor
Ed Jackson to appoint him to the vacant seat. Beveridge, however,
was not interested. If appointed, he would have to run in the 1926
primaries and election for the last two years of Ralston's term and
then run again in 1928 for a full term. That would make two primaries
and two elections following on each other's heels, with Watson working underground to betray him. If he was going back into politics, he
would rather run against Watson in 1926 for a full six-year term. But
for reasons of pride, he confided to Shaffer, "I WOULD VERY MUCH
LIKE TO HAVE THE APPOINTMENT OFFERED ME PUBLICLY SO THAT I COULD
DECLINE IT PUBLICLY."[5]

Shaffer was so hopeful that Jackson would make the appointment
and so insistent that Beveridge take the place that Beveridge grudgingly agreed he would accept if offered the position. But Jackson

---

3. Beveridge to Glossbrenner [24 August 1925], BP.
4. Beveridge to Glossbrenner, 10 October 1925, BP.
5. Beveridge to Shaffer, 15 October 1925, BP.

named Arthur R. Robinson, a power in the Indiana Klan. He was indebted to the Klan for its support in his election as governor. He himself had ambitions to run for the Senate in 1928 when his term as governor expired, and he knew that Beveridge, if appointed, would seek election for the full term. Party regulars still remembered Beveridge's past insurgency, and his attacks upon the administration-backed proposal for American adherence to the World Court reinforced their doubts. And though Watson disclaimed any hand in the selection, Beveridge found signs of his influence in blocking his appointment. Although Shaffer was bitterly disappointed, Beveridge claimed to be "tremendously relieved."[6]

For a time, he remained receptive to a draft to run against Watson in the primary. Reports began to fill the newspapers that he was planning to make the race. Beveridge-for-senator clubs sprang up anew across the state. And the Watson forces, expecting a battle, readied their organization. But when the New-Goodrich-Hays people insisted that Beveridge would have to make an active campaign to win, he decided to give up the race rather than lose the two years of labor he had put in upon the Lincoln. To leave no possible doubt, he made public in mid-January of 1926 his reply to a telegram from his supporters urging his candidacy, announcing his decision not to make the race.[7] Although the anti-Watson leaders continued to hope, despite his announcement, that he might yet be induced to run, Beveridge stood firm. Finally a young Indianapolis lawyer named Claris Adams, the former Marion County prosecuting attorney, undertook to make the race. Although taking no active part in the campaign, Beveridge privately wished Adams well and was disappointed—but not surprised—at Watson's triumph.

Beveridge's anxieties about the future of "free institutions" were heightened by the reports of new scandals: the corrupt expenditure of money in the 1926 Pennsylvania primary, Gifford Pinchot's payment while governor of the Keystone State of state officials out of a private fund, and the revelations about the millions of dollars spent by the Anti-Saloon League in its lobbying activities—including large payments to members of Congress. Beveridge assailed the order by the head of the federal prohibition bureau making local officials

---

6. Beveridge to John N. Dyer, 22 October 1925, BP.
7. *Indianapolis Star*, 19 January 1926.

federal officers in enforcing the Volstead Act as a dangerous step toward "excessive consolidation" destructive of local self-government. And he was furious when the administration resorted to cloture —"gag rule," he charged—to push through the Senate approval of United States adherence to the World Court.[8]

Despite appeals from friends that he make a few speeches in Indiana to keep himself in favor with the regular Republican organization in case he wished to try for a political comeback in 1928, Beveridge decided not to campaign. He was, he explained, too busy trying to finish the second volume of the life of Lincoln; he was not physically up to campaigning; he could not possibly support Watson after his past actions; the party was so divided on the leading issues that there was nothing he could say; the State Committee had not even asked him to speak; and he was appalled by the reports of widespread corruption involving high Republican officials and Klan leaders coming out in the wake of D. C. Stephenson's murder conviction. Above all, he had at last freed himself from the political virus. "There is nothing big—hardly anything worthwhile—in the political mixup just now," he wrote Shaffer. ". . . There seems to be nothing at present but retail politics."[9]

His resolve to turn his back on politics and push forward with the Lincoln work was strengthened by the painful realization that he did not have too many years left. His long-time friend Judge John H. Baker had died in 1915. Remembering how the kindly older man had acted as a second father to him when he first practiced as a lawyer, he was "grieved beyond words to express." His own mother followed three years later. She had been living at Sullivan, Illinois with the daughter of her first marriage. Throughout the years, he had remained in close touch, visiting when he could and contributing to her support.[10]

George W. Perkins died on 18 June 1920. Beveridge's resentment over Perkins's high-handed and dictatorial behavior in the last days of the Progressive party had chilled their former friendship. But a

---

8. Beveridge to B. F. Lawrence, 11 July 1926; to Mark Sullivan, 4 February 1926, BP. *Indianapolis Star*, 3 June 1926.
9. Beveridge to Shaffer, 30 September 1926, BP.
10. Beveridge to Francis E. Baker, 22 October 1915 (telegram), 8 April 1918, BP.

reconciliation had been arranged before Perkins's death. The sudden death of long-time *Indianapolis Star* editor Ernest Bross in February, 1923, came "like a blow in the face."[11] He was even more shocked when Charles W. Miller committed suicide that same month. Judge Francis E. Baker died in March 1924, Boston lawyer Arthur Lord in April 1925, publisher Frank Munsey that December, and his loyal friend and adviser, Indianapolis publisher W. C. Bobbs, two months later. Perhaps the sharpest personal blow was the death in September 1924 of the faithful Leopold G. Rothschild.

Those "in our little circle who are left," Beveridge wrote Worthington C. Ford after the death of their friend Arthur Lord, "must stick closer together than ever."[12] He kept in touch with editor Albert Shaw, asking his advice on the Lincoln work, urging him to watch his health, congratulating him upon his work in the *Review of Reviews*. He resumed his friendship with Gifford Pinchot, broken as a result of the squabbles that had wracked the Progressive Party. His ties with John C. Shaffer had grown stronger with time. Even their differences over the League of Nations did not cool their feelings for one another.

Most important to Beveridge was his own family. Hard as he worked on Lincoln, he still had more time to spend with them than he would have had if he had returned to politics. His children were growing up—"like splendid flowers," he wrote his brother-in-law— and the doting father was determined to give them the advantages he had not had when a boy. He sent his daughter Abby to a private girls' school in Indianapolis and then to Foxcroft, a fashionable finishing school near Washington, and watched with pride as she blossomed into a lovely young lady. And his wife, he rhapsodized to former comrade-in arms Moses Clapp, "is more beautiful even than she was when you knew her in Washington, and gets more lovely all the time. . . . I feel that I am greatly blessed, and am appreciative of and grateful for it."[13]

The apple of his eye was Albert, Jr. Beveridge sent him to the exclusive Episcopalian boarding school, Saint Mark's, at Southborough, Massachusetts, and had his heart set on his going to Harvard.

---

11. Beveridge to Shaffer, 7 February 1923, BP.
12. Beveridge to Worthington C. Ford, 13 April 1925, BP.
13. Beveridge to Spencer Eddy, 3 August 1913; to Moses Clapp, 10 July 1925, BP.

He could not deny the boy his slightest wish; he even let him have an automobile while at prep school. But parental overindulgence had its harmful side. Too accustomed to having his own way, young Albert lacked self-discipline and failed to buckle down to his studies. Beveridge hired tutors to assist him, wrote lengthy letters of exhortation, was quick to praise when he showed improvement, and boasted to his friends about his achievements. "As the days and nights go by," he assured him after his return to prep school, "I miss you more than ever. . . . My best love, dear Albert, and always remember that I am for you and will stick by you through thick and thin."[14]

As with the Marshall biography, Beveridge set out in writing second volume of the Lincoln work to place his subject within the larger context of his times. Thus, he included a chapter on the struggle over the Compromise of 1850, although Lincoln was no more than a distant onlooker. He devoted some fifty pages to the passage of the Kansas-Nebraska bill, and followed with a detailed reexamination of the ensuing struggle on the plains of Kansas. A separate chapter dealt with the Dred Scott case. When his readers complained that Lincoln tended to become lost in the mass of detail, Beveridge replied that the average reader could not understand what Lincoln did or why without this background. If not for the turmoil in Kansas, for example, there would have been no Republican party, and if no Republican party, no Lincoln as president. "To tell nothing except what Lincoln looked like, what he did, and what he said," he explained to Samuel Eliot Morison, "is as if Hamlet were to be played without his mother, the King, Ophelia, Laertes, Polonius or even the ghost—just Mr. Hamlet suddenly strutting out before the footlights and delivering soliloquies."[15]

In filling in this background, Beveridge displayed sympathies strange for a biographer of Lincoln. In his first chapter, "Seeds of War: Abolition Attack and Southern Defence," he painted a strikingly favorable picture of Southern society in the years before the Civil War and placed the blame for that conflict upon the abolitionists. If not for the "fear and anger" their "violence" and "vituperation" aroused in the South, he wrote, "it is not altogether impossible that there would have been no war and that slavery would in time have

---

14. Beveridge to Albert J. Beveridge, Jr., 22 September 1923, BP.
15. Beveridge to Samuel Eliot Morison, 1 July 1926, BP.

given way to the pressure of economic forces." Privately he was even more hostile toward the abolitionists—"'fanatical reformers," he termed them, so filled with self-righteousness that they were "past reasoning with." "The deeper I get into this thing," he told Charles A. Beard, "the clearer it becomes to me that the whole wretched mess would have been straightened out without the white race killing itself off, if the abolitionists had let matters alone.[16]

His Southern readers were enthusiastic. Many of his Northern readers, however, complained about his pro-Southern bias. Arthur C. Cole felt that he had leaned over backward "toward a rather pro-slavery position." J. Franklin Jameson complained that he had exaggerated "the agreeable side of slavery" and "the merits of Southern society," and declared that the evidence gave "no support" to Beveridge's argument that if not for the abolitionists the South would have eliminated slavery on its own. Samuel Eliot Morison joined in challenging Beveridge's assumption of the inevitable natural death of slavery: "Granted that the abolitionists made the war, slavery made the abolitionists. Softer methods had been tried previously . . . ; but every attempt to end slavery by peaceful means was thwarted by the cotton States."[17]

Beveridge denied that he was taking sides, intruding his preconceptions, or presenting an "interpretation." His credo, he affirmed, was that the historian must avoid propagandizing—"must watch his step all the time" so that he does not fall into the trap of "championing what he thinks a good cause, and opposing what he thinks a bad cause." The "facts . . . interpret themselves" provided "ALL the facts" have been presented. The historian's duty was "to state exactly what happened," and he was not to blame if the facts showed the South in a more favorable light. "The heart of my troubles in this hard and heavy task," he told a sympathetic H. J. Eckenrode, "is the question as to whether the actual facts shall be told . . . or whether one must compromise with legends that grew out of sheer propaganda."[18]

More sophisticated historians retorted that the mere arrangement

16. *Lincoln*, 2: 19–20. Beveridge to Morison, 19 February 1926; to Charles A. Beard, 16 March 1926, BP.
17. Arthur C. Cole to Beveridge, 5 April 1926; J. Franklin Jameson to Beveridge, 24 May 1926; Morison to Beveridge, 23 February 1926, BP.
18. Beveridge to Theodore C. Pease, 7 May 1925; to Frank Owsley, 30 April 1926; to James A. Woodburn, 26 July 1926; to H. J. Eckenrode, 10 November 1926, BP.

of facts constituted an interpretation. And notwithstanding his protests, Beveridge did start out believing that previous historians had
not treated the South "fairly or adequately."[19] The more difficult
question is, Why this pro-Southern bias? A complex of factors was
involved. His nationalist sensibilities were affronted by the disunionist preachments of the more extreme abolitionists. His irritation at the
mid-Victorians who had deified and distorted Lincoln extended to
their pro-abolitionist sympathies. When he discovered that the facts
did not substantiate the legends propagated by Republican bloody-
shirt orators of his youth, he overreacted. "It is," he exclaimed in
disgust, "enough to make a man sick at heart and at his stomach too,
to find out that everything he was taught was, in fact, just the other
way around."[20]

At the same time, he was influenced by the writing of contemporary
historians who were revising the existing stereotypes about Southern
society and the causes of the Civil War—Ulrich Phillips's work on
slavery, Justin Smith's *The War with Mexico*, and Mary Scrugham's
The Peaceable Americans. He was at first impressed with Charles A.
Beard's argument that the clash of economic interests lay behind the
slavery issue. But further research convinced him that economic
considerations could not explain why the mass of nonslaveholders
in the South had rallied to the Confederacy. "I have reluctantly
come to the conclusion which Professor Phillips insists upon so
powerfully," he confessed, "that the ultimate roots of the war on the
part of the South—not all the roots, but the deepest roots—were
racial."[21]

As an Anglo-Saxon supremacist, he could not but sympathize with
the Southerners' determination to keep the South a white man's
country. As a Republican, he deplored the solid South. As an American nationalist, he had long denounced sectional—no less than class
—divisions in the United States and lamented the continuance into
the twentieth century of the North-South split growing out of the
Civil War. He had even proclaimed that a leading aim of the Progressive party was to remove this "abnormal and hurtful sectionalism."[22]
Thus he looked upon the Civil War with mixed emotions. On the

---

19. Beveridge to John Rutherfoord, 31 January 1925, BP.
20. Beveridge to Frank H. Hodder, 27 January 1927, BP.
21. Beveridge to Thomas Frothingham, 14 December 1925, BP.
22. Beveridge, "A Progressive Promise," *Collier's*, 18 January 1913, p. 8.

one hand, the conflict had saved the Union. On the other, he regretted that the situation had been allowed to come to that pass. "The idea of brothers cutting one anothers' throats," he confessed to William E. Dodd, "is repellent to me."[23]

Thus Beveridge became a pioneer exponent of the "repressible conflict" school of Civil War historiography. The hero of his chapter on the Compromise of 1850 was Daniel Webster. By saving the day for the Compromise, Webster "had saved the Union." And the attacks upon him by the abolitionists were like "strokes of adders." In contrast, the villains of the Kansas-Nebraska story were the antislavery heroes Salmon P. Chase and Charles Sumner. Their charges of a Southern plot to extend slavery were "wholly false." Nor was the uprising in the North that followed the bill's passage motivated "exclusively" by hostility to slavery expansion. Know-nothingism, prohibition, hard-times, the demand for river and harbor improvements, and "practical politics" were "almost as potent."[24]

He went on to deflate the abolitionist legends about "bleeding Kansas." He showed how many of the free state men were animated more by anti-Negro bias and hopes for financial gain than by antislavery feelings; he blamed many of the difficulties in the territory upon rival land and town-site speculations; and he accused the Republicans in Congress of magnifying and distorting what happened for political gain. He even sympathized with "Bully" Brooks against Sumner. He dismissed the Dred Scott case as a fictitious suit arranged to further antislavery propaganda; exonerated President Buchanan and the members of the Supreme Court from any conspiracy; blamed the dissents filed by Justices Curtis and McLean upholding the constitutionality of the Missouri Compromise for forcing the majority to deal with that question; and found scant evidence of popular excitement over the decision until the Republicans took up the cry of a proslavery conspiracy for partisan advantage.

Emerging as the hero of the story was not Lincoln but Stephen A. Douglas. Beveridge painted a startlingly new picture of the Little Giant. He was no longer the self-seeking politician whose ambitions for the presidency had brought on the Civil War through his repealing of the Missouri Compromise. Beveridge followed University of

---

23. Beveridge to William E. Dodd, 31 January 1925, Dodd Papers.
24. *Lincoln*, 2: 127–28, 185. Beveridge to Owsley, 30 April 1926; to Shaffer, 4 July 1926, BP.

Kansas historian Frank H. Hodder in emphasizing Douglas's interest in the construction of a transcontinental railroad as "a dominant motive" in his introduction of the Kansas-Nebraska bill. Personally convinced—as was Douglas—that as *a practical matter* slavery could not flourish in the new territories, Beveridge defended Douglas as "one of the greatest patriots the country ever produced—and not only that but one of the very, very few statesmen we have had"—who wished to avert a bloody conflict by removing the slavery issue from the political arena.[25]

Throughout Beveridge's account of the 1850s, Douglas continued to hold the center of the stage. "How tremendously Douglas looms up in the period on which I am now at work!" he exclaimed. "What a mighty man he was!" His admiration went out to Douglas for his valiant fight to stem the tide against the Democrats in Illinois after the Kansas-Nebraska bill. He affirmed that Douglas's attack upon the Emigrant Aid Company for fostering trouble in Kansas "stated the facts." He thought Douglas's "doctrine of friendly legislation" in reply to the Dred Scott decision "right" as "a matter of law, as well as a matter of fact." Remembering his own insurgency over the Payne-Aldrich tariff, he identified with Douglas in his break with Buchanan over the Lecompton Constitution and battle for reelection in the face of administration knifing. "The more I read the 'facts' concerning this amazing man," he confessed, "the more I admire him, and the stronger becomes my feeling that he has been shamefully used by sentimental writers calling themselves 'historians,' who, in order to write Lincoln up, felt that it was necessary to write everybody else down."[26]

What about Lincoln? He remained the hesitant and calculating politician who "neither led nor retarded mass movements, but accurately registered . . . dominant popular thought and feeling." He refused to leave the Whig party or speak out on the Kansas troubles until the assault upon Sumner "and the increasing disturbances beyond the Missouri border had aroused the North and made possible the success of the Republican Party." He repeatedly assured the voters that he did not favor Negro equality. He did not accuse the Supreme

25. *Lincoln*, 2: 171. Beveridge to Morison, 28 February 1926; to Louis Howland, 4 March 1927, BP.

26. *Lincoln*, 2: 337. Beveridge to William L. Patton, 9 February 1926; to William O. Lynch, 31 January 1925, BP.

Court of complicity in a plot to nationalize slavery through the Dred
Scott decision until Republican leaders in the Senate took up that cry
"as a matter of party strategy." Ambitious for the presidency after
the support given him for the vice-presidential nomination at the
1856 Republican national convention, he geared his "every word and
act" during the next four years to attaining that ambition.[27]

At the same time, Beveridge did find growing evidence of Lincoln's
future greatness. In his "First Great Speech," at Springfield in
October 1854, attacking the Kansas-Nebraska bill, he displayed that
"exalted yet restrained eloquence," that "breadth, sympathy, and
tolerance," and that "generosity of spirit which is to be fully realized
in the Second Inaugural." His efforts to consolidate the unstable
coalition that would become the Republican party by avoiding such
divisive issues as prohibition and Know-nothingism showed "the
wisdom of the statesman as well as the astuteness of the politician."
Thus, in the 1856 campaign he "stuck to two great issues—slavery
must not be extended, the Union must be preserved." And in his
speeches he set forth "that purpose which he was to carry out as
President, the purpose to put down secession by force—if the South
should go out of the Union, the North would bring it back at the
point of the bayonet."[28]

Despite his hopes of making the work definitive, Beveridge made
his mistakes. Thus, for example, he accepted without reservations
and quoted at length from the subsequently "discredited" Henry
Clay Whitney version of Lincoln's "Lost Speech" at the Bloomington
Convention on 29 May 1856. In his reaction against the excessive
glorification of Lincoln by previous biographers, he exaggerated
Lincoln's slowness in coming over to the new Republican party.
And, to quote a later scholar, he "simply misread the evidence" in
picturing Lincoln's nomination for the senatorship by the Republican
state convention in June 1858 as purely and simply a move to block
the ambitions of "Long John" Wentworth rather than a rebuke by
angry Illinois Republicans to those Eastern Republicans calling for
a partnership with Douglas. Nor has more recent scholarship found
"the slightest evidence" that Lincoln by 1858 had his eye upon the
White House and that his famous House Divided speech was, as

---

27. *Lincoln,* 2: 143, 297, 400, 519–20.
28. Ibid., 2: 218, 245, 297, 410, 419.

Beveridge held, "his most important move in the game for the Presidency" even at the risk of losing the senate race.[29]

To speed up the work on Lincoln, Beveridge greatly reduced his outside activities. But he was so exhausted by his labors that his friends warned him to let up. He planned to go to Europe over the summer of 1926 for a rest, but his wife would not leave until the children went back to school and he would not go alone. By the fall, he found himself so far behind in his schedule that he canceled the trip. He was laid up for three weeks for an infected antrum and was suffering so badly from arthritis that his doctor insisted that he go to Chicago for three months' treatment by a specialist. He grudgingly went, but while there he combined the treatments with research on the 1858 senatorial contest between Lincoln and Douglas. He hoped to finish volume two, bringing Lincoln up to his election to the presidency, by June, and then spend another full year making the final revisions.

He returned to Indianapolis at the beginning of April and resumed his normal schedule—getting up at seven, taking a two-mile walk, getting down to work before nine, and continuing except for breaks for lunch and dinner until one or two in the morning. Although he reassured his friends about his health, he was stricken on 14 April 1927, with a severe heart attack. While confined to bed, he had his wife read to him from the chapter on the Dred Scott case. He appeared to be recovering. On the evening 26 April, he even had friends in and talked in his familiar buoyant fashion. At 6:10 the following morning, however, he died following another attack.

After a private Episcopalian service at his home and a public service at the Meridian Street Methodist Church, Beveridge was buried on 29 April 1927 in Crown Hill cemetery outside Indianapolis. The flags on public buildings were lowered to half staff in his honor; nearly all governmental business in the city was halted for the afternoon of his funeral; and friend and foe, Democrat and Republican, from President Coolidge to the Hoosier man-in-the-street, joined in

---

29. For criticism of Beveridge *re* the Whitney version of Lincoln's "Lost Speech," see Randall and Current, *Lincoln the President*, 1: 99. For Beveridge's exaggerating Lincoln's slowness in joining the Republican Party, misreading the evidence about his nomination for the senatorship, and misinterpreting the House Divided speech, see Don E. Fehrenbacher, *Prelude to Greatness: Lincoln in the 1850's* (Stanford, Cal., 1962), pp. 42–43, 66, 73, 97. Beveridge's comment about Lincoln's purposes in the House Divided speech is in *Lincoln*, 2: 585.

expressing their shock and loss. While acknowledging Beveridge's political achievements, the obituaries concluded that his *Life of John Marshall* would stand as his most lasting monument. And eulogist after eulogist lamented that death had cut short his last and greatest undertaking.

Although Beveridge had finished only the first half of the first draft of the chapter on the Lincoln-Douglas debates, his widow decided to publish the work as far as he had gone. Worthington C. Ford worked with Beveridge's former secretary to prepare the manuscript for publication, and wrote, on the basis of his research notes, a concluding summary taking Lincoln up to his election as president.

A near-unanimous chorus of praise greeted its publication. Poet and Lincoln buff Edgar Lee Masters hailed the work as a landmark in Lincoln studies that would "supplant all previous performances." The reviewer for the *Chicago Tribune* extolled the volumes as "a stupendous piece of work." *The Nation* called the work "learned," "masterly," and "mercilessly dispassionate." The *Springfield (Mass.) Union and Republican* praised the volumes as "the most exact and authoritative narrative of Lincoln's early life now available." The *Times Literary Supplement* of London found the work a "vivid picture, full of stir and life," of the world "in which Lincoln lived and moved." Claude G. Bowers applauded Beveridge's achievement in revealing "the Lincoln of reality." Samuel Eliot Morison declared his account "incomparably the greatest story of Lincoln's life before his presidency." Ralph Henry Gabriel of Yale mourned the author's premature death as "a real loss to historical scholarship."[30]

Even Lincoln specialists joined in the praise. Though differing with Beveridge on many details, William E. Barton thought the volumes "a magnificent piece of work" of "permanent value." Though concluding that Beveridge had not attained the definitiveness he had aimed for, Paul M. Angle praised him for having "probably utilized more source material than any other student who has written

---

30. *New York Herald Tribune*, 9 September 1928. *Chicago Tribune*, 29 September 1928. *The Nation*, 10 October 1928, pp. 368, 370. *Springfield (Mass.) Union and Republican*, 30 September 1928. *Times Literary Supplement* (of London), 18 October 1928, pp. 741–42. *New York World*, 23 September 1928. *The New Republic*, 12 December 1928, pp. 117–20. *Yale Review* 18 (December 1928): 370–72.

on the subject," for his literary skill in making the volumes "eminently readable," for his sure touch in presenting "Lincoln the politician," for his giving Stephen A. Douglas at last his due, and for his success in presenting Lincoln "in the proper historical perspective." Benjamin P. Thomas hailed the volumes as a "truly monumental" achievement that "had put the romanticists to rout," applauded his success in making Lincoln "a living, breathing man," and rejoiced that his broad life-and-times approach had "brought Lincoln scholarship out of the sheltered eddy, where it had been circling, back into the full current of the historical stream." And David M. Potter of Stanford has concluded that the work "still remains far the best account of Lincoln's political career up to the moment of his entry upon the national stage . . . the first biographical treatment which combined extensive original investigation with critical capacity of a high order."[31]

---

31. William E. Barton, "A Noble Fragment: Beveridge's Life of Lincoln," *MVHR* 15 (March 1929): 497–510. Paul M. Angle, "The Beveridge 'Lincoln,'" Lincoln Centennial Association *Bulletin,* No. 13 (1 December 1928): 1–8. Thomas, *Portrait for Posterity,* pp. 263, 265–66. David M. Potter, *The South and the Sectional Conflict* (Baton Rouge, La., 1968), p. 172.

23

Retrospect

The sixty-four years of Albert J. Beveridge's life witnessed the transformation of the United States from a largely rural and small-town land to a modern industrialized and urbanized society. The speed and complexity of the changes taking place aroused widespread anxieties about the future of traditional American values and institutions. Beveridge shared many of these anxieties. But he realized that an unbending stand-pattism was self-defeating. And in dealing with the challenges facing the country, he took as his touchstone what he saw as the national interest. As he boasted, he was first, last, and always "an American Nationalist—an American Nationalist with a big 'A' and a big 'N.' "[1]

Beveridge was reared in the faith that the G.O.P. was the savior of the Union, the Democrats the party of treason, and the protective tariff the foundation of national prosperity. At college, he was educated in the dogmas of a "clerical laissez-faire" drawn from a simpler, bygone age. He was a living exemplar of the Horatio Alger myth of the farm boy who made good in the city. As

1. Beveridge to Edward S. Corwin, 4 January 1919, BP.

a prospering young lawyer in Indianapolis during the 1890s, he was shocked by the bloody and violent strikes and the farmers' revolt of those grim depression years. With repudiation, even revolution, threatening, he rallied behind William McKinley and sound money.

In the years before and after the Spanish-American war, Beveridge was a leading apostle of America's imperial destiny. Overseas expansion would prevent future depressions by supplying new markets for the nation's surplus of farm and factory. Perhaps even more important, looking outward would restore the national unity so badly splintered by the class and sectional antagonisms of the 1890s. Inculcated from youth with a belief in the United States as the home of God's chosen people, he preached this country's duty to uplift and succor less fortunate peoples. After the waning of popular enthusiasm for expansion, Beveridge tempered his imperialism. But his faith in America's millennial role had not dimmed—and would take on renewed life amid the troubles in Mexico during the Wilson administration.

At the same time, Beveridge hewed to the traditional idea that the successful working out of America's divinely-appointed mission required separation from the corruption and snares of the Old World. His isolationism vis-à-vis Europe was reinforced by his suspicions of, and hostility toward, Great Britain. Thus, before this country's entry into the First World War, he advocated strict neutrality. And when Woodrow Wilson championed the League of Nations as the fulfillment of America's redemptive mission to save the world, Beveridge remained faithful to the older—and more widely accepted—view that this country's true role was to stand apart as the city upon the hill "working out our American institutions of orderly freedom" to provide a model for the world to follow.[2]

Beveridge came to the Senate a stalwart apologist for business America. The old guard leaders of the upper chamber considered the youthful Hoosier a promising recruit. But alarmed by the growing popular restiveness in the years after the turn of the century, Beveridge moved to reform. He saw in Theodore Roosevelt a kindred spirit—a man who, like himself, wished to save the masters of capital from their own shortsightedness. His progressivism brought him into worsening conflict with the standpat majority within the G.O.P.

---

2. Beveridge, "To the Women of America," *Collier's,* 12 June 1920, p. 42.

who remained blind to the dangers which moved Beveridge. This conflict fed back into Indiana politics, giving a new sharpness and bitterness to the long-standing factional rivalry within Hoosier Republicanism. The climax was the break in the Republican party in 1912.

Like most of his fellow progressives, Beveridge had no fundamental quarrel with the existing social and economic structure of the time. His purpose was to lead the popular discontent along safe lines. He pushed for federal regulation of giant corporations to forestall any wholesale trustbusting. He wished to alleviate the lot of America's less fortunate citizens to undercut the appeal of socialism. His fight for a tariff commission and against the Payne-Aldrich bill was aimed at safeguarding the protective system. And he coupled his demands for reform with exhortations to his fellow Americans to subordinate their differences to the higher national interest. Even in the heyday of his insurgency, he continued to regard himself as a "moderate conservative."[3]

As a Hamiltonian, he favored strengthening the federal government to halt corporate wrongdoing. But he was not against business, not even big business. Viewing the concentration and consolidation of industry as inevitable and beneficent, he accepted labor unions as a legitimate weapon of worker self-defense. But he feared lest unrestrained big labor become an even more dangerous threat to the public weal than unrestrained big business. He supported federal intervention to protect those—like child laborers—who could not protect themselves. His guiding vision, however, remained the neutral state administered by men such as himself, standing above the clash of selfish interests and devoted to the national good. So, not surprisingly, he shrank from the new directions in which reform was moving in the 1920s.

Beveridge was bewitched by the will-o'-the-wisp of the presidency until near the end of life. His political ambitions were repeatedly frustrated. Ironically, he gained his most lasting triumphs in what he had taken up as a temporary sideline. He was drawn to write his *Life of John Marshall* because of his lifelong admiration for the great chief justice as the foremost exponent of his own nationalist faith. The resulting massive four volumes are testimony to his energy,

---

3. Beveridge to E. M. Lee, 16 March 1910, BP.

scholarly zeal, and literary skill. Self-taught in historical method, Beveridge had his faults as a biographer: his hero-worshipping of Marshall, his bias against Jefferson, his tendency to excessive detail and quotation, and his weakness in dealing with the technical side of Marshall's decisions. Despite these shortcomings, however, the work stands to this day as the standard biography—the starting point for all later writers on Marshall.[4]

After the failure of his political comeback, Beveridge devoted his last years to writing a biography of Abraham Lincoln. He started out an admirer of Lincoln as the man who had carried on and brought to fulfillment Marshall's, and his own, nationalist philosophy, but he was sadly disillusioned to find the Lincoln of the 1850s not the heroic Lincoln of boyhood legend. His premature death left the work, in William E. Barton's phrase, "a noble fragment."

---

4. Robert K. Faulkner, *The Jurisprudence of John Marshall* (Princeton, N.J., 1968), p. xi.

Bibliographical Notes

The basic source for this biography is the Albert J. Beveridge Papers in the Library of Congress. This massive collection, consisting of approximately 350 boxes of material, includes an uncompleted autobiography, a scrapbook of newspaper clippings from the years before Beveridge became senator, his incoming correspondence from roughly 1890 on, the bulk of his outgoing correspondence from 1898 on, and drafts of many of his speeches.

The *Indianapolis News, Indianapolis Journal* (to June 1904), *Indianapolis Press* (December 1899–April 1901), and *Indianapolis Star* (from June 1903) provided indispensable information about Indiana politics, reported Beveridge's activities in the Senate, and published, in part or whole, many of his speeches. For Beveridge's years in the Senate, I have also relied upon U.S., Congress, Senate, *Congressional Record*.

A number of Beveridge's speeches were separately published. In addition, because he was financially dependent upon his writing, he was a prolific author of books and articles. Most of his books, articles, and published speeches are listed below in the bibliographical notes for the individual chapters.

Those not so listed are: *The Bible as Good Reading* (Philadelphia, 1907); *Work and Habits* (Philadelphia, 1908); "Address by Albert J. Beveridge," in *Addresses at the Dinner in honor of Albert J. Beveridge February fifth Nineteen seventeen* [Indianapolis, 1917], pp. 37–41 (copy in ISL); and the following *Saturday Evening Post* articles: "Contemporary Great Men," 4 August 1900, pp. 2–3; "Great Men of Our Day—Diaz," 11 August 1900, pp. 2–3; and "The Lincoln Highway," 20 March 1915, pp. 9–10, 69–70, 72–74. An essay written for publication in 1909 in the *Chicago Tribune* was later published as "Lincoln an Example to Young Men," *The Magazine of History* 32 (Extra Number—no. 125, 1926): 22–32.

The abbreviations used in the bibliographical notes are explained on p. xi.

CHAPTER 1

For Beveridge's genealogy, see: George F. Black, "The Surnames of Scotland, Their Origin, Meaning, and History," pt. 4, *Bulletin of the New York Public Library* 47 (November 1943): 846; Charles A. Hoppin, *The Washington Ancestry and Records of the McClain, Johnson and Forty Other Colonial American Families* (3 vols., Greenfield, Ohio, 1932); and Claude G. Bowers, *Beveridge and the Progressive Era* (Boston, 1932). For further details, see 1840, 1850, 1860, 1870, and 1880 Censuses and the Pension Records of Thomas Henry Beveridge, National Archives; Deed and Mortgage Records and Auditor's Tax Duplicates, Highland County, Ohio; Probate Court Records, Warren County, Ohio; and Deed, Mortgage, Probate Court, and Treasurer's Records, Moultrie County, Illinois.

In 1908, Beveridge's friend, *Saturday Evening Post* editor George H. Lorimer, urged him to write his autobiography. After his defeat for reelection to the Senate in 1910, he wrote the first chapter of what he titled the "Autobiography of an American Boy." He then prepared a revised draft in response to Lorimer's suggestions, but finally abandoned the project. Although untrustworthy on details, this second draft—cited in the footnotes as MS Autobiography, BP (Box 324)—is invaluable for insight into the forces that shaped Beveridge's personality and mind.

The next most important sources of information about Beveridge's boyhood and college years are Herold T. Ross's "The Oratorical Career of Albert Jeremiah Beveridge" (Ph.D. diss., State University of Iowa, 1932), and his "Albert Jeremiah Beveridge at DePauw (unpublished MS, 1935; microfilm copy in DePauw University Archives).

Reminiscences of Beveridge by two fellow DePauw students are given in David Graham Phillips, "Albert J. Beveridge," *Success Magazine* 8 (August 1905), 526–28, and Clarence W. Hall, *Samuel Logan Brengle: Portrait of a Prophet* (New York, 1933).

Additional sources for Beveridge's youth are: Bowers, *Beveridge and the Progressive Era;* John A. Coffin, "The Senatorial Career of Albert J. Beveridge" [Part I], *IMH* 24 (September 1928), 139–47; William Warren Sweet, *Indiana Asbury–DePauw University, 1837–1937: A Hundred Years of Higher Education in the Middle West* (New York, Cincinnati, and Chicago, 1937); Robert Shackleton, "The New Senator from Indiana," *SEP,* 8 September 1900, pp. 8–10; Richard Lloyd Jones, "The Beginnings of Beveridge," *Collier's,* 15 October 1910, pp. 21–22; "When Beveridge Was the 'Boy Orator,'" *Literary Digest,* 4 June 1927, p. 34; and the *Indianapolis News,* 11 January 1899.

CHAPTER 2

Copies of many of Beveridge's articles and speeches from the years between his graduation from DePauw and his election to the Senate are in Boxes

297 and 326, Beveridge Papers. A scrapbook (Box 327) contains newspaper clippings from these years. His correspondence for 1890–98 are in Boxes 111–21, but consist mostly of incoming letters. A letterbook for 1898 is in Box 266. Important letters from Beveridge are in the John C. Shaffer Papers (ISL) and Louis T. Michener Papers (LC).

A number of his speeches from these years were published: "Response of Hon. Albert J. Beveridge," *Twelfth Annual Celebration of the New England Society of St. Louis . . . December 21, 1896* (Saint Louis, 1897), pp. 10–20 (copy in ISL); *The Vitality of the American Constitution an Address Delivered before the Allegheny County Bar Association . . . Pittsburgh, Pennsylvania, January 4th, 1898. . . .* (Pittsburgh [1898]; copy in ISL); and "Grant, The Republican." *Address . . . At the Banquet of the Middlesex Club of Massachusetts, Boston, Mass. , . . . April 27, 1898* ([Boston, 1898]; copy in ISL).

Additional sources are: MS Autobiography; Bowers, *Beveridge and the Progressive Era;* Ross, "The Oratorical Career of Albert Jeremiah Beveridge"; Shackleton, "The New Senator from Indiana"; the *Indianapolis News* and *Indianapolis Journal;* and the *Indiana Reports.* Recollections of friends are given in *Dinner and Toasts in Honor of Senator Albert J. Beveridge . . . January 13, 1899* (Indianapolis [1899]) and *Addresses at the Dinner in honor of Albert J. Beveridge February fifth Nineteen seventeen* (copies in ISL).

On Indianapolis, see Frederick D. Kershner, Jr., "A Social and Cultural History of Indianapolis, 1860–1914" (Ph.D. diss., University of Wisconsin, 1950). For background on American expansion, I have used Julius W. Pratt, *Expansionists of 1898: The Acquisition of Hawaii and the Spanish Islands* (Baltimore, 1936), and Foster Rhea Dulles, *The Imperial Years* (New York, 1956).

CHAPTER 3

Major sources for Republican factionalism in Indiana during the 1880s and 1890s are the Walter Q. Gresham Papers (LC), Benjamin Harrison Papers (LC), Louis T. Michener Papers, Robert S. Taylor Papers (ISL), and Harry S. New Papers (LC). But probably the single most important source is the Charles W. Fairbanks Papers. The larger part is in the Lilly Library, Indiana University; the rest is in the Indiana Historical Society. There are some important Fairbanks letters in the papers of his uncle, William Henry Smith, in the Indiana Historical Society.

The best available published account of G.O.P. factionalism is in Russel M. Seeds, *History of the Republican Party of Indiana* (Indianapolis, 1899). See also: Matilda Gresham, *Life of Walter Q. Gresham, 1832–1895* (2 vols., Chicago, 1919); Harry J. Sievers, S. J., *Benjamin Harrison, Hoosier Statesman: From the Civil War to the White House, 1865–1888* (New York,

1959), and *Benjamin Harrison, Hoosier President: The White House and After* (Indianapolis, Kansas City, and New York, 1968); Herbert J. Rissler, "Charles Warren Fairbanks: Conservative Hoosier" (Ph.D. diss., Indiana University, 1961); and A. Dale Beeler, ed., "Letters to Colonel William R. Holloway, 1893–1897," *IMH* 36 (December 1940): 371–96.

Beveridge's speech opening the 1898 Indiana G.O.P. campaign was published as *"The March of the Flag"* . . . *Speech by Hon. Albert Beveridge Opening the Indiana Republican Campaign, at Tomlinson Hall, Indianapolis, Friday, September 16, 1898* ([Indianapolis, 1898]; copy in ISL). On Beveridge's role as a local opinion-maker on imperialism, see Ernest R. May, *American Imperialism: A Speculative Essay* (New York, 1968).

For Beveridge's strategy in the senatorial contest, see BP, Boxes 120–24, 266–67. For his campaign managers' promises of offices, see the Nicholas Filbeck Papers (LL).

See also *Indianapolis News, Indianapolis Journal,* Fairbanks Papers (LL and IHS), Taylor Papers, and David W. Henry Papers (ISL).

The account in Bowers, *Beveridge and the Progressive Era,* is based on interviews with surviving participants. Coffin, "The Senatorial Career of Albert J. Beveridge" [pt. I], pp. 147–65, relies upon the newspaper reports. Charles F. Remy, one of Beveridge's inner circle of supporters, wrote "The Election of Beveridge to the Senate," *IMH* 36 (June 1940): 123–35. After reading a draft of Remy's article, Harry S. New wrote his own recollections of the election. This is in the Harry S. New Papers (ISL), along with correspondence with Remy and James M. Huff, Posey's campaign manager.

Beveridge set down his precepts for a successful orator in two articles: "Public Speaking," *SEP,* 6 October 1900, pp. 2–3, and "The Art of Public Speaking," ibid., 26 April 1924, pp. 3–4, 146–48, 151. The latter was published in book form: *The Art of Public Speaking* (Boston and New York, 1924).

For the Beveridge-Phillips correspondence, see Box 276, BP; for the Beveridge-Shaffer correspondence, Boxes 278–82, BP, and the Shaffer Papers; for the Beveridge-Perkins correspondence, Boxes 275–76, BP, and the George W. Perkins Papers (Columbia University Library); for the Beveridge-Shaw correspondence, Boxes 282–83, BP, and the Beveridge file, Albert Shaw Papers (New York Public Library); for the Beveridge-Lorimer correspondence, Boxes 271–72, BP, and the Beveridge file, George H. Lorimer Papers (Historical Society of Pennsylvania).

On Phillips, see Isaac F. Marcosson, *David Graham Phillips and his Times* (New York, 1932), and Kenneth S. Lynn, *The Dream of Success: A Study of the American Imagination* (Boston and Toronto, 1955); on Shaffer, *Indianapolis Star,* 6 October 1943 and *Who's Who in America;* on Perkins, John A. Garraty, *Right-Hand Man: The Life of George W.*

Perkins (New York, 1960); on Shaw, Frank L. Mott, *A History of American Magazines* (5 vols., Cambridge, Mass., 1930–68), 4: 657–64; on Lorimer, John Tebbel, *George Horace Lorimer and the Saturday Evening Post* (Garden City, N.Y., 1948).

CHAPTER 4

For details on Beveridge's trip to the Philippines, see: Bowers, *Beveridge and the Progressive Era*. Beveridge's *SEP* articles on the Philippines are: "The American Soldier in the Philippines," 17 March 1900, pp. 834–35, 851; "With Our Fighters in the Philippines," 31 March 1900, pp. 881–83; and "The American Army Officer in Action," 5 May 1900, pp. 1018–20. For his impressions of Ito, see: "Great Men of Our Day—Ito," *SEP*, 18 August 1900, p. 2.

On the attitudes of McKinley and congressional leaders toward Beveridge, see: Cortelyou Diary, George B. Cortelyou Papers (LC); Henry Cabot Lodge, ed., *Selections from the Correspondence of Theodore Roosevelt and Henry Cabot Lodge* (2 vols., New York, 1925); Sam H. Acheson, *Joe Bailey: The Last Democrat* (New York, 1932); Charles G. Dawes, *A Journal of the McKinley Years*, ed. Bascom Timmons (Chicago, 1950); and Margaret Leech, *In the Days of McKinley* (New York, 1959).

For the Puerto Rican tariff fight, see: Leech, *In the Days of McKinley;* H. Wayne Morgan, *William McKinley and His America* (Syracuse, N.Y., 1963); Richard C. Baker, *The Tariff under Roosevelt and Taft* (Ph.D. diss., Columbia University; Hastings, Neb., 1941); Phillip C. Jessup, *Elihu Root* (2 vols., New York, 1938); Everett Walters, *Joseph Benson Foraker: An Uncompromising Republican* (Columbus, Ohio, 1948); Dawes, *A Journal of the McKinley Years;* and the Cortelyou Diary. See the Fairbanks Papers (LL) for the reaction to the measure in Indiana.

On the Hay-Pauncefote treaty, see: J. A. S. Grenville, "Great Britain and the Isthmian Canal, 1898–1901," *American Historical Review* 61 (October 1955): 48–69; Leech, *In the Days of McKinley;* Charles S. Campbell, Jr., *Anglo-American Understanding, 1898–1903* (Baltimore, 1957). On the opposition to ratification, see: Howard K. Beale, *Theodore Roosevelt and the Rise of America to World Power* (Baltimore, 1956), and the Frederick W. Holls Papers (Columbia University Library).

On Cuban policy, see: Leech, *In the Days of McKinley;* Jessup, *Elihu Root;* David F. Healy, *The United States in Cuba, 1898–1902: Generals, Politicians, and the Search for Policy* (Madison, Wis., 1963); and Russell H. Fitzgibbon, *Cuba and the United States, 1900–1935* (Menasha, Wis., 1935). For Beveridge's regrets over the Teller Amendment, see Beveridge, *For the Greater Republic, Not for Imperialism. An Address Delivered . . . at the Union League of Philadelphia, February 15, 1899* [Philadelphia, 1899]; for his defense of the Platt Amendment, "Cuba and Congress,"

North American Review 172 (April 1901): 535–50. For Beveridge's belief in the "*ultimate* annexation of Cuba," see: "Americans of To-Day and To-Morrow," *SEP*, 19 September 1903, pp. 10–11.

CHAPTER 5

On the Philippine civil government act, see: Garel A. Grunder and William E. Livezey, *The Philippines and the United States* (Norman, Okla., 1951), and William Howard Taft Papers (LC). On the Philippine atrocity issue, see: Jessup, *Elihu Root;* John A. Garraty, *Henry Cabot Lodge: A Biography* (New York, 1953); and U.S., Congress, Senate, Committee on the Philippines, *Affairs in the Philippine Islands. Hearings,* 57 Cong., 1st sess., S. Doc. 331 (3 vols., Washington, 1902). Beveridge's defense of the army on the Senate floor was reprinted as *The Philippine Situation . . . ,* 57th Cong., 1st sess., S. Doc. 422 (Washington, 1902). On the clash with Bailey, see Acheson, *Joe Bailey.*

On the Far Eastern situation, see: Edward H. Zabriskie, *American-Russian Rivalry in the Far East: A Study of Diplomacy and Power Politics, 1895–1914* (Philadelphia, 1946), and Beale, *Theodore Roosevelt and the Rise of America to World Power.*

For Beveridge's plea for a Russian-American deal, see "Russia and America: The Two Youths among the Nations," *SEP*, 9 June 1900, pp. 1146–47. Letters from Beveridge while on Russian and Far East trip are in the Albert Shaw Papers, Harry S. New Papers (LC), and Elihu Root Papers (LC). After his return, he wrote the following series of articles for *SEP*: "The White Invasion of China," 23 November 1901, pp. 1–2, 30 November 1901, pp. 3–5, 7 December 1901, pp. 1–3, 14 December 1901, pp. 6–7, 14–15; "A Diplomatic Game for an Empire," 18 January 1902, pp. 3–5; "The March of a Nation to the Sea," 25 January 1902, pp. 1–2; "The Coming War between Russia and Japan," 8 February 1902, pp. 1–3; "The War Cry of the German Empire in the East," 15 March 1902, pp. 3–4, 18; "Winning the Markets of the Orient," 22 March 1902, pp. 1–2, 12 April 1902, pp. 1–2, 19 April 1902, pp. 10–11; "Two Great Men of Russia 1. Witte," 26 July 1902, pp. 3–4; and "Two Great Men of Russia II. Pobedo-nosteff," 2 August 1902, pp. 6–7. Beveridge brought these articles together, with some additional material, in a book entitled *The Russian Advance* (New York and London, 1903). As the tensions between Russia and Japan heightened, Beveridge renewed his plea against this country's making any premature commitments in "The Hand of Russia in the Far East," *SEP*, 12 December 1903, pp. 1–2, 21.

For a criticism of Beveridge's favorable impressions of imperial Russia, see William English Walling, *Russia's Message: The True World Import of the Revolution* (New York, 1908).

On the 1906 Cuban crisis, see: Fitzgibbon, *Cuba and the United States,*

1900–1935; the Theodore Roosevelt Papers (LC); and Elting E. Morison, *et al.*, eds., *The Letters of Theodore Roosevelt* (8 vols., Cambridge, Mass., 1951–54), vol. 5. On the decline of popular interest in overseas expansion: Dulles, *The Imperial Years,* and Louis Hartz, *The Liberal Tradition in America: An Interpretation of American Political Thought since the Revolution* (New York, 1955).

For Beveridge's continuing enthusiasm for America's imperial mission, see: "Americans of To-Day and To-Morrow," *SEP,* 8 August 1903, pp. 1–2, 5 September 1903, pp. 4–5, 19 September 1903, pp. 10–11; "The Young Man in the World," ibid., 1 July 1905, pp. 1–3, 19; "National Integrity: What Is a Nation Profited, If It Shall Gain the Whole World and Lose Its Own Soul?" *The Reader* 7 (May 1906): 569–73; "The Development of a Colonial Policy for the United States," *Annals of the American Academy of Political and Social Science* 30 (July 1907): 3–15; "True Liberty under Law" ("The Government of Dependencies 'Imperialism': The Fifth in the Series of Articles on the Problems of the People"), *The Reader* 10 (July 1907): 148–56; and "Senator Beveridge's Reply" ("The Government of Dependencies 'Imperialism': The Sixth in the Series of Articles on the Problems of the People"), ibid. (August 1907): 259–69; and *Americans of To-Day and To-Morrow* (Philadelphia, 1908).

For Beveridge's lack of interest in the work of the Senate Foreign Relations Committee, see Shelby M. Cullom, *Fifty Years of Public Service* (Chicago, 1911).

CHAPTER 6

Beveridge's most important correspondents regarding Indiana politics (Boxes 122–148) were Henry W. Bennett, John R. Bonnell, Charles W. Miller, Henry C. Pettit, and Leopold G. Rothschild. His correspondence with Gifford Pinchot is in Box 276; with Theodore Roosevelt, in Box 277. Additional Beveridge letters are in the Theodore Roosevelt Papers, George W. Perkins Papers, Albert Shaw Papers, John C. Shaffer Papers, and Gifford Pinchot Papers (LC). For Beveridge's relations with the Senate leaders, see: the Orville H. Platt Papers (Connecticut State Library) and Nelson W. Aldrich Papers (LC).

For Indiana politics in this period, see: Frank Munger, "Two-Party Politics in the State of Indiana" (Ph.D. diss., Harvard University, 1955), and Clifton J. Phillips, *Indiana in Transition: The Emergence of an Industrial Commonwealth, 1880–1920* (Indianapolis, 1968). See also Louis Ludlow, *From Cornfield to Press Gallery: Adventures and Reminiscences of a Veteran Washington Correspondent* (Washington, 1924). The Fairbanks Papers (LL) contains a wealth of material on Republican factionalism. Rissler, "Charles Warren Fairbanks: Conservative Hoosier," is a biography based upon the Lilly Library collection. William Henry Smith, *The*

Life and Speeches of the Hon. Charles Warren Fairbanks (Indianapolis, 1904), is a laudatory campaign biography. On Fairbanks's secret ownership of the *Indianapolis News,* see: Hilton U. Brown, *A Book of Memories* (Indianapolis, 1951); the Delavan Smith Papers (Indiana Historical Society); and *United States* v. *Delavan Smith,* U.S. District Court, Indianapolis (1919), Federal Records Center, Chicago. Additional materials on Indiana politics are in the David W. Henry Papers and Lucius C. Embree Papers (ISL).

On the working of the Republican party machinery, see: Jesse Macy, *Party Organization and Machinery* (New York, 1904); Charlotte E. Bruce, "A Review of Indiana Election Laws, 1889–1935" (M.A. thesis, Butler University, 1935; copy in ISL); J. F. Connell, "Indiana Primary Laws," *IMH* 18 (September 1922): 224–38; *Laws of the State of Indiana . . . 1901* (Indianapolis, 1901), pp. 495–505, and *Laws of the State of Indiana . . . 1905* (Indianapolis, 1905), pp. 122–27; and the Will H. Hays Papers (ISL).

For Beveridge's activities on behalf of his constituents, see: Wayne E. Fuller, *RFD: The Changing Face of Rural America* (Bloomington, Ind., 1964); Lorenz G. Schumm Collection (Indiana Historical Society); and O. H. Hasselman Collection (Indiana Historical Society).

Beveridge set forth his version of the gospel of success in the following *SEP* articles: "The Young Man and the World," 7 July 1900, pp. 3–5; "The World and the Young Man," 1 September 1900, pp. 4–5; "Great Chances for New-Century Americans," 22 September 1900, pp. 2–3; "Facing the World at Fifty," 29 September 1900, pp. 3–4; "The Young Lawyer and His Beginnings," 27 October 1900, pp. 1–3; "The Young Man Out of Business Hours," 1 December 1900, pp. 8–9; "The Young Man and College Life," 10 June 1905, pp. 1–3, 21; and "The Young Man in the World," 20 May 1905, pp. 1–3, 26–27; 1 July 1905, pp. 1–3, 19; 15 July 1905, pp. 1–2, 20; 2 September 1905, pp. 1–3, 24; 30 September 1905, pp. 2–4. He brought much of this material together in book form: *The Young Man and the World* (New York, 1905).

Beveridge coupled predictions of America's future world greatness with warnings against class divisions within the country in another series of *SEP* articles: "Americans of To-Day and To-Morrow," 28 February 1903, pp. 1–2; 11 April 1903, pp. 1–2, 47–48; 16 May 1903, pp. 1–2; 6 June 1903, pp. 1–2; 4 July 1903, pp. 1–2; 8 August 1903, pp. 1–2; 5 September 1903, pp. 10–11. These articles were brought together in book form: *Americans of To-Day and To-Morrow* (Philadelphia, 1908).

A collection of his speeches was published under the title *The Meaning of the Times and Other Speeches* (Indianapolis, 1908), but, since many of these were edited after delivery, I have for the most part relied upon the newspaper reports.

Two of Beveridge's speeches from these years were separately published in pamphlet form: *Republicanism: The Spirit of Conservative Progress . . . . Speech . . . Indiana State Republican Convention, at Indianapolis, Ind., April 23d, 1902 . . .* ([Indianapolis, 1902]; copy in ISL), and *Address . . . at the Dedication of Indiana's Monuments on the Battlefield of Shiloh, Tennessee, April 6, 1903* (Indianapolis [1903]; copy in LC).

On the ship subsidy bill, see Herbert Croly, *Marcus Alonzo Hanna: His Life and Work* (New York, 1912). Biographies of other Senate leaders are: Louis A. Coolidge, *An Old Fashioned Senator: Orville H. Platt of Connecticut* (New York and London, 1910); Nathaniel W. Stephenson, *Nelson W. Aldrich: A Leader in American Politics* (New York, 1930); Dorothy G. Fowler, *John Coit Spooner: Defender of Presidents* (New York, 1961); and Leland L. Sage, *William Boyd Allison: A Study in Practical Politics* (Iowa City, 1956).

On Roosevelt, see: John M. Blum, *The Republican Roosevelt* (Cambridge, Mass., 1954); George E. Mowry, *The Era of Theodore Roosevelt, 1900–1912* (New York, 1958); and William H. Harbaugh, *Power and Responsibility: The Life and Times of Theodore Roosevelt* (New York, 1961). Roosevelt's messages to Congress are published in Theodore Roosevelt, *State Papers as Governor and President, 1899–1909*, vol. 15 of *The Works of Theodore Roosevelt*, ed. Hermann Hagedorn, National Edition, 20 vols. (New York, 1926).

During the 1904 campaign, Beveridge wrote the following articles extolling T.R.: "Following Roosevelt as President," *SEP*, 10 September 1904, pp. 1–3, 23; "Why a Young Man Should Vote the Republican Ticket," ibid., 1 October 1904, pp. 1–3, 15; and "A Republican View of the Campaign Issues," *Harper's Weekly*, 29 October 1904, pp. 1650–52.

CHAPTER 7

The material in this chapter appeared in somewhat different form, with full documentation, in John Braeman. "Albert J. Beveridge and Statehood for the Southwest, 1902–1912," *Arizona and the West* 10 (Winter 1968): 313–42. For T.R.'s position, see the Theodore Roosevelt Papers and Morison, *The Letters of Theodore Roosevelt;* his messages to Congress are in Roosevelt, *State Papers as Governor and President.*

For the omnibus bill, see U.S. Congress, House, Committee on the Territories, *Admission of Certain Territories into the Union: Report to Accompany H.R. 12543*, 57th Cong., 1st sess., 1902, H. Rept. 1309 (Washington, 1902); for the accompanying measure giving the Indian Territory territorial status: Committee on the Territories, *Territory of Jefferson and Government for the Same: Report to Accompany H.R. 12268*, 57th Cong., 1st sess., 1902, H. Rept. 956 (Washington, 1902). The hearings conducted by Beveridge are published as Committee on Territories, *New Statehood*

Bill: Hearings . . . on House Bill 12543 . . . , 57th Cong., 2nd sess., 1902, S. Doc. 36 (Washington, 1902). The majority report of the Senate Committee on Territories is given in Committee on Territories, *New Statehood Bill: Report to Accompany H.R. 12543,* 57th Cong., 2nd sess., 1902, S. Rept. 2206, Part 1 (Washington, 1902). For the final compromise requiring a referendum in Arizona and New Mexico on jointure, see U.S., Congress, Committee of Conference, *Statehood Bill: Conference Report to Accompany H.R. 12707,* 59th Cong., 1st sess., 1906, H. Rept. 4925 (Washington, 1906).

Background on the statehood controversy is drawn from: Howard R. Lamar, 'The Reluctant Admission: The Struggle to Admit Arizona and New Mexico to the Union," in Robert G. Ferris, ed., *The American West: An Appraisal* (Santa Fe, N.M., 1963), pp. 163–75; Lamar, *The Far Southwest, 1846–1912: A Territorial History* (New Haven, 1966); and Donald D. Leopard, "Joint Statehood: 1906" (M.A. thesis, University of New Mexico, 1958). A summary of Leopard's thesis was published under the same title in the *New Mexico Historical Review* 34 (October 1959): 241–47.

For further details on New Mexico, see: Marion Dargan, "New Mexico's Fight for Statehood, 1895–1912," *New Mexico Historical Review* 14 (January 1939): 1–33; (April 1939): 121–42; 15 (April 1940): 133–87; 16 (January 1941), 70–103; (October 1941), 379–400; 18 (January 1943), 60–96; (April 1943): 148–175; Robert E. Larson, 'Statehood for New Mexico, 1888–1912," ibid. 37 (July 1962): 161–200; Larson, "Taft, Roosevelt, and New Mexico Statehood," *Mid-America* 45 (April 1963): 99–114; Larson, *New Mexico's Quest for Statehood, 1846–1912* (Albuquerque, N.M., 1968); Miguel A. Otero, *My Nine Years as Governor of the Territory of New Mexico, 1897–1906,* ed. Marion Dargan (Albuquerque, N.M., 1940); Ralph E. Twitchell, *The Leading Facts of New Mexican History* (5 vols., Cedar Rapids, Iowa, 1911–17), 2; H. B. Hening, ed., *George Curry, 1861–1947: An Autobiography* (Albuquerque, N.M., 1958); and the Herbert J. Hagerman Papers (New Mexico State Records Center and Archives, Santa Fe, N.M.).

On Arizona: La Moine Langston, "Arizona's Fight for Statehood in the Fifty-Seventh Congress" (M.A. thesis, University of New Mexico, 1959); George H. Kelly, *Legislative History: Arizona, 1864–1912* (Phoenix, 1926); Richard E. Sloan, *Memories of an Arizona Judge* (Stanford University, 1932); Rufus K. Wyllys, *Arizona: History of a Frontier State* (Phoenix, 1950); "Territorial Sentiment on the Statehood Question," *Literary Digest,* 23 December 1905, pp. 947–48; H. A. Hubbard, "The Arizona Enabling Act and President Taft's Veto," *Pacific Historical Review* 3 (September 1934): 307–22; Howard R. Lamar, "Carpetbaggers Full of Dreams: A Functional View of the Arizona Pioneer Politician," *Arizona and the West* 7 (Autumn 1965): 187–206; and Steven A. Fazio, "Marcus Aurelius Smith: Arizona's Delegate and Senator," ibid. 12 (Spring 1970): 23–62.

On Oklahoma–Indian Territory: Roy Gittinger, *The Formation of the State of Oklahoma* (Berkeley, 1917); Grant Foreman, *A History of Oklahoma* (Norman, Okla., 1942); Edward C. McReynolds, *Oklahoma: A History of the Sooner State* (Norman, Okla., 1954); and Amos Maxwell, "The Sequoyah Convention," *Chronicles of Oklahoma* 28 (Summer 1950): 161–92; (Autumn 1950): 299–340.

For data on leading participants in the congressional battle, see: W. H. Hutchinson, *Oil, Land and Politics: The California Career of Thomas Robert Bard* (2 vols., Norman, Okla., 1965), and Waldemar Westergaard, "Senator Bard and the Arizona–New Mexico Statehood Controversy," *Annual Publications of the Historical Society of Southern California* 11, pt. 2 (1919): 9–17; the Orville H. Platt Papers; Walters, *Joseph Benson Foraker;* and Oscar D. Lambert, *Stephen Benton Elkins* (Pittsburgh, 1955). For Quay's approval of the compromise worked out by the Senate Republican leaders to resolve the controversy by joining the four territories into two states, see *Philadelphia Press*, 4, 23–26 February 1903. The activities of the leading Senate spokesman for Arizona's opposition to joint statehood can be followed through the Joseph B. Foraker Papers (Cincinnati Historical Society).

CHAPTER 8

Beveridge's two *SEP* articles foreshadowing his turning toward progressivism are: "Private Fortune a Public Trust," 18 November 1905, pp. 4–5, and "The Rich Man in Public Life," 16 June 1906, pp. 3–4, 16. For his hesitancy over publishing the second article and the reaction to its appearance, see Beveridge's correspondence with Lorimer, Box 271, BP.

On the rising tide of discontent in Indiana and throughout the nation, see: Mowry, *The Era of Theodore Roosevelt;* Phillips, *Indiana in Transition;* and Ora E. Cox, "The Socialist Party in Indiana since 1896," *IMH* 12 (June 1916): 95–130.

For background on the Smoot case, see M. Paul Holsinger, "For God and the American Home: The Attempt to Unseat Senator Reed Smoot, 1903–1907," *Pacific Northwest Quarterly* 60 (July 1969): 154–60. The hearings are published as U.S., Congress, Senate, Committee on Privileges and Elections, *Proceedings . . . in the Matter of Protests against the Right of Hon. Reed Smoot, a Senator from Utah, to Hold His Seat,* 59th Cong., 1st sess. (4 vols., Washington, 1906). Beveridge's speech in Smoot's defense is in *CR*, 59th Cong., 2nd sess., 1907, 41, pt. 4: 3408–12.

For the background on the Hepburn act, see John M. Blum, "Theodore Roosevelt and the Hepburn Act: Toward an Orderly System of Control," in Morison, *The Letters of Theodore Roosevelt*, 6: 1558–71. Aldrich's outburst is described in Stephenson, *Nelson W. Aldrich*, p. 266.

A fully documented account of the background and passage of the meat inspection law is John Braeman, "The Square Deal in Action: A Case Study in the Growth of the 'National Police Power,'" in Braeman *et al.*, eds., *Change and Continuity in Twentieth-Century America* (Columbus, Ohio, 1964), pp. 35–80. On the pure food and drug law, see Oscar E. Anderson, Jr., *The Health of a Nation: Harvey W. Wiley and the Fight for Pure Food* (Chicago, 1958).

Major sources for the meat inspection law fight are: the Beveridge Papers; Theodore Roosevelt Papers; Morison, *The Letters of Theodore Roosevelt;* Wadsworth Family Papers (LC); Office of the Secretary of Agriculture, R.G. 16, Solicitor's Office Correspondence (National Archives); and *CR* (Senate and House), 59th Cong., 1st sess., 1905–6, 40 (11 vols., Washington, 1906). Additional details drawn from the Chicago newspapers, and U.S., Congress, House, Committee on Agriculture, *Hearings . . . on the So-called "Beveridge Amendment" to the Agricultural Appropriation Bill (H.R. 18537) . . .*, 59th Cong., 1st sess., 1906 (Washington, 1906).

For the first report from the House Committee on Agriculture, see U.S., Congress, House, Committee on Agriculture, *Amendments to Agricultural Appropriation Bill: Report to Accompany H.R. 18537,* 59th Cong., 1st sess., 1906, H. Rept. 4935, [pt. 1] (Washington, 1906). Roosevelt's special message to Congress with the text of the Neill-Reynolds report is U.S., Congress, House, *Conditions in Chicago Stock Yards: Message from the President . . . Transmitting the Report of Mr. James Bronson Reynolds and Commissioner Charles P. Neill . . .*, 59th Cong., 1st sess., 1906, H. Doc. 873 (Washington, 1906).

On Beveridge's unsuccessful efforts to improve the bill at subsequent sessions of Congress, see: *CR*, 59th Cong., 2nd sess., 1906–7, 41 (6 vols., Washington, 1907), and 60th Cong., 1st sess., 1907–8, 42 (9 vols., Washington, 1908).

CHAPTER 9

The material in this chapter appeared in somewhat different form, with full documentation, in John Braeman, "Albert J. Beveridge and the First National Child Labor Bill," *IMH* 60 (March 1964): 1–36.

For background, see: Elizabeth S. Johnson, "Child Labor Legislation," in John R. Commons, et al., *History of Labor in the United States* (4 vols., New York, 1926–35), 3: 403–56; Elizabeth H. Davidson, *Child Labor Legislation in the Southern Textile States* (Chapel Hill, N.C., 1939); and Robert H. Bremner, *From the Depths: The Discovery of Poverty in the United States* (New York, 1956).

The bulk of Beveridge's correspondence *re* his child labor bill is filed under that heading in Boxes 156 and 161, BP. Beveridge's speech before the National Child Labor Committee's annual convention was reprinted as "Child Labor and the Nation," *Annals of the American Academy of Political and Social Science* 29 (January 1907): 115–24; his child labor speech in the Senate was published as *Employment of Child Labor. Speech . . . in the Senate of the United States, January 23, 28, and 29, 1907* (Washington, 1907; copy in LC). Beveridge summarized his constitutional arguments for the bill in "The Position of Child Labor Legislation," *The Independent*, 21 February 1907, pp. 434–36. And when Mrs. Van Vorst published her articles in book form, he wrote the "Introduction," Mrs. John Van Vorst, *The Cry of the Children: A Study of Child Labor* (New York, 1908), pp. ix–xxiii. On the activities of the National Child Labor Committee, see National Child Labor Committee Papers (LC). On McKelway, see Herbert J. Doherty, "Alexander J. McKelway: Preacher to Progressive," *Journal of Southern History* 24 (May 1958): 177–90. McKelway recounts his lobbying for the Beveridge bill in "Legislative Hints for Social Reformers," Alexander J. McKelway Papers (LC). His account of the passage of the 1916 law is "Another Emancipation Proclamation: The Federal Child Labor Law," *American Review of Reviews* 54 (October 1916): 423–26.

For the A. F. of L.'s attitude, see Eva M. Valesh, "Child Labor," *American Federationist* 14 (March 1907): 157–73. Bryan's support of the bill is in "Mr. Bryan's Reply" ["The Nation versus State's Rights: The Second in the Series of Articles on the Problems of the People"], *The Reader* 9 (April 1907): 465.

On Murphy, see: Maud King Murphy, *Edgar Gardner Murphy: From Records and Memories* (New York, 1943); Hugh C. Bailey, *Edgar Gardner Murphy: Gentle Progressive* (Coral Gables, Fla., 1968); and Edgar Gardner Murphy Papers (Southern Historical Collection, University of North Carolina Library). Murphy set forth his opposition to the Beveridge measure in *The Federal Regulation of Child Labor: A Criticism of the Policy Represented in the Beveridge-Parsons Bill* [Montgomery, Ala., 1907].

CHAPTER 10

For the discontent with the tariff status quo, see; "Shall the Tariff Be Revised?" *The Outlook*, 25 October 1902, pp. 444–52; Wolf von Schierband, "Our Tariff Differences with Germany," *American Monthly Review of Reviews* 32 (August 1905): 205–07; W. M. Corwine, "Does the Country Want Tariff Readjustment?" ibid. 36 (July 1907): 47–50; H. Parker Willis, "The Impending Tariff Struggle," *Journal of Political Economy* 17 (January 1909): 1–18; Henry T. Wills, *Scientific Tariff*

Making: A History of the Movement to Create a Tariff Commission (New York, 1913); F. W. Taussig, *The Tariff History of the United States* (8th rev. ed., New York, 1931); Baker, *The Tariff under Roosevelt and Taft;* L. Ethan Ellis, *Print Paper Pendulum: Group Pressures and the Price of Newsprint* (New Brunswick, N.J., 1948); Robert H. Wiebe, *Businessmen and Reform: A Study of the Progressive Movement* (Cambridge, Mass., 1962); Joseph F. Kenkel, "The Tariff Commission Movement: The Search for a Nonpartisan Solution of the Tariff Question" (Ph.D diss., University of Maryland, 1962); Richard M. Abrams, *Conservatism in a Progressive Era: Massachusetts Politics, 1900–1912* (Cambridge, Mass., 1964); *Chicago Tribune,* 17–18 August 1905; Theodore Roosevelt Papers; Charles W. Fairbanks Papers (LL); Orville H. Platt Papers; Nelson W. Aldrich Papers; and Jonathan P. Dolliver Papers (State Historical Society of Iowa). The leading organ of the defenders of the existing protective system was the *American Economist.*

The bulk of Beveridge's correspondence re the tariff commission is in folders marked "Tariff Commission" and "H. E. Miles" in Boxes 159 and 164–65, BP.

Beveridge set forth his proposal for a tariff commission in the following articles: "Revision Necessary—By Commission" ["The Tariff—Help or Hindrance?: The Ninth in the Series of Articles on the Problems of the People"], *The Reader* 10 (November 1907): 612–18; "Senator Beveridge's Reply" ["The Tariff—Help or Hindrance?: The Tenth in the Series of Articles on the Problems of the People"], ibid. 11 (December 1907): 73–81; and "A Permanent Tariff Commission," *Annals of the American Academy of Political and Social Science* 32 (September 1908): 409–28. For the influence of the German example, see Beveridge to John C. O'Laughlin, 30 August 1913, BP. On the Indiana manufacturing situation, see: Phillips, *Indiana in Transition,* and John D. Barnhart, *Indiana from Frontier to Industrial Commonwealth* (4 vols., New York, 1954), 2.

Re the N.A.M.'s activities in behalf of the tariff commission, see: *Proceedings of the Tenth Annual Convention of the National Association of Manufacturers . . . 1905* (New York [1905]); *Proceedings of the Twelfth Annual Convention . . . 1907* (New York [1907]); *Proceedings of the Thirteenth Annual Convention . . . 1908* (New York [1908]). In 1913, congressional investigators of N.A.M. lobbying published the correspondence in the N.A.M. files—much of it dealing with its tariff commission activities—in U.S., Congress, Subcommittee of the Senate Committee on the Judiciary, *Maintenance of a Lobby to Influence Legislation: Appendix,* 63rd Cong., 1st sess. (4 vols., Washington, 1913–14).

For details on the deal involving the Aldrich currency bill, see: Stephenson, *Nelson W. Aldrich;* Beveridge to Jeannette P. Nichols, 27 January 1927, Beveridge Papers; and the letters and telegrams from George W.

Perkins, Charles Steele and Beveridge in Box 19, George W. Perkins Papers.

On the tariff commission convention, see file marked "Tariff Com. Convention and J. W. Van Cleave," Box 170, BP.

CHAPTER 11

Beveridge's correspondence with his political lieutenants in Indiana— Henry W. Bennett, Charles W. Miller, Elam H. Neal, H. C. Pettit, and Leopold G. Rothschild—for the years 1905-8 is in Boxes 149-65, BP. His most important confidants outside Indiana on public and personal matters were: John C. Shaffer (Boxes 279-80, BP, and Shaffer Papers); George W. Perkins (Box 275, BP, and Perkins Papers); Gifford Pinchot (Box 276, BP, and Pinchot Papers); and Albert Shaw (Boxes 282-83, BP). For his relations with Roosevelt, see Box 227, BP, and Theodore Roosevelt Papers.

Beveridge's magazine articles during these years include: "The Senate: A Mirror of Our National Ideals," *SEP*, 16 June 1906, pp. 3-4, 24; "The Vicious Fear of Losing," ibid., 6 October 1906, pp. 17-19; "The Demagogue in Public Life," ibid., 27 October 1906, pp. 17-18; and "Shall None but Millionaires Run the Government?" *Appleton's Magazine* 9 (March 1907): 259-64.

Probably the fullest exposition of Beveridge's views on the public questions of the time was in his debate with Democratic leader William Jennings Bryan in *The Reader*:

"The Nation versus State's Rights: The First Debate in the Series on the Problems of the People," 9 (March 1907): Bryan, "Our Dual Government," pp. 349-56; Beveridge, "The Nation," pp. 356-64. "The Nation versus State's Rights: The Second in the Series of Articles on the Problems of the People," 9 (April 1907): "Mr. Bryan's Reply," pp. 461-65; "Senator Beveridge's Reply," pp. 465-71. "Trusts and Their Treatment: The Third in the Series of Articles . . . ," 9 (May 1907): Bryan, "Dissolution and Prevention," pp. 573-78; Beveridge, "Regulation, Not Extermination," pp. 579-88, "Trusts and Their Treatment: The Fourth . . . ," 10 (June 1907): "Mr. Bryan's Reply," pp. 34-40; "Senator Beveridge's Reply," pp. 40-46. "The Government of Dependencies 'Imperialism': The Fifth . . . ," 10 (July 1907): Bryan, "Weakening the Republic," pp. 142-48; Beveridge, "True Liberty under Law," pp. 148-56. "The Government of Dependencies 'Imperialism': The Sixth . . . ," 10 (August 1907): "Mr. Bryan's Reply," pp. 255-59; "Senator Beveridge's Reply," pp. 259-69. "The Relation of the State to Labor: The Seventh . . . ," 10 (September 1907): Bryan, "The Spirit of Brotherhood," pp. 372-77; Beveridge, "Mutual Confidence and Consideration," pp. 377-86. "The Relation of the State to Labor: The Eighth . . . ," 10 (October 1907): "Mr. Bryan's Reply," pp. 478-81;

"Senator Beveridge's Reply," pp. 481–85. "The Tariff—Help or Hindrance?: The Ninth . . . ," 10 (November 1907): Bryan, "Tariff for Revenue, not for Protection," pp. 612–18; Beveridge, "Revision Necessary —By Commission," pp. 618–26. "The Tariff—Help or Hindrance?: The Tenth . . . ," 11 (December 1907): "Mr. Bryan's Reply," pp. 68–73; "Senator Beveridge's Reply," pp. 73–81. "The State and Swollen Fortunes: The Eleventh . . . ," 11 (January 1908): Bryan, "Prevention More than Penalty," pp. 145–51; Beveridge, "Restoring the Unearned Increment," pp. 151–58. "The Railroads' Power in the State: The Twelfth . . . ," 12 (February 1908): Bryan, "What the People Should Demand of the Railroads," pp. 288–93; Beveridge, "Supervision, Not Ownership," pp. 294–205.

Beveridge's stands on labor questions are detailed in Theodore Perry, et al., *Beveridge's Labor Record* ([Indianapolis, 1910]; copy in ISL). For background on the injunction issue, see: Mark Karson, *American Labor Unions and Politics, 1900–1918* (Carbondale, Ill., 1958), and Bernard Mandel, *Samuel Gompers: A Biography* (Yellow Springs, Ohio, 1963).

The split in the national G.O.P. is described by Mowry, *The Era of Theodore Roosevelt.* For background on the four-battleship fight, see: Raymond A. Esthus, *Theodore Roosevelt and Japan* (Seattle and London, 1966); Charles E. Neu, *An Uncertain Friendship: Theodore Roosevelt and Japan, 1906–1909* (Cambridge, Mass., 1967); Harold and Margaret Sprout, *The Rise of American Naval Power* (Princeton, N.J., 1942); and Merle Curti, *Peace or War: The American Story* (reprint ed., Boston, 1959).

Phillips, *Indiana in Transition,* surveys the Indiana political and newspaper situation in these years. See also John O. Carrington, "The Foreign Policy of the Indianapolis Star, 1918–1939" (Ph.D. diss., University of Kentucky, 1958). For information on Beveridge's factional rivals in Indiana, see Rissler, "Charles Warren Fairbanks" and Charles W. Fairbanks Papers (LL); for the political situation as viewed by two independent, reform-minded, pro-Roosevelt figures, see the William Dudley Foulke Papers (LC and ISL) and Lucius B. Swift Papers (ISL).

Re the primary election law, see the correspondence between Beveridge and Charles O. Roemler, Box 158, BP, and *Laws of the State of Indiana . . . 1907* (Indianapolis, 1907), pp. 627–52. On the temporary chairmanship of the 1908 G.O.P. national convention, see Memorandum, 15 February 1930, Harry S. New Papers (ISL). Beveridge's low opinion of the vice-presidency is given in his "The Fifth Wheel in Our Government," *Century Magazine* 79 (December 1909): 208–14.

Beveridge's speaking itinerary in the 1908 campaign is given in Ross, "The Oratorical Career of Albert Jeremiah Beveridge," Appendix 2: 215. On the temperance issue in Indiana politics, see Charles E. Canup, "The

Temperance Movement in Indiana," *IMH* 16 (June 1920): 112–51. On the 1908 election see: Charles M. Thomas, *Thomas Riley Marshall: Hoosier Statesman* (Oxford, Ohio, 1939); James E. Watson, *As I Knew Them: Memoirs of James E. Watson* (Indianapolis and New York, 1936); *Maintenance of a Lobby to Influence Legislation: Appendix;* Keith S. Montgomery, "Thomas R. Marshall's Victory in the Election of 1908," *IMH* 53 (June 1957): 147–66; and Lawrence M. Bowman, "Stepping Stone to the Vice Presidency: A Study of Thomas Riley Marshall's 1908 Gubernatorial Victory" (M.A. thesis, University of Kansas, 1967).

CHAPTER 12

On the Payne-Aldrich tariff, see: H. Parker Willis, "The Tariff of 1909: 1. Analysis of the Act," *Journal of Political Economy* 17 (November 1909): 589–619; "The Tariff of 1909: 2. The Legislative History of the Act," ibid. 18 (January 1910): 1–33; "The Tariff of 1909: 3. The Effect of the Act upon Foreign Relations," ibid. (March 1910): 173–96; Taussig, *The Tariff History of the United States;* Ellis, *Print Paper Pendulum;* Baker, *The Tariff under Roosevelt and Taft;* Mark Sullivan, *Our Times* (6 vols., New York, 1925–35), 4; and Kenneth Hechler, *Insurgency: Personalities and Politics of the Taft Era* (New York, 1940).

The bulk of Beveridge's correspondence re the bill is in the file "Tariff 1909" in Box 170, BP. Beveridge complained about New England domination of the Senate in "The Control of the Senate," *SEP,* 5 June 1909, pp. 6–7. He reviewed the battle in three *SEP* articles: "The Insurgents," 16 October 1909, pp. 3–5, 58–60; "The Tariff Commission: The Natural History of a Reform," 17 September 1910, pp. 3–5, 45–46; and "The Tariff Commission: The Downs and Ups of the Tariff Commission Idea," 24 September 1910, pp. 8–9, 57–58.

On Taft, see: Presidential Letterbooks, William Howard Taft Papers; William H. Taft, *Presidential Addresses and State Papers* (Garden City, N.Y., 1910); [Archibald W. Butt], *Taft and Roosevelt: The Intimate Letters of Archie Butt, Military Aide* (2 vols., Garden City, N.Y., 1930); Henry F. Pringle, *The Life and Times of William Howard Taft: A Biography* (2 vols., New York and Toronto, 1939); Stanley D. Solvick, "William Howard Taft and Cannonism," *Wisconsin Magazine of History* 48 (Autumn 1964): 48–58; and Solvick, "William Howard Taft and the Payne-Aldrich Tariff," *Mississippi Valley Historical Review* 50 (December 1963): 424–42.

On the old guard, see: the Nelson W. Aldrich Papers; Stephenson, *Nelson W. Aldrich;* and Lodge, *Selections from the Correspondence of Theodore Roosevelt and Henry Cabot Lodge.* On the insurgents, see: James Holt, *Congressional Insurgents and the Party System, 1909–1916* (Cambridge, Mass., 1967); Joseph L. Bristow Papers (Kansas State Historical

Society) and A. Bower Sageser, *Joseph L. Bristow: Kansas Progressive* (Lawrence, Kans., and London, 1968); Jonathan P. Dolliver Papers and Thomas R. Ross, *Jonathan Prentiss Dolliver: A Study in Political Integrity and Independence* (Iowa City, 1958); Robert M. La Follette, *La Follette's Autobiography* (paperback ed., Madison, Wisc., 1963), and Belle C. and Fola La Follette, *Robert M. La Follette* (2 vols., New York, 1953); Calvin P. Armin, "Coe I. Crawford and the Progressive Movement in South Dakota," South Dakota Department of History, *Report and Historical Collections* 32 (1964): 23–231; and Martin W. Odland, *The Life of Knute Nelson* (Minneapolis, 1926).

For information on the income tax, see: Acheson, *Joe Bailey*, and Sidney Ratner, *American Taxation: Its History as a Social Force in Democracy* (New York, 1942). On the tariff commission, see: Kenkel, "The Tariff Commission Movement," and *Maintenance of a Lobby to Influence Legislation: Appendix.*

CHAPTER 13

On the politics of insurgency, see George E. Mowry, *Theodore Roosevelt and the Progressive Movement* (Madison, Wis., 1946); on Taft, Stanley D. Solvick, "William Howard Taft and the Insurgents," *Papers of the Michigan Academy of Science, Arts, and Letters* 48 (1963): 279–95.

For the differences between the House and Senate bills, compare U.S., Congress, House, Committee on the Territories, *Statehood for the Territories: Report to Accompany H.R. 18166*, 61st Cong., 2nd sess., H. Rept. 152 (Washington, 1910), with U.S., Congress, Senate, Committee on Territories, *An Act Enabling the People of New Mexico and Arizona to Form a Constitution and State Government, Etc.: Report to Accompany H.R. 18166*, 61st Cong., 2nd sess., S. Rept. 454 (Washington, 1910). On Beveridge's delaying action on the New Mexico constitution, see W. H. Andrews to Thomas B. Catron, 24 February, 11 March 1911, Marion Dargan Papers (University of New Mexico Library).

On the Alaskan government bill, see: Atherton Brownell, "Wanted: A Government for Alaska," *The Outlook*, 26 February 1910, pp. 431–40; Jeannette P. Nichols, *Alaska: A History of Its Administration, Exploitation and Industrial Development during Its First Century under the Rule of the United States* (Cleveland, 1924); Ernest Gruening, *The State of Alaska* (New York, 1954); and Marian C. McKenna, *Borah* (Ann Arbor, Mich., 1961).

For Beveridge's friendship with Gifford Pinchot, see Box 276, BP, and Gifford Pinchot Papers. On his support for Pinchot's conservation policies in the Senate, see Gifford Pinchot, *Breaking New Ground* (New York, 1947).

For information on the postal-savings bank bill, see the Thomas H.

Carter Papers (LC). On the railroad legislation of 1910, see: Frank H. Dixon, "The Mann-Elkins Act, Amending the Act to Regulate Commerce," *Quarterly Journal of Economics* 24 (August 1910): 593–633; William Z. Ripley, *Railroads: Rates and Regulations* (New York, 1912); I. L. Sharfman, *The Interstate Commerce Commission: A Study in Administrative Law and Procedure* (4 parts in 5 vols., New York, 1931–37), 1; and Gabriel Kolko, *Railroads and Regulation, 1877–1916* (Princeton, N.J., 1965).

The activities of the tariff board are described in Kenkel, "The Tariff Commission Movement." For complaints about its activities, see the *American Economist;* for the dissension within the N.A.M. and its withdrawal from active leadership of the tariff commission movement, see: *Proceedings of the Fourteenth Annual Convention of the National Association of Manufacturers . . . 1909* (New York [1909]); *Proceedings of the Fifteenth . . . 1910* (New York [1910]); and *Proceedings of the Sixteenth . . . 1911* (New York [1911]). Material on the lobbying by the National Tariff Commission Association is in *Maintenance of a Lobby to Influence Legislation: Appendix*. Taft's special message urging a $250,000 appropriation to continue the existing tariff board is in U.S., Congress, Senate, *The Tariff Board: Message from the President . . .* , 61st Cong., 2nd sess., S. Doc. 463 (Washington, 1910).

CHAPTER 14

Beveridge's correspondence with Henry W. Bennett, John F. Hayes, E. M. Lee, Charles W. Miller, H. C. Pettit, and Leopold G. Rothschild are in Boxes 166–83, BP. On Indiana patronage matters, see the Frank H. Hitchcock file, Box 174, ibid.; on the *Indianapolis Star* litigation, see Beveridge's correspondence with John C. Shaffer, Box 280, ibid. Beveridge stressed the growing importance of independent voting in "Political Parties," *SEP*, 26 February 1910, pp. 3–5, 41.

Additional material on the 1910 campaign is in the William Dudley Foulke Papers (LC and ISL); Lucius B. Swift Papers; William Allen White Papers; and Joseph L. Bristow Papers. For T.R.'s role, see: Mowry, *Theodore Roosevelt and the Progressive Movement;* Theodore Roosevelt Papers; and Morison, *The Letters of Theodore Roosevelt*.

A review of the Indiana political situation sympathetic to Beveridge is Samuel G. Blythe, "Insurgent Indiana," *SEP*, 2 April 1910, pp. 3–4. On Beveridge's old guard factional rivals, see: Rissler, "Charles Warren Fairbanks"; Charles W. Fairbanks Papers (LL); Lucius C. Embree Papers; William Howard Taft Papers; and Charles D. Hilles Papers (Yale University Library). On the Democrats, see: Thomas, *Thomas Riley Marshall;* Claude G. Bowers, *The Life of John Worth Kern* (Indianapolis, 1918); and Samuel M. Ralston Papers (LL).

CHAPTER 15

For further details on the tariff commission bill, see: *Maintenance of a Lobby to Influence Legislation; Appendix;* Kenkel, "The Tariff Commission Movement"; *The National Tariff Commission Association Convention: A Complete Record of the Proceedings, Washington, D.C., January 11, 12, 1911* (Washington, 1911); and Presidential Series #2, Files 167, 652, and 656, Taft Papers. The House bill is given in U.S., Congress, House, Committee on Ways and Means, *Tariff Board: Report to Accompany H.R. 32010,* 61st Cong., 3rd sess., H. Rept. 1979 (Washington, 1911). For the compromise accepted by Taft for a $400,000 appropriation to continue the existing tariff board, see U.S., Congress, House, Committee on Appropriations, *Sundry Civil Appropriation Bill: Report to Accompany H.R. 32909,* 61st Cong., 3rd sess., H. Rept. 2235 (Washington, 1911), p. 2. This sum was subsequently reduced in conference to $250,000: U.S., Congress, Committee of Conference, *Sundry Civil Appropriation Bill: Conference Report to Accompany H.R. 32909,* 61st Cong., 3rd sess., H. Rept. 2303 (Washington, 1911), p. 1.

On Canadian reciprocity, see: Hechler, *Insurgency,* and L. Ethan Ellis. *Reciprocity 1911: A Study in Canadian-American Relations* (New Haven, Toronto, and London, 1939). Beveridge's support for the treaty is expressed in his "Canadian Reciprocity: Its Influence on the Cost of Living," *SEP,* 25 March 1911, pp. 3–5, 53–54. For his awareness of the opposition to reciprocity north of the border, see his "Canada's Tariff Policy—The Old East Versus the New West," *American Review of Reviews* 43 (June 1911): 695–700.

For background on the Lorimer case, see: Irving Dilliard, "William Lorimer," *Dictionary of American Biography: Supplement One* (New York, 1954), pp. 511–12; William T. Hutchinson, *Lowden of Illinois* (2 vols., Chicago, 1957); James W. Neilson, *Shelby M. Cullom: Prairie State Republican* (Urbana, Ill., 1962); Morison, *The Letters of Theodore Roosevelt;* and *The Outlook,* 7 January 1911, pp. 13–14, 11 March 1911, pp. 521–22. For Beveridge's work on the case, see Boxes 273–74, BP.

CHAPTER 16

Beveridge's articles on Canada are: "Our Canadian Cousins," *SEP,* 17 June 1911, pp. 3–5, 40–42; 1 July 1911, pp. 10–11, 44–45; 22 July 1911, pp. 10–12, 32–33; 26 August 1911, pp. 18–19, 36–37; 9 September 1911, pp. 26–27, 53; 23 September 1911, pp. 26–27, 74; "Canada's Tariff Policy —The Old East versus the New West," *American Review of Reviews* 43 (June 1911): 695–700; "Federalism in Canada and in the United States," ibid. 44 (October 1911): 471–76; "Canada's Government Railway: An Experiment in Public Ownership and Operation," ibid. 46 (November

1912): 585–93; and "Canada's System of Responsible Government," *McClure's Magazine* 37 (July 1911): 330–37.

Letters from Beveridge while in Switzerland are in the Albert Shaw Papers, Gifford Pinchot Papers, George W. Perkins Papers, Lucius B. Swift Papers, and David M. Parry Papers (in possession of Mr. Milton Rubincam, West Hyattsville, Maryland).

General surveys of the contest over the 1912 Republican presidential nomination and the launching of the Progressive Party are: Mowry, *Theodore Roosevelt and the Progressive Movement;* Holt, *Congressional Insurgents and the Party System;* and Norman A. Wilensky, *Conservatives in the Progressive Era: The Taft Republicans of 1912* (Gainesville, Fla., 1965). On Osborn's role, see Robert M. Warner, "Chase S. Osborn and the Presidential Campaign of 1912," *MVHR* 46 (June 1959): 19–45. Two illuminating contemporary accounts by Samuel G. Blythe are "The Republican Situation," *SEP,* 20 April 1912, pp. 3–4, 43–45, and "Post-Mortem: What Happened at Chicago," ibid., 27 July 1912, pp. 3–5, 35.

Carl Painter, "The Progressive Party in Indiana," *IMH* 16 (September 1920): 173–283, is based upon the accounts in the Indianapolis newspapers. For the struggle in Indiana from the Roosevelt side, see the: Beveridge Papers, Shaw Papers, Theodore Roosevelt Papers and Morison, *The Letters of Theodore Roosevelt,* and William Dudley Foulke Papers (LC); from the Taft side, see the William H. Taft Papers, Charles W. Fairbanks Papers (LL), Charles D. Hilles Papers, and Harry S. New Papers (ISL). The *Indianapolis News* was bitterly anti-Roosevelt throughout; the *Indianapolis Star* started out opposing Roosevelt because of his stand in favor of the recall of judicial decisions, but by the time of the G.O.P. national convention had switched to his support and thereafter became the leading Indiana organ of the Progressive Party.

On Beveridge's warning T.R. that he could not win the nomination and remonstrating against his bolting to form the Progressive Party, see Beveridge to Mark Sullivan, 12 August 1925, BP. James R. Parker, "Beveridge and the Election of 1912: Progressive Idealist or Political Realist," *IMH* 63 (June 1967): 103–14, is a somewhat different account from mine about Beveridge's behavior in 1912.

For the conflict over the Sherman Act plank in the Progressive Party's national platform, see Garraty, *Right-Hand Man,* and Amos R. E. Pinchot, *History of the Progressive Party, 1912–1916,* ed. Helene M. Hooker (New York, 1958). Beveridge set forth his criticisms of the Sherman law in his "Modern Business and Medieval Law," *SEP,* 6 January 1912, pp. 6–7, 52; his protests against the plank reported from the resolutions committee are recounted in Chester H. Rowell to William Allen White, 29 November 1919, Rowell Papers (Bancroft Library, University of California— Berkeley).

Beveridge's *Speech . . . Accepting the Nomination for Governor by the Progressive Party at the Indiana State Convention August 1, 1912* ([Indianapolis, 1912]; copy in ISL), includes a copy of the Progressive state platform. His keynote address before the Progressive national convention was reprinted as *"Pass Prosperity Around" Speech of Albert J. Beveridge Temporary Chairman of Progressive National Convention* (New York, [1912]; copy in LC).

The 1912 election contest in Indiana is examined in Samuel G. Blythe, "A Mere Matter of Figures: But Are You Sure Your Arithmetic Is on Straight?" *SEP*, 5 October 1912, pp. 16–17, 48–49, and "Before the Battle: A Final View of the Struggle That Will Come in November," ibid., 26 October 1912, pp. 10–11, 38–39. Oscar K. Davis, *Released for Publication: Some Inside Political History of Theodore Roosevelt and His Times, 1898–1918* (Boston and New York, 1925), has some valuable sidelights about Beveridge and the campaign. Re the campaign contributions investigation, see U.S., Congress, Senate, *Campaign Contributions: Testimony before a Subcommittee of the Committee on Privileges and Elections . . . ,* 62nd Cong., 3rd sess. (2 vols., Washington, 1913). On organized labor's position nationally, see Karson, *American Labor Unions and Politics;* in Indiana, see *Official Proceedings of the Twenty-Eighth Annual Convention Indiana State Federation of Labor* [Evansville, Ind., 1912]. The official election results are published in *Biennial Report of . . . Secretary of State of the State of Indiana* (Indianapolis, 1912), pp. 92–139.

CHAPTER 17

For Beveridge's long-time interest in writing a biography of John Marshall, see Beveridge to Joe Mitchell Chapple, 2 April 1920, BP. Re his approaching the editors of the *Century Magazine* in 1908, see his correspondence with Robert U. Johnson in the Century Collection (New York Public Library).

The bulk of Beveridge's correspondence re the research on and writing of the first two volumes of the Marshall biography is in files marked "Life of Marshall," Boxes 194, 199, 203, and 206, Beveridge Papers. There are important Beveridge letters on this subject in the William E. Dodd Papers (LC). His correspondence with J. Franklin Jameson has been published: Elizabeth Donnan and Leo F. Stock, eds., "Senator Beveridge, J. Franklin Jameson, and John Marshall," *MVHR* 25 (December 1948): 463–92. Beveridge described some of the new materials he had found in "Some New Marshall Sources," *Annual Report of the American Historical Association . . . 1915* (Washington, 1917), pp. 201–5. His account of Marshall's life up to the ratification of the federal constitution is published as Beveridge, *The Life of John Marshall* (4 vols., Boston and New York, 1916–19), 1.

Mowry, *Theodore Roosevelt and the Progressive Movement,* is the fullest available account of the Progressive Party. On Roosevelt's attitude, see Morison, *The Letters of Theodore Roosevelt;* for the refusal of the bulk of the Republican insurgents to join the new party, see Holt, *Congressional Insurgents and the Party System.* Information about the controversy over Perkins's role is in Garraty, *Right-Hand Man,* and Pinchot, *History of the Progressive Party.* Beveridge's defense of Perkins is related in the Gifford Pinchot Diary, Pinchot Papers. For his temporary break with Gifford Pinchot over the affair, see Box 276, Beveridge Papers.

Re the Progressive Party in Indiana, see: Painter, "The Progressive Party in Indiana"; *Indianapolis Star; Indianapolis News;* and Beveridge Papers. Beveridge extolled the new party's future potential in: "The Future of the Progressive Party," *SEP,* 28 December 1912, pp. 3–4, 36–37; "A Progressive Promise," *Collier's,* 18 January 1913, pp. 8–9, 24; *Senator Beveridge's Lincoln Day Speech Hotel Astor, New York City February 12, 1913 (Progressive Service Documents D 3—March, 1913)* ([New York, 1913]; copy in ISL); and "The Progressive-Republican Merger," *SEP,* 28 June 1913, pp. 3–5, 49–52. His "A Party Afraid of Itself," *Collier's,* 31 January 1914, pp. 7–8, 24–26, assails the G.O.P. national committee's refusal to call a special national convention.

Beveridge's speech opening the 1914 campaign was published as *"Permanent Prosperity" Speech by Albert J. Beveridge, Progressive Candidate for Senator, Opening the State Campaign at Terre Haute, September 14, 1914* ([Indianapolis, 1914]; copy in ISL). He explained, in a pamphlet entitled *Initiative, Referendum and Recall* ([Indianapolis, 1914]; copy in ISL), the Progressive Party's position on these questions. The major themes of Beveridge's 1914 campaign speeches are summarized in "Permanent Prosperity," *SEP,* 31 October 1914, pp. 14–15, 49–50.

For the domestic and foreign policies of the Wilson administration, see Arthur S. Link, *Woodrow Wilson and the Progressive Era, 1910–1917* (New York, 1954); for Samuel M. Ralston's achievements as governor, see Phillips, *Indiana in Transition.* On Hays's rebuilding of the state G.O.P., see Will H. Hays, *The Memoirs of Will H. Hays* (Garden City, N.Y., 1955), and Garlan C. Routt, "Will Hays: A Study in Political Leadership and Management" (M.A. thesis, University of Chicago, 1937); re Hugh T. Miller, see Richard H. Gemmecke, "W. G. Irwin and Hugh Thomas Miller: A Study in Free Enterprise in Indiana" (Ph.D. diss., Indiana University, 1955).

Samuel G. Blythe, "An Off Year That Was On," *SEP,* 12 December 1914, pp. 23–25, analyzes the Progressive debacle in the 1914 elections. Beveridge gave his own assessment, stressing the Hinman affair, in "The Launching and Wrecking of the Progressive Party," in "G. H. Lorimer 1916" file, Box 206, BP. The official Indiana election returns are published in *Bien-*

nial Report of . . . Secretary of the State of Indiana . . . 1914 (Indianapolis, 1914), pp. 140–93.

CHAPTER 18

Boxes 328–37, BP, contain materials on his trip to Europe as a war correspondent for *Collier's*. These include six bound volumes containing correspondence, a diary, his notes, copies of his interviews corrected and approved by the interviewees, and the manuscript draft of his war book; and four boxes of miscellaneous printed matter and photographs. Bowers, *Beveridge and the Progressive Era*, has excerpts from Beveridge's letters to his wife while abroad.

The eight *Collier's* articles are: "On the Doorstep of War," 6 February 1915, pp. 5–6, 30–31; "In the German Trenches," 13 March 1915, pp. 5–7, 31, 34–35; "A Visit to the Kaiser and His War Lords," 27 March 1915, pp. 5–7, 29; "What a Battle Looks Like," 24 April 1915, pp. 5–6, 20–21, 24–25; "A Nation United," 1 May 1915, pp. 7–8, 26, 28–31; "German Thought Back of the War," 8 May 1915, pp. 8–9, 20–22, 24–26; "Why France Fights On," 22 May 1915, pp. 8–9, 24, 26–28, 30; and "British War Opinion," 12 June 1915, pp. 7–8, 28–30. The three articles published in the *American Review of Reviews* are: "As Witnessed in Germany," 51 (May 1915): 557–67; "As Witnessed in France," 51 (June 1915): 699–708; and "War Opinion in England—Some Contrasts," 52 (July 1915): 49–58. Beveridge described the growing trend toward "collectivism" resulting from the war in his "Democracy the Conqueror," *SEP,* 19 June 1915, pp. 23–26. He brought this material together in his book *What Is Back of the War* (Indianapolis, 1915).

On Beveridge's pro-German sentiments during the war, see: William Dudley Foulke to Theodore Roosevelt, 7 December 1914, Foulke Papers (LC), and Lucius B. Swift to Mrs. Theodore Roosevelt, 17 June 1922, Swift Papers. For his difficulties with *Collier's* over the articles, see his correspondence with Mark Sullivan, Box 204, BP; re his efforts to promote the sales of the book, see his correspondence with W. C. Bobbs, Box 202, BP.

Beveridge appealed to the American people to avoid foreign entanglements and concentrate on putting things at home in shape in his "Preparedness for Peace," *SEP,* 16 February 1916, pp. 6–7, 48–50. For *Post* editor George H. Lorimer's turning down a stronger plea of his for neutrality, see Lorimer to Beveridge, 28, 30 March 1916, BP.

For the research on and writing of the second volume of the Marshall, see bibliographical note to chap. 17. On the house at Beverly Farms, see Bowers, *Beveridge and the Progressive Era*. Beveridge's account of Marshall's life from the ratification of the federal constitution to his appointment as chief justice is in *The Life of John Marshall*, 2. Reexaminations of different aspects of Marshall's career on the occasion of the bicentennial of his birth are in W. Melville Jones, ed., *Chief Justice John Marshall: A Reappraisal* (Ithaca, N.Y., 1956).

On the death of the Progressive Party nationally, see Mowry, *Theodore Roosevelt and the Progressive Movement;* in Indiana, see: Painter, "The Progressive Party in Indiana"; *Indianapolis Star; Indianapolis News;* William Dudley Foulke Papers (ISL); Lucius B. Swift Papers; and Beveridge Papers. For the negotiations leading to Beveridge's return to the G.O.P., see his correspondence with W. C. Bobbs (Box 204), George W. Perkins (Box 276), and John C. Shaffer (Box 281), Beveridge Papers.

For Beveridge's concern over the need for increased protection against postwar foreign dumping, see his "War and the Tariff," *SEP,* 4 December 1915, pp. 25–28. His criticism of Wilson's Mexican policy is in: "*Kept Out of War*" ([Indianapolis, 1916]; copy in ISL) and "What to Do about Mexico: An Important Aspect of Our Present War Problem," *Collier's,* 19 May 1917, pp. 5–7, 27.

On the 1916 campaign in Indiana, see Samuel G. Blythe, "Consider Indiana," *SEP,* 21 October 1916, pp. 6–7, 56. One of Beveridge's campaign speeches was published by the Hughes Alliance of Indiana: *Speech of Hon. Albert J. Beveridge at Formal Opening of the Republican Speaking Campaign . . . Chicago, on the Night of October 5, 1916* ([Indianapolis, 1916]; copy in ISL).

CHAPTER 19

The bulk of Beveridge's correspondence re the research on and writing of volumes three and four of the Marshall biography is in files marked "Life of Marshall," Boxes 210, 212–13, 216–17, and 222, BP. Additional Beveridge letters are in the Edward S. Corwin Papers (Princeton University Library), William E. Dodd Papers, and James A. Woodburn Papers (LL). Beveridge's account of Marshall's years as chief justice is in *The Life of John Marshall,* 3 and 4. For his efforts to promote the sales of the work, see the Ferris Greenslet–Houghton Mifflin files, Boxes 221 and 226, BP.

Tracy E. Strevey, "Albert J. Beveridge," in William T. Hutchinson, ed., *The Marcus W. Jernegan Essays in American Historiography* (Chicago, 1937), pp. 374–93, appraises Beveridge as an historian-biographer. Corwin's argument about *Marbury* v. *Madison* is in Edward S. Corwin, *The Doctrine of Judicial Review: Its Legal and Historical Basis and Other Essays* (Princeton, N.J., 1914), pp. 1–78; his criticism of Marshall's ruling in the Burr case is in Corwin, *John Marshall and the Constitution* (New Haven, 1919). A recent defense of Marshall's opinion is Robert Faulkner, "John Marshall and the Burr Trial," *Journal of American History* 53 (September 1966): 247–58. C. Peter McGrath, *Yazoo: Law and Politics in the*

New Republic, The Case of Fletcher v. Peck (Providence, R.I., 1966), reexamines that case, while Charles G. Haines, *The Role of the Supreme Court in American Government and Politics, 1789–1835* (Berkeley and Los Angeles, 1944), criticizes Marshall's opinion in the Dartmouth College case. Gustavus Myers's attack upon Marshall re the Fairfax case is in his *History of the Supreme Court of the United States* (Chicago, 1925).

For background on the fight over the League of Nations, see: D. F. Fleming, *The United States and the League of Nations, 1918–1920* (New York, 1932); Ruhl H. Bartlett, *The League to Enforce Peace* (Chapel Hill, N.C., 1944); and Thomas A. Bailey, *Woodrow Wilson and the Lost Peace* (New York, 1944) and *Woodrow Wilson and the Great Betrayal* (New York, 1945).

Beveridge's speeches attacking the League and the Treaty of Versailles are reported in the *Indianapolis Star*. See also: Beveridge, "The School and the Nation," *National Education Association of the United States: Addresses and Proceedings . . . 1917* (Washington, 1917), pp. 678–90; Speech before the Massachusetts Bar Association, 6 December 1918, in *CR*, 65th Cong., 3rd sess., 1919, 57, pt. 3: 2113–15; Speech before the Pennsylvania Bar Association, 24 June 1919, in *CR*, 66th Cong., 1st sess., 1919, 58, pt. 2: 1721–25; "Pitfalls of a 'League of Nations,'" *North American Review* 209 (March 1919): 305–14; and his correspondence with William E. Borah (Boxes 211 and 214), Frank Brandegee (Box 214), Albert B. Cummins (Box 214), George Harvey (Box 215), Will H. Hays (Box 215), Philander C. Knox (Boxes 212 and 215), Hiram Johnson (Box 215), Henry Cabot Lodge (Box 216), Medill McCormick (Boxes 212 and 216), Frank A. Munsey (Box 216), Harry S. New (Box 217), Theodore Roosevelt (Box 277), and John C. Shaffer (Box 281), BP.

CHAPTER 20

For information on Indiana politics during these years, the *Indianapolis Star* and *Indianapolis News* are indispensable. On Goodrich's record as governor, see Phillips, *Indiana in Transition*, re Hays, see James O. Robertson, "Progressives Elect Will H. Hays Republican National Chairman, 1918," *IMH* 64 (September 1968): 173–90. For the rivalry between the Watson and Hays-Goodrich factions, see the Will H. Hays Papers. On Beveridge's rapprochement with Hays and Goodrich, see his correspondence with W. C. Bobbs (Boxes 208 and 214), James P. Goodrich (Boxes 209 and 215), Will H. Hays (Boxes 209 and 215); and E. Vernon Knight (Box 209).

Beveridge eulogized Roosevelt's achievements in his "The Roosevelt Period," *SEP*, 5 April 1919, pp. 10, 49–50, 53–54, and "The Statesmanship of Theodore Roosevelt," in Theodore Roosevelt, *Thomas Hart Benton [and] Gouverneur Morris,* vol. 7 of *The Works of Theodore Roosevelt,* National Edition, pp. ix–xxviii.

Wesley M. Bagby, *The Road to Normalcy: The Presidential Campaign of 1920* (Baltimore, 1962), is the fullest available account of the contest over the 1920 Republican presidential nomination and the ensuing campaign. Re Beveridge's dark-horse presidential aspirations in 1920, see his correspondence with George Harvey (Box 221), Frank A. Munsey (Boxes 216 and 222), John C. Shaffer (Box 281), and Thomas R. Shipp (Box 223), BP. Shaffer's maneuvering to gain for Beveridge the temporary chairmanship can be followed in the Hays Papers. On Beveridge's selection as one of the delegates-at-large from Indiana, see Edmund M. Wasmuth to Will H. Hays, 19 July 1938, Harry S. New Papers (ISL). For the rejection of Beveridge as temporary and even permanent chairman of the G.O.P. national convention, see the *New York Times* and Arthur W. Dunn, *From Harrison to Harding: A Personal Narrative, Covering a Third of a Century, 1888–1921* (2 vols., New York and London, 1922).

Beveridge set for his views on the issues in his speeches reported in the *Indianapolis Star;* "To the Women of America," *Collier's,* 12 June 1920, pp. 8, 38, 40, 42, 44; *Address of Albert J. Beveridge at the Celebration of the 299th Anniversary of the Landing of the Pilgrims . . . Plymouth, Mass. December 22nd, 1919* (n.p., n.d.; copy in ISL); *Address of Hon. Albert J. Beveridge at the McKinley Day Celebration of the Detroit Republican Club Detroit, Michigan January 29, 1920* (n.p., [1920]; copy in LC) and *Speech of Former Senator Albert J. Beveridge of Indiana . . . Opening the Michigan Republican Campaign . . . . January 29th, 1920 . . .* ([Detroit, 1920]; copy in ISL); *Sons of the Revolution in the State of New York Addresses Delivered by Ex-Senator Albert J. Beveridge of Indiana on Washington's Birthday February 22, 1921* (n.p., [1921]; copy in LC); *Forward to Prosperity Speech of Ex-Senator Albert J. Beveridge at Fort Wayne, Indiana March 9th, 1922* ([Indianapolis, 1922]; copy in ISL); and *Address of Albert J. Beveridge at Evansville Indiana September 26th, 1922* ([Indianapolis, 1922]; copy in ISL). His Bar Association speech was published as *The Assault upon American Fundamentals Address of Albert J. Beveridge at the Annual Meeting of the American Bar Association St. Louis, August 26, 1920* (n.p., [1920]; copy in ISL); his correspondence re the research on and writing of that speech is in files marked "American Bar Association Address August 26, 1920," Box 218, BP.

For the details on the activities of Beveridge's supporters in preparing for the 1922 primary race, see his correspondence with Willitts A. Bastian (Boxes 219 and 225), W. C. Bobbs (Boxes 219 and 225), A. M. Glossbrenner (Box 226), Charles W. Miller (Boxes 222 and 228); Clarence R. Martin (Box 228), and Leopold G. Rothschild (Boxes 223 and 229), BP.

The most important sources for the 1922 primary contest and the general election are the *Indianapolis Star, Indianapolis News,* and Boxes 230–41, BP. For information on the primary battle from the New forces side, see: Joseph I. Irwin Papers (LL); Richard Lieber Papers (LL); and Hays Papers. The Democratic campaign strategy can be followed in the Samuel M. Ralston Papers.

Comments upon the significance of Beveridge's primary victory are in: the *New York Times;* "Weathercocks of the Harding Administration," *Current Opinion* 73 (July 1922): 1–5; "Mr. Beveridge's Victory," *The Outlook,* 17 May 1922, pp. 96–97; "Mr. Beveridge's Choice," *The Nation,* 17 May 1922, pp. 586; "Beveridge Comes Back," *The New Republic,* 17 May 1922, pp. 331–33.

For the attitude of farm organizations and journals, see: *Journal of Proceedings of the Indiana State Grange Fifty-Second Annual Session . . . 1922* (Columbus, Ind., [1922]) and *Indiana Farmer's Guide;* for organized labor hostility toward the G.O.P. generally and Beveridge particularly, see: *Official Proceedings of the Thirty-Eight Annual Convention of the Indiana State Federation of Labor . . . 1922* (Evansville, [1922]); *Report of Proceedings of the Forty-Second Annual Convention of the American Federation of Labor . . . 1922* (Washington, 1922); *American Federationist; Labor;* and Samuel Gompers to W. H. Davis, 18 September 1922, Gompers Papers (LC). On the Ku Klux Klan, see: Norman Weaver, "The Knights of the Ku Klux Klan in Wisconsin, Indiana, Ohio, and Michigan" (Ph.D. diss., University of Wisconsin, 1954); David M. Chalmers, *Hooded Americanism: The First Century of the Ku Klux Klan, 1865–1965* (Garden City, N.Y., 1965); and Kenneth L. Jackson, *The Ku Klux Klan in the City, 1915–1930* (New York, 1967).

The official primary and general election results are published in the *Yearbook of the State of Indiana . . . 1922* (Indianapolis, 1923), pp. 11–22, 49–83.

CHAPTER 21

The bulk of Beveridge's correspondence re the research on and writing of his biography of Lincoln is filed alphabetically, with separate folders for the more important correspondents, in boxes marked "Lincoln Correspondence," Boxes 285–96, BP. Drafts of his chapters with his readers' comments are in boxes marked "Critics' Notes & Comments," Boxes 9–18, Beveridge Papers, Accession 9648 (LC). Beveridge explained his method and philosophy of writing biography in his "The Making of a Book," *SEP,* 23 October 1926, pp. 14–15, 182, 185–186. The first two volumes carrying the biography up to the Lincoln-Douglas debates was published posthumously as *Abraham Lincoln, 1909–1858* (2 vols., Boston and New York, 1928).

Additional Beveridge letters are in the William E. Barton Papers (University of Chicago Library), William E. Dodd Papers, and Beveridge file, Illinois Historical Survey Records (University of Illinois Library, Urbana-Champaign). His correspondence with J. Franklin Jameson is published in Elizabeth Donnan and Leo F. Stock, eds., "Senator Beveridge, J. Franklin Jameson, and Abraham Lincoln," *MVHR* 25 (March 1949): 639–73; with Jacob M. Dickinson, in William T. Alderson and Kenneth K. Bailey, eds., "Correspondence between Albert J. Beveridge and Jacob M. Dickinson on the Writing of Beveridge's Life of Lincoln," *Journal of Southern History* 20 (May 1954): 210–237. Excerpts from his correspondence with David Rankin Barbee, managing editor of the *Ashville (N.C.) Citizen,* were published in pamphlet form under the title *An Excursion in Southern History* . . . (Asheville, N.C., 1928).

Surveys of Lincoln historiography that place Beveridge's work in the context of previous and later scholarship are: Paul M. Angle, *A Shelf of Lincoln Books: A Critical Selective Bibliography of Lincolniana* (New Brunswick, N.J., 1946); Benjamin P. Thomas, *Portrait for Posterity: Lincoln and His Biographers* (New Brunswick, N.J., 1947); D. E. Fehrenbacher, *The Changing Image of Lincoln in American Historiography* (Oxford, 1968); and David M. Potter, "The Lincoln Theme and American National Historiography," *The South and Sectional Conflict* (Baton Rouge, La., 1968), pp. 151–76.

On the Bartlett collection, see Carl Sandburg, *Lincoln Collector: The Story of Oliver R. Barrett's Great Private Collection* (New York, 1949); on the Robert Todd Lincoln collection, see David C. Mearns, ed., *The Lincoln Papers: The Story of the Collection with Selections to July 4, 1861* (2 vols., Garden City, N.Y., 1948), 1: 3–140.

A legend has grown up that Robert Todd Lincoln closed the papers to keep Beveridge from seeing the collection because of his anger upon learning that Beveridge was using the Herndon manuscripts and that he even consulted an actuary as to Beveridge's life expectancy before fixing the twenty-one-year limit. Mearns speculates (1: 134) that "it may have been more than a coincidence that [his refusal to Beveridge] was written on the same day he signed the deed of gift, decreeing that the papers should be locked away for a generation." But Robert Todd Lincoln's biographer finds "no evidence that Lincoln had had anything in particular" against Beveridge: John S. Goff, *Robert Todd Lincoln: A Man in His Own Right* (Norman, Okla., 1969), p. 191. And Mearns shows that Lincoln, from the start, refused to allow anybody, except Nicolay and Hay, to see the papers because of his anxiety that materials therein might reflect adversely upon still living persons and concludes (1: 105) that his action in closing the papers "was entirely consonant with his lifelong purpose to avoid personal injury."

For a criticism of Beveridge's excessive reliance upon the Herndon manuscripts, see William E. Barton, "A Noble Fragment: Beveridge's Life of Lincoln," *MVHR* 15 (March 1929): 497–510. David Donald, *Lincoln's Herndon* (New York, 1948), on the whole supports Beveridge's favorable opinion of Herndon's own accuracy. Paul M. Angle's refutation of the Ann Rutledge myth was published as "Lincoln's First Love?" Lincoln Centennial Association *Bulletin*, no. 9 (1 December 1927): 1–8; a full analysis of the evidence, including a criticism of Beveridge's account, is in J. G. Randall and Richard N. Current, *Lincoln the President* (4 vols., New York, 1945–55), 2: 321–42. For the refutation of "the fatal first of January" legend and a more sympathetic treatment of Mrs. Lincoln generally, see Carl Sandburg and Paul M. Angle, *Mary Lincoln: Wife and Widow* (New York, 1932).

For Beveridge's role in obtaining the Harmsworth professorship for Morison, see his correspondence with Morison, Box 228, BP; on his recommending Nathaniel W. Stephenson to write the authorized biography of Senator Nelson W. Aldrich, see his correspondence with Abby A. Rockefeller, Box 246, BP. His review of Jesse W. Weik's *The Real Lincoln* is "Lincoln as His Partner Knew Him," *Literary Digest International Book Review* 1 (September 1923): 33–35, 51; his review of Stephenson's volume, "A New Portrayal of Abraham Lincoln," ibid. 1 (March 1923): 14–15, 64. For his friendship with Claude G. Bowers, see Boxes 219, 225, 231, 242, 248, and 255, BP.

Material on his work in behalf of the American Historical Association's endowment fund drive is in two boxes titled "Correspondence American Historical Association," Boxes 268–69, BP; *Annual Report of the American Historical Association . . . 1924* (Washington, 1929), *Annual Report . . . 1925* (Washington, 1929), and *Annual Report . . . 1926* (Washington, 1930); and *New York Times*.

His *SEP* articles are: "In or Out," 17 November 1923, pp. 3–4, 133–34, 136–38; "Common Sense and the Constitution," 15 December 1923, pp. 25, 119, 121–22, 125–26, 129; "Steady as She Goes," 26 January 1924, pp. 6–7, 60, 63, 65, and 2 February 1924, pp. 25, 42, 44, 46; "Republic or Bureaucracy," 15 March 1924, pp. 33, 189–90, 193–94, 197; and "Mr. President," 12 April 1924, pp. 16–17, 81–82, 84. These were published as a book: *The State of the Nation* (Indianapolis, 1924). For additional expressions of his views on public questions, see: *"An Appeal to Plain Americans" Address of Albert J. Beveridge at the Annual Banquet of the Indiana Society, Chicago December 9, 1922 . . .* (n.p., n.d.; copy in ISL), and the reports of his speeches in the *Indianapolis Star*.

For background on domestic and foreign policies during these years, see: Donald R. McCoy, *Calvin Coolidge: The Quiet President* (New York and London, 1967); Betty Glad, *Charles Evans Hughes and the Illusions of Innocence: A Study in American Diplomacy* (Urbana, Ill., and London, 1966); and L. Ethan Ellis, *Republican Foreign Policy, 1921–1933* (New Brunswick, N.J., 1968). On Indiana politics, see the *Indianapolis Star* and *Indianapolis News.*

For Beveridge's continuing political ambitions, see his correspondence with W. C. Bobbs (Boxes 242 and 248), E. Vernon Knight (Box 244), Clarence R. Martin (Boxes 245 and 251), Leopold G. Rothschild (Box 246), and John C. Shaffer (Box 282), BP. On his withdrawing his name from a petition urging the release of wartime political prisoners, see his correspondence with Mrs. Mary Fendall and Gilson Gardner, Box 243, BP. Re the talk of Beveridge as the vice-presidential nominee, see the *New York Times.*

CHAPTER 22

For the major sources on the research on and writing of the second volume of the Lincoln biography, see the bibliographical note for chap. 21. Worthington C. Ford's correspondence while Ford was preparing Beveridge's manuscript for publication is in the Box 270, BP.

Two recent studies that revise Beveridge at a number of points are Randall and Current, *Lincoln the President,* and Don E. Fehrenbacher, *Prelude to Greatness: Lincoln in the 1850's* (Stanford, Cal., 1962). Thomas J. Pressly, *Americans Interpret Their Civil War* (Princeton, N.J., 1954), and Potter, "The Literature on the Background of the Civil War," *The South and the Sectional Conflict,* pp. 87–150, place Beveridge's work in the context of the historiography of the Civil War.

For Beveridge's continuing defense of the direct primary, see his "Of, by and for the People—Yes or No?" *SEP,* 11 December 1926, pp. 8–9, 109–10; 18 December 1926, pp. 14–15, 80, 83, 86. For his views on public questions, see " 'Steady as She Goes'—Abstract," *National Education Association of the United States: Addresses and Proceedings . . . 1925* (Washington, 1925), pp. 81–84; *Sources of the Declaration of Independence an Address Delivered by Hon. Albert J. Beveridge before the Historical Society of Pennsylvania June 2, 1926* ([Philadelphia, 1926]; copy in ISL); and the reports of his speeches in the *Indianapolis Star.*

The *Indianapolis Star* and *Indianapolis News* remain indispensable for Indiana politics in these years. See also the *New York Times* re the Robinson appointment. For information on Beveridge's possibly trying for the senatorial nomination in 1926, his decision not to run, and his refusal to campaign, see his correspondence with W. C. Bobbs (Box 255), A. M. Glossbrenner (Boxes 256 and 261), Fred Joss (Boxes 256 and 261), Clarence R. Martin (Boxes 257 and 262), and John C. Shaffer (Box 282), BP.

Index

359